Topics at the Grammar-Discourse Interface

Editors: Philippa Cook (University of Frankfurt), Anke Holler (University of Göttingen), Cathrine Fabricius-Hansen (University of Oslo)

In this series:

1. Song, Sanghoun. Modeling information structure in a cross-linguistic perspective.

Modeling information structure in a cross-linguistic perspective

Sanghoun Song

language science press

Sanghoun Song. 2017. *Modeling information structure in a cross-linguistic perspective* (Topics at the Grammar-Discourse Interface 1). Berlin: Language Science Press.

This title can be downloaded at:
http://langsci-press.org/catalog/book/111
© 2017, Sanghoun Song
Published under the Creative Commons Attribution 4.0 Licence (CC BY 4.0):
http://creativecommons.org/licenses/by/4.0/
ISBN: 978-3-946234-90-6 (Digital)
    978-3-944675-97-8 (Hardcover)
    978-3-946234-64-7 (Softcover)
DOI:10.5281/zenodo.818365

Cover and concept of design: Ulrike Harbort
Typesetting: Sanghoun Song
Proofreading: Amr El-Zawawy, Andreas Hölzl, Christian Döhler, Evans Gesure, Gerald Delahunty, Ikmi Nur Oktavianti, Natsuko Nakagawa, Jean Nitzke, Ken Manson
Fonts: Linux Libertine, Arimo, DejaVu Sans Mono
Typesetting software: X∃LATEX

Language Science Press
Unter den Linden 6
10099 Berlin, Germany
langsci-press.org

Storage and cataloguing done by FU Berlin

Language Science Press has no responsibility for the persistence or accuracy of URLs for external or third-party Internet websites referred to in this publication, and does not guarantee that any content on such websites is, or will remain, accurate or appropriate.

Contents

Acknowledgments — ix

Abbreviations — xiii

1 **Introduction** — 1
   1.1 Motivations — 2
   1.2 Grammar engineering — 3
   1.3 Outline — 5

2 **Preliminary notes** — 7
   2.1 Examples — 7
   2.2 Terminology — 9

3 **Meanings of information structure** — 11
   3.1 Information status — 12
   3.2 Focus — 14
      3.2.1 Definition — 14
      3.2.2 Subtypes of focus — 15
      3.2.3 Linguistic properties of focus — 18
      3.2.4 Tests for Focus — 22
   3.3 Topic — 23
      3.3.1 Definition — 23
      3.3.2 Subtypes of topic — 25
      3.3.3 Linguistic properties of topic — 27
      3.3.4 Tests for topic — 30
   3.4 Contrast — 32
      3.4.1 Definition — 32
      3.4.2 Subtypes of contrast — 35
      3.4.3 Linguistic properties of contrast — 35
      3.4.4 Tests for contrast — 37
   3.5 Background — 42
   3.6 Summary — 43

Contents

4	**Markings of information structure**			**45**
	4.1	Prosody		45
		4.1.1	Prosody as a widespread means of marking	46
		4.1.2	Mappings between prosody and information structure	47
		4.1.3	Flexible representation	48
	4.2	Lexical markers		49
		4.2.1	Multiple markers	51
		4.2.2	Positioning constraints	52
		4.2.3	Categorical restriction	53
		4.2.4	Interaction with syntax	53
	4.3	Syntactic positioning		53
		4.3.1	Focus position	57
		4.3.2	Topic position	63
		4.3.3	Contrast position	67
	4.4	Summary		69
5	**Discrepancies between meaning and marking**			**71**
	5.1	Ambivalent lexical markers		71
	5.2	Focus/Topic fronting		74
	5.3	Competition between prosody and syntax		76
	5.4	Multiple positions of focus		78
	5.5	Summary		80
6	**Literature review**			**83**
	6.1	Information structure in HPSG		83
		6.1.1	Sentential forms	85
		6.1.2	Location within the feature geometry	87
		6.1.3	Underspecification	88
		6.1.4	Marking vs. meaning	93
	6.2	Information structure in MRS		94
	6.3	Phonological information in HPSG		96
	6.4	Information structure in other frameworks		99
		6.4.1	CCG-based studies	99
		6.4.2	LFG-based studies	102
	6.5	Summary		104
7	**Individual CONStraints: fundamentals**			**105**
	7.1	Minimal Recursion Semantics		105

	7.2	Motivations	108
		7.2.1 Morphosyntactic markings vs. Semantic representation	108
		7.2.2 Underspecification	109
		7.2.3 Binary relations	110
		7.2.4 Informative emptiness	112
		7.2.5 Summary	113
	7.3	Information structure (*info-str*)	113
		7.3.1 ICONS	116
		7.3.2 ICONS-KEY and CLAUSE-KEY	118
		7.3.3 Summary	121
	7.4	Markings (*mkg*)	121
	7.5	Sentential forms (*sform*)	124
	7.6	Graphical representation	133
	7.7	Summary	135
8	**Individual CONStraints: specifics of the implementation**		**137**
	8.1	Lexical types	137
		8.1.1 Nominal items	138
		8.1.2 Verbal items	140
		8.1.3 Adpositions	147
		8.1.4 Determiners	147
		8.1.5 Adverbs	148
		8.1.6 Conjunctions	149
	8.2	Phrasal types	150
	8.3	Additional constraints on configuring information structure	152
		8.3.1 Periphery	152
		8.3.2 Lightness	155
		8.3.3 Phonological structure	158
	8.4	Sample derivations	158
		8.4.1 English	159
		8.4.2 Japanese and Korean	161
		8.4.3 Russian	167
	8.5	Summary	170
9	**Multiclausal constructions**		**171**
	9.1	Complement clauses	172
		9.1.1 Background	172
		9.1.2 Analysis	174

Contents

	9.2	Relative clauses	175
		9.2.1 Background	176
		9.2.2 Analysis	180
	9.3	Adverbial clauses	182
		9.3.1 Background	183
		9.3.2 Analysis	183
	9.4	Summary	186
10	**Forms of expressing information structure**		**187**
	10.1	Focus sensitive items	187
		10.1.1 Quantifiers	189
		10.1.2 *Wh*-words	189
		10.1.3 Negative expressions	193
	10.2	Argument optionality	193
	10.3	Scrambling	196
	10.4	Cleft constructions	202
		10.4.1 Properties	202
		10.4.2 Subtypes	203
		10.4.3 Components	205
		10.4.4 *It*-clefts in the ERG	209
	10.5	Passive constructions	211
	10.6	Fronting	214
	10.7	Dislocation	215
	10.8	Summary	217
11	**Focus projection**		**219**
	11.1	Parse trees	220
	11.2	F(ocus)-marking	220
		11.2.1 Usage of MRS	222
		11.2.2 Languages without focus prosody	222
		11.2.3 Lexical markers	222
	11.3	Grammatical relations	223
	11.4	An analysis	225
		11.4.1 Basic data	225
		11.4.2 Rules	226
		11.4.3 Representation	228
		11.4.4 Further question	230
	11.5	Summary	231

12 Customizing information structure — 233
- 12.1 Type description language — 237
- 12.2 The questionnaire — 238
  - 12.2.1 Focus — 238
  - 12.2.2 Topic — 239
  - 12.2.3 Contrastive focus — 240
  - 12.2.4 Contrastive topic — 241
- 12.3 The Matrix core — 241
  - 12.3.1 Fundamentals — 241
  - 12.3.2 Lexical types — 242
  - 12.3.3 Lexical rules — 243
  - 12.3.4 Phrase structure rules — 243
- 12.4 Customized grammar creation — 244
  - 12.4.1 Lexical markers — 245
  - 12.4.2 Syntactic positioning — 247
- 12.5 Regression testing — 250
  - 12.5.1 Testsuites — 250
  - 12.5.2 Pseudo grammars — 251
  - 12.5.3 Processing — 252
- 12.6 Testing with Language CoLLAGE — 252
  - 12.6.1 Languages — 254
  - 12.6.2 Testsuites — 255
  - 12.6.3 Comparison — 255
  - 12.6.4 Information structure in the four languages — 257
  - 12.6.5 Summary — 258
- 12.7 Live-site — 258
- 12.8 Download — 259

13 Multilingual machine translation — 261
- 13.1 Transfer-based machine translation — 261
- 13.2 Basic machinery — 262
- 13.3 Processor — 265
- 13.4 Evaluation — 266
  - 13.4.1 Illustrative grammars — 266
  - 13.4.2 Testsuites — 267
  - 13.4.3 An experiment — 268
- 13.5 Summary — 270

Contents

14 Conclusion   273
    14.1 Summary 273
    14.2 Contributions 274
    14.3 Future Work 275

List of references   277

Bibliography   277

Index   297
    Name index 297
    Language index 303
    Subject index 305

Acknowledgments

First and foremost, I would like to express my deep gratitude to my wonderful PhD adviser, Emily M. Bender. She has introduced me to the study of information structure and provided me with tremendous help in modeling information structure from a cross-linguistic perspective.

I have received such wonderful support from all of the faculty members of the Dept. of Linguistics, University of Washington. I am deeply grateful to Toshiyuki Ogihara, Fei Xia, Gina-Anne Levow, Sharon Hargus, Richard Wright, Ellen Kaisse, Alicia Beckford Wassink, and Julia Herschensohn. I have received great assistance from Mike Furr and Joyce Parvi. I am also full of appreciation to fellow students: Joshua Crowgey, Woodley Packard, Lisa Tittle Caballero, Varya Gracheva, Marina Oganyan, Glenn Slayden, Maria Burgess, Zina Pozen, Ka Yee Lun, Naoko Komoto, Sanae Sato, Prescott Klassen, T.J. Trimble, Olga Zamaraeva, David Inman, and, deeply, Laurie Poulson.

After having completed my PhD, I worked as a research fellow at Nanyang Technological University in Singapore. The experience at NTU provided me with the opportunity to improve my understanding of grammar engineering as well as grammatical theory across languages. I would like to express special thanks to my great supervisor, Francis Bond. I have also received such kind assistance from my colleagues at NTU: Michael Wayne Goodman, Luis Morgado da Costa, František Kratochvíl, Joanna Sio Ut Seong, Giulia Bonansinga, Chen Bo, Zhenzhen Fan, David Moeljadi, Tuấn Anh Lê, Wenjie Wang, and Takayaki Kuribayashi.

I participated in many helpful discussions with the DELPH-IN developers. Ann Copestake and Dan Flickinger suggested using Individual Constraints to represent information structure. While discussing this matter with Dan Flickinger, I was able to improve my analysis on how to model information structure from the perspective of grammar engineering. Stephan Oepen helped me improve functionality of the information structure library. I also had productive discussions with Antske Fokkens, Tim Baldwin, Berthold Crysmann, Ned Letcher, Rebecca Dridan, Lars Hellan, and Petya Osenova.

I have also received important aid from many linguists. Stefan Müller provided me such meaningful assistance with my study of information structure. I

Acknowledgments

had a great opportunity to discuss with Nancy Hedberg, which helped me understand better the interaction between prosody and information structure in English. Yo Sato let me know his previous comparative study of information structure marking in Japanese and Korean. Bojan Belić helped me understand information structure properties in Bosnian Croatian Serbian. Of course, they do not necessarily agree with my analysis.

I cannot miss my deep appreciation to the editors of this book series "Topics at the Grammar-Discourse Interface". Philippa Cook (Chief Editor) kindly helped me develop my manuscript. Felix Bildhauer and the other anonymous reviewer gave me a number of great comments, which gave me one more chance to improve my idea, though it should be noted that I could not fully accommodate them in this book. Thanks to Sebastian Nordhoff's kind help and other proofreaders' assistance, I could finish this book. Additionally, I would like to express thanks to Anke Holler, Cathrine Fabricius-Hansen. Needless to say, all remaining errors and infelicities are my own responsibility.

Since becoming interested in linguistic studies, I have been receiving invaluable guidance from many Korean linguists. Most of all, I would like to express my respect to my MA adviser, Jae-Woong Choe. If it had not been for his tutelage, I would not have made such progress in linguistic studies. Jong-Bok Kim provided me with the opportunity to participate in the KRG project. This led me to the study of HPSG/MRS-based language processing. Seok-Hoon You introduced me to the study of linguistics when I was an undergraduate and opened to door to this academic field I enjoy today. Eunjeong Oh was my wonderful mentor when I started my graduate courses. She helped raise me higher than I could have done on my own. Suk-Jin Chang, Kiyong Lee, and Byung-Soo Park formed the basis of HPSG-based studies in Korean, on which I could build up my own understanding of HPSG-based linguistic models. I would like to thank other Korean linguists who helped me so much: Ho-Min Sohn, Chungmin Lee, Beom-mo Kang, Chung-hye Han, Hee-Rahk Chae, Tosang Chung, Sang-Geun Lee, Myung-Kwan Park, Jin-ho Park, Hae-Kyung Wee, Young Chul Jun, Hye-Won Choi, Eun-Jung Yoo, Minhaeng Lee, Byong-Rae Ryu, Sae Youn Cho, Jongsup Jun, Incheol Choi, Kyeong-min Kim, and many others.

After I joined Incheon National University, I have been supported by the faculty members of the Dept. of English Language and Literature. I give my thanks to Hyebae Yoo, Hwasoon Kim, Jung-Tae Kim, Yonghwa Lee, Seenhwa Jeon, So-yeon Yoon, and Hwanhee Park. I also want to express thanks to Kory Lauzon.

Lastly and most importantly, I would like to say that I love Ran Lee and Aaron Song so much.

This material is based upon work supported by the National Science Foundation under Grant No. 0644097. Any opinions, findings, and conclusions or recommendations expressed in this material are those of the author and do not necessarily reflect the views of the National Science Foundation.

Abbreviations

1/2/3	first/second/third	IOBJ	indirect object
ABS	absolutive	LE	*le* in Chinese
ACC	accusative	LOC	locative
AG	agentive	LV	light verb
AUX	auxiliary	NEG	negative
CF	contrastive focus	NOM	nominative
CLF	classifier	NONTOP	non-topic
CLITIC/CL	clitic	NULL	zero morpheme
COMP	complementizer	NUN	(*n*)*un* in Korean
COP	copula	OBJ	object
DAT	dative	PART	particle
DECL	declarative	PAST/PST	past
DEF	definite	PERF/PRT	perfective
DET	determiner	PL	plural
DE	*de* in Chinese	POLITE	polite
DIR	direction	PRES/PRS	present
DOBJ	direct object	PROG	progressive
ERG	ergative	PRON/PRO	pronoun
FOC/FC	focus	QUES	question
FUT	future	REFL	reflexive
GEN	genitive	REL	relative
HON	honorific	SG	singular
IMPF/IMP	imperfective	SHI	*shì* in Chinese
INF	infinite	TOP	topic
		WA	*wa* in Japanese

1 Introduction

Human languages consist of various structures, among which syntactic structure and semantic structure are particularly well known. The present study is primarily concerned with information structure, and the ways in which it could be leveraged in natural language processing applications.

Information structure is realized by prosodic, lexical, or syntactic cues which constrain interpretation to meet communicative demands within a specific context. Information structure is comprised of four primary components: focus, topic, contrast, and background. Focus marks what is new and/or important in a sentence, while topic marks what the speaker wants to talk about. Contrast, realized as either contrastive focus or contrastive topic, signals a contextually contrastive set of focus or topic items respectively. That which is not marked as either focus or topic is designated as background information.

Information structure affects the felicity of using a sentence in different discourse contexts, as exemplified in (1).

(1) a. Kim reads the book.

b. It is Kim that reads the book.

c. It is the book that Kim reads.

Though the sentences in (1b–c) are constructed using the same lexical items and describe the same state of affairs as sentence (1a), they differ with respect to how information is packaged: 'Kim' is focused in (1b), while 'the book' is focused in (1c). This difference in information structure means that (1b) would be a felicitous answer to *Who is reading the book?* and (1c) would be a felicitous answer to *What is that book?*, but not vice versa.

Furthermore, information structure can be key to finding felicitous translations (Paggio 1996; Kuhn 1996). Since languages vary in the ways they mark information structure, a model of information structure meanings and markings is a key component of a well-constructed grammar. For example, the simple English sentence (2a) can be translated into at least two Japanese allosentences

1 Introduction

(close paraphrases which share truth-conditions, Lambrecht 1996), with the nominative marker *ga* or with the so-called topic (and/or contrast) marker *wa*.

(2) a. I am Kim.

   b. watashi ga/wa   Kim desu.
       I   NOM/WA Kim COP [jpn]

The choice between alternatives is conditioned by context. Marking on the NP hinges on whether *watashi* 'I' functions as the topic or not. If the sentence is an answer to a question like *Who are you?*, *wa* is preferred. If the sentence is instead a reply to a question like *Who is Kim?*, answering using *wa* sounds unnatural.

This difference in felicity-conditions across languages should be taken into consideration in computational linguistics; in particular in machine translation. When machine translation systems cannot accurately model information structure, resulting translations may sound rather unnatural to native speakers. Successful translation requires reshaping how information is conveyed in accordance with the precepts of the target language and not simply changing words and reordering phrases in accordance with syntactic rules. Better accuracy in translation requires the incorporation of information structure.

1.1 Motivations

The nature of information structure is less understood than that of syntactic and semantic structures. For many languages the full range of information structure markings remains unknown. Furthermore, the integration of information structure has been rather understudied in computational linguistic investigations to date, despite its potential for improving machine translation, Text-to-Speech, automatic text summarization, and many other language processing systems.

There are several opportunities for improved incorporation of further exploration of information structure. First, the absence of cross-linguistic findings results in less use of the information in practical systems. In order for language processing systems to provide more fine-grained results and work truly language-independently, acquiring knowledge across languages is required (Bender 2011). Second, distributional findings obtained from language data are still insufficient. Several previous studies exploit language data for the study of information structure, but use merely monolingual or bilingual texts (Komagata 1999; Johansson 2001; Bouma, Øvrelid & Kuhn 2010; Hasegawa & Koenig 2011), so a larger picture of how information structure works across a range of languages is still elusive. Third, existing proposals for representing information structure within a grammatical framework for natural language processing remain somewhat underdeveloped and insufficiently tested. Previous literature, including King (1997), Steedman (2000), and Bildhauer (2007), provides a variety of formalisms to represent information structure, but none of them has been shown to be cross-linguistically valid. Moreover, their formalisms have never been implemented into a practical system in a fully comprehensive way. Lastly, largely for the reasons presented thus far, the potential improvement to machine translation and language processing systems derivable from using information structure has not yet been shown. If the contribution of information structure to improvement of practical applications were to be quantitatively substantiated through experimentation, this would motivate further development of information structure-based applications.

The central goal of this book is to create a computational model to handle information structure from a multilingual perspective within the HPSG (Head-driven Phrase Structure Grammar, Pollard & Sag 1994) framework, using the MRS (Minimal Recursion Semantics, Copestake et al. 2005) formalism, and contributing to the LinGO Grammar Matrix system (Bender et al. 2010).

1.2 Grammar engineering

In a nutshell, grammar engineering is the process of creating machine-readable implementations of formal grammars. In order to understand what grammar engineering is, it is necessary to define what language is. Since the early days of generative study in linguistics, language has been defined as (i) an infinite set of strings (ii) accepted as grammatical by (iii) native speakers, and grammar engineering has embraced this definition. (i) Given that the number of sentences in human language is assumed to be nonfinite, grammar engineering takes the generative capacity of grammar into account in sentence-generation as well as sentence-parsing. (ii) Since formulating grammatical well-formedness in a language is crucial, grammar engineering is fundamentally concerned with constructing a linguistically-precise and broad-coverage grammar. (iii) Finally, grammaticality has to be judged by native speakers. The judgment can be made either via linguistic intuition or with reference to language data such as corpora. Intuition-based and data-based methodologies complement each other in grammar engineering.[1]

---

[1] Baldwin et al. (2005), in the context of grammar engineering, discuss this spirit in an overall sense and conduct an evaluation using the ERG (English Resource Grammar, Flickinger 2000) and the BNC (British National Corpus, Burnard 2000). They substantiate the interaction of two sources of linguistic findings, namely acceptability judgments and corpus data.

1 Introduction

The main goal of grammar engineering is to build up reusable computational grammar resources. Ideally, the empirical description of the grammar resources is linguistically motivated. A grammar is to be described in a linguistically well-elaborated way, and on a large enough scale to cover the linguistic phenomena in a human language. For this purpose, grammar engineering also utilizes various types of linguistic data such as (machine-readable) dictionaries, corpora (Nichols et al. 2010; Song et al. 2010), testsuites (Oepen 2001), treebanks (Oepen et al. 2004; Bond, Fujita & Tanaka 2006), and wordnets (Bond et al. 2009; Pozen 2013). The described grammar should be able to run on a computer in order to prove its mathematical tractability as well as its potential for utilization. The constructed grammar has to be reusable for other studies with varied research goals.[2] Building upon the grammar resources, grammar engineering facilitates parsing and generation, which can be used for several practical applications such as machine translation, grammar checking, information extraction, question-answering, etc.

Within the field of grammar engineering, there are several competing theories of grammar, including HPSG, LFG (Lexical-Functional Grammar, Bresnan 2001), CCG (Combinatory Categorial Grammar, Steedman 2001), and TAG (Tree-Adjoining Grammar, Joshi & Schabes 1997). HPSG, which employs typed feature structures as a mathematical foundation, has been used for creation of reusable computational grammars in many languages. Those who study grammar engineering within the HPSG framework have cooperated with each other, by forming a consortium called DELPH-IN (DEep Linguistic Processing with HPSG - INitiative, http://www.delph-in.net).[3] DELPH-IN, in the spirit of open-source NLP (Pedersen 2008), provides research and development outcomes in a readily available way. These are largely gathered in the LOGON repository (http://moin.delph-in.net/LogonTop).[4] LOGON includes a collection of computational

---

[2] Bender (2008: 16) offers an explanation about how grammar engineering can be used for linguistic hypothesis testing: "[L]anguages are made up of many subsystems with complex interactions. Linguists generally focus on just one subsystem at a time, yet the predictions of any particular analysis cannot be calculated independently of the interacting subsystems. With implemented grammars, the computer can track the effects of all aspects of the implementation while the linguist focuses on developing just one."

[3] There are other initiatives based on HPSG as well as other frameworks, such as CoreGram for HPSG-based implementations (http://hpsg.fu-berlin.de/Projects/CoreGram.html) using the TRALE system (http://www.sfs.uni-tuebingen.de/hpsg/archive/projects/trale), and ParGram in LFG-based formalism (http://pargram.b.uib.no). There are also other HPSG-based grammars such as Enju for English (http://www.nactem.ac.uk/enju, Miyao & Tsujii 2008), and a Chinese grammar constructed in a similar way to Enju (Yu et al. 2010).

[4] Note that not all DELPH-IN resources are in the LOGON repository. For example, the collection of *Language CoLLAGE* is not in the repository, but is readily available (Bender 2014).

grammars, e.g., ERG for English (Flickinger 2000), Jacy for Japanese (Siegel, Bender & Bond 2016), KRG for Korean (Kim et al. 2011), GG for German (Crysmann 2003; 2005b,a), SRG for Spanish (Marimon 2012), LXGram for Portuguese (Branco & Costa 2010), Norsource for Norwegian (Hellan 2005), BURGER for Bulgarian (Osenova 2011), ZHONG for the Chinese languages (Fan, Song & Bond 2015a,b), INDRA for Indonesian (Moeljadi, Bond & Song 2015), and so forth, processors, e.g., LKB (Copestake 2002), PET (Callmeier 2000), etc., and other software packages, e.g., [incr tsdb()] (Oepen 2001).

One of the major projects under the DELPH-IN consortium is the LinGO Grammar Matrix (Bender et al. 2010). The LinGO Grammar Matrix customization system is an open source starter kit for the rapid development of HPSG/MRS-based grammars (http://www.delph-in.net/matrix/customize). The grammars created by the system are to be rule-based, scalable to broad-coverage, and cross-linguistically comparable. The main idea behind the system is that the common architecture simplifies exchange of analyses among groups of developers, and a common semantic representation speeds up implementation of multilingual processing systems such as machine translation.

The current work is largely dependent upon the results of the DELPH-IN consortium. First, I make use of the DELPH-IN formalism to construct the HPSG/MRS-based information structure library from a multilingual perspective on grammar engineering. Second, I refer to the comprehensive DELPH-IN grammars (i.e. resource grammars, such as the ERG and the Jacy) during the construction. Finally, I utilize the DELPH-IN tools to check the feasibility of what I propose and conduct several types of evaluations.

1.3 Outline

This book is divided into three parts, dedicated to exploring solutions to each of the problems mentioned in Section 1.1 individually from a perspective of grammar engineering (Section 1.2).

The first part explores various information structure meanings and markings and how they are related to each other within and across different languages. This is done through a review of previous studies on information structure as well as through a survey of various types of languages and their information structure systems. Building on this initial work and additional evidence, a more cross-linguistically valid explanation of information structure is provided. Chapter 3 lays out the meanings each component of information structure conveys, and Chapter 4 looks into three forms of expressing information structure, namely

1 Introduction

prosody, lexical markings, and sentence position. Chapter 5 discusses the discrepancies in meaning-form mapping of information structure.

The second part presents a formal architecture for representing information structure within the HPSG/MRS-based formalism. Several previous studies on information structure are surveyed in Chapter 6. After that, I propose the definition of a new constraint type and feature hierarchy for modeling information structure in HPSG/MRS. ICONS (mnemonic for Individual CONStraints) is presented as an extension to MRS in Chapters 7 and 8. Chapter 7 presents the fundamentals of representing information structure via ICONS, and Chapter 8 goes into the particulars of how ICONS works with some sample derivations. Chapter 9 shows how information structure in multiclausal utterances can be represented via ICONS, and Chapter 10 delves into several means of expressing information structure with reference to ICONS. Chapter 11 explores how focus projection can be supported by underspecification.

The third part is devoted to the implementation of an information structure-based computational model and evaluates the model. The present study is concerned with the LinGO Grammar Matrix system, especially aiming to create a library for information structure and add that library into the customization system (Bender & Flickinger 2005; Drellishak 2009; Bender et al. 2010). I discuss how the library for information structure is built up and how an information structure-based system works for multilingual machine translation. Chapter 12 builds up a grammar library for information structure and Chapter 13 addresses how machine translation can be improved using ICONS.

2 Preliminary notes

2.1 Examples

For ease of exposition, several typeface conventions are employed in this book to represent properties of information structure in examples. First, if a word (or phrase) bears the accent responsible for conveying focus, it is marked in SMALL CAPS. Second, **boldface** denotes an accent conveying topic. Third, [$_f$] stands for focus projection. For example, in the English Q/A pair in (1), DOG and **Kim** bear the A and B accents (Jackendoff 1972), respectively, and the focus that DOG (with the A-accent) conveys is projected to the VP *chased the* DOG.

(1) Q: What about Kim? What did Kim do?
     A: **Kim** [$_f$ chased the DOG].

Fourth, # means that a sentence sounds infelicitous in the given context, though the sentence itself is syntactically legitimate. Finally, ~~strike~~ means either a constituent is informatively empty or the given utterance cannot be generated from the semantic representation (i.e. MRS).

The examples that previous studies offer, as far as possible, are cited without any change. Thus, glossing conventions may not be consistent across examples. For example, the past morpheme may be glossed as PST in one article or PAST in another. All the examples created by me for the present study use the gender neutral names *Kim, Lee* and *Sandy* for any people, and the name *Fido* for any dog. When an example is excerpted from previous literature, the proper names in the example are not modified at all.

Where I have needed to modify an example from the source, the example has been judged by a native speaker of the language. Any sentences provided by native speaker consultants have also been faithfully reproduced. Every example presented in the present study has been taken from literature as is or verified by at least one native speaker. In the cases of Korean examples (a language of which I am a native speaker), examples were again, either taken from previous literature or created by me and judged by another Korean native speaker.

2 Preliminary notes

Table 2.1: Catalogue of languages

name	ISO 639-3	language family
Abma	app	Austronesian/Oceanic
Akan	aka	Niger-Congo/Kwa
Armenian	hye	Indo-European
Basque	eus	unknown
Bosnian Croatian Serbian	hbs	Indo-European/Slavic
Breton	bre	Indo-European/Celtic
Buli	bwu	Niger-Congo/Gur
Cantonese	yue	Sino-Tibetan
Catalan	cat	Indo-European/Romance
Cherokee	chr	Iroquoian
Chicheŵa	nya	Niger-Congo/Bantu
Czech	ces	Indo-European/Slavic
Danish	dan	Indo-European/Germanic
Ditammari	tbz	Niger-Congo/Gur
(Northern) Frisian	frr	Indo-European/Germanic
French	fra	Indo-European/Romance
Georgian	kat	Kartvelian
German	ger	Indo-European/Germanic
Greek	ell	Indo-European/Hellenic
Hausa	hau	Afro-Asiatic/Chadic
Hungarian	hun	Uralic
Ilonggo	hil	Austronesian/Philippine
Ingush	inh	Ingush
Italian	ita	Indo-European/Romance
Japanese	jpn	unknown
Korean	kor	unknown
Lakota	lkt	Siouan
Mandarin Chinese	cmn	Sino-Tibetan/Chinese
Miyako	mvi	Japonic
Moroccan Arabic	ary	Afro-Asiatic/Semitic
Navajo	nav	Athabaskan
Ngizim	ngi	Afro-Asiatic/Chadic
Nishnaabemwin	ojg/otw	Algic
Norwegian	nor	Indo-European/Germanic
Paumarí	pad	Arauan
Portuguese	por	Indo-European/Romance
Rendile	rel	Afro-Asiatic/Cushitic
Russian	rus	Indo-European/Slavic
Spanish	spa	Indo-European/Romance
Standard Arabic	arb	Afro-Asiatic/Semitic
Tangale	tan	Afro-Asiatic/Chadic
Turkish	tur	Turkic
Vietnamese	vie	Austro-Asiatic/Vietic
Wolof	wol	Niger-Congo/Senegambian
Yiddish	ydd	Indo-European/Germanic

Lexical markers in Korean and Japanese have been dealt with in different ways by previous literature. Because the current work aims to contribute to DELPH-IN grammars, I follow the approaches that Jacy (Siegel, Bender & Bond 2016) and KRG (Kim et al. 2011) are based on. KRG identifies the lexical markers in Korean (e.g. *i* / *ka* for nominatives, (*l*)*ul* for accusatives, and -(*n*)*un* for topics) as affixes responsible for syntactic (and sometimes semantic) functions of the phrases that they are attached to. In contrast, the lexical markers in Japanese (e.g. *ga*, *o*, and *wa*) have been treated as adpositions by Jacy, which behave as a syntactic head. In the literature, postpositions in Japanese, such as *ga* and *wa* are sometimes attached to NPs with a hyphen (e.g. *inu-ga* 'dog-NOM'), and sometimes separated by white space (e.g. *inu ga*). In extracted Japanese examples the presence/absence of the hyphen reflects its presence/absence in the original source. In any Japanese examples created by me, I make use of white space instead of a hyphen, following Jacy convention. Note that, different glossing formats notwithstanding, Japanese lexical markers are all implemented as adpositions (i.e. separate lexical items) in the current work. In Korean examples, following the convention in previous literature, hyphens are made use of (e.g. *kay-ka* 'dog-NOM') without any white space before lexical markers. Unlike the lexical markers in Japanese, those in Korean are dealt with and implemented as affixes.

Lastly, note that ISO 639-3 codes, such as [spa] for Spanish, [rus] for Russian, [eus] for Basque, [jpn] for Japanese, [kor] for Korean, [cmn] for Mandarin Chinese, [yue] for Cantonese, etc., are attached to all examples not in English. The language catalogue is provided in Table 2.1.

2.2 Terminology

In addition to differences in glossing conventions, there is also some variation in the terminology used by previous research into information structure. First, the distinction between focus *vs.* topic has sometimes been regarded as a relationship between rheme and theme, a distinction originally conceptualized by the Prague School. Within this framework, theme is defined as the element with the weakest communicative dynamism in a sentence, while rheme is defined as the element with the strongest communicative dynamism (Firbas 1992: 72).

Using slightly different terminologies, Vallduví (1990) considers focus to be the prime factor of information structure. A sentence, in Vallduví's schema, can be divided into focus and ground, and ground can be divided again into link and tail. Link is roughly equivalent to topic in this book, with tail corresponding to the remaining portion of the sentence. For example, in (2), *the* DOG functions as

2 Preliminary notes

the focus of the sentence and ***Kim chased*** is the ground of the sentence which comprises the link ***Kim*** and the tail *chased*.

(2) Q: What about Kim? What did Kim chase?
    A: [[**Kim**]~LINK~ chased]~GROUND~ the DOG.

Lastly, there is also some variation in labels for denoting contrast. Vallduví & Vilkuna (1998) use the term 'kontrast' in order to emphasize a different semantic behavior from non-contrastive focus. Instead of using theory-specific terms (e.g. rheme, theme, link, tail, kontrast), the current work, makes use of the most widespread and common terms for referring to components of information structure: focus, topic, contrast, and background.

On the other hand, to avoid potential confusion, the present work provides alternate terminology for several morphosyntactic phenomena. First, there are the OSV constructions in English as exemplified in (3b), which are sometimes cited as examples of 'topicalization' in the sense that *Mary* in (3a) is topicalized and preposed.

(3) a. John saw Mary yesterday.
    b. Mary, John saw yesterday. (Prince 1984: 213)

Instead, the present study calls such a construction 'focus/topic fronting' taking the stance that constructions like (3b) are ambiguous. Because a fronted phrase such as *Mary* in (3b) can be associated with either focus or topic, the term 'topicalization' cannot satisfactorily represent the linguistic properties of such a construction. Second, *wa* in Japanese and -*(n)un* in Korean have been labelled as 'topic markers' by many previous studies. However, they are not used exclusively to mark topics. They are sometimes employed in establishing contrastive focus. Thus, 'topic-marker' is not an appropriate name (see Section 5.1). Instead, the present study uses just *wa*-marking and *(n)un*-marking in order to avoid confusion. In the IGT (Interlinear Glossed Text) format of Japanese and Korean examples, even if the source of the IGT says TOP, they are glossed as WA and NUN unless there is a particular reason for saying TOP.

3 Meanings of information structure

The present study regards focus, topic, contrast, and background as the main categories of information structure, though there is a no broad consensus on these categories in many previous studies (Lambrecht 1996; Gundel 1999; Féry & Krifka 2008). (i) Focus means what is new and/or important in the sentence. (ii) Topic refers to what the sentence is about. (iii) Contrast applies to a set of alternatives, which can be realized as either focus or topic. (iv) Background is neither focus nor topic.

The main criterion for classifying components of information structure in the present study is the linguistic forms. If a particular language has a linguistically encoded means of marking an information structure meaning, the information structure category exists in human language as a cross-cutting component of information structure. This criterion is also applied to the taxonomy of information structure in each language. If a language has a linguistic means of expressing a type of information structure meaning, the corresponding component is assumed to function as an information structure value in the language.

The current analysis of information structure meanings builds on the following assumptions: (i) Every sentence has at least one focus, because new and/or important information plays an essential part in information processing in that all sentences are presumably communicative acts (Engdahl & Vallduví 1996; Gundel 1999). (ii) Sentences do not necessarily have a topic (Büring 1999), which means that there are topicless sentences in human language. (iii) Contrast, contra Lambrecht (1996), is treated as a component of information structure given that it can be linguistically expressed.[1] (iv) Sometimes, there is a linguistic item to which neither focus nor topic are assigned (Büring 1999), which is called background (also known as 'tail' in the schema of Vallduví & Vilkuna) hereafter.

Building upon the taxonomy presented above, the present study makes three fundamental assumptions. First, focus and topic cannot overlap with each other

---

[1]Lambrecht (1996: 290–291) says "Given the problems involved in the definition of the notion of contrastive, I prefer not to think of this notion as a category of grammar. To conclude, contrastiveness, unlike focus, is not a category of grammar but the result of the general cognitive processes referred to as conversational implicatures."

3 Meanings of information structure

in a single clause (Engdahl & Vallduví 1996).² That means there is no constituent that plays both roles at the same time in relation to a specific predicate.³ The information structure meaning of a constituent within a clause should be either, or neither of them (i.e. background). Second, as constituents that can receive prosodic accents presumably belong to informatively meaningful categories (Lambrecht 1996), contentful words and phrases either bear their own information structure meanings or assign an information structure meaning to other constituents. Finally, just as informatively meaningful categories exist, there are also lexical items to be evaluated as informatively meaningless. The informatively void items themselves cannot be associated with any component of information structure, though they can function in forming information structure.

3.1 Information status

Before discussing information structure meanings, it is necessary to go over information status such as givenness (i.e. new vs. old). It is my position that information structure interacts with but is distinct from information status.

Information status has been widely studied in tandem with information structure (Gundel 2003). For instance, Halliday (1967) claims that focus is not recoverable from the preceding discourse because what is focused is new. Cinque (1977) argues that the leftmost NPs and PPs in dislocation constructions have a restriction on information status in some languages. According to Cinque, in Italian, a required condition for placing a constituent to the left peripheral position of a sentence is that the constituent should deliver old information. Thus, NPs and PPs conveying new information cannot be detached from the rest of a sentence in Italian. This assumes that information status is represented by information structure meanings so that new information bears focus, and topic is something given in the context. However, there are more than a few counterexamples to this generalization (Erteschik-Shir 2007): New information can occasionally convey topic meaning, and likewise focus does not always carry new information.

Definiteness, upon which the choice of determiners is dependent, has also been assumed to have an effect on articulation of information structure: Definite

---

²There are alternative conceptions to this generalization, such as Krifka (2008): (i) Contrast is not a primitive. (ii) Alternatives are always introduced by focus. (iii) Contrastive topics contain a focus. (iv) Focus and topic are thus not mutually exclusive. The distributional and practical reasons for not taking these conceptions in the current work are provided in the remainder of this book from a special perspective of multilingual machine translation.

³Chapter 9 looks into two or more different information structure values that a constituent can have with respect to different clauses (i.e. multiclausal constructions).

3.1 Information status

NPs carry old information, and indefinite NPs carry new information. Thus, it has been thought that indefinite NPs cannot be the topic of a sentence, unless used for referencing generics (Lambrecht 1996). In particular, topic-comment structures have a tendency to assign a topic relation to only definite NPs. Kuroda (1972), for instance, claims that *wa*-marked NPs in Japanese, widely assumed to deliver topic meaning, can be only translated into definite NPs or indefinite non-specific NPs in English, while *ga*-marked NPs (i.e. ordinary nominatives) do not have such a correspondence restriction in translation. A similar phenomenon can be found in Chinese. Chinese employs three types of word orders such as SVO (unmarked), SOV, and OSV, but the ordering choice is influenced by the definiteness of the object: The preverbal object in SOV and OSV constructions seldom allows an indefinite non-specific expression.

(1) a. wo zai zhao yi-ben xiaoshuo.
 I at seek one-CL novel
 'I am looking for a novel.' (SVO)

 b. *wo yi-ben xiaoshuo zai zhao.
 I one-CL novel at seek (SOV)

 c. *yi-ben xiaoshuo, wo zai zhao.
 one-CL novel I at seek (OSV) [cmn]

 (Huang, Li & Li 2009: 200)

However, there are quite a few counterarguments to the generalization that topic is always associated with definiteness. Erteschik-Shir (2007) argues that the correspondence between marking definiteness and topichood is merely a tendency. This argument is supported for several languages. First, Yoo, An & Yang (2007), exploiting a large English-Korean bilingual corpus, verify there is no clear-cut corresponding pattern between (in)definite NPs in English and the NP-marking system (e.g. *i* / *ka* for nominatives vs. -(*n*)*un* for topics or something else) in Korean. Thus, we cannot say that the correlation between expressing definiteness and topichood is cross-linguistically true. Second, since some languages (e.g. Russian) seldom use definite markers, we cannot equate definiteness with topichood at the surface level. Definiteness is presumed to be a language universal. Every language has (in)definite phrases in interpretation, even though this is not necessarily overtly expressed in a languages. Of particular importance to the current work are the overt marking systems of definiteness in some languages. For instance, distinctions between different types of determiners (e.g.

3 Meanings of information structure

the/*a(n)* in English) do not have a one-to-one correspondence with information structure components. So that in English, for example, not all NPs specified with *the* deliver a topic meaning, and NPs with *a(n)* have topic meaning in certain circumstances.

I conclude that information status is neither a necessary nor a sufficient condition for identifying information structure; the relationship between the two is simply a tendency and quite language-specific. For this reason, in the present work, I downplay the discussion of information status, and instead pay more attention to information structure.

3.2 Focus

3.2.1 Definition

Focus, from a pragmatic point of view, refers to what the speaker wants to draw the hearer's attention to (Erteschik-Shir 2007; Féry & Krifka 2008). Lambrecht (1996) regards the basic notion of focus in (2).

(2) a. Pragmatic Presupposition: the set of presuppositions lexicogrammatically evoked in an utterance which the speaker assumes the hearer already knows or believes or is ready to take for granted at the time of speech. (Lambrecht 1996: 52)

　　b. Pragmatic Assertion: the presupposition expressed by a sentence which the hearer is expected to know or believe or take for granted as a result of hearing the sentence uttered. (Lambrecht 1996: 52)

　　c. Focus: the semantic component of a pragmatically structured proposition whereby the assertion differs from the presupposition. (Lambrecht 1996: 213)

In a nutshell, focus encompasses what speakers want to say importantly and/or newly, and this is influenced by both semantics and pragmatics. Building upon (2), the current work represents information structure within the MRS (Minimal Recursion Semantics, Copestake et al. 2005) formalism. In the following subsection, approaches to the taxonomy of focus are provided on different levels of classification (syntactic, semantic, and pragmatic). Among them, I mainly adapt Gundel's classification, because it is based on linguistic markings. Ultimately, semantic focus (also known as non-contrastive focus) and contrastive focus are distinguishably marked in quite a few languages, and they exhibit different linguistic behaviors from each other across languages.

3.2.2 Subtypes of focus

3.2.2.1 Lambrecht (1996)

Lambrecht classifies focus into three subtypes depending on how focus meaning spreads into larger phrases; (a-i) argument focus, (a-ii) predicate focus, and (a-iii) sentential focus. The main classification criterion Lambrecht proposes is sentential forms, which suggests that how a sentence is informatively articulated largely depends on the scope that the focus has in a sentence. For argument focus, the domain is a single constituent such as a subject, an object, or sometimes an oblique argument. Predicate focus has often been recognized as the second component of 'topic-comment' constructions. That is, when a phrase excluding the fronted constituent is in the topic domain, the rest of the sentence is an instance of predicate focus. Sentential focus's domain is the entire sentence.

This notion has been developed in quite a few studies. For instance, Paggio (2009) offers a type hierarchy for sentential forms, looking at how components of information structure are articulated and ordered in a sentence.[4] In the taxonomy of Paggio (2009), there are two main branches, namely focality and topicality. As subtypes of focality, Paggio presents narrow focus and wide focus. Note that argument focus is not the same as narrow focus. The former means that an argument (i.e. NP) of the predicate is marked as the focus of the clause, while the latter means that a single word is marked as the focus of the clause. Thus, non-nominal categories such as verbs, adjectives, and even adverbs can be narrowly focused. The same goes for the distinction between predicate focus and wide focus. Predicate focus literally means that the predicate plays the core role of focus, and the focus is spread onto the larger VPs. Wide focus and predicate focus both involve focus projection, but the core of wide focus can be from various lexical categories, including nominal ones (e.g. common nouns, proper names, pronouns, etc.). In other words, argument focus is a subset of narrow focus; predicate focus is a subset of wide focus, and a narrow focus is not necessarily an argument focus; a wide focus does not necessarily involves a predicate focus.

---

[4]The type hierarchy that Paggio proposes is presented in Chapter 6 with discussion about which implication it has on the current work.

3 Meanings of information structure

3.2.2.2 É. Kiss (1998)

É. Kiss, in line with alternative semantics (Rooth 1992), suggests a distinction between (b-i) identificational focus and (b-ii) informational focus.

(3) An identificational focus represents a subset of the set of contextually or situationally given elements for which the predicate phrase can potentially hold. (É. Kiss 1998: 245)

(3) implies that identificational focus has a relation to a powerset of the set consisting of all the elements in the given context. Thus, the elements in the alternative set of identificational foci are already introduced in the context, while those of informational foci are not provided in the prior context. The difference between them can be detected in the following sentences in Hungarian; (4a–b) exemplify identificational focus and informational focus, respectively.

(4) a. Mari EGY KALAPOT nézett ki magának.
　　　 Mary a　 hat.ACC　picked out herself.ACC
　　　 'It was A HAT that Mary picked for herself.'

　　b. Mari ki nézett magának　 EGY KALAPOT.
　　　 Mary out picked herself.ACC a　 hat.ACC
　　　 'Mary picked for herself A HAT.' [hun] (É. Kiss 1998: 249)

According to É. Kiss, (4a) sounds felicitous in a situation in which Mary was trying to pick up something at a clothing store, which implies that she chose only one hat among the clothes in the store, and nothing else. (4b), by contrast, does not presuppose such a collection of clothes, and provides just new information that she chose a hat. In other words, there exists an alternative set given within the context in (4a), which establishes the difference between identificational focus and informational focus.

3.2.2.3 Gundel (1999)

Gundel, mainly from a semantic standpoint, divides focus into (c-i) psychological focus, (c-ii) semantic focus (also known as non-contrastive focus), and (c-iii) contrastive focus. Psychological focus, according to Gundel's explanation, refers to the current center of attention, and has to do with unstressed pronouns, zero anaphora, and weakly stressed constituents. Among the three subtypes that Gundel presents, the current work takes only the last two as the subtypes of focus, because psychological focus seems to related to information status, rather than information structure.

Gundel offers some differences between semantic focus and contrastive focus. First, semantic focus is the most prosodically and/or syntactically prominent.[5] This is in line with Givón's claim that the most important element in a cognitive process naturally has a strong tendency to be realized in the most marked way. This property of focus is also argued by Büring (2010) as presented in (5).

(5) Focus Prominence: Focus needs to be maximally prominent. (Büring 2010: 277)

Second, semantic focus does not necessarily bring an entity into psychological focus, whereas contrastive focus always does. Finally, semantic focus is truth-conditionally sensitive, while contrastive focus has a comparably small influence on the truth-conditions (Gundel 1999).[6]

3.2.2.4 Gussenhoven (2007)

Gussenhoven classifies focus in English into seven subtypes in terms of its functional usage within the context. These include (d-i) presentational focus, (d-ii) corrective focus, (d-iii) counterpresupposition focus, (d-iv) definitional focus, (d-v) contingency focus, (d-vi) reactivating focus, and (d-vii) identificational focus. (d-i) Presentational focus is a focused item corresponding to *wh*-words in questions. (d-ii) Corrective focus and (d-iii) counterpresupposition focus appear when the speaker wants to correct an item of information that the hearer incorrectly assumes. In the current study, these subtypes are regarded as contrastive focus such that the correction test can be used as a tool to vet contrastive focus (Gryllia 2009). (d-iv) Definitional focus and (d-v) contingency focus, which usually occur with an individual-level predicate, aim to inform the hearer of the attendant circumstances: For example, *Your EYES are BLUE.* states that the eye-color of the hearer is generically blue. (d-vi) Reactivating focus, unlike other subtypes of focus, is assigned on given information and is realized by the syntactic device called focus/topic fronting in the present study. Finally, (d-vii) identificational focus (É. Kiss 1998) is realized within clefts (e.g., *It is JOHN who she dislikes.*). The taxonomy provided by Gussenhoven has its own significance in that it shows the

---

[5] Of course, contrastive focus is also prosodically and/or morphosyntactically marked. What is to be noted is that semantic focus is assigned to the most prominent constituent in a sentence.
[6] It is reported that contrastive focus is sometimes relevant to the truth-conditions. Suffice it to say that semantic focus is highly and necessarily sensitive to the truth-conditions.

3 Meanings of information structure

various functions that focus performs, but the present study does not directly use it. Gussenhoven's subtypes seem to be about the way in which focus is used to different communicative ends (i.e. pragmatics), which is not synonymous with focus as defined in the current work. Recall that I restrict the subtypes of information structure components to those which are signaled by linguistic marking in human languages.

3.2.2.5 Summary

Regarding the subtypes of focus, the present study draws primarily from Gundel (1999), except for psychological focus which has more relevance to information status. The present study classifies focus into semantic focus (also known as non-contrastive focus) and contrastive focus for two main reasons. First, in quite a few languages, these focus types are distinctively expressed via different lexical markers or different positions in a clause. Second, they show clearly different behaviors. In particular, semantic focus is relevant to truth-conditions, while contrastive focus is not so much. In contrast, Lambrecht (1996) provides a classification in terms of how a sentence is configured. The classification has to do with focus projection and the ways in which focus spreads from a core onto a larger phrase. The classification that É. Kiss (1998) proposes has not been applied to the basic taxonomy of focus in the present study, but the key distinction (i.e. identificational vs. informational) is reviewed in the analysis of cleft constructions. Gussenhoven's subtypes show various properties of focused elements, but they are not also straightforwardly incorporated into the analysis of focus herein. This is mainly because they are seldom linguistically distinguishable.

3.2.3 Linguistic properties of focus

There are three major properties of focus realization; (i) inomissibility, (ii) felicity-conditions, and (iii) truth-conditions.

3.2.3.1 Inomissibility

Information structure is a matter of how information that a speaker bears in mind is articulated in a sentence. Thus, formation of information structure has to do with selecting the most efficient way to convey what a speaker wants to say. Focus is defined as what is new and/or important in an utterance and necessarily refers to the most marked element in an utterance (Gundel 1999; Büring 2010).

3.2 Focus

Due to the fact that if the maximally prominent information is missing, a conversation becomes void and infelicitous, focus can never be dropped from the utterance.[7] For this reason, inomissibility has been commonly regarded as the universal factor of focus realization in previous literature (Lambrecht 1996; Rebuschi & Tuller 1999): Only non-focused constituents can be elided. Lambrecht, for instance, suggests an ellipsis test. In (6), *John* and *he* convey topic meaning, and *he* can be elided as shown in (6A2). In contrast, if the subjects are focused, elision is disallowed as shown in (7A2).[8]

(6) Q: What ever happened to John?
    A1: John married ROSA, but he didn't really LOVE her.
    A2: John married ROSA, but didn't really LOVE her.
                    (Lambrecht 1996: 136)

(7) Q: Who married Rosa?
    A1: JOHN married her, but he didn't really LOVE her.
    A2: *?JOHN married her, but didn't really LOVE her.
                    (Lambrecht 1996: 136)

For this reason, the present study argues that (8) is the most important property of focus.

(8) Focus is an information structure component associated with an inomissible constituent in an utterance.

This property can also be straightforwardly applied to contrastive focus. Constituents associated with contrastive focus cannot be elided, either.[9] This is the main distinction between contrastive focus and contrastive topic. As mentioned before, contrast is realized as either contrastive focus or contrastive topic. In other words, a constituent conveying contrastiveness should be either of these. In some cases, because many languages use the same marking system to express both contrastive focus and contrastive topic and they share a large number of properties, it would be hard to discriminate them using existing tests. However,

---

[7] Note that this distinguishes focus as a component of information structure from the information status *in focus*, since referents that are *in focus* can often be referred to with zero anaphora (Gundel 2003).

[8] It appears that the acceptability of (7A2) differs by different speakers. Suffice it to say that (7A2) sounds less acceptable than (7A1).

[9] In terms of the HPSG formalism, because contrastive focus is also a specific type of focus, linguistic features plain focus involves are directly inherited into contrastive focus.

3 Meanings of information structure

when we test whether a constituent is omissible or not, they are distinguishable. A constituent with contrastive focus cannot be dropped, whereas one with contrastive topic can. This difference between them is exemplified in Chapter 5 (p. 72) with reference to discrepancies between meanings and markings.

The fact that focus can only be assigned to constituents which are contextually inomissible logically entails another theorum that dropped elements in subject/topic-drop languages can never be evaluated as conveying focus meaning. It is well known that subjects in some languages such as Italian and Spanish can be dropped, which is why they are called subject-drop languages. What should be noted is that there is a constraint on dropping subjects. Cinque (1977: 406) argues that subject pronouns in Italian are omissible everywhere unless the subjects give new information (i.e. focus from the perspective of the current study).

I argue that *pro*-drop is relevant to expressing information structure, mainly focusing on argument optionality (Saleem 2010; Saleem & Bender 2010): Some languages often and optionally drop NPs with non-focus meaning. That is, dropped arguments in *pro*-drop languages must be non-focus. *Pro*-drop can be divided into two subtypes: subject-drop and topic-drop.[10] Typical examples of topic-drop are shown in (9) (a set of multilingual translations, excerpted from *The Little Prince* written by *Antoine de Saint-Exupéry*). (9) are answers in English, Spanish, Korean, and (Mandarin) Chinese to a *wh*-question like *What are you doing there?*.

(9) a. I am drinking.

    b. ∅ Bebo.
       (I) drink.1SG.PRES [spa]

    c. ∅ swul   masi-n-at.
       (I) alcohol drink-PRES-DECL [kor]

    d. (wǒ) hē   jiǔ.
       I   drink alcohol [cmn]

The subjects in (9a–d) are all first person, and also function as the topic of the sentences. The different languages have several different characteristics. (i) The

---

[10] We cannot equate topics with a single grammatical category like subjects at least in English, Spanish, Korean, and Chinese. Linguistic studies, nonetheless, have provided ample evidence that topics and subjects have a close correlation with each other across languages: Subjects normally are the most unmarked topics in most languages (Lambrecht 1996; Erteschik-Shir 2007). Therefore, in more than a few cases, it is not easy to make a clear-cut distinction between subject-drop and topic-drop, which stems from the fact that subjects display a tendency to be interpreted as topics.

use of 'I' in (9a) is obligatory in English. (ii) The subject in Spanish, a morphologically rich language, can be freely dropped as shown in (9b). (iii) The subject in Korean is also highly omissible as shown in (9c), though Korean does not employ any agreement in the morphological paradigm. (iv) Chinese, like English, is morphologically impoverished, and also is like Korean in that it does not have inflection on the verb according to the subject. The subject in Chinese (e.g. wǒ 'I' in 9d) can be dropped as well. The subjectless sentences exemplified in (9c–d) in Korean and Chinese have been regarded as instances of topic-drop in quite a few previous studies in tandem with the subjectless sentences in subject-drop languages (e.g. Spanish) (Li & Thompson 1976; Huang 1984; Yang 2002; Alonso-Ovalle et al. 2002).

3.2.3.2 Felicity-conditions

Felicity is conditioned by how a speaker organizes an utterance with respect to a particular context. For this reason, information structure generally affects felicity conditions. That is, information structure should be interpreted with respect to the contexts in which an utterance of a particular form can be successfully and cooperatively used.

Information structure has often been studied in terms of allosentences. These are close paraphrases which share truth-conditions (Lambrecht 1996). Engdahl & Vallduví (1996) begin their analysis with a set of allosentences though they do not use that terminology. Allosentences (10a–b) differ in the way their content is packaged: (10a) in which the object is focused is an appropriate answer to a question like *What does he hate?*, while (10b) in which the verb is focused is not. Propositions in (10a–b) have in common what they assert about the world (i.e. the same truth-condition), but differ in the way the given information is structured.

(10) a. He hates CHOCOLATE.

   b. He HATES chocolate.

   c. Chocolate he LOVES. (Engdahl & Vallduví 1996: 2)

In a nutshell, allosentences are sentences which differ only in felicity-conditions. Although a set of allosentences is comprised of exactly the same propositional content, the sentences convey different meanings from each other, and the differences are caused by how focus is differently expressed.

3 Meanings of information structure

3.2.3.3 Truth-conditions

Information structure can also impact truth conditions (Partee 1991; Gundel 1999). Beaver & Clark (2008) claim that focus sensitive items deliver complex and nontrivial meanings which differ from language to language, and their contribution to meaning is rather difficult to elicit. What is notable with respect to focus sensitive items is that if there is an item whose contribution to the truth-conditional semantics (e.g., where it attaches in the semantic structure) is focus-sensitive, then changes in information structure over what is otherwise the same sentence containing that item should correlate with changes in truth-conditions.

Focus sensitive items related to truth-conditions include modal verbs (e.g. *must*), frequency adverbs (e.g. *always*), counterfactuals, focus particles (e.g. *only, also,* and *even*), and superlatives (e.g. *first, most,* etc.) (Partee 1991). One well known example is shown in (11), originally taken from Halliday (1970).

(11) a. Dogs must be CARRIED.

    b. DOGS must be carried. (Partee 1991: 169)

They are respectively interpreted as (a) MUST(dog(x) & here(x), x is carried) and (b) MUST(here(e), a dog or dogs is/are carried at e) or MUST(you carry x here, you carry a dog here) (Partee 1991: 169). In other words, the focused items in (11a–b) differ, and they cause differences in truth-conditions. To take another example, the sentences shown in (12b–c) do not share the same truth-conditions due to two focus-sensitive operators *most* and *first*. They convey different meanings depending on which item the A-accent (H* in the ToBI format, Bolinger 1961; Jackendoff 1972) falls on.

(12) a. The most students got BETWEEN 80 AND 90 on the first quiz.

    b. The most students got between 80 and 90 on the FIRST quiz. (Partee 1991: 172)

3.2.4 Tests for Focus

As exemplified several times so far, *wh*-questions are commonly used to probe meaning and marking of focus (Lambrecht 1996; Gundel 1999). The phrase answering the *wh*-word of the question is focused in most cases; the focused part of the reply may be either a word (i.e. narrow focus, or argument focus), a phrase consisting of multiple words (i.e. wide focus, or predicate focus), or a sentence including the focused item (i.e. all focus, or sentence focus). For instance, if a *wh*-question is given like *What barks?*, the corresponding answer to the *wh*-word bears the A-accent, such as *The DOG barks*.

It seems clear that using *wh*-questions is a very reliable test for identifying focus in the sense that we can determine which linguistic means are used in a language. Yet, there are also instances in which *wh*-questions cannot be used. In particular, it is sometimes problematic to use *wh*-questions to locate focused constituents in running texts, which do not necessarily consist of Q/A pairs. Moreover, it can be difficult to pinpoint focused elements unless the marking system used is orthographically expressed. For instance, since the primary way to express information structure meanings in English is prosody, *wh*-questions are unlikely to be determinate when analyzing written texts in English.[11]

In order to make up for the potential shortcomings of the *wh*-test, the present study employs the deletion test, leveraging the fact that focused items are inomissible. As illustrated in the previous subsection (Section 3.2.3.1), inomissibility is an essential linguistic property of focus.[12]

3.3 Topic

3.3.1 Definition

Topic refers to what a sentence is about (Strawson 1964; Lambrecht 1996; H.-W. Choi 1999), which can be defined as (13).

(13) An entity, E, is the topic of a sentence, S, iff in using S the speaker intends to increase the addressee's knowledge about, request information about, or otherwise get the addressee to act with respect to E. (Gundel 1988: 210)

There is an opposing point of view to this generalization. Vermeulen (2009) argues that what the sentence is about is not necessarily the topic of the sentence. Vermeulen does not analyze the subject *he* in (14A) as the topic of, even though

---

[11] This problem is also raised by Gracheva (2013), who utilizes the Russian National Corpus for a study of contrastive structures in Russian. She points out that it is troublesome to apply existing tests of information structure, such as *wh*-questions, to naturally occurring speech. This is because, when working with running text, it is actually impossible to separate a single sentence from the context and test it independently.

[12] Another test for focus is identifying the strongest stress (Rebuschi & Tuller 1999), but Casielles-Suárez (2004) provides a counterexample to this test. Casielles-Suárez reveals that primary stress does not always guarantee the focus even in English. In particular, finding the more remarkable stress is not available for the present study that basically aims at text processing.

3 Meanings of information structure

the sentence is about the subject. According to Vermeulen, *he* is an anaphoric item that merely refers back to the so-called discourse topic *Max* in (14Q).

(14) Q: Who did Max see yesterday?
A: He saw Rosa yesterday.

However, this analysis is not adopted by the current work for two reasons: First, Vermeulen's argument runs counter to the basic assumption presented by Lambrecht (1996), who asserts that a topic has to designate a discourse referent internal to the given context. Second, if the answer (14A), given to a question like *Who did Max see yesterday?*, is translated into Korean in which the *-(n)un* marker is used in complementary distribution with the nominative marker *i / ka*, *ku* 'he' can be combined with only the *-(n)un* marker as shown in (14').

(14') Q: Mayksu-nun/ka ecey mwues-ul po-ass-ni?
Max-NUN/NOM yesterday what-ACC see-PST-QUES
'What did Max see yesterday.'
A: ku-nun/#ka ecey losa-lul po-ass-e.
he-NUN/NOM yesterday Rosa-ACC see-PST-DECL
'He saw Rosa yesterday.' [kor]

That is to say, though *he* in (14A) is an anaphoric element connecting to the discourse topic *Max*, it can function as the topic in at least one language with relatively clear marking of topic.

There is another question partially related to (13): Are there topicless sentences? There are two different viewpoints on this. Erteschik-Shir (2007) argues that every sentence has a topic, though the topic does not overtly appear, and a topic that covertly exists is a so-called stage topic. According to Erteschik-Shir's claim, topic is always given in sentences in human language, because topic is relevant to knowledge the hearer possesses. In contrast, Büring (1999) argues that topic may be non-existent, in terms of sentential forms. Büring assumes that sentences, in terms of information structure, are composed of focus, topic, and background, and a sentence may be either an all-focus construction, a bipartite construction (i.e. lacking topic), or a tripartite construction consisting of all three components, including background. In fact, these arguments are not incompatible with Erteschik-Shir simply putting more emphasis on psychological status, and Büring emphasizing form. The present study follows Büring's argument, because I am interested in mapping linguistic forms to information structure meaning.

3.3.2 Subtypes of topic

Given that contrast is one of the cross-cutting categories in information structure, topics can be divided into two subtypes: contrastive topic and non-contrastive topic (here renamed aboutness-topic in line with H.-W. Choi's claim that aboutness is the core concept of regular topics). In comparison with other components of information structure, contrastive topic has been relatively understudied, with a few notable exceptions. Contrastive topic has been addressed in Japanese and Korean in reference to *wa* and *-(n)un* (also known as topic markers) (Kuno 1973; H.-W. Choi 1999). Additionally, Arregi (2003) identifies clitic left dislocation in Spanish and other languages as a syntactic operation to articulate contrastive topic.

In addition to those outlined above, Féry & Krifka (2008) present another subtype of topics: frame-setting topics. Chafe (1976: 50) defines a frame-setting topic as an element which sets "a spatial, temporal or individual framework within which the main predication holds", and it can be formally defined as (15).

(15) Frame-setting: In (X Y), X is the frame for Y iff X specifies a domain of (possible) reality to which the proposition expressed by Y is restricted. (J. Jacobs 2001: 656)

This terminology is not directly included into the taxonomy of information structure meanings (i.e. the type hierarchy of information structure) in the current work, but its linguistic constraints are incorporated into the information structure library. This is mainly because frame-setting topics are redundant with other topic types (particularly, contrastive topic) with respect to semantic representation.

Frame-setting topics are universally associated with sentence-initial adjuncts (Lambrecht 1996: 118) though not all sentence-initial adjuncts are necessarily frame-setting topics (i.e., the relation is not bidirectional). In other words, frame-setting topics have one constraint on sentence positioning; they should be sentence-initial. Féry & Krifka (2008) give an example of frame setting as shown in (16), in which the sentence talks about the subject *John*, but is only concerned with his health. Thus, the aboutness topic is assigned to *John*, but frame setting narrows down the aspect of description.[13]

---

[13] In a similar vein but from a different point of view, J. Jacobs (2001: 656) argues that frame-setting is divergent from the other topics in terms of dimensions of Topic-Comment: "..., frame-setting is not a feature of all instances of TC but just one of the dimensions of TC that may or may not occur in TC sentences."

3 Meanings of information structure

(16) Q: How is John?
     A: {Healthwise}, he is FINE (Féry & Krifka 2008: 128).

As mentioned above, the present work does not regard frame-setting topics as one of the cross-cutting components that semantically contribute to information structure. Since the property of frame-setting topics refers to a syntactic operation expressing information structure, hereafter it is referred to as a frame-setter. Various types of constructions can be used as a frame-setter. First, the 'as for ...' construction in English serves as a frame-setter as exemplified in (16) and (17).

(17) Q: How is John?
     A: {As for his health}, he is FINE (Féry & Krifka 2008: 128).

Second, adverbial categories (e.g. *Healthwise* in 16A) can sometimes serve as frame-setters. For instance, regarding (i), in (18) in German, where *gestern abend* 'yesterday evening' and *körperlich* 'physically' are fronted, the frame-setting topic is assigned to the adverbials. This property is conjectured to be applicable to all other languages (Chafe 1976; Lambrecht 1996).

(18) a. Gestern abend haben wir Skat gespielt.
        yesterday evening have we Skat played
        'Yesterday evening, we played Skat.'

     b. Körperlich geht es Peter sehr gut.
        physically goes it Peter very well
        'Physically, Peter is doing very well.' [ger] (Götze, Dipper & Skopeteas 2007: 169)

An adjunct NP can sometimes be a frame-setter, if and only if it appears in the sentence-initial position. In the Japanese sentence (19) below, the genuine subject of the sentence is *supiido suketaa* 'speed skater', while *Amerika* 'America' restricts the domain of what the speaker is talking about. Note that since frame-setters are realized as a topic, they are normally realized by the *wa*-marking.

(19) Amerika wa supiido suketaa ga hayai.
     America WA speed skater NOM fast
     'As for America, the speed skaters are fast.' [jpn]

Therefore, the first NP combined with *wa* is interpreted as topic, whereas the second phrase with the nominative marker *ga*, which functions as the subject, does not convey topic meaning. Adjunct clauses which set the frame to restrict the temporal or spatial situation of the current discourse also have a topic relation with the main clause. Haiman (1978) and Ramsay (1987) argue that sentence-initial conditional clauses function as the topic of the whole utterance. The same goes for sentence-initial temporal clauses. For instance, in (20), taken from the translation of *The Little Prince* written by *Antoine de Saint-Exupéry*, the entire temporal clause *when he arrived on the planet* is dealt with as the frame-setter of the sentence.

(20) When he arrived on the planet, he respectfully saluted the lamplighter.

In sum, frame-setters must show up before anything else, and this holds true presumably across all languages (Chafe 1976; Lambrecht 1996). The role of frame-setters is assigned to sentence-initial constituents which narrow down the domain of what the speaker is talking about as defined in (15). It can be assigned to various types of phrases including adverbs and even adjunct clauses. The syntactic restrictions on frame-setters are not reflected in the current classification of topics, because the present work intends to provide a semantics-based classification of information structure components. The only semantic distinctions between frame-setter and other topics are orthogonal to information structure.

3.3.3 Linguistic properties of topic

This subsection discusses several linguistic properties which should be taken into consideration in the creation of a computational model for the realization of topics; (i) scopal interpretation relying on the topic relation, (ii) clausal constraints, (iii) multiple topics, and (iv) verbal topics.

3.3.3.1 Scopal interpretation

Many previous studies argue that topics take wide scope. For instance, according to Büring (1997), if a rise-fall accent contour in German co-occurs with negation, the prosodic marking disambiguates a scopal interpretation. For example, (21a) would have two scopal readings if it were not for prosodic marking, but in (21b), in which '/' and '\' stand for rise and fall respectively, there is only a single available meaning.

(21) a. Alle Politiker sind nicht korrupt.
    all politicians are not corrupt
    (a) $\sqrt{\forall} > \neg$ 'For all politicians, it is not the case that they are corrupt.'
    (b) $\sqrt{\neg} > \forall$ 'It is not the case that all politicians are corrupt.'

3 Meanings of information structure

    b. / A<small>LLE</small> Politiker   sind N<small>ICHT</small> \ korrupt.
       all   politicians are not   corrupt
       *∀>¬, √¬>∀ [ger] (Büring 1997: 175)

3.3.3.2 Clausal constraints

Topics can appear in non-matrix clauses, but there are some clausal constraints. Lambrecht (1996: 126) offers an observation that some languages mark the difference in topicality between matrix and non-matrix clauses by morphosyntactic means. To take a well known example, Kuno (1973) argues that the topic marker *wa* in Japanese tends not to be attached to NPs in embedded clauses, and it is my intuition that Korean shares the same tendency. Yet, a tendency is just a tendency. Some subordinate clauses are evaluated as containing topic. (22) presents two counterexamples from Korean.

(22) a. hyangki-nun coh-un   kkoch-i   phi-n-ta.
       scent-N<small>UN</small>   good-R<small>EL</small> flower-N<small>OM</small> bloom-P<small>RES</small>-D<small>ECL</small>
       'A flower with a good scent blooms.'

    b. Chelswuka-ka insayng-un yuhanha-tako malha-yss-ta.
       Cheolsoo-N<small>OM</small> life-N<small>UN</small>   limited-C<small>OMP</small> say-P<small>ST</small>-D<small>ECL</small>
       'Cheolsoo said that life is limited.' [kor] (Lim 2012: 229)

First, Lim argues that -(*n*)*un* can be used in a relative clause as given in (22a) when the (*n*)*un*-marked NP conveys a contrastive meaning (i.e. a contrastive focus in this case). The relative clause in (22a), which modifies the following NP *kkoch* 'flower', conveys a meaning like *The flower smells good, but contrastively it does not look so good.*, and -(*n*)*un* attached to *hyangki* 'scent' is responsible for the contrastive reading. If *hyangki* is combined with a nominative marker *ka*, instead of *nun*, the sentence still sounds good as presented in (22'a), but the contrastive meaning becomes very weak or just disappears.

(22') a. hyangki-ka coh-un   kkoch-i   phi-n-ta.
       scent-N<small>OM</small>   good-R<small>EL</small> flower-N<small>OM</small> bloom-P<small>RES</small>-D<small>ECL</small>
       'A flower with a good scent blooms.' [kor]

Second, if the main predicate is concerned with speech acts (e.g. *malha* 'say') as is the case in (22b), non-matrix clauses can have topicalized constituents.

    The relationship between topic and clausal types has been discussed in previous literature with special attention to the so-called root phenomena (Haegeman 2004; Heycock 2007; Bianchi & Frascarelli 2010; Roberts 2011). Roberts, for instance, provides several English examples in which the topic shows up in the non-matrix clauses.

(23) a. Bill warned us that **flights to Chicago** we should try to avoid. (Emonds 2004: 77)

b. It appears that **this book** he read thoroughly. (Hooper & Thompson 1973: 478)

c. I am glad that **this unrewarding job**, she has finally decided to give up. (Bianchi & Frascarelli 2010: 69)

These examples imply that left-dislocated constituents can appear in embedded clauses even in English, if the main predicate denotes speech acts (e.g. *warn* in 23a), quasi-evidentials (e.g. *it appears* in 23b), or (semi-)factives (e.g. *be glad* in 23c).

This property of topics in non-matrix clauses needs to be considered when I build up a model of information structure for multiclausal utterances. The relevant constraints are reexamined in Chapter 9 in detail.

3.3.3.3 Multiple topics

Bianchi & Frascarelli (2010) argue that aboutness topics (A-Topics in their terminology) can appear only once, while other types of topics, such as contrastive topics (C-Topics), can turn up multiple times. The present study looks at the difference in terms of discrepancies between marking and meaning of information structure. As discussed previously at the beginning of this chapter, topic-marked elements may or may not occur in a single clause. Notably, they can appear multiple times as exemplified in (24).

(24) Kim-un chayk-un ilk-ess-ta.
Kim-NUN book-NUN read-PST-DECL
'Kim read the book.' [kor]

However, the (*n*)*un*-marked NPs in (24) do not carry the same status with respect to information structure. The (*n*)*un*-marked subject *Kim-un* in situ in (24) can be either an aboutness topic or a contrastive topic, because Korean is a topic-first language (Sohn 2001). In contrast, the (*n*)*un*-marked object *chayk-un* has a contrastive meaning, because (*n*)*un*-marked non-subjects in situ are normally associated with contrastive focus (H.-W. Choi 1999; Song & Bender 2011). In short,

3 Meanings of information structure

(*n*)*un*-marked (i.e. topic-marked) constituents can occur multiple times, but not all of them are necessarily associated with topic. Thus, topic marker is not an appropriate name at least for -(*n*)*un* in Korean (and *wa* in Japanese). Section 5.1 provides more discussion on meanings that -(*n*)*un* and *wa*-marked items in Korean and Japanese carry.

3.3.3.4 Verbal topics

Topic-marking on verbal items is rare, but a cross-linguistic survey of information structure markings provides one exceptional case: Paumarí does employ a verbal topic marker, which cannot co-occur with a nominal topic marker in the language (Chapman 1981). Therefore, the present study assumes that topic can be assigned to verbal items, and the possibility is one of the language-specific parameters that needs to be considered when I describe and implement the web-based questionnaire (Section 12.2). In the questionnaire, I let users choose a categorical constraint on focus and topic. Although topics are normally assigned to NPs, users are able to choose verbal markings of topic.

3.3.4 Tests for topic

Given that the treatment of aboutness as the semantic core of topics is supported by many previous studies, Reinhart (1981) and H.-W. Choi (1999) suggest a diagnostic to identify topic, namely the *tell-me-about* test. For instance, a reply to *Tell me about the dog* will contain a word with the B-accent (L+H*) in English, such as *The dog* BARKS. This test can be validly used across languages. For example in Korean, the word that serves as the key answer to *tell-me-about* must not be realized with case markers that have the non-topic relation, as exemplified in (25).

(25) Q: ku kay-ey tayhayse malha-y cwu-e.
the dog-DAT about talk-COMP give-IMP
'Tell me about the dog.'

A: ku kay-#ka/nun cacwu cic-e.
the dog-NOM/NUN often bark-DECL
'The **dog** often barks.' [kor]

Nonetheless, there are a few opposing claims (Vermeulen 2009), and several additional tests have been devised that take notice of the relationship between topichood and aboutness. Roberts (2011), in line with Reinhart (1981) and Gundel

(1985), provides four paraphrasing tests for topic in English as follows, which differ subtly in their felicity-conditions. If a left-dislocated NP conveys a meaning of topic, the constituent can be paraphrased as at least one of the constructions presented below.

(26) a. **About** Coppola, he said that he found him to be ...

b. **What about** Coppola? He found him to be ...

c. **As for** Coppola, he found him to be ...

d. **Speaking of** Coppola, he found him to be ... (Roberts 2011: 1916)

As Roberts (2011) explains, those tests may not be straightforwardly applicable to other languages because translations can vary in accordance with fairly delicate differences in felicity. Oshima (2009) suggests using the *as-for* test (which can be translated into *ni-tsuite-wa*) to test for topic in Japanese. The test can be defined as (27) with examples in Japanese given in (28). For example, *Ken-wa* in (28a) and *Iriasu-wa* (28c) are evaluated as containing topic meaning because they pass the *as-for* test.

(27) The *as for* test: If an utterance of the form: [$_{S_1}$ ... X ...] can be felicitously paraphrased as [*As for* X, S_2] where S_2 is identical to S_1 except that X is replaced by a pronominal or empty form anaphoric to X, X in S_1 is a topic. (Oshima 2009: 410)

(28) a. Ken-wa Iriasu-o yomi-mashi-ta.
Ken-WA Iliad-ACC read-POLITE-PST
'Ken read Iliad.' [jpn]

b. Ken-ni-tsuite-wa, Iriasu-o yomi-mashi-ta.
Ken-ni-tsuite-WA Iliad-ACC read-POLITE-PST
'As for Ken, he read Iliad.' [jpn]

c. Iriasu-wa Ken-ga yomi-mashi-ta.
Iliad-WA Ken-NOM read-POLITE-PST
'As for Iliad, Ken read it.' [jpn]

d. Iriasu-ni-tsuite-wa, Ken-ga yomi-mashi-ta.
Iliad-ni-tsuite-WA Ken-NOM read-POLITE-PST
'As for Iliad, Ken read it.' [jpn] (Oshima 2009: 410)

3 Meanings of information structure

Given that aboutness is the semantic core of topic from a cross-linguistic view, the current work employs the diagnostics presented by Roberts (2011) as exemplified in (26). In the current work, topic is assumed to be assigned to an entity that can pass one of the paraphrasing tests in Roberts.

3.4 Contrast

3.4.1 Definition

In the present work, contrast is treated as a cross-cutting information structure component, which contributes the entailment of an alternative set (Molnár 2002; Krifka 2008). Since contrast can never show up out of the blue (Erteschik-Shir 2007: 9), the existence of an alternative set within the discourse is essential for contrast.

A so-called alternative set which posits focus semantic values is suggested within the framework of alternative semantics (Rooth 1985; 1992). What follows briefly shows how focus alternatives are calculated. In line with Rooth's proposal, a sentence S has three semantic values; the ordinary value $[\![S]\!]^o$, the focus value $[\![S]\!]^f$, plus the topic value $[\![S]\!]^t$. The ordinary value is a proposition, and the focus value is a set of propositions, and the topic value is a set of sets of propositions (Nakanishi 2007: 184). For example, given that a discourse D involves an ontology D consisting of {John, Bill, David, Sue}, the semantic values with respect to (29b) are composed of elements in the alternative set (29c). Note that the element in the focus domain (i.e. *Bill*) is altered into other elements in the ontology.

(29) a. Who did John introduce to Sue?

b. **John** introduced [$_f$ BILL] to Sue.

c. $[\![(29a)]\!]^o$ = who did John introduce to Sue

d. $[\![(29b)]\!]^f$ = { [John introduced John to Sue], [John introduced Bill to Sue], [John introduced David to Sue], [John introduced John to Sue] }

e. $[\![(29b)]\!]^t$ = { { [John introduced John to Sue], [John introduced Bill to Sue], [John introduced David to Sue], [John introduced John to Sue] }, { [Bill introduced John to Sue], [Bill introduced Bill to Sue], [Bill introduced David to Sue], [Bill introduced John to Sue] }, ... }

3.4 Contrast

If the alternative set is invoked in the given discourse with an exclusive meaning, we can say *Bill* in (29b) is contrastively focused. That is, the focus value and the topic value define the alternative set, with respect to an ontology D.

This notion is actually very similar to (or even the same as) the so-called trivialization set proposed by Büring (1999). It can be formulated as the following rule relating a *wh*-question to its corresponding reply, given that $\cup[\![S]\!]^f$ is as informative as the solicited question.

(30) A sentence A can be appropriately uttered as an answer to a question Q iff $\cup[\![A]\!]^f = \cup[\![Q]\!]^o$

Building upon (30), the following Q/A pairs are ill-formed. The question in the second pair, for instance, does not presuppose the pop stars wore caftans, but the answer does with narrowly focusing on the color of caftans.

(31) Q: What kind of caftans did the pop stars wear?
      A: #All the pop stars wore [$_f$ dark CAFTANS].
      Q: What did the pop stars wear?
      A: #All the pop stars wore [$_f$ DARK] caftans. (Büring 1999: 144)

Turning back to the alternative set, CAFTAN and DARK with the A-accent in (31a–b) respectively are not included in the alternative set of the given discourse. Thus, they can be focused neither non-contrastively nor contrastively, because they do not invoke any alternative set. In sum, the existence of an alternative set is essential for articulating the information structural meaning of contrast.

As with non-contrastive topic and focus, contrast may be marked by virtually any linguistic means (prosodic, lexical, and/or syntactic) across languages, and the same device may mark both non-contrastive and contrastive constituents. For example, Gundel (1999: 296) argues that placing a constituent in a specific sentence position (e.g. the sentence-initial position in English) can be used to mark either non-contrastive focus or purely contrastive focus. Topic can also have a contrastive meaning, and sometimes non-contrastive topic and contrastive topic share the same linguistic means. For example, Korean which employs -(n)un can express contrastive topic as shown in (32); the answer conveys an interpretation like *I surely know Kim read a book, but I think Lee, contrastively, might not have*.

(32) Q: Kim-kwa Lee-nun mwuess-ul ilk-ess-ni?
        Kim-and Lee-NUN what-ACC read-PST-QUES
        'What did Kim and Lee read?'

3 Meanings of information structure

    A: Kim-un   chayk-ul ilk-ess-e.
       Kim-NUN book-ACC read-PST-DECL
       'Kim read a book.' [kor]

Lambrecht (1996) regards 'contrastiveness' as a merely cognitive concept, yet there are quite a few counterexamples to the claim from a cross-linguistic perspective. Some languages have a linguistic means of marking contrast in a distinctive way from non-contrastive topic and focus. For instance, Vietnamese uses a contrastive-topic marker *thì* (Nguyen 2006) as shown in (33). The contrast function is shown by the alternative set evoked in (33), while the distinctiveness from focus is shown by the fact that *thì*-marked NPs cannot be used to answer *wh*-questions.

(33) Nam thì đi Hà Nội
      Nam TOP go Ha Noi
      'Nam goes to Hanoi(, but nobody else).' [vie] (Nguyen 2006: 1)

We also find syntactic marking of contrast in several languages. In Standard Arabic, for instance, contrastively focused items are normally preposed to the sentence-initial position, while non-contrastively focused items which convey new information (i.e. semantic focus in Gundel's terminology) are in situ with a specific pitch accent, as exemplified in (34a–b) respectively (Ouhalla 1999).

(34) a. RIWAAYAT-AN ʔallat-at   Zaynab-u
           novel-ACC   wrote-she Zaynab-NOM
          'It was a NOVEL that Zaynab wrote.'

      b. ʔallat-at   Zaynab-u   RIWAAYAT-an
           wrote-she Zaynab-NOM novel-ACC
          'Zaynab wrote a NOVEL.' [arb] (Ouhalla 1999: 337)

Similarly, in Portuguese, contrastive focus precedes the verb, while non-contrastive focus follows the verb (Ambar 1999), as exemplified in (35A). If *a tarte* 'a pie' conveys a contrastive meaning as implied in the translation 'What else she ate, I don't know.', it cannot be preceded by the verb *comeu* 'ate'.

(35) Q: Que comeu a   Maria?
         what ate   the Mary
         'What did Mary eat?'

> A: #A Maria comeu a tarte.
> the Mary ate the pie.
> 'Mary ate the pie (What else she ate, I don't know.)' [por] (Ambar 1999: 28–29)

In Russian, contrastive focus is preposed, while non-contrastive focus shows up clause-finally (Neeleman & Titov 2009). For example, in (36), JAZZ-PIANISTA 'jazz-pianist' in initial position shows a contrast with *jazz-gitarista* 'jazz-guitarist'.

> (36) JAZZ-PIANISTA mal'čiki slyšali vystuplenie
> jazz-pianist.GEN boys listened performance.ACC
> (a ne jazz-gitarista).
> (and not jazz-guitarist.GEN)
> 'The boys listened to the performance of the jazz pianist.' [rus] (Neeleman & Titov 2009: 519)

3.4.2 Subtypes of contrast

Contrast can be used with either focus or topic, resulting in two subtypes: contrastive focus and contrastive topic. These may co-occur in a single clause. For example, in (37) taken from van Valin (2005), Mary and Sally are contrastively focused, whereas book and magazine are contrastively topicalized.

> (37) Q: Who did Bill give the book to and who did he give the magazine to?
>
> A: He gave the **book** to MARY and the **magazine** to SALLY. (van Valin 2005: 72)

3.4.3 Linguistic properties of contrast

In addition to the distributional facts presented in §3.4.1, which substantiate the existence of contrast as a component of information structure, there is also an argument that contrast behaves differently from non-contrastive focus (or topic) in the semantics.

Gundel (1999) provides several differences between contrastive focus and non-contrastive focus, as already presented in Section 3.2.2.3. The different behavior between them is also exemplified in (38) taken from Partee (1991). (38a) can be ambiguously interpreted depending on where the accent is assigned. (38d), in which the subscript $_{CF}$ stands for a specific accent responsible for contrastive focus, has the same truth-conditions as (38c), but not (38b).

3 Meanings of information structure

(38) a. The largest demonstrations took place in Prague in November (in) 1989.

b. The largest demonstrations took place in PRAGUE in November (in) 1989.

c. The largest demonstrations took place in Prague in NOVEMBER (in) 1989.

d. The largest demonstrations took place in PRAGUE$_{CF}$ in NOVEMBER (in) 1989. (Gundel 1999: 301–302)

Nakanishi (2007) compares contrastive topic with thematic topic (also known as non-contrastive topic or aboutness topic in the present study) in Japanese from several angles, since *wa* can be used for either the theme or the contrastive element of the sentence. From a distributional viewpoint, a non-contrastively *wa*-marked constituent can be either anaphoric (i.e. previously mentioned) or generic, whereas a contrastive element with *wa* can be generic, anaphoric, or neither. (39) is an example in which a contrastively *wa*-marked NP conveys neither an anaphoric interpretation nor a generic one.

(39) oozei-no   hito-wa   paatii-ni kimasi-ta
     many-GEN   people-WA   party-to   come-PST
     ga   omosiroi   hito-wa   hitori   mo   imas-en-desita.
     but   interesting people-WA   one-person   even   be-NEG-PST
     'Many people came to the party indeed but there was none who was interesting.' [jpn] (Kuno 1973: 270)

From a phonological stance, if *wa* is used for a thematic interpretation, the highest value of F0 contour after *wa* is as high as or even higher than the highest value before *wa*. In contrast, if it denotes a contrastive meaning, *wa* is realized with a dramatic downslope of F0 contour. From a semantic perspective, it turns out that the two versions of the marker have different scopal interpretations when they co-occur with negation. The scopal interpretation driven by the relationship with focus and negation was originally captured by Büring (1997) as exemplified earlier in (21). Nakanishi, in line with the claim of Büring, compares two types of *wa*-marked topics in Japanese as shown in (40): Thematic *wa* in (40a) and contrastive *wa* in (40b) have the opposite scopal reading to each other.

(40) a. Minna-wa   ne-nakat-ta.
        everyone-WA sleep-NEG-PAST
        'Everyone didn't sleep.'
        (thematic *wa*) $\sqrt{\forall > \neg}, {}^{*}\neg > \forall$

b. [Minna-wa]$_T$ ne-[nakat]$_F$-ta.
everyone-WA sleep-NEG-PAST
'Everyone didn't sleep.'
(contrastive *wa*) *$\forall>\neg$, √$\neg>\forall$ (Nakanishi 2007: 187–188)

Compared to non-contrastive topics, contrastive topics tend to have relatively weak constraints on positioning and the selection of NP. H.-W. Choi (1999) provides an analysis of scrambling (i.e. OSV) in Korean, which reveals that contrastive focus can freely scramble, while completive focus (also known as non-contrastive focus or semantic focus) cannot scramble. Erteschik-Shir (2007) argues that in Danish contrastive topic can be associated with non-specific indefinites, whereas non-contrastive topic cannot, as shown in (41). *En pige* 'a girl' in (41a) cannot play the non-contrastive topic role, because its interpretation is non-specifically indefinite. In contrast, *et museum* 'a museum' in (41b) can be the topic of the sentence, because it has an alternative *en kirke* 'a church'.

(41) a. #En pige mødte jeg i går.
 a girl met I yesterday
 'I met a girl yesterday.'

 b. Et museum besøgte jeg allerede i går,
 a museum visited I already yesterday
 en kirke ser jeg først i morgen.
 a church see I only tomorrow
 'I visited a museum already yesterday, I will see a church only tomorrow.' [dan] (Erteschik-Shir 2007: 8–9)

3.4.4 Tests for contrast

Gryllia (2009: 42–43) provides six tests to vet the meaning and marking of contrastive topic and contrastive focus as follows.[14]

(42) a. *Wh-questions*: A contrastive answer is not compatible with a common *wh*-question.

 b. *Correction test*: A contrastive focus can be used to answer a yes-no question correcting part of the predicate information of the question.

---

[14]For more elaborated explanation and examples for each of them, see Chapter 3 in Gryllia (2009). This subsection, for brevity, provides only the definition and representative examples focusing on correction test.

3 Meanings of information structure

    c. Choice test: When answering an alternative question, one alternate is contrasted to the other.

    d. Accommodation focus test: When the discourse is accommodated in such a way that the initial *wh*-question can be interpreted as containing a positive and a negative question (e.g. *who came?, who did not come?*), then the focus in the answer is contrastive.

    e. Substitution test: If two terms are interpreted with a 'List Interpretation', then they can be substituted with *the former* and *the latter*.

    f. Right dislocation: Contrast is incompatible with right dislocation.

    g. Implicit subquestion test: (i) When a *wh*-question can be split into subquestions and the answer is organized per subquestion, then, there is a contrastive topic in the answer. (ii) When a question can be interpreted as containing more than one implicit subquestion, and the answer addresses only one of these subquestions, rather than the general question, then, this answer contains a contrastive topic.

Some of the diagnostics above, however, are not cross-linguistically valid. In non-Indo-European languages, such as Korean, only some work. For example, the *wh*-question test does not work for English and Korean in the same manner, as exemplified below.

(43) Q: Who came?

    A: Well, KIM came, I know that much, but I can't tell you about anyone else.

(44) Q: nwuka o-ass-ni?
       who   come-PST-QUES
      'Who came?'

    A: Kim-i/un   o-ass-e.
       Kim-NOM/NUN come-PST-DECL
      'Kim came.' [kor]

Kim with *-(n)un* in (44A) can be an appropriate answer to the question, and it involves a contrastive interpretation (i.e. conveying a meaning like *I know that* *at least Kim came, but I'm not sure whether or not others came.*). In this case, the replier alters the information structure articulated by the questioner arbitrarily in order to offer a more informative answer to the solicited question. Note that contrastiveness is basically speaker-oriented (Chang 2002). In other words, contrast is primarily motivated by the speaker's necessity to attract the hearer's special attention at a particular point in the discourse. Thus, speakers may change the stream of information structure as they want.

The right dislocation test, on the other hand, seems valid in Korean as well. The (*n*)*un*-marked NP can be used in the right dislocation constructions in Korean as given in (45Q1). Yet, if an alternative set is entailed as shown in (45Q2), right dislocation sounds absurd.

(45) Q1: cangmi-nun ettay?
rose-NUN about
'How about the rose?'

A: coh-a, cangmi-nun.
good-DECL rose-NUN
'It's good, the rose.'

Q2: kkoch-un ettay?
flower-NUN about
'How about the flowers?'

A1: #coh-a, cangmi-nun.
good-DECL rose-NUN

A2: cangmi-nun coh-a.
rose-NUN good-DECL [kor]

The most convincing and cross-linguistically applicable tests among the tests in (42) is the correction test, as exemplified in (46) in Italian (47) in Greek, and (48) in Korean.

(46) Q: L' ha rotto Giorgio, il vaso?
it has broken Giorgio the vase
'Has Giorgio broken the vase?'

A: [Maria]$_{C\text{-Foc}}$ ha rotto il vaso.
Maria has broken the vase
'It is Maria who has broken the vase.' [ita] (Gryllia 2009: 32)

3 Meanings of information structure

(47) Q: Thelis   tsai?
     want.2SG tea.ACC
     'Would you like tea?'

   A1: Ohi, thelo   [kafe]_{C-Foc}.
       no   want.1SG coffee.ACC
       'No, I would like coffee.'

   A2: Ohi, [kafe]_{C-Foc} thelo
       no   coffee.ACC want.1SG [ell] (Gryllia 2009: 44)

(48) Q: chayk ilk-ess-ni?
     book read-PST-QUES
     'Did you read a book?'

   A: ani, capci-lul/nun   ilk-ess-e.
      no   magazine-ACC/NUN read-PST-DECL
      'No, (but) I read a magazine.' [kor]

Gussenhoven (2007), in a similar vein, suggests corrective focus as a subtype of focus in English as presented below.

(49) A: What's the capital of Finland?

   B: The CAPital of FINland is [HELsinki]_{FOC}

   A′: The capital of Finland is OSlo.

   B′: (NO.) The capital of Finland is [HELsinki]_{CORRECTIVE} (Gussenhoven 2007: 91)

Gussenhoven also provides a similar example in Navajo. Navajo has two negative modifiers; one is neutral, *doo ... da* in (50a), and the other expresses corrective focus, *hanii* in (50b). That is, *hanii* serves to mark a contrastive focus in Navajo.

(50) a. Jáan doo chidí yiyíiłchø'-da.
        John NEG car   3RD.PAST.wreck-NEG
        'John didn't wreck the car.'

b. Jáan hanii chidí yiyíiłchø'.
John NEG car 3RD.PAST.wreck
'JOHN didn't wreck the car (someone else did).' [nav] (Gussenhoven 2007: 91)

Wee (2001) proposes a test with conditionals, in which a contrastive topic is paraphrased into a conditional clause as exemplified in (51B″). That is, -(n)un which can convey contrast meaning in Korean can be altered into a conditional marker *lamyen*, which also has an alternative set drawn by *nobody* in (51A) and functions to make a correction to the presupposition given in (51A).

(51) A: Nobody can solve the problem.

B: Peter would solve the problem.

B′: Peter-nun ku muncey-lul phwul-keya.
Peter-NUN the problem-ACC solve-would
'Peter would solve the problem.'

B″: Peter-lamyen, ku muncey-lul phwul-keya.
Peter-if the problem-ACC solve-would
'If Peter were here, he would solve the problem.' [kor]

von Fintel (2004) and J. Kim (2012) suggest a test for contrast called "Hey, wait a minute!", which serves to cancel or negate presupposed content in the previous discourse. In other words, the contrastive marking acts as the key for correcting the inaccurate part in a presupposition. Likewise, Skopeteas & Fanselow (2010), exploring focus positions in Georgian, define contrastive focus as a "corrective answer to truth value question". This definition is also in line with my argument that the correction test can be reliably used to vet contrastive focus.

The present study makes use of the correction test to scrutinize contrast. However, that does not means that recognizing corrections is the only use of contrastive focus. Note that use for corrections is a sufficient condition for expressing contrastive focus, but not a necessary condition.

Lastly, because foci are inomissible while topics are not, if a constituent that passes the correction test cannot be elided, it is evaluated as conveying contrastive focus. If a constituent passes the correction test but can be dropped, it is regarded as contrastive topic.

3 Meanings of information structure

3.5 Background

We can say a constituent is in the background when it conveys a meaning of neither focus nor topic. In terms of linguistic forms, background constituents typically do not involve additional marking but may be forced into particular positions in a sentence. Background is in complementary distribution to both topic and focus and adds no information structure meaning to the discourse. Focus, topic, and background are mutually exclusive, and thereby cannot overlap with each other.[15]

Background can often be found in cleft sentences. Clefts refer to (copula) constructions consisting of a main clause and a dependent clause (e.g. a relative clause), in which a constituent in the main clause is narrow-focused.[16] The narrow foci in cleft constructions can be easily identified by means of a deletion test. As noted before, focus means a constituent that can never be elided, which is one of the main behaviors distinguishing focus from topic and background. Thus, any other constituent in (52-53), except for the narrowly focused ones *Kim* and *from her*, can be freely eliminated.

(52) Q: Who reads the book?
A1: It is Kim that reads the book.
A2: It is Kim.
A3: Kim.

(53) Q: Where did you have my address from?
A1: It was from her that I had your address.
A2: It is from her.
A3: From her.

Clefts typically put the part of the sentence after the focused item into background. Since the remaining part of the sentence (i.e. the cleft clause) such as *that reads the book* and *that I had your address* in each cleft sentences can be freely dropped, it can be regarded as either topic or background. Moreover, the constituents in cleft clauses are rarely (*n*)*un*-marked in Korean, as shown in (54).

(54) a. ku chayk-ul/*un ilk-nun salam-i/un Kim-i-ta.
the book-ACC/NUN read-REL person-NOM/NUN Kim-COP-DECL
'It is Kim that reads the book.'

---

[15] As aforementioned, there exists an opposing view to this generalization (Krifka 2008).
[16] The focused item in clefts does not need to be an argument focus, because non-nominal categories such as adverbs and information status is represented can sometimes take place in the main clause of clefts as given in (53).

b. Kim-i/*un   ilk-nun kes-i/un   ku chayk-i-ta.
   Kim-NOM/NUN read-REL thing-NOM/NUN the book-COP-DECL
   'It is the book that Kim reads.' [kor]

As discussed thus far, -(n)un in Korean assigns either topic or contrast, or both (i.e. contrastive topic) to the word it is attached to. The marker -(n)un cannot be used within the cleft clauses as shown in (54). Thus, NPs in cleft clauses are usually identified as background (i.e. non-focus and non-topic, simultaneously), at least in Korean. Cleft clauses can contain a focused constituent in some languages as exemplified in (55), however.

(55) Q: Does Helen know JOHN?

   A: It is John/JOHN she DISLIKES.

   Q: I wonder who she dislikes.

   A: It is JOHN she dislikes. (Gussenhoven 2007: 96)

Thus, we cannot say cleft clauses are always in background, and more discussion about cleft clauses is given in Section 10.4.3.4 (p. 209).

3.6 Summary

This chapter has reviewed the primary components of information structure (focus, topic, contrast and background), including definitions of the concepts and explorations of sub-classifications, associated linguistic phenomena and potential tests. The assumptions presented in the previous section are as follows: First, I establish that information status is not a reliable means of identifying information structure since the relationship between the two is simply a tendency. Second, I define focus as what is new and/or important in a sentence, and specify that a constituent associated with focus cannot be eliminated from a sentence. I present two subtypes of focus; semantic focus (lacking a contrastive meaning) and contrastive focus. Tests to vet focus marking and meaning include *wh*-questions and the deletion test. Third, I define topic as what a speaker is talking about. While every sentence presumably has at least one focus, topic may or may not appear in the surface form. I outline two subtypes; aboutness topic (also known as thematic topic or non-contrastive topic) and contrastive topic. Frame-setters, which serve to restrict the domain of what is spoken (temporal, spatial, conditional, manner, etc.), are always external (not an argument of the predicate) and

3 Meanings of information structure

sentence-initial. In contrast to previous work, frame-setters are not treated as a subtype of topic here. Because the semantic core of topic is aboutness, the tools for identifying topics are the *tell-me-about* test and several paraphrasing tests such as *as for ..., speaking of ...,* and *(what) about ....* Next, I explicate the ways in which contrast always entails an alternative set, which can be realized as either contrastive focus or contrastive topic. The most reliable and cross-linguistically valid diagnosis for contrast is the correction test, because correction necessarily requires an alternative. Finally, I define background as neither focus nor topic, and posit that any constituent associated with it can be freely elided without loss of information delivery. These cross-linguistic generalizations help provide linguistic generalizations to be used in creating HPSG/MRS-based constraints on information structure. Moreover, they are also used to design the library of information structure for the LinGO Grammar Matrix system.

4 Markings of information structure

The main goal of this chapter is to find the range of possible expressions with respect to information structure. Different languages employ different marking systems, and the linguistic means of conveying information structure meanings includes: (i) prosody, (ii) lexical markers, (iii) syntactic positioning, and (iv) combinations of these (Gundel 1999). This chapter explores how these meanings are specifically realized in various languages. This contributes to typological studies of human languages, and also carries weight with implementing a grammar library for information structure within the LinGO Grammar Matrix customization system (Bender & Flickinger 2005; Drellishak 2009; Bender et al. 2010). Because users of that system are referencing the actual linguistic forms in their language it is important that the library that they use systematize linguistic realizations in a sufficiently fine-grained way.

This chapter is structured as follows: Section 4.1 addresses prosodic means of expressing information structure. The present work does not directly implement constraints on prosodic patterns into the system, but presents a flexible representation for them to set the ground work for a further developed system. Section 4.2 looks into lexical markers responsible for focus and topic from a cross-linguistic viewpoint. These are classified into three subclasses: affixes, adpositions, and modifiers. Section 4.3 surveys positioning constraints on information structure components in human language.

4.1 Prosody

In much of the previous work on this topic, prosody has been presumed to be the universal means of marking information structure (Gundel 1999; Büring 2010). Many previous papers have studied information structure with special reference to how it is marked by prosody. Bolinger (1958) argues that there are two types of pitch accents in English; the A and B-accents (i.e. H* and L+H* in the ToBI format respectively). Jackendoff (1972) creates a generalization about the correlation between pitch accents and information structure components: A and B-accents in

4 Markings of information structure

English are responsible for marking constituents as focus and topic respectively.[1] The way in which A and B accents structure information is exemplified in (1), in which SMALL CAPS represents the A-accent, and **boldface** represents the B-accent. The constituent semantically associated with aboutness bears the B-accent in English, and because it refers to aboutness, is identified as the topic in the present study. The constituent corresponding to the *wh*-word in the question *What did Kim read?* bears the A-accent, which gives a focus meaning.

(1) Q: What about Kim? What did Kim read?
    A: **Kim** read the BOOK.

In the following subsections I explore the details of three perspectives on incorporating prosodic information into grammatical structures. This is done with an emphasis on application in the creation of an information structure library as a tool for grammar engineering.

4.1.1 Prosody as a widespread means of marking

Since Jackendoff (1972), quite a few studies have explored the connection between prosodic patterns and information structure in languages, including English (Steedman 2000), German (Büring 2003), Portuguese (Frota 2000), Japanese and Korean (Ueyama & Jun 1998). However we should not assume that every language employs prosody for marking information structure. In fact there are several counterarguments to treating prosody as a language-universal way to express focus and/or topic.

My cross-linguistic survey reveals several languages with no means of expressing information structure through prosody. For instance, it is reported that Yucatec Maya employs no prosodic marking for expressing information structure. Instead, syntactic functions indicate these relations without an interaction with prosody (Kügler, Skopeteas & Verhoeven 2007). In Akan, prosodic patterns also have little to do with expressing focus, and instead a focused item must occupy the clause-initial position with one of several morphological markers (Drubig 2003). Likewise, Catalan, in which syntactic operation is responsible for marking information structure, has a rather weak (or even null) correlation between

---

[1] Admittedly, there are quite a few recent and comprehensive studies of the interaction between prosody and information structure, such as Ladd (2008), Chen (2012), and many others. Their analyses may help model information structure in a cross-linguistic perspective. Nonetheless, the present study does not enter into the deeper details of them, mainly because the current model basically aims to be used for text-based processing systems.

prosody and information structure meanings (Engdahl & Vallduví 1996). Hence, the assumption that prosody is a language-universal means of marking information structure is not valid. That is to say, using prosody for expressing information structure is clearly widespread, but not universal (Drellishak 2009).

4.1.2 Mappings between prosody and information structure

There seems to be no clear consensus with respect to mappings between prosody and information structure even in English. Contra to Jackendoff's claim, (i) Kadmon (2001), Büring (2003), and Oshima (2008) argue that B-accents are specifically responsible for contrastive topics, rather than topic in a broad sense. (ii) Steedman (2000) argues that B-accents mark theme, and additionally associates information structure meanings with boundary tones. (iii) Hedberg (2006) regards the use of a B-accent as a contrastive marker for both focus and topic (i.e. either or contrastive topic). (iv) More recently, Constant (2012) explores how semantic and pragmatic behavior is influenced by a specific prosodic 'rise-fall-rise' pattern in English (transcribed in the ToBI format as [L*+H L- H%]), as illustrated in (2). That is, there are three components: The first 'rise' corresponds to [L*+H], 'fall' to [L-], and the second 'rise' to [H%].[2]

(2) A: Why isn't the coffee here?
 B: I don't know. I was *expecting* there to be coffee ...
                          L*+H   L-   H%
     (Constant 2012: 409)

Constant investigates the correlations between 'rise-fall-rise' intonation and contrastive topic intonation. Constant denies the previous assumption that the former is a subclass of the latter.

Among the varied claims, I follow Hedberg's argument, mainly because Hedberg's classification is firmly based on an acoustic analysis of naturally occurring spoken data (Hedberg & Sosa 2007): A-accents are responsible for non-contrastive focus, while B-accents are responsible for topic and contrast in English.

The debate presented above is largely concerned with which prosodic pattern has which effect on information structure, and the nature of the mapping between prosody and information structure. However, there exist some circum-

---

[2]The main argument Constant (2012) provides is that the 'rise-fall-rise' intonation involves a regular conventional implicature, acting as a focus sensitive quantifier over assertable alternative propositions.

4 Markings of information structure

stances in which prosody is not involved in the articulation of information structure (even in English). Féry & Krifka (2008) argue prosodic patterns are not obligatorily related to information structure even in English. For example, the association between prosody and focus can be canceled in the context of Second Occurrence Focus. A second occurrence focus is an expression that falls within the scope of a focus sensitive operator (e.g. *only* in English), but is a repeat of an earlier focused occurrence (Partee 1999; Beaver et al. 2007; Féry & Ishihara 2009). The repeatedly focused item prosodically differs from the previously focused one (i.e. ordinarily focused), and is normally devoid of a specific pitch accent responsible for marking focus. Because *vegetables* in (3b) is combined with a focus sensitive item *only*, it would be interpreted as containing focus meaning, but that meaning is already given in (3a).

(3) a. Everyone already knew that Mary only eats [vegetables]$_F$.

b. If even [Paul]$_F$ knew that Mary only eats [vegetables]$_{SOF}$, then he should have suggested a different restaurant. (Partee 1999: 215–216)

(3) is a clear counterexample to Halliday's claim that what is focused should carry new information as 'vegetables' in (3b) has already been mentioned. In addition, while the *vegetables* in (3a) bears an A-accent, the repeated occurrence in (3b) does not. According to Féry & Krifka (2008: 132), "there are only weak correlates of accent, and no pitch excursions in the postnuclear position.". This means that the focus meaning in this case is not directly invoked by the A-accent.

These findings indicate that prosodic patterns do not always reliably reveal information structure.[3] In other words, prosodic prominence is merely a tendency; it is neither a sufficient nor a necessary condition for conveying information structure meanings even in languages whose markings are largely dependent on prosody (e.g. English) (Rochemont 1986; Drubig 2003).

4.1.3 Flexible representation

Prosody makes a contribution to information structure in many languages, even if the relationship between prosodic marking and information structure is com-

---

[3]Fanselow (2007) provides a view against this. The claim is that the connection between information structure and syntax is mediated by prosody, with no direct link between information structure and syntax. I do not follow this, because my cross-linguistic survey reveals that some languages, such as Catalan (Engdahl & Vallduví 1996), Akan (Drubig 2003), and Yucatec Maya (Kügler, Skopeteas & Verhoeven 2007), have a system with very weak or no interaction between prosody and syntax with respect to focus.

plicated. However, in some contexts, especially processing of texts that were originally written (rather than transcribed speech), we do not have access to prosodic information anyway. Given that our processing system is usually text-based, currently it is almost impossible for us to resolve the phonological patterns of sentences, including intonation contour and pitch accents. The best way to handle prosodic marking is to allow for underspecification in such a way that prosodic information can be later added into the formalism. Kuhn (1996) in the same context suggests an underspecified representation for information structure, noting that even prosodic marking of information structure often yields ambiguous meanings, which cannot in general be resolved in sentence-based processing. The present work employs underspecification for representing information structure when the meaning is not fully solved by prosody. In principle, this would allow for refining the representation monotonically.

4.2 Lexical markers

According to my cross-linguistic survey, there are three subtypes of lexical markers that assign information structure roles; (i) affixes, (ii) adpositions, and (iii) modifiers.

Quite a few languages have specific affixes to signal focus, topic, and contrast, as exemplified in the following Rendile (Cushitic, Afro-Asiatic, spoken in northern Kenya) examples, in which two affixes are used to express an argument focus (i.e. é by an enclisis process) and a predicate focus (i.e. á by a proclisis process) respectively (Lecarme 1999).

(4) a. ínam-é yimi
   boy-FOC came
   'THE BOY came.'

b. ínam á-yimi
   boy FOC-came
   'The boy CAME.' [rel] (Lecarme 1999: 277)

Some languages use affixes responsible for topic meanings; for instance, -(n)un in Korean is used to signal information structure meanings (*contrast-or-topic* in the current work), and is in complementary distribution with ordinary case morphemes (e.g. *i / ka* for nominatives, *(l)ul* for accusatives).

4 Markings of information structure

(5) ku kay-nun cic-e
    DET dog-NUN bark-DECL
    'The **dog** barks.' [kor]

Unlike the focus affixes used in (4) (i.e. *é* and *á*) which directly signal the information structure roles of the constituent, *-(n)un* in Korean is not deterministic. The word which *-(n)un* is attached to can be ambiguously interpreted. This is addressed in Section 5.1 in detail.

Clitics are also often employed to express information structure. A clitic, somewhere between morpheme and word, is a linguistic item that is syntactically independent, but phonologically dependent. Clitics used for information structure markings can be subclassed into two types; adpositions and modifiers.[4] Adpositions are responsible for information structure markings in Japanese. In (6), the adposition *wa* is responsible for conveying contrast or topic.

(6) inu wa hoeru.
    dog WA bark
    'The **dog** barks.' [jpn]

On the other hand, clitics that have nothing to do with case marking can also be used as lexical markers for information structure. They are regarded as modifiers in the current work. For instance, Man (2007) presents two types of Cantonese lexical particles that mark NPs for information structure roles: *aa4* and *ne1* as the topic marker and *aa3*, *laa1*, and *gaa3* as focus markers, respectively.

(7) a. nei1 bun2 syu1 **aa4** ngo5 tai2gwo3 hou2do1 ci3
       DEF CLF book PART 1SG read.EXP many times
       'As for this book, I have read it for many times.' [yue]

    b. keoi5 **aa3** bun2 syu1 ngo5 bei2zo2
       3.SG PART CLF book 1SG give.PERF
       'It is him/her who I have given the book to.' [yue] (Man 2007: 16)

Clitics are made use of to designate the topic and/or the focus in other languages, too. For example, Cherokee (a native American language (Iroquoian), still spoken in Oklahoma and North Carolina) employs a second-position clitic *=tvv* as the focus marker, meaning it immediately follows the focused word as shown below (Montgomery-Anderson 2008).

---

[4]Note that I do not argue that all adpositions are necessarily enclitics.

4.2 Lexical markers

(8) a. ayv=tvv yi-tee-ji-hnooki
    1PRO=FC IRR-DST-1A-sing.IMM
    'I am going to sing it.'

   b. noókwu=tvv ji-tee-a-asuúla-a
       now=FC   REL-DST-3A-wash.hands:IMM-IMM
       'He just washed his hands.' [chr] (Montgomery-Anderson 2008: 152)

As noted above, the present study defines three subtypes of lexical markers for expressing information structure: (i) affixes, (ii) adpositions, and (iii) modifiers.[5]

The differences among them are as follows: First, (i) affixal markers such as -(n)un in Korean always behave dependently within the morphological system (as shown in 5). In contrast, adpositions (e.g. lexical markers in Japanese) and modifiers (e.g. particles in Cantonese and Cherokee) are dealt with as separate words in the language. Second, if a language employs a non-affixal marker to express information structure, there are two options: (ii) If a non-suffixal marker is used to express information structure and the language employs adpositions, the marker is regarded as an adposition, too. In other words, when a language makes use of case-marking adpositions, and the adpositions are in complementary distribution with a lexical marker of information structure (as in Japanese), the marker is subtyped as an adposition. (iii) Otherwise, the lexical marker is regarded as a modifier.

According to my survey, there are four constraints on lexical markers for information structure. They are presented in the following subsections.

4.2.1 Multiple markers

Human languages can have multiple lexical markers for expressing either focus or topic, with different syntax from each other. Turning back to the Rendile example (4), *é* is used for nominals, while *á* is a verbal focus marker. There are similar cases in other languages, too: For example, Akan employs two focus markers; one is *na* that appears only in sentential replies, and the other is *a* that shows up only with a short answer (Drubig 2003: 4).

---

[5]Someone may claim that what I regard as an adposition in a given language is a modifier or something. Admittedly, I am concerned with finding the full range of potential ways to mark information structure. This enables the users of the LinGO Grammar Matrix system to have flexibility in describing what they see in their language following the meta-modeling idea of Poulson (2011).

4 Markings of information structure

(9) Q: Hena na Ama rehwehwɛ?
who FOC Ama is.looking.for
'Who is it that Ama is looking for?'

A1: Kofi na *(Ama rehwehwɛ)
Kofi FOC Ama is.looking.for

A2: Kofi a (*Ama rehwehwɛ)
Kofi FOC
'(It is) KOFI (that Ama is looking for)' [aka] (Drubig 2003: 5)

Sometimes, multiple lexical markers can be used simultaneously: Schneider (2009) argues that Abma has four markers expressing information structure: *ba* as a comment marker, and *tei* as a focus marker. *Ba* and *tei* can appear together before the predicate to designate comment plus focus (i.e. predicate focus), but the latter should be immediately preceded by the former as presented in (10) below.

(10) ... ba tei te ba=i=te Liwusvet=nga.
COMM FOC 3SG.PFV NEG.1=be=PART Liwusvet=NEG.2
'... but it wasn't Liwusvet.' [app] (Schneider 2009: 5)

4.2.2 Positioning constraints

Lexical markers can occur before or after a phrase that is assigned an information structure role by the markers. For instance, in Rendile, *é* in (4a) is a suffix, and *á* in (4b) is a prefix. (11) is an example in Buli, in which the focus marker *kà* precedes the focused constituent. In contrast, the focus marker *nyā* in Ditammari is preceded by the focused constituent, as shown in (12). [6]

(11) Q: What did the woman eat?

A: ò ŋòb kà túé.
3SG eat FM beans
'She ate BEANS.' [bwu] (Féry & Krifka 2008: 133)

(12) Q: What did the woman eat?

A: ò dī yātūrà nyā.
3SG eat beans FM
'She ate BEANS.' [tbz] (Féry & Krifka 2008: 133)

---
[6]Both languages belong to the language family of Niger-Congo/Gur.

4.2.3 Categorical restriction

There is a categorical restriction on the phrases with which lexical markers can be combined. Phrases can be nominal, verbal, and even adverbial; for instance, adverbial categories in Korean and Japanese can be *wa* and *(n)un*-marked. Choice of lexical markers can also be dependent on category; in Rendile as shown in (4), an affix *é* is attached to only nouns such as *ínam* 'boy', while a prefix *á* is exclusively used with verbs such as *yimi* 'came'. That means, each lexical marker has a constraint on which category it can be used for, which also needs to be represented as lexical information.

4.2.4 Interaction with syntax

In some languages that employ lexical markers for expressing information structure, lexical markers interact with syntactic operations. One well known case of this interplay between lexical markers and syntactic positioning is scrambling constructions in Korean and Japanese (H.-W. Choi 1999; Ishihara 2001). Similarly, in Akan, focused items obligatorily (i) occupy sentence-initial position and (ii) immediately precede focus markers such as *na* and *a* as already illustrated in (9) (Drubig 2003: 4). A comparable phenomenon can be found in the Buli example (11): According to Féry & Krifka (2008), if a focused constituent is sentence-initial, the focus marker *kà* can be used. Cherokee, as demonstrated in (8), employs the clitic *tvv* to signal focus, and the focused constituent with *tvv* should be followed by any other constituents in the sentence (i.e. it should be clause-initial).

4.3 Syntactic positioning

Information structure roles are often associated with specific positions in a clause. It is well-documented that the realization of information structure has much to do with word order, and this relationship can be cross-linguistically captured (Zubizarreta 1998; van Valin 2005; Mereu 2009). For example, although word order in Spanish is relatively free in comparison with English, there are still ordering constraints in Spanish that hinge on information structure (Zagona 2002). Moreover, according to Li & Thompson (1976), every language has one or more syntactic device(s) for expressing information structure.

Before discussing specific syntactic positions, it is necessary to look into how information is structured in the basic word order in a language. Languages have different unmarked focus positions, depending largely, but not entirely, on their neutral word order. For example, in English, narrow focus on the object is a case

4 Markings of information structure

of unmarked narrow focus, while narrow focus on the subject is a case of marked narrow focus. An ordinary example of a narrow focus can be found in Q/A pairs in which the object plays the role of focus as provided in (13).

(13) Q: What did Kim read?
A: Kim read the BOOK.

van Valin (2005) captures a generalization about the relationship between word order type and the most unmarked position of narrow focus: In SVO languages, it is the last position in the core clause (e.g. English) or the immediate postverbal position (e.g. Chicheŵa). In verb-final languages, the unmarked focus position is the immediate preverbal position (e.g. Korean and Japanese). In VOS languages, it is the immediate postverbal position (e.g. Toba Batak).

The present study does not place an information structure constraint on sentences in the unmarked word order for two reasons.

First, the clause-initial items in subject-first or V2 languages are ambiguous when it comes to focus/topic fronting. For instance, note (14) in Yiddish. Given that declarative clauses in Yiddish are both SVO and V2 (N. G. Jacobs 2005), the constituent that occurs in the sentence-initial position is the subject in the default word order. What is to be considered at the same time is that focus/topic fronting is productively used in Yiddish as exemplified below (N. G. Jacobs 2005).

(14) a. Der lerər šrajbt di zacn mit krajd afn tovl.
'The teacher writes the sentences with chalk on the blackboard.' (neutral)

b. Di zacn šrajbt der lerər mit krajd afn tovl.
the sentences writes the teacher with chalk on the blackboard
'It's the sentence (not mathematical equations) that the teacher is writing with chalk on the blackboard.'

c. mit krajd šrajbt der lerər di zacn afn tovl.
with chalk writes the teacher the sentences on the blackboard
'It's with chalk (not with a crayon) that that the teacher is writing the sentence on the blackboard.'

d. afn tovl šrajbt der lerər di zacn mit krajd.
on the blackboard writes the teacher the sentences with chalk
'It's on the blackboard (not the notepad) that that the teacher is writing the sentence with chalk.' [ydd] (N. G. Jacobs 2005: 224)

4.3 Syntactic positioning

Thus, without reference to the context, we cannot clearly say which information structure meaning the subject carries when the sentence is in V2 order. That is, the subject *Der lerər* in (14a) may or may not be associated with focus. Another example can be found in Breton (a V2 language). In the Q/A pair, what is focused in (15A) is the fronted item *Marí* (the rheme and the new information in Press's terminology). In this case, the word order of the sentence is SVO.

(15) Q: Pív   a wel Yanníg?
       who sees Yannig
       'Who sees Yannig?'

   A: Marí a wel Yanníg
      Marie sees Yannig
      'Maries sees Yannig.' [bre] (Press 1986: 194)

However, the sentence *Marí a wel Yanníg* itself, if it were not for the contextual information, sounds ambiguous. Press argues that in the sentence *Yanníg* could well be the subject of the sentence (i.e. in an OVS order). If *Yanníg* is the subject, focus is assigned to the fronted object *Marí*. In other words, a Breton sentence *Marí a wel Yanníg* conveys two potential meanings like either *It is Marie who sees Yannig.* (when the sentence is SVO) or *It is Marie who Yannig sees.* (when the sentence is OVS). Note that (15A) in which the focus is associated with the subject is ambiguous because Breton is a V2 language, and therefore the subject, in itself, can be interpreted as either as focused or just unknown. In the analysis I propose later the information structure value of the constituents in situ (e.g. the subjects in 14 and 15A) is left underspecified.

Second, unmarked focus positions in different languages also deeply interact with phonological variation.[7] Ishihara (2001) argues that two types of stresses have an effect on the unmarked position; one is N-stress (Nuclear stress), and the other is A-stress (Additional stress). According to Ishihara, A-stress is not required, while every sentence presumably bears N-stress, and the position of the N-stress is rather fixed in a language.[8] Thus, N-stress is realized in the same

---

[7] This has to do with the so-called p-movement (Zubizarreta 1998), which indicates an indirect interface between information structure and syntax. Given that nuclear-stress position is relatively fixed (in some languages at least; cf. non-plastic accent, Vallduví 1990) and focus should be maximally prominent (Büring 2010), the focused item needs to be in the right (i.e. stressed) position.

[8] Ishihara (2001) offers this argument based on a lot of previous phonological studies, but not seeing a large number of languages (e.g. Japanese, Korean, Basque, etc.). Thus, we may not say that these rules are meant to be universals. Nonetheless, Ishihara's argument still has a significance in that it is well discussed how different types of sentential stresses impact forming information structure of sentences in a default word order.

4 Markings of information structure

position almost invariably even if constituents shift their order (e.g. through inversion, scrambling, etc.). For example, the following sentences in Japanese (16) and Ondarroa Basque (17), in which ´ and ˆ stand for the N-stress in each language, show that the position of N-stress (preverbal in both languages) does not shift to reflect the change in word order.

(16) a. Taro-ga   kyoo hón-o   katta
       Taro-NOM today book-ACC bought
       'Taro bought a book today.'

   b. Taro-ga   hon-o   kyóo katta
      Taro-NOM book-ACC today bought [jpn] (Ishihara 2001: 145)

(17) a. Jonek   Mîren ikusí ban.
       John.ERG Miren see.TU AUX.PST
       'Jon saw MIREN.'

   b. Miren   Jônek ikusí ban.
      Miren.ERG John see.TU AUX.PST
      'JON saw Miren.' [eus] (Arregi 2000: 22)

N-stress has a tendency to fall on the preverbal position in OV languages as shown in *hón-o* and *kyóo* (16) and *Mîren* and *Jônek* in (17), while it tends to fall on the postverbal position in VO languages (e.g. English). By contrast, since A-stress lays an additional emphasis on a specific word, its position can vary depending on what the speaker wants to emphasize (i.e. focus). With respect to the presence of A-stress, Ishihara proposed a rule: Any material that follows an A-stress must be deaccented.

Combining the three factors presented thus far, (i) basic word order, (ii) N and A-stresses, and (iii) the unmarked position for narrow focus, we can explain the reason why an object normally bears the focus of a sentence in an unmarked way at least in the languages presented so far. A-stress, as mentioned, does not show up unless it is necessary for the speaker to emphasize something. In the absence of an A-stress, the word with N-stress is the most stressed constituent in the sentence. N-stress in a sentence has a strong tendency to fall on the object in both OV and VO languages. In addition, subjects have a strong tendency to be topics. Most languages have a spot in the syntactic structure which is the unmarked position for topics, and subjects tend to fall in that part of the syntactic

4.3 Syntactic positioning

structure (Lambrecht 1996). Hence, the unmarked marking of focus tends to fall on objects.

The present study does not deal with the unmarked positions of topic and focus. We cannot identify them without deterministic clues that reveal their information structure meanings. The different positions of focus outlined in the next section are those which are not in the most neutral word order in each language.

4.3.1 Focus position

Some languages assign a specific position to signal focus. It is evident that the position in this case is primarily motivated by the necessity to mark narrow focus on a single constituent in the non-neutral word order. For example, if a language employs SVO by default, and the canonical focus position of the language is clause-final, then the object in SVO is not considered as necessarily containing focus. This is because sentences in the default word order allow for all possibilities in information structure.

According to Féry & Krifka (2008) and my own survey, there are four positions that human languages employ to designate narrow focus; (i) clause-initial, (ii) clause-final, (iii) preverbal, and (iv) postverbal. In the following subsections, each position is exemplified and the languages that use the strategy are enumerated.

4.3.1.1 Clause-initial position

Narrow focus can be assigned to the clause-initial position in some languages, including English (e.g. focus/topic fronting constructions), Ingush (Nichols 2011), Akan (Drubig 2003), Breton (Press 1986), Yiddish (N. G. Jacobs 2005), and Hausa (Hartmann & Zimmermann 2007; Büring 2010).

The representative example in (18) is from Ingush (a Northeast Caucasian language, spoken in Ingushetia and Chechnya). Ingush is a head-final language except for predominantly V2 order in main clauses (Nichols 2011). In (18), the first element in each sentence is associated with focus.

(18) a. Cuo   diicar   suona jerazh.
       3s.ERG D.tell.WP 1s.DAT these
       '*She* told me them (=stories).' (focus on *she*)

   b. Suona diicar   cuo   yzh.
       1s.DAT D.tell.WP 3s.ERG 3p
       'She told *me* them (=stories).' (focus on *me*) [inh] (Nichols 2011: 687)

4 Markings of information structure

Hausa is also known to use the clause-initial position for marking focus (Büring 2010). As is exemplified in the Q/A pair presented in (19Q-A1) and (19Q-A12, the focused constituent in Hausa (replying to the *wh*-question) can appear first or can be realized in situ. That is to say, there are two types of foci in Hausa, namely ex situ focus (19A1) and in situ focus (19A2) (Hartmann & Zimmermann 2007).

(19) Q: Mèe sukà kaamàa?
what 3PL.REL.PERF catch
'What did they catch?'

A1: **Kiifii** (nèe) sukà kaamàa.
fish PRT 3PL.REL.PERF catch
'They caught FISH.'

A2: Sun kaamàa **kiifii**.
3PL.ABS.PERF catch fish
'They caught FISH.' [hau] (Hartmann & Zimmermann 2007: 242–243)

There are two types of languages with respect to focus position. One obligatorily places focused elements in a specific position, and the other optionally does. Hausa is of the latter type. Ingush and English belong to former.

Even if a language does not always assign focus to the clause-initial position, it can sometimes make use of clause-initial focus, which is called focus/topic fronting in the current analysis.[9] Old information is sometimes focus-marked as in (20) where the replier wants to say that *she* does not merely know *John*, but dislikes him.[10]

(20) Q: Does she know JOHN?
A: JOHN she DISLIKES. (Gussenhoven 2007: 96)

Hence, an English sentence in which the object is not in situ (e.g., *John she dislikes.*), if we do not consider the accents, can be read ambiguously (e.g., either *It is John who she dislikes.* or *As for John, she dislikes him.*). These matters are revisited in the next chapter in terms of discrepancies between meaning and marking of information structure. For the moment, suffice it to say that the clause-initial position can be employed to narrowly mark the focus of the sentence in many languages including English.

---

[9] As mentioned several times, this kind of syntactic operation is often called topicalization (Prince 1984; Man 2007).

[10] Another example is already given in (3), which is called Second Occurrence Focus (Section 4.1.2).

4.3.1.2 Clause-final position

Second, narrow focus can be licensed in clause-final position in some languages. These include Russian (Neeleman & Titov 2009),[11] Bosnian Croatian Serbian, American Sign Language (Petronio 1993; Churng 2007), and some Chadic languages such as Tangale and Ngizim (Drubig 2003). For example, in Russian, if (i) a constituent corresponds to the *wh*-word in a given question, and thereby is narrowly focused and (ii) the accent does not designate the focus, it can occupy the clause-final position as presented below.[12]

(21) Q: Kto dal Kate knigu?
   who gave Kate.DAT book.ACC
   'Who gave a book to Kate?'

   A: Kate knigu dala ANJA.
   Kate.DAT book.ACC gave Anna
   'ANNA gave a book to Kate.' (focus on the subject)

   Q: Čto Anja dala Kate?
   what.ACC Anna gave Kate.DAT
   'What did Anna give to Kate?'

   A: Anja dala Kate KNIGU.
   Anna gave Kate.DAT book.ACC
   'Anna gave a BOOK to Kate.' (focus on the direct object)

   Q: Komu Anja dala knigu?
   who.DAT Anna gave book.ACC
   'Who did Anna give a book to?'

   A: Anja dala knigu KATE.
   Anna gave book.ACC Kate.DAT
   'Anna gave a book to KATE.' (focus on the indirect object) [rus] (Neeleman & Titov 2009: 515)

Russian, in which the most unmarked word order is SVO, is known for its free word order of constituents. However, Rodionova (2001), exploring variability of word order in Russian declarative sentences, concludes that the word order in

---

[11] In Russian, non-contrastive focus (i.e. *semantic-focus* in the taxonomy of the present study) shows up sentence-finally, whereas contrastive focus is fronted (Neeleman & Titov 2009).
[12] The second answer in (21) is in the most unmarked word order in Russian.

4 Markings of information structure

Russian is influenced by different types of focus, namely narrow, predicate, and sentential focus.

The same phenomenon holds in Bosnian Croatian Serbian as exemplified in (22); (22a) represents an unmarked word order in the language (SVO), but the subject in (22b) *Slavko* is postposed to mark focus meaning overtly through syntax.

(22) a. Slavk-o vid-i Olg-u
Slavko.M-SG.NOM see-3SG Olg-3.F.SG.ACC
'Slavko sees OLGA' (the unmarked word order)

b. Olg-u vid-i Slavk-o
Olga.F-SG.ACC see-3SG Slavko.M-SG.NOM
'SLAVKO sees Olga.' (focus on the subject) [hbs]

4.3.1.3 Preverbal position

Third, the (immediately) preverbal position is another site that signals focus. Languages that assign narrow focus to the preverbal position include Basque (Ortiz de Urbina 1999), Hungarian (É. Kiss 1998; Szendrői 2001), Turkish (İşsever 2003), and Armenian (Comrie 1984; Tamrazian 1991; 1994; Tragut 2009; Megerdoomian 2011). Basque, for instance, is a language in which focus marking heavily depends on sentence positioning. This is similar to the situation in Catalan (Vallduví 1992; Engdahl & Vallduví 1996) and Yucatec Maya (Kügler, Skopeteas & Verhoeven 2007). The syntactic device for marking narrow focus in Basque is to assign focus immediately to the left of the verb as exemplified in (23). While (23a) conveys neutral information structure (i.e., all constituents are underspecified from the view of the present study.), in (23b–c), the subject *Jonek* 'Jon', being adjacent to the verb *irakurri* 'read', should be read as conveying focus meaning.

(23) a. Jonek eskutitza irakurri du
Jon letter read has
'Jon has read the letter.' (SOV)

b. Jonek irakurri du eskutitza
Jon read has letter
'JON has read the letter.' (SVO)

c. Eskutitza, Jonek irakurri du
letter Jon read has
'JON has read the letter.' (OSV) [eus] (Ortiz de Urbina 1999: 312)

4.3 Syntactic positioning

Crowgey & Bender (2011) also employ the *wh*-test for identifying focus in Basque: Both (24b–c) are grammatical sentences in Basque, but (24c) cannot be used as an answer to (24a). This distinction in felicity-conditions shows that focused constituents should appear in the immediately preverbal position.

(24) a. Liburu bat   nork   irakurri du?
       book one.ABS.SG who.ERG.SG.FOC read.PERF 3SGO.PRES.3SGA
       'Who has read one book?'

   b. Liburu bat   Mirenek   irakurri du.
       book one.ABS.SG Mary.ERG.SG.FOC read.PERF 3SGO.PRES.3SGA
       'Mary has read one book.'

   c. Mirenek   liburu bat   irakurri du.
       Mary.ERG.SG.FOC book one.ABS.SG read.PERF 3SGO.PRES.3SGA
       'Mary has read one book.' [eus] (Crowgey & Bender 2011: 48–49)

Hungarian is a well known language as fixed focus position.[13] The constituent order in Hungarian can be schematized as '(Topic*) Focus V S O' (Büring 2010), as exemplified in (25).

(25) a. Mari   fel hívta Pétert.
       Mary-NOM VM rang Peter-ACC

   b. MARI$_F$ hívta fel Pétert.
       Mary-NOM rang VM Peter-ACC

   c. *MARI   fel hívta Pétert.
       Mary-NOM VM rang Peter-ACC
       'Mary rang up Peter' [hun] (Szendrői 1999: 549)

(25a) is encoded as the basic word order, in which a marker *fel* occurs between the subject *Mari* 'Mary' and the main verb *hívta* 'rang'. If *Mari* is focused, the verb *hívta* should immediately follow the focused item as given in (25b), and if not as shown in (25c), it sounds bad as. É. Kiss (1998) states that focus in Hungarian can appear either in situ or immediately preverbally.[14] Szendrői (2001) argues that

---

[13] Some counterarguments to this generalization have been reported: The so-called focus position in Hungarian has been claimed to encode exhaustiveness rather than identificational focus (Horvath 2007; Fanselow 2008).

[14] That indicates informational focus and identificational focus, respectively. According to É. Kiss (1998), the preverbal focus in Hungarian (i.e. identificational focus) is almost the same as cleft constructions in English.

4 Markings of information structure

focus in Hungarian tends not to be in situ, and that preverbal positioning has to be phonologically licensed (marked with small caps above).

According to Tamrazian (1991), Armenian also places focused constituents in the immediately preverbal position: Both sentences (26a–b) sound natural in Armenian, but the first one is in the basic word order without a focused element. In contrast, the preverbal item SURKIN in (26b) is focused, which is signaled by the adjacent auxiliary *e*. The auxiliary *e* should immediately follow the focused item. For instance, (26c) in which an accent falls on SURKIN but *e* appears after the main verb *sirum* 'like' is ill-formed.

(26) a. siranə surikin sirum e
   Siran(NOM) Surik(ACC) like is
   'Siran likes Surik'

  b. siranə SURIKIN e sirum
   Siran(NOM) Surik(ACC) is like
   'Siran likes SURIK'

  c. *siranə SURIKIN sirum e
   Siran(NOM) Surik(ACC) like is [hey] (Tamrazian 1991: 103)

4.3.1.4 Postverbal position

Finally, the (immediate) postverbal position is responsible for marking narrow focus in several languages. These include Portuguese (Ambar 1999), Toba Batak, and Chicheŵa (van Valin 2005). For example, Ambar claims that non-contrastive focus is preceded by the verb in Portuguese. An example is presented below, in which the focused item *a Joana* (functioning as the subject) follows the verb *comeu* 'ate'. If the subject with focus meaning precedes the verb, the sentence sounds infelicitous in the context, as shown in (27A3-A4).

(27) Q: Quem comeu a tarte?
   who ate the pie
   'Who ate the pie?'

 A1: Comeu a Joana.
   ate the Joana

 A2: A tarte comeu a Joana.

 A3: #A Joana comeu.

 A4: #A Joana comeu a tarte. [por] (Ambar 1999: 27)

4.3 Syntactic positioning

4.3.2 Topic position

Topic is also associated with a specific position in some languages. For example, according to Ambar (1999), topics in Portuguese cannot follow the verb as shown in (28).

(28) Q: Que comeu a   Maria?
       what ate   the Mary
       'What did Mary eat?'

   A1: Comeu a tarte.

   A2: A Maria comeu a tarte.

   A3: #A tarte comeu a Maria.

   A4: #Comeu a Maria a tarte. [por] (Ambar 1999: 28)

In (28), *Maria* 'Mary' plays the topic role in the answers. The word should either disappear (as shown in 28A1) or precede the verb *comeu* 'ate' (as presented in 28A2). The sentences in which the topic is preceded by the verb sound infelicitous (as provided in 28A3-A4).

4.3.2.1 Topic-first restriction

Previous studies have assumed the canonical position of topic to be sentence-initial. In fact, quite a few languages have been reported as having a strong tendency towards topic-fronting. Nagaya (2007) claims that topics in Tagalog canonically appear sentence-initially, Chapman (1981) says topics in Paumarí appear sentence-initially, and Casielles-Suárez (2003) states that topics should be followed by focus (i.e. *topic-focus*) in the canonical word order in Spanish. In Bosnian Croatian Serbian, if a constituent as in *Olg-u* is given in the previous sentence as the focus as shown in (29a), it appears sentence-initially in the following sentence such as (29b) when functioning as the topic. Since focused constituents in that language appear in the clause-final position (as mentioned in Section 4.3.1.2), *mi* 'we' in (29b) is associated with focus (marked in small caps in the translation).[15] That is, in Bosnian Croatian Serbian, topics appear first, and foci occur finally.

---

[15] In (29b), *i* 'as well' enforces the focus effect on *mi* 'we' in the final position. That means *i* in the sentence behaves as a focus particle, similarly to 'also' in English.

4 Markings of information structure

(29) a. Slavk-o vid-i Olg-u
Slavko.M-SG.NOM see-3.SG Olg-3.F.SG.ACC
'Slavko sees OLGA'

b. Olg-u vid-imo i mi
Olg.F-3 SG.ACC as well 1.PL.NOM
'WE see Olga, too' [hbs]

In some languages including Japanese and Korean, it is the case that (non-contrastive) topics are required to be sentence-initial (Maki, Kaiser & Ochi 1999; Vermeulen 2009). Maki, Kaiser & Ochi argue that a *wa*-marked phrase can be interpreted as a topic if and only if it turns up in initial position. Otherwise, the *wa*-marked phrase in a clause-internal position should be evaluated as conveying a contrastive meaning.

(30) a. John-wa kono hon-o yonda.
John-WA this book-ACC read
'As for John, he read this book.'

b. Kono hon-wa John-ga yonda.
this book-WA John-NOM read
'As for this book, John read it.'

c. John-ga kono hon-wa yonda.
John-NOM this book-WA read
'John read this book, as opposed to some other book.'
'*As for this book, he read this it.' [jpn] (Maki, Kaiser & Ochi 1999: 7–8)

The same goes for Korean in my intuition. Féry & Krifka (2008) provide a *prima facie* counterexample to this claim as shown in (31), in which *disethu* 'dessert' is combined with -(*n*)*un*.

(31) nwukwuna-ka disethu-nun aiswu khwulim-ul mek-ess-ta.
everyone-NOM dessert-NUN ice.cream-ACC eat-PST-DECL
'As for dessert, everyone ate ice cream.' [kor] (Féry & Krifka 2008: 130)

However, -(*n*)*un* is not always compatible with the information structure meaning of topic. That is, there is a mismatch between form and meaning. The (*n*)*un*-marked *disethu* in (31), in my intuition, fills the role of contrastive topic, rather than aboutness topic. Contrastive topics cross-linguistically have no constraint

4.3 Syntactic positioning

on position in word order (Erteschik-Shir 2007; Roberts 2011). In conclusion, aboutness topics in Korean and Japanese should be sentence-initial.

Other studies, however, indicate that topics are not necessarily sentence-initial (Erteschik-Shir 2007; Féry & Krifka 2008). According to Erteschik-Shir's analysis, topic fronting is optional in Danish, and topics can be marked either in an overt way (i.e. topicalization in or in situ as shown in 32a–b).

(32) a. Hun hilstepå Ole. **Ham** havde hun ikke mødt før...
    She greeted Ole. **Him** had she not met before

  b. Hun hilstepå Ole. Hun havde ikke mødt **ham** før...
    She greeted Ole. She had not met **him** before
    [dan] (Erteschik-Shir 2007: 7)

Erteschik-Shir asserts that so-called topicalization in Danish, which dislocates the constituent playing the topic role to the left periphery, is used only for expressing the topic in an overt way. In other words, topics in Danish are not necessarily sentence-initial.

Building on the analyses presented so far, the present study argues that the canonical position of aboutness topics is language-specific: In some languages such as Japanese and Korean aboutness topics must appear in the initial position, while in other languages such as Danish they do not.

4.3.2.2 Right dislocation

It is necessary to take one more non-canonical topic position into account. Topics can also appear sentence-finally. This phenomenon is called right dislocation (Cecchetto 1999; Law 2003), sentence-final topic (Féry & Krifka 2008), anti-topic (Chafe 1976; Lambrecht 1996), or postposing (T. Kim 2011).

(33) a. Left dislocation: This book, it has the recipe in it.

  b. Right dislocation: You should go to see it, that movie. (Heycock 2007: 185–186)

Gundel (1988) regards this construction as a peculiar construction within the comment-topic structure contrasting it to the ordinary topic-comment structure. There must be an intonational break (i.e. a prosodic phrase marked as $_p$) which

4 Markings of information structure

separates the topic from the prior parts of the given sentence. Such constructions exist cross-linguistically as exemplified in (34)[16] in Korean and (35)[17] in Cantonese and French.

(34) a. kumyen, kuke-n com saki-nte.
   if.so that-NUN a.little fraud-be.SEM
   'If so, that is a kind of fraud, I think.'

b. kumyen, com saki-nte, kuke-n
   if.so a.little fraud-be.SEM that-NUN
   'If so, that is a kind of fraud, I think.' [kor] (T. Kim 2011: 223–224)

(35) a. ((Go loupo)$_P$ (nei gin-gwo gaa)$_P$, ([ni go namjan ge]$_T$)$_P$)$_I$.
   CLF wife 2.SG see-EXP DSP this CLF man DSP
   'The wife you have seen, of this man.' [yue]

b. ((Pierre l' a mangée)$_P$, ([la pomme]$_T$)$_P$)$_I$.
   Peter it-ACC has eaten, the apple
   'Peter has eaten the apple.' [fra] (Féry & Krifka 2008: 130)

Despite the difference in positioning, right dislocation has much in common with left dislocation. At first appearance, right dislocation looks like a mirror image of left-dislocation, in that the topic is apparently separate from the main clause and it is not likely that there is a missing function in the preceding sentence. In fact, Cecchetto (1999) proposes the so-called mirror hypothesis, which implies right dislocation is tantamount to a mirror image of left-dislocation.

The current study hence regards right dislocation as a non-canonical variant of left dislocation. Lambrecht (1996) provides a counterargument to this hypothesis, but the difference between left/right dislocations in Lambrecht's analysis appears to be contextual, rather than the result of a morphosyntactic operation. As the present study is not directly concerned with pragmatic constraints, the mirror hypothesis is still applicable to the current work. The difference between them seems to be trivially influenced by the degree of speaker's attention to the conversation: Left dislocation would be used for the purpose of restricting the

---

[16] The suffix -n in (34) is an allomorph of -(n)un, which mostly shows up in spoken data.

[17] Féry & Krifka (2008) state a boundary tone that is created by the lexical markers responsible for information structure meanings (e.g. ge in Cantonese as given in 35a) allows the topic to be added into the final position.

4.3 Syntactic positioning

frame of what the speaker wants to talk about in advance, whereas right dislocation is just an afterthought performing almost the same function. A piece of evidence that supports this argument is provided by a corpus study which exploits a monolingual but fully naturally occurring text. T. Kim (2011) scrutinizes several spoken data in Korean, and concludes that right dislocation (postposing, in his terminology) such as (34b) is largely conditioned by how accessible and/or urgent the information is: If the information is not uttered within several neighboring preceding sentences and is thereby less accessible in the speaker's consciousness, it tends to be easily postposed. These findings lend further support for the argument that the choice between left and right dislocation is determined by only contextual conditions.

4.3.3 Contrast position

Contrastive topics have a weaker constraint on order than non-contrastive topics (i.e. aboutness topics) (Erteschik-Shir 2007; Bianchi & Frascarelli 2010). Contrastive topics have a tendency to precede aboutness topics in some languages (Bianchi & Frascarelli 2010), but this generalization has not been verified in all languages. With respect to sentence positioning of contrastive focus, there are two types of languages. The first, in which contrastive focus shares the same position as non-contrastive focus, is more common. A typical language of this type is English, in which contrastive focus is not distinguishable from non-contrastive focus in terms of sentence position. The second type of language selects two distinctive positions from among the ordinary focus positions given earlier; (i) clause-initial, (ii) clause-final, (iii) preverbal, and (iv) postverbal. The languages that belong to this type include Georgian (preverbal vs. postverbal, Skopeteas & Fanselow 2010), Portuguese (preverbal vs. postverbal, Ambar 1999), Russian (clause-initial vs. clause-final, Neeleman & Titov 2009), Ingush (immediately preverbal vs. clause-initial, Nichols 2011), and so on. For example, (36) shows preverbal focus and postverbal focus in Georgian.

(36) a. kal-i   kotan-s u-q'ur-eb-s.
       woman-NOM pot-DAT (IO.3)OV-look.at-THM-PRS.S.3SG

   b. kal-i   u-q'ur-eb-s   kotan-s.
       woman-NOM (IO.3)OV-look.at-THM-PRS.S.3SG pot-DAT
       'The woman looks at the pot.' [kat] (Skopeteas & Fanselow 2010: 1371)

According to Skopeteas & Fanselow, both sentences in (36) are legitimate in Georgian. The difference between them is where the narrowly focused item appears in a sentence; either in the immediately preverbal position or in a postverbal position. That is, *kotan-s* ' pot-DAT' in (36a) is a preverbal focus (necessarily), while the subject *kal-i* 'woman-NOM' and the object *kotan-s* in (36b) can be interpreted as preverbal focus and postverbal focus (sufficiently), respectively. Skopeteas & Fanselow argue that focus in the preverbal position normally bears contrastiveness (i.e. contrastive focus). Thus, the positions that non-contrastive focus and contrastive focus canonically occupy are different in Georgian.

This distinction between two types of foci requires the grammar library for information structure to allow users to select (a) whether a language uses the same position for both kinds of focus, and (b) if not, which type occupies which position.

Additionally, a given language might have two (or more) ways of expressing contrastive meaning, and this also has to be considered in modeling information structure in a cross-linguistic perspective. For example, Ingush marks contrastive focus by two means; via the use of a clitic =*m*, and via word order, as exemplified in (37a–b) respectively.

(37) a. Suona=m xoza di xet, hwuona myshta dy xaac (suona).
 1s.DAT=FOC nice day think, 2s.DAT how D.be.PRS know.PRS (1s.DAT)
 'I don't know what you think, but *I* think it's a nice day.' (Nichols 2011: 721)

 b. Pacchahw **uqazahw** hwavoagha
 king here DX.V.come.PRS
 'The king is coming *here* (he was expected to go somewhere else).' [inh]
 (Nichols 2011: 690)

The ordinary contrastive focus, as shown in (37b) where focus is in boldface, occupies the immediate preverbal position in Ingush, and this position is different from the non-contrastive focus position, which occurs clause-initially. According to Nichols, the use of a clitic as given in (37a) is motivated by the necessity to express contrastive meaning in a more marked way.

In sum, the canonical position for contrastive focus is language specific; contrastive focus can either share the same position with non-contrastive focus (e.g. English, Greek (Gryllia 2009), etc.) or show up in another position (e.g. Portuguese (Ambar 1999), Russian (Neeleman & Titov 2009), Georgian (Skopeteas & Fanselow 2010), Ingush (Nichols 2011), etc.). Contrastive topics have no rigid restrictions on position (Erteschik-Shir 2007; Bianchi & Frascarelli 2010).

4.4 Summary

There are three linguistic forms of expressing information structure: prosody, lexical markers, and syntactic positioning.[18] The use of prosody to mark topic and focus is widespread but not universal. The best way to handle prosodic marking in the current work is to allow for underspecification in such a way that prosodic information can be added into the formalism at a later point. Lexical markers of information structure can be affixes, adpositions, and modifiers. Information-structure marking adpositions are in complementary distribution with ordinary case-marking adpositions in a language. With respect to sentence positioning, I argue that information structure of sentences in the basic word order is necessarily underspecified. When a constituent is ex situ and narrowly focused, four positions can be used: clause-initial, clause-final, preverbal, and postverbal. Topics canonically appear sentence-initially in some languages, but the topic-first restriction is not necessarily a property of all languages. Contrastive focus may or may not share the same position as non-contrastive focus (i.e. semantic focus). Lastly, contrastive topic does not enforce strong constraints on position across languages.

---

[18]There are also special constructions of expressing information structure, such as clefting. The construction will be addressed later in Chapter 10.

5 Discrepancies between meaning and marking

Bolinger (1977) claims that the existence of one meaning per one form and vice versa (i.e. an isomorphism between formal and interpretive domains) is the most natural state of human language. Natural human languages, however, provide many counterexamples to this notion. At the lexical level, homonymy and polysemy are two widespread examples of a single ability to convey two or more meanings. Moreover, mismatches between meaning and form can sometimes be caused by grammatical elements. For example, English shows discrepancies between form and meaning in counterfactuals, constructions in which the speaker does not believe the given proposition expressed in the antecedent is true. The most well known factor which deeply contributes to the counterfactual meaning in many languages is the past tense morpheme (e.g. '-ed' in English) (Iatridou 2000). The past tense morpheme in counterfactuals (also known as fake past tense) does not denote an event that actually happened in the past as exemplified in (1). Thus, the mapping relationship between morphological forms and their meaning in counterfactual sentences is not the same as that in non-counterfactual sentences.

(1) a. If he were smart, he would be rich.
(conveying "He isn't smart." and "He isn't rich.")
b. I wish I had a car.
(conveying "I don't have a car now.") (Iatridou 2000: 231–232)

As with other grammatical phenomena, information structure also exhibits discrepancies in form-meaning mapping. This chapter presents several types of mismatches between the forms that express information structure and the information structure meanings conveyed by those forms.

5.1 Ambivalent lexical markers

In some languages, one lexical marker can correspond to meanings of several components of information structure (i.e. no one-to-one correspondence between

5 Discrepancies between meaning and marking

form and meaning). One such mismatch caused by lexical markers is exhibited in Japanese and Korean. As is well known, *wa* in Japanese and *-(n)un* in Korean are regarded as lexical markers to express the topic of the sentence, but they can also sometimes be used for conveying contrastive focus.

(2) Q: Kim-i   onul o-ass-ni?
    Kim-NOM today come-PST-INT
    'Did Kim come today?'

   A: ani. (Kim-un) ecey-nun   o-ass-e.
      No. Kim-NUN yesterday-NUN come-PST-DECL
      'No. Kim came yesterday.' [kor]

The lexical marker *-(n)un* in Korean appears twice in (2A); one occurrence is with the subject *Kim*, and the other is combined with an adverb *ecey* 'yesterday'. Although the same lexical marker is used, they do not share the same properties of information structure. It is clear that topic is assigned to *Kim-un* in that the word is already given in the question and as indicated by the parentheses, it is optional. By contrast, the *(n)un*-marked *ecey* is newly and importantly mentioned by the replier, and thereby it should be evaluated as containing a meaning of focus rather than topic. Moreover, if *ecey-nun* disappears, the answer sounds infelicitous within the context, which clearly implies it is focused. Recall that I define focus as an information structure component associated with an inomissible constituent. Furthermore, (2) passes the correction test to vet contrastive focus (Gryllia 2009). Since *onul* 'today' in the question and *ecey* 'yesterday' in the reply constitute an alternative set, *ecey* in (2A) has a contrastive meaning. As a consequence, the information structure role of *ecey* in (2A) is contrastive focus, even though the so-called topic marker *-(n)un* is attached to it.

This *(n)un*-marked constituent associated with contrastive focus is realized differently from the one associated with contrastive topic. In (3A), the *(n)un*-marked element in the first position can be dropped as the parentheses imply. When *ku chack-un* appears, the fronted constituent is associated with contrast. This finding echoes H.-W. Choi's argument. She claims that only elements with contrastive meaning can be scrambled in Korean, which means *ku chack-un* 'the book-NUN' in (3A) gives contrastive meaning.

(3) Q: nwuka ku chayk-ul ilk-ess-ni?
       who   the book-ACC read-PST-INT
       'Who read the book?'

5.1 Ambivalent lexical markers

A: (ku chayk-un) Kim-i   ilk-ess-e.
   the book-NUN Kim-NOM read-PST-DECL
   '(As for the book,) Kim read it.' [kor]

In fact, H.-W. Choi does not concede the existence of contrastive topic in Korean, and the scrambled and (n)un-marked constituents are analyzed as only contrastive focus in her proposal. However, this notion is contradictory to the definition that focus cannot be elided. Given that *ku chayk-un* in (3A) can felicitously disappear, we cannot say that it is associated with focus. Since contrast should be realized as either contrastive focus or contrastive topic, *ku chayk-un* in (3A) must be evaluated as a contrastive topic.

Therefore, -(n)un in Korean can assign three meanings to an adjoining NP: aboutness topic, contrastive topic, and contrastive focus. In other words, -(n)un provides constraints, but only partial ones, which cause discrepancies between form and meaning. Because this marker can be combined with constituents that are not topics, it is my position that 'topic-marker' is not an appropriate label. The same goes for *wa* in Japanese. It should also be noted that case markers in these languages (e.g. *i* / *ka* and *ga* for nominatives) also convey an ambiguous interpretation, either focus or background (i.e. non-topic).

In some languages, a lexical marker known for marking topic coincides with cleft constructions which clearly carry a focus meaning. (4) in Ilonggo (also known as Hiligaynon, an Austronesian language spoken in the Philippines) exemplifies such a mismatch (Schachter 1973). In Ilonggo, the topic marker *ang* is in complementary distribution with case markers similarly to *wa* in Japanese and -(n)un in Korean. One difference is that the case relation is marked by an affix attached to the verb (e.g. the agentive marker *nag-* in 4).

(4) a. nag-   dala ang babayi sang   bata
       AG.TOP- bring TOP woman NONTOP child
       'The woman brought a child.'

   b. ang babayi ang nag-   dala sang   bata
       TOP woman TOP AG.TOP- bring NONTOP child
       'It was the woman who brought a child.' [hil] (Croft 2002: 108)

(4a) is a topicalized construction in which the topic marker *ang* is combined with *babayi* 'woman'. (4b) is a focused construction, in which the topic marker *ang* is still combined with the focused constituent *babayi*, and one more topic marker appears at the beginning of the cleft clause *nag- dala sang bata*, which implies that the so-called topic marker does not necessarily express topic meaning.

5 Discrepancies between meaning and marking

5.2 Focus/Topic fronting

My cross-linguistic survey of focus/topic fronting draws a tentative conclusion: If focus and topic compete for the sentence-initial position, topic always wins. To take an example, in Ingush, both topic and focus can precede the rest of the clause, but a focused constituent must follow a constituent conveying topic, as exemplified in (5).

(5) Jurta   jistie
    town.GEN   nearby
    (topic)
    joaqqa   sag   ull   cymogazh   jolazh.
    J.old   person   lie.PRS   sick.CVsim J.PROG.CVsim
    (focus)
    'In the next town an old woman is sick (is lying sick).'
    Mista   xudar   myshta   duora?
    sour   porridge   how   D.make.IMPF
    (topic)   (focus)
    'How did they make sour porridge? (How was sour porridge made?)'
    [inh] (Nichols 2011: 683)

This means that if topic and (narrow) focus co-occur, topic should be followed by focus even in languages which place focused constituents in the clause-initial position. The same phenomenon can be found in many other languages. For example, in Nishnaabemwin (an Algic language spoken in the region surrounding the Great Lakes, in Ontario, Minnesota, Wisconsin, and Michigan), if both the subject and the object of a transitive verb appear preverbally, the first is marked for topic and the second for focus (Valentine 2001). No counterexamples to this generalization have been observed, at least among the languages I have examined hitherto.

Yet, there are some cases in which it is unclear which role (i.e. focus or topic) the fronted constituent is assigned. I would like to label the constructions in which this kind of ambiguity takes place 'focus/topic fronting' (also known as Topicalization). Prince (1984) provides two types of OSV constructions in English, and argues that the change in word order is motivated by marking information status, such as new and old information.

(6) a. John saw Mary yesterday.

   b. Mary, John saw yesterday.

   c. Mary, John saw her yesterday. (Prince 1984: 213)

5.2 Focus/Topic fronting

Both (6b–c) relate to (6a), but (6b) is devoid of the resumptive pronoun in the main clause, whereas (6c) has *her* referring to *Mary*. These are called Topicalization and Left-Dislocation by Prince,[1] but I use the label focus/topic fronting for the first type of syntactic operation.

The focus/topic fronting constructions have two potential meanings, as exemplified in (7). That is, (7a) can be paraphrased into either (7b) or (7c), whose information structures differ.

(7) a. The book Kim read.
    b. It was the book that Kim read.
    c. As for the book, Kim read it.

If the fronted NP is focused, its configuration is the same as cleft constructions (7b). If it behaves as the topic within the context, the sentence can share the same information structure as (7c). This means (7a) in itself would sound ambiguous, in the absence of contextual information. Gundel (1983), in order to distinguish the different structures, makes use of the two terms Focus Topicalization and Topic Topicalization, suggesting that OSV constructions like (7a) are ambiguous. Gussenhoven (2007) also takes notice of such an ambiguity, and regards the constructions like (7a) as containing 'reactivating focus'.

(8) Q: Does she know JOHN?
    A: JOHN she DISLIKES. (Gussenhoven 2007: 96)

Nevertheless, it is my position that the terms that Gundel and Gussenhoven make use of still lead to confusion.[2]

---

[1] Prince (1984) argues that the choice of one over another is not random but is influenced by the information status of what the speaker is talking. According to Prince, Topicalization has two characteristics; one is that it is used to mark information status of the entity itself, and the other is that it involves an open proposition. In short, in Prince's analysis, information status factors (e.g. new vs. given), have an effect on the composition in the OSV order, which removes the fronted NP referring to a discourse-new entity from a syntactic position that disfavours it. As indicated in Chapter 3 (Section 3.1), since the present study is not concerned with information status, such a distinction based on new information vs. given information is not used in the present work.

[2] From a different point of view, some English native speakers say that (7c) does not look like a proper paraphrasing of (7a). Intuitively, the fronted item *The book* conveys only focus meaning. If this thought holds true, the focus/topic fronting constructions are actually equivalent to cleft constructions, like a pair of (7a–b). In fact, other native speakers who read focus/topic constructions in other languages have similar thoughts. For instance, one Cantonese informant says that (9) in Cantonese can convey both meanings, but the first reading is predominant. For now, I cannot draw a conclusion about which one is a sound interpretation, but what is important is that the name 'Topicalization' is not appropriate in any cases.

5 Discrepancies between meaning and marking

Other languages also have the focus/topic fronting constructions. In the following Cantonese example, the fronted constituent *nei1 bun2 syu1* 'this book' can play the role of either focus or topic of the sentence, and the choice between the two readings hinges on the context.

(9) Nei1 bun2 syu1   ngo5 zung1ji3
    DEF CLF book   1.SG like
    (a) 'It is this book that I like.' or
    (b) 'As for this book, I like it.' [yue] (Man 2007: 16)

The same phenomenon can also be observed in Nishnaabemwin. Information structure in Nishnaabemwin, whose basic word order is VOS, is also accomplished via syntactic means. If a verbal argument appears before the verb, then it is marked for information structure. Its meaning, just as in the previous examples in English and Cantonese, becomes ambiguous only if one argument is preverbal (Valentine 2001). In fact, this kind of ambiguity frequently happens in languages in which focus shows up clause-initially (e.g. Ingush).

In brief, a single form has two different information structure meanings; the construction often refered to as Topicalization (Prince 1984) sounds ambiguous unless the given context is ascertained. Regarding the selection of terminology, the present study calls such a construction focus/topic-fronting, because (i) this explicitly displays the ambiguous meaning, and (ii) the previous terminology (i.e. topicalization) confuses syntactic and pragmatic notions.

5.3 Competition between prosody and syntax

There are potentially three subclasses of the connection between prosody and syntax. First, some languages have a system with very weak or no interaction between prosody and syntax with respect to focus. These include Catalan (Engdahl & Vallduví 1996), Akan (Drubig 2003), and Yucatec Maya (Kügler, Skopeteas & Verhoeven 2007). In those languages, displacing constituents is the only way to identify focused elements. The second subclass assigns focus to a particular position. Constraints on this position necessarily correlate with phonological marking in the second type of languages. Hungarian belongs to this type, in which the focused and accented item appears immediately prior to the verb (É. Kiss 1998; Szendrői 2001). The third type, which occasionally brings about a mismatch between form and meaning, includes languages in which prosody and syntax compete in expressing focus. That is, in this type of language, either prosodic or syntactic structure can be used to mark focus, depending on the construction.

5.3 Competition between prosody and syntax

Büring (2010) calls the third type 'Mixed Languages' and draws the following generalization about them.

(10) MARKED WORD ORDER → UNMARKED PROSODY: Marked constituent order may only be used for focusing X if the resulting prosodic structure is less marked than that necessary to focus X in the unmarked constituent order. (Büring 2010: 197)

Büring argues that mixed languages include Korean, Japanese, Finnish, German, European Portuguese, and most of the Slavic languages. According to my survey, Russian and Bosnian Croatian Serbian (i.e. the Slavic languages) clearly fall under this third mixed type: as they can either (i) employ a specific accent to signal focus or (ii) assign the focused constituent to the clause-final position. For instance, the subject *sobaka* 'dog' in (11a) can have focus meaning if and only if it bears the accent for focus, which means (11a) is informatively ambiguous in the absence of information about accent. In contrast, (11b) where the subject is in the final position sounds unambiguous, and *sobaka* is evaluated as focused.

(11) a. Sobaka laet.
       dog   bark
       'The dog bark.'

   b. Laet sobaka.
      bark dog
      'The DOG bark.' [rus]

The distinction between (11a–b) is more clearly shown with the *wh*-test. If the question is *Who barks?* as given in (12Q1), both sentences can be used as the reply. If the reply is (11a) in the neutral word order, the verb *laet* bears an accent. In contrast, if the question is (12Q2), which requires the predicate to be focused, (11b) cannot be an appropriate answer and also there should be no sentential stress on the verb *laet*.

(12) Q1: Kto laet?
        who barks
        'Who barks?'

   A1: Sobaka laet. / Laet sobaka.

5 Discrepancies between meaning and marking

Q2: Čto delaet sobaka?
what doing dog
'What does the dog do?'

A2: Sobaka laet. / #Laet sobaka. [rus]

The same holds true for Bosnian Croatian Serbian. When the question is given as (13Q2), the sentence in which the subject is not in situ sounds infelicitous, and the verb *laje* is not allowed to bear a sentential stress.

(13) Q1: Ko laje?
who barks
'Who barks?'

A1: Pas laje. / Laje pas.
dog barks. / barks dog.
'The dog barks.'

Q2: Šta(Što) radi pas?
what doing dog
'What does the dog do?'

A2: Pas laje. / #Laje pas. [hbs]

In summary, in the third type of language, prosody takes priority over syntax in the neutral word order with respect to expressing focus (i.e., the prosodic marking wins). In contrast, when the sentence is not in the default word order, syntactic structure wins. Since sentences in an unmarked word order are normally ambiguous along these lines, focus position is not defined for sentences with unmarked word order, only for those with other word orders.

5.4 Multiple positions of focus

Even if a language employs a specific position for expressing focus, the focused constituent does not necessarily take that position, as exemplified by Russian in the previous section. That is, focus can be assigned to multiple positions. For instance, the focus in Russian may not be clause-final (as presented in 11), if the accent falls on another constituent. In this case, clause-final focus does not seem to be the same as cleft constructions in Russian, and the accented constituent

5.4 Multiple positions of focus

in situ is not also necessarily equivalent to informational focus. A more complex phenomenon with respect to syntactic operations on focus is exemplified by Greek (Gryllia 2009). In Greek, whose basic word order is VSO or SVO, focus can be both preverbal and postverbal and there is no informative difference between them.

(14) Q: Thelis   kafe   i   tsai?
     want.2SG coffee.ACC or tea.ACC
     'Would you like coffee or tea?'

  A1: Thelo   [kafe]$_{C\text{-Foc}}$.
      want.1SG coffee.ACC
      'I would like coffee.'

  A2: [Kafe]$_{C\text{-Foc}}$ thelo.
      coffee.ACC want.1SG
      'Coffee I would like.' [ell] (Gryllia 2009: 44)

The preverbal focus, shown on *kafe* in (14A2), is not in situ, because verbs precede objects in the neutral word order in Greek. Yet, there is no evidence that preverbal focus plays the role of identification and this sentential form is informatively the same as cleft constructions in Greek. Gryllia, moreover, argues that focused elements in both positions can receive the interpretation of contrastive focus as well as non-contrastive focus. That is, there are options for focus realization in Greek; (i) preverbal non-contrastive focus, (ii) preverbal contrastive focus,(iii) postverbal non-contrastive focus, and (iv) postverbal contrastive focus. The multiple focus positions in Greek demonstrate convincingly that forms which express information structure are not in a one-to-one relation with information structure components and thereby cannot unambiguously mark a specific information structure meaning.

Another important phenomenon related to focus positions can be found in Hausa. According to Hartmann & Zimmermann (2007), Hausa employs two strategies for marking focus. One is called ex situ focus, and the other is in situ focus. They are exemplified in (15A1-A2), respectively.

(15) Q: Mèe sukà   kaamàa?
     what 3PL.REL.PERF catch
     'What did they catch?'

5 Discrepancies between meaning and marking

> A1: **Kiifii** (nèe) sukà kaamàa.
> fish PRT 3PL.REL.PERF catch
> 'They caught FISH.'
>
> A2: Sun kaamàa **kiifii**.
> 3PL.ABS.PERF catch fish
> 'They caught FISH.' [hau] (Hartmann & Zimmermann 2007: 242–243)

In situ focus in Hausa does not require any special marking, whereas ex situ focus in the first position is prosodically prominent. Moreover, Hausa employs two focus particles *nèe* and *cèe*, but they can co-occur with only ex situ focus as shown in (15A1).[3] For this reason, Büring (2010) regards Hausa as a language without a specific marking system for focus. This analysis of focus realization in Hausa implies that some languages can assign focus to a constituent in situ without the help of pitch accents.

The examples presented in this section motivate flexible representation of information structure, particularly for sentences in unmarked word order. That is to say, in some circumstances, we cannot exactly say where focus is signaled.

5.5 Summary

Just as with other grammatical phenomena, there are discrepancies between forms and meanings with respect to information structure. This chapter has looked at several cases in which there are mismatches in mapping between information structure markings and meanings. First, lexical markers that express information structure occasionally cause such a mismatch. For example, *wa* and *-(n)un* in Japanese and Korean respectively are topic markers in these languages, but they can sometimes be used for expressing contrastive focus. Second, topic and focus appear sentence-initially in quite a few languages, but there are some cases in which we cannot decisively state whether the fronted item is associated with topic or focus. Such a construction has often been called 'Topicalization' in previous literature, but I use different terminology in order to be more accurate and I treat these constructions as examples of focus/topic fronting. Third, if prosody and syntax compete for expressing information structure, prosody takes

---

[3] This is an intriguing phenomenon, because in other languages in situ foci in the unmarked word order normally require an additional constraint, such as pitch accents. In other words, as shown in the examples of the Slavic languages (presented in the previous section), it is common that focused constituents in the default position need to be accented if the language uses multiple strategies for marking focus or topic.

5.5 Summary

priority in most cases. Finally, many languages place a focused constituent in a specific position, but this placement is optional in some languages. The last two properties are related to expressing focus in sentences in default word order. Information structure in unmarked sentences is also addressed in Section 7.2.2 (p. 109) in terms of the implementation.

6 Literature review

This chapter surveys previous literature based on HPSG (Head-driven Phrase Structure Grammar, Pollard & Sag 1994), MRS (Minimal Recursion Semantics, Copestake et al. 2005), and other frameworks. First, Section 6.1 investigates HPSG-based studies on information structure, which are largely based on a pioneering study offered by Engdahl & Vallduví (1996). Section 6.2 looks into how several previous studies represent information structure using the MRS formalism, and how they differ from the current model. Section 6.3 surveys prior studies of how phonological structure interacts with information structure in HPSG. Section 6.4 offers an explanation of how other frameworks treat information structure within their formalism, and what implications they have for the current model.

6.1 Information structure in HPSG

To my knowledge, Engdahl & Vallduví (1996) is the first endeavor to study information structure within the HPSG framework. This pioneering work has had a great effect on most subsequent HPSG-based studies of information structure. The main constraints Engdahl & Vallduví (1996) propose are conceptualized in (1) and (2). Many HPSG-based studies on information structure, irrespective of whether they use MRS, present a variant version of (1) and (2) as a means of encoding information structure. For this reason, they show a certain degree of overlap in the way they represent information structure and calculate information structure values.

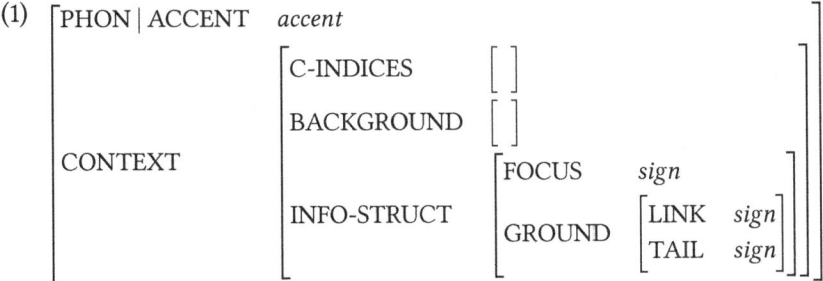

6 Literature review

(2) a. $\boxed{1}\begin{bmatrix} \text{PHON} \mid \text{ACCENT} & a \\ \text{INFO-STRUCT} \mid \text{FOCUS} & \boxed{1} \end{bmatrix}$

b. $\boxed{1}\begin{bmatrix} \text{PHON} \mid \text{ACCENT} & b \\ \text{INFO-STRUCT} \mid \text{GROUND} \mid \text{LINK} & \boxed{1} \end{bmatrix}$

c. $\begin{bmatrix} \text{PHON} \mid \text{ACCENT} & u \end{bmatrix}$

Engdahl & Vallduví (1996) regard information structure as an interface across different layers in human language. This notion can be more precisely explained within the HPSG framework, because HPSG accounts for various structural layers (e.g. phonology, morphosyntax, semantics, and pragmatics) in an interactive way. Regarding information structure in English, Engdahl & Vallduví pay particular attention to the co-operation between phonological behaviors and contextual information. In their proposal, *accent* has three subtypes in English. They use the traditional distinction between the A and B accents as shown in (2) (Bolinger 1958; Jackendoff 1972); a for A-accented words, b for B-accented ones, and u for unaccented ones. In order to determine if their constraints work analogously cross-linguistically, they also analyze sentences in Catalan, in which information structure is expressed without reference to prosodic patterns. Unlike English, Catalan does not place a constraint on PHON to instantiate information structure. INFO-STRUCT in Catalan, instead, is expressed via SUBCAT (SUBCATegorization) and phrasal types of daughters. Although their analysis dwells on left/right dislocation constructions in Catalan, their approach has had a strong influence on following HPSG-based studies, including De Kuthy (2000) for German, Bildhauer (2007) for Spanish, Chang (2002) and Chung, Kim & Sells (2003) for Korean, Ohtani & Matsumoto (2004) and Yoshimoto et al. (2006) for Japanese, and many others.

These previous studies share a common proposal that information structure is an independent module within a grammatical framework that should be represented separately from CAT (CATegory) and CONT (CONTent): Either under SYNSEM|CONTEXT (Engdahl & Vallduví 1996; Chang 2002; Ohtani & Matsumoto 2004; Yoshimoto et al. 2006; Paggio 2009) or outside of SYNSEM (De Kuthy 2000; Chung, Kim & Sells 2003; Bildhauer 2007). The current analysis, however, merges information structure into CONT (i.e. MRS).

On the other hand, previous studies are differentiated from each other in the values the relevant types utilize in formalizing components of information structure. In other words, it is necessary to determine whether the value of the information-structure related features is a whole sign or whether that value is something semantic (i.e. MRS). The traditional means of formalizing information structure values is to use coreferences between the whole sign and a value listed for FOC(US) and TOP(IC). Engdahl & Vallduví (1996) make use of this method, and Chung, Kim & Sells (2003) and Ohtani & Matsumoto (2004) utilize the same method for handling information structure in Korean and Japanese, respectively. Recently, several studies co-index something inside of MRS with a value in the list of FOCUS, TOPIC, and others. In Yoshimoto et al. (2006), Bildhauer (2007), and Sato & Tam (2012), the RELS itself has a structure-sharing with a value in the lists of components of information structure. Paggio (2009) also utilizes MRS, but the values in the lists of components of information structure are co-indexed with the value of INDEX (e.g. *x1*, *e2*, etc.). These two methods represent just two of many methods for representing information structure in HPSG and MRS. Taking a different approach, Chang (2002) represents information structure using just a string. J.-B. Kim (2007) and J.-B. Kim (2012) use a boolean feature as the value of FOCUS and TOPIC, and these features are under an independent structure called INFO-ST. Sometimes, a specific feature structure is introduced, which represents logical forms (Webelhuth 2007; De Kuthy & Meurers 2011).

6.1.1 Sentential forms

Engdahl & Vallduví (1996) argue that information structure is an integral part of grammar. In a similar vein, Lambrecht (1996) regards information structure as a subtype of sentential grammar.

There exist various suggestions on how information structure affects forms at the sentence level, such as topic-comment and focus-ground (i.e. bipartite structures). There are two basic components in the proposal by Engdahl & Vallduví; focus and ground. While ground acts as an usher for focus, focus is defined as the actual information or update potential of a sentence. Ground, consisting of link and tail, is viewed as something already subsumed by the input information state.[1] This definition implies that a sentence can have a ground if and only if the informative content guarantees its use. For example, sentences with sentential focus (*all-focus* in the present study) – such as a reply to questions like *What happened?*, are not required to include ground. Since they divide ground into link and tail, in line with Vallduví (1990), they make use of a tripartite structure consisting of different combinations of focus, link, and tail.[2] Building upon

---

[1] Note that ground is not the same as background. Ground is thought of as opposite to focus, while background is neither focus nor topic.
[2] Büring (2003) suggests another tripartite structure such as topic-focus-background.

6 Literature review

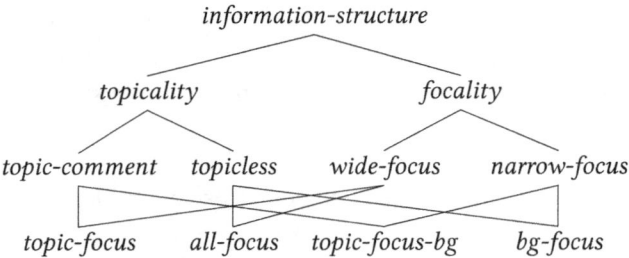

Figure 6.1: Type hierarchy of Paggio (2009)

some extra constraints such as barring focus from preceding link (i.e. linear order in instantiating information structure, such as link > focus > tail), they propose four types of sentential forms; link-focus, link-focus-tail, focus-tail, and all-focus. For example, (3A1) is a link-focus construction, while (3A2) is a link-focus-tail construction.

(3) Q1: So tell me about the people in the White House. Anything I should know?
A1: Yes. The **president** [$_f$ hates the Delft CHINE SET]. Don't use it.
Q2: In the Netherlands I got a big Delft china tray that matches the set in the living room. Was that a good idea?
A2: Maybe. The **president** [$_f$ HATES] the Delft chine set. (but the **first lady** LIKES it.) (Engdahl & Vallduví 1996: 5)

This classification is similarly implemented as a hierarchy in Paggio (2009), though the terms are different (i.e. *topic* for link, and *bg* for tail). The type hierarchy Paggio (2009: 140) proposes for Danish is shown in Figure 6.1, and the lowest subtypes are exemplified in (4) respectively.

(4) a. (Hvad lavede børnene?)   [$_T$ De] [$_F$ spiste is].
    (what did   children.DEF)   they   ate   icecream
    'What did the children do? They ate icecream.' (*topic-focus*)

b. (Hvad spiste børnene?)   [$_{BG}$ [$_T$ De] spiste] [$_F$ is].
    (what ate   children.DEF)   they ate   icecream
    'What did the children eat? They ate icecream.' (*topic-focus-bg*)

c. (Hvem har spist isen?)   [$_{BG}$ Det har] [$_F$ børnene].
    (who   has eaten icecream.DEF)   that have   children.DEF
    'Who has eaten the icecream? The children did.' (*bg-focus*)

d. (Hvad skete der?) [$_F$ Børnene spiste] is].
   (what happened there) children.DEF ate icecream
   'What happened? The children ate icecream.' (*all-focus*) [dan] (Paggio 2009: 139)

The present study concurs that information structure needs to be investigated as a subtype of sentential grammar (Lambrecht 1996; Engdahl & Vallduví 1996; Paggio 2009). However, the type hierarchy given in Figure 6.1 is altered in the current analysis to accommodate a cross-linguistic perspective. In particular, it is necessary to delve into whether or not the hierarchy for sentential forms has to deal with the linear order of components of information structure. At first glance, *bg-focus* in Figure 6.1 might look inconsistent with the focus-tail construction presented by Engdahl & Vallduví. As exemplified in (4c), a constituent associated with *bg* can precede other constituents associated with *focus* in Danish, which means the linear ordering constraint (i.e. link > focus > tail) is language-specific. The different linear orders notwithstanding, the present study claims that *bg-focus* in Figure 6.1 is actually the same as focus-tail. Paggio (2009) calls the identificational focus of (4c) *bg-focus* that serves to identify a referent as the missing argument of an open proposition (Lambrecht 1996: 122).[3] For this reason, the type hierarchy for sentential forms in the current work is built up without an ordering constraint, exclusively considering which components participate in forming information structure.

6.1.2 Location within the feature geometry

Previous literature commonly introduces an independent typed feature structure for information structure into *sign*. The independent structure is either CXT (ConteXT) dealing with pragmatic (i.e. contextual) information or just INFO-ST; Chang (2002) employs PRA|DF|TFA in (6), Ohtani & Matsumoto (2004) uses CONX|INFO-ST, and J.-B. Kim (2007) uses just INFO-ST immediately under *sign*. Similar structures are used in other papers: SYNSEM|LOC|CONTEXT|INF-ST (Yoshimoto et al. 2006), SYNSEM|IS (Bildhauer & Cook 2010), CTXT|IS (Bjerre 2011), INFO-STRUC (De Kuthy & Meurers 2011), etc. The functionality of these features has one thing in common: Information structure is separately represented from both morphosyntactic structure (i.e. CAT) and semantic structure (i.e. CONT).

Information structure as presented here is an independent module in grammar, however, that does not necessarily mean that information structure should

---
[3]The *bg-focus* sentential form is similar to cleft constructions.

6 Literature review

be separately represented on AVMs. Unless there is a necessity to separate components of information structure from CONT(ent), the independent structure is redundant. In seeking a minimal solution, is it possible to represent information structure without introducing additional structure? Partee (1991) also addresses this with her observations that information structure is not independent of truth-conditions. If information structure is truth-conditionally relevant, it should be represented in the semantics. Engdahl & Vallduví (1996), nevertheless, invoke a separate representation in the belief that information structure and logical semantics have to be represented in the grammar in a modular manner. They leave the final resolution of these two components as a question for future work. My understanding is that most subsequent HPSG-based studies on information structure do not attempt to answer how final meanings are arrived at.[4] The next chapter shows information structure can be fully represented without using CTXT or introducing an independent structure.

Representing information structure within CONT (i.e. MRS) has another important merit in the context of multilingual machine translation. As stated earlier, the present study argues that translation means reshaping the packaging of the information of a sentence. Thus, one of the most important considerations in representing information structure is its availability in multilingual machine translation as a computational model. Because all ingredients relevant to translation must be accessible in MRS within our transfer-based system (Oepen et al. 2007), information structure should be accessible in MRS.

6.1.3 Underspecification

One of the main motivations for and advantages in using the HPSG/MRS formalism is underspecification. The value of a particular attribute can be left underspecified in a description unless a constraint identifies the value with a more specific type. This makes grammatical operation more flexible and more economical. For example, (2c) means that unaccented words leave their information structure value underspecified, facilitating varied meanings of an unmarked expression. Kuhn (1996) argues that using underspecification is a more effective way to represent information structure; especially for the purpose of implementing HPSG-based NLP applications (e.g. machine translation, TTS (Text-To-Speech) systems, etc.). However, underspecification has been scarcely used in previous HPSG-based studies on information structure. The current model relies on un-

---

[4]To my knowledge, one exceptional study is Webelhuth (2007), in which information structure components are dealt with under CONT.

6.1 Information structure in HPSG

derspecified values of components of information structure. More specific justifications as to why underspecification is crucial for representing information structure are discussed in the following subsections.

6.1.3.1 Prosody

In most HPSG-based studies of information structure, a typed feature structure for representing prosody is commonly introduced. The interface between information structure and prosody has been studied for many Indo-European languages as well as in non-Indo-European languages such as Korean and Japanese. (5), taken from Chang (2002), stands for a typed feature structure for prosody in Korean which has two key attributes TC (Terminal Contour) and STR (STRess). The values of the former include falling (HL%), neutral (H%), and rising (LH%), and those of the latter stand for four levels of stress.

(5) $\begin{bmatrix} ppm \\ \text{PROS} \begin{bmatrix} pros \\ \text{TC} & \langle \searrow, \rightarrow, \nearrow \rangle \\ \text{STR} & \langle 0, 1, 2, 3 \rangle \end{bmatrix} \end{bmatrix}$

In his formalism, this structure has a correlation with another typed feature structure, namely PRA (PRAgmatics). Information structure values, such as topics and foci, are gathered into the lists under PRA|DF|TFA as presented in (6)[5].

(6) $\begin{bmatrix} pra \\ \text{SA} & sa \\ \text{DF} & \begin{bmatrix} \text{TFA} & \begin{bmatrix} \text{TOP} & list(phon) \\ \text{FOC} & list(phon) \end{bmatrix} \\ \text{POV} & list(ref) \\ \text{CTR} & list(ref) \end{bmatrix} \\ \text{BKG} & bkg \end{bmatrix}$

---

[5] DF stands for Discourse Function, and TFA means Topic-Focus Articulation. Additionally, SA is short for Speech Act, BKG is for BacKGround, POV is for Point-Of-View, and CTR is for CenTeR.

6 Literature review

For example, -(n)un and i / ka in Korean have one of the feature structures presented in (7a) and (7b), respectively. In (7), the PHON structure is the same as the STEM structure in `matrix.tdl` of the LinGO Grammar Matrix system. That is, the value type of PHON is just string. Despite the name, it is not directly related to any phonological information.

(7) a. i. Zero Topic
$$\begin{bmatrix} \text{STR} & \langle 0 \rangle \\ \text{PHON} & \langle \boxed{1} \rangle \\ \text{TFA} & [\text{TOP} \langle \boxed{1} \rangle] \end{bmatrix}$$

ii. (Thematic) Topic
$$\begin{bmatrix} \text{STR} & \langle 1 \rangle \\ \text{PHON} & \langle \boxed{1} \rangle \\ \text{TFA} & [\text{TOP} \langle \boxed{1} \rangle] \end{bmatrix}$$

iii. Contrastive Topic
$$\begin{bmatrix} \text{STR} & \langle 3 \rangle \\ \text{PHON} & \langle \boxed{1} \rangle \\ \text{TFA} & [\text{TOP} \langle \boxed{1} \rangle] \end{bmatrix}$$

b. i. (Narrow) Focus
$$\begin{bmatrix} \text{STR} & \langle 2 \rangle \\ \text{PHON} & \langle \boxed{1} \rangle \\ \text{TFA} & [\text{FOC} \langle \boxed{1} \rangle] \end{bmatrix}$$

ii. Contrastive Focus
$$\begin{bmatrix} \text{STR} & \langle 3 \rangle \\ \text{PHON} & \langle \boxed{1} \rangle \\ \text{TFA} & [\text{FOC} \langle \boxed{1} \rangle] \end{bmatrix}$$

Ohtani & Matsumoto (2004), similarly, analyzed *wa*-marked and *ga*-marked NPs in Japanese: *Wa*-marked NPs are interpreted as either topic, restrictive focus or non-restrictive focus,[6] whereas *ga*-marked NPs are interpreted as either restrictive focus or all focus. Similarly to (7) in Korean, in the formalism Ohtani & Matsumoto propose *wa* and *ga* can have one of the feature structures in (8a) and (8b), respectively.

---

[6] In Ohtani & Matsumoto (2004: 95), restrictive focus means wide focus.

6.1 Information structure in HPSG

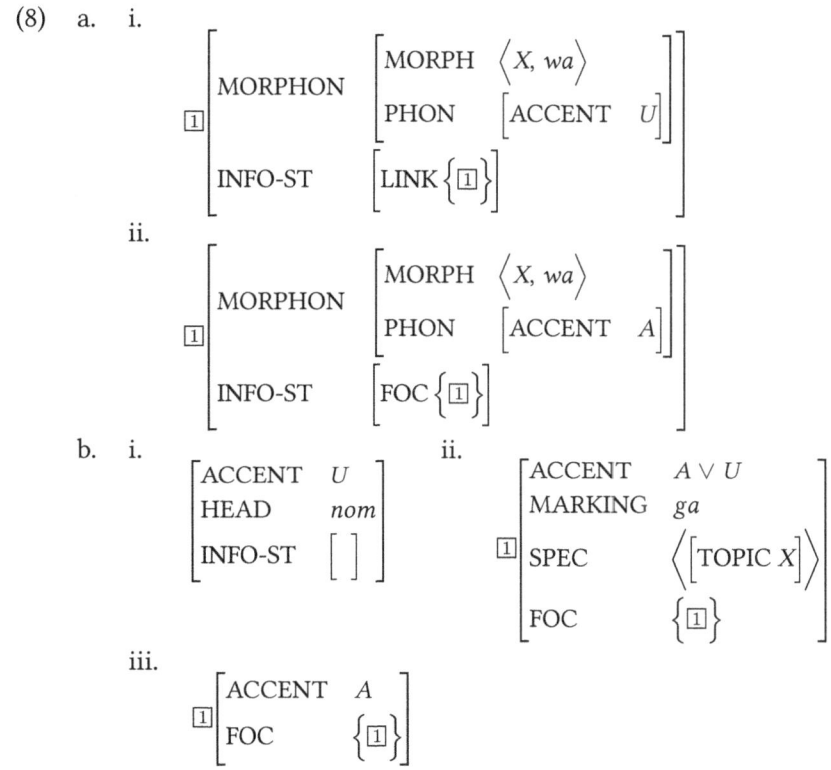

(7) and (8), though their formats are slightly different, are actually the Korean and Japanese variants of (2) in English. Bildhauer (2007) argues that it is rather unclear where the information about accents comes from. This criticism seems appropriate when we think of the current computational environments for sentence processing. Because our applications are mostly text-based, for now it would be quite difficult to resolve for accent type within the text domain. Nonetheless, the criticism seems rather shortsighted when we consider the future direction of language applications. Even in the absence of an implementation that connects the HPSG grammar to ASR (Automatic Speech Recognition) systems to prosody extraction or TTS (Text-To-Speech) systems with prosody generation, if there is a robust correlation between information structure and prosodic accents, the grammar can leverage information about stress to yield higher performance. Hence, it is important to allow the grammar formalism to model prosodic information using underspecification (Kuhn 1996). I believe that this strategy contributes to the long-term task of refining meaning representation via prosodic information.

6 Literature review

However, there is a remaining controversial point embedded in (7) and (8). In fact, they are tantamount to redundantly introducing *i / ka* and *-(n)un* in Korean, and *ga* and *wa* in Japanese into the lexicon. For example, (7a) implies that the morphemes for introducing a zero topic *-(n)un*, a thematic topic *-(n)un*, and a contrastive topic *-(n)un* are three separate homonyms. The use of multiple rules for *-(n)un* and *wa* is an undesirable choice which should be avoided if possible. Korean and Japanese very productively employ *-(n)un* and *wa*, respectively, which means that having multiple lexical entries for *wa* and *-(n)un* items in the respective grammars causes problematic amounts of spurious ambiguity.[7] In other words, if we include all the rules in (7a), every *(n)un*-marked constituent produces spurious parse trees. As a result, the number of parse trees can sometimes grow too large to handle.[8] If there is something that the multiple-entry approach captures that the single-entry approach does not, then we should use the former, because there could be a loss in information processing. Yet, as discussed hitherto, the lexical markers (e.g. *-(n)un* and *wa*) and the prosodic patterns each contribute only partial information. In other words, neither of them can be a decisive clue for identifying which information structure meaning is assigned to a given constituent.

To sum up, my alternate approach for constraining lexical markers (especially in Japanese and Korean) is as follows: First, there is one and only one entry for each marker. Second, the lexical rules include prosodic structures in principle, but they are preferentially underspecified. Third, the meaning that each marker potentially conveys is flexibly and tractably represented to cover all the partial information.

6.1.3.2 Ambiguity

In many previous studies across theories of grammar, so-called F(ocus)-marking is represented as a boolean feature (i.e. [FOCUS *bool*]) as proposed in Zubizarreta (1998). Handling information structure via a boolean feature is also common in other unification-based frameworks. For instance, H.-W. Choi (1999), within the

---

[7] Exploring the *Sejong* Korean Treebank reveals that subjects in Korean are combined with *-(n)un* more than twice than the ordinary nominative marker *i / ka*.

[8] In fact, this is one of the major problems that cause a bottleneck in parsing and generation in the old version of Korean Resource Grammar. It had two types of *-(n)un*; one for topic, and the other for contrast. These two *-(n)un* sometimes had an adverse effect on system performance. Occasionally, even not a long sentence could have a large number of parse trees if *-(n)un* occurs multiple times in the sentence. Accordingly, the sentence could not be generated in most cases because of memory overflow. For more information, see Song et al. (2010).

6.1 Information structure in HPSG

framework of LFG (Lexical-Functional Grammar Bresnan 2001), makes use of [± New] and [± Prom] as presented later in (17). Other components of information structure are also similarly marked. These include [TOPIC *bool*], [CONTRAST *bool*], [HIGHLIGHT *bool*], and so on. For instance, J.-B. Kim (2007) claims that *beer* in (9A) is constrained as in (10). Since *beer* in (9A) is contrastively focused (i.e. an answer to an alternative question Gryllia 2009), it has both [HIGHLIGHT +] and [FOCUS +] in his analysis. Note that [HIGHLIGHT *bool*] in (10) indicates whether or not the constituent conveys a contrastive meaning, which is almost the same as [CONTRAST *bool*].

(9) Q: Did John drink beer or coke?
    A: John drank beer. (J.-B. Kim 2007: 229)

(10) $\begin{bmatrix} \text{PHON} & \langle \text{beer} \rangle \\ \text{SYN | HEAD | POS} & \textit{noun} \\ \text{SEM} & \begin{bmatrix} \text{INDEX} & i \\ \text{RELS} & \left\langle \begin{bmatrix} \text{PRED} & \textit{beer-rel} \\ \text{ARG1} & i \end{bmatrix} \right\rangle \end{bmatrix} \\ \text{INFO-ST} & \begin{bmatrix} \text{HIGHLIGHT} & + \\ \text{FOCUS} & + \end{bmatrix} \end{bmatrix}$

In contrast, the present work does not use boolean features for representing information structure meaning. This is mainly because using boolean features would not allow us to represent information structure as a relationship between an entity and a clause. The current work encodes information structure into the semantic representation via ICONS (Individual CONStraints). The main motivation for ICONS is the ability to encode information structure values as a relationship with the clause an information structure-marked constituent belongs to, rather than as simply a property of the constituent itself. Chapter 7 provides the fundamentals of ICONS in detail.

6.1.4 Marking vs. meaning

Most of the previous formalisms are exclusively concerned with markings, as the name F(ocus)-marking implies. Hence, they are rather ill-suited to deal with any discrepancies between the forms expressing information structure and the meanings expressed. The lexical markers *wa* and *-(n)un* in Japanese and Korean

6 Literature review

are typical cases showing this kind of mismatch, and (10) illustrates via an example from Korean. If -(n)un in Korean is used contrastively and an NP with it is focused, then the NP in J.-B. Kim's AVMs would be constrained as either (i) [HIGHLIGHT +, TOPIC +] focusing on the NP-marking system or (ii) [HIGHLIGHT +, FOCUS +] putting more weight on the meaning. Another potential constraint on the NP would be [HIGHLIGHT +, FOCUS +, TOPIC +], but this analysis fails with respect to the basic assumption the present study is built on: topic and focus are mutually exclusive.[9]

The present study proposes two strategies as an alternative method. First, information structure markings should be separately specified from information structure meanings. The former should be constrained using a morphosyntactic feature that can be language-specific. The latter should be attributed within the semantics (i.e. under CONT), and rely on a cross-linguistically valid type hierarchy. Second, there are more than a few cases in which we cannot convincingly say which element is associated with which information structure meaning. Therefore, it is necessary to specify information structure values as flexibly as possible. This is particularly important when creating a robust computational model of information structure.

6.2 Information structure in MRS

The present study, unlike previous HPSG-based studies including Engdahl & Vallduví (1996), does not introduce another structure and instead represents information structure within the MRS semantic representations. There are two motivations for doing so. The first motivation is that information structure impacts semantic properties. As discussed previously, information structure (especially, semantic focus) is sometimes relevant to truth-conditions (Gundel 1999) and scopal interpretation (Büring 1997; Portner & Yabushita 1998; Erteschik-Shir 1999; 2007; Bianchi & Frascarelli 2010). Hence, it is right to incorporate information structure into the meaning representation in a direct manner. The second motivation is strictly practical: The infrastructure for machine translation does MRS-based transfer (Oepen et al. 2007), therefore encoding information structure into MRS facilitates its immediate availability for use in machine translation.

Previous HPSG-based studies can be divided into two subgroups: One represents information structure without reference to MRS (De Kuthy 2000; Chang

---

[9] As stated earlier, there exist counterarguments to this generalization (Krifka 2008).

6.2 Information structure in MRS

2002; Chung, Kim & Sells 2003; Ohtani & Matsumoto 2004; Webelhuth 2007; J.-B. Kim 2007; 2012), and the other links information structure values in an independent typed feature structure to MRS (e.g. INDEX or RELS) (Wilcock 2005; Yoshimoto et al. 2006; Paggio 2009; Bildhauer & Cook 2010; Sato & Tam 2012).

Wilcock (2005), to my knowledge, is the first attempt to use MRS for representing information structure, modeling the scope of focus analogously to quantifier scope (i.e. HCONS).

(11) a. The president [$_f$ hates the china set].

b. 1:the(x,2), 2:president(x), 3:the(y,4), 4:china(y), 4:set(y), 5:hate(e,x,y)
TOP-HANDLE:5, LINK:1, FOCUS:3,5 (wide focus)

This is similar to the basic idea of the current analysis, in that information structure can be represented as a list of binary relations in the same way as HCONS is. The difference between Wilcock's proposal and that of the current analysis is that information structure in his model is represented as handles, whereas the current model represents the relationships between individuals and clauses as binary relations. This facilitates scaling to multiclausal constructions. For instance, (11b) taken from Wilcock (2005: 275) represents the wide focus reading of (11a) (i.e. from 3 to 5). Note that in this representation, LINK (*topic* in this paper) and FOCUS have no relation to the clause or its head (*hate*).

Yoshimoto et al. (2006) use MRS, too. In their model, information structure values are unified with whole MRS predications rather than just indices. Based on this assumption, they apply the information structure values to analyzing floating quantifiers in Japanese. However, their AVM does not look like a standard MRS representation, and it is rather unclear how their model could be used for practical purposes.

Paggio (2009) also models information structure with reference to the MRS formalism, but the components of information structure in Paggio's proposal are represented as a part of the context, not the semantics. Though each component under CTXT|INFOSTR involves co-indexation with individuals in MRS, her approach cannot be directly applied to the LOGON MT infrastructure which requires all transfer-related ingredients to be accessible in MRS (Oepen et al. 2007).

Bildhauer & Cook (2010) offer another type of MRS-based architecture: Information structure in their proposal is represented directly under SYNSEM (i.e.

6 Literature review

SYNSEM|IS) and each component (e.g. TOPIC, FOCUS) has a list of indices identified with ones that appear in EPs in RELS, which is not applicable to the LOGON infrastructure for the same reason as the Paggio (2009) model.[10]

Among the various methods presented so far, the method used by the present study most closely resembles that of Paggio (2009) in that individuals (the value type of INDEX) are constrained for representation of information structure (i.e. Individual CONStraints). The main differences between Paggio's approach and mine are as follows: First, I place the feature whose value represents information structure inside of CONT. Second, I represent information structure values using a type hierarchy of *info-str*. Third, the features to represent information structure involve a binary relation between individuals and clauses. Chapter 8 enters into the implementation details.

6.3 Phonological information in HPSG

Quite a few HPSG-based studies explore the effect of phonological behaviors on the structuring of information in a sentence. However, this subsection surveys only Bildhauer's proposal.

Though the current model does not devote much attention to phonological constraints on information structure, it is still necessary to formalize some prosodic information in relation to information structure markings for at least two reasons. First, focus projection has been considered to be triggered by prosody. Second, as Kuhn (1996) and Traat & Bos (2004) point out, TTS (Text-To-Speech) synthesizers and automatic speech recognizers can be improved by using information structure. Thus, it is my expectation that including prosodic information in the HPSG formalism facilitates the use of HPSG-based grammars for those kinds of systems in the long term.

According to the account of Bildhauer (2007), there are three HPSG-based approaches to phonology; (i) metrical tree-based approaches (Klein 2000; Haji-Abdolhosseini 2003), (ii) grid-only approaches (Bonami & Delais-Roussarie 2006), and (iii) hybrid approaches that take advantage of the two former approaches (Bildhauer's own). According to Bildhauer (2007: 160), the metrical tree-based approach provides a representation of prosodic consistency, but deploys only nested structure. This is a drawback when it comes to handling intonational tunes. Bildhauer also argues that while the grid-only approach of Bonami &

---

[10]This, of course, does not mean that every grammar should be compatible with the LOGON infrastructure. The ultimate goal of the present study is creating a computational library within the Grammar Matrix, which can be effectively used to enhance performance of HPSG/MRS-based MT systems. Given that LOGON, for now, is the readily available infrastructure for the purpose, the present study follows the requirements as far as possible.

6.3 Phonological information in HPSG

Delais-Roussarie involves a basically flat representation, it is too language-specific to be straightforwardly applied to other languages. The three basic approaches outlined by Bildhauer each yield their own explanation about how phonological information can be calculated within the HPSG framework in a general sense, and how the information co-operates with information structure.

Another approach to the HPSG-based interface between prosody and syntax is provided in Yoshimoto (2000). Its basic assumption is that P(rosodic)-structure and C(onstituent)-structure form a bistratal phase with each other. The bistratal approach is not considered in the present study for two reasons. First, Yoshimoto's proposal is not directly concerned with information structure. Second, although the interaction between prosodic and syntactic structures is examined, the analysis is rather language-specific (i.e. for Japanese) as implied by the name of the typed feature that plays the key role (MORA).

The present analysis, largely accepting the hybrid approach, keeps an eye towards being compatible with the HPSG-based formalism Bildhauer (2007) proposes. Bildhauer's account is divided into two layers. One is the PHON list which is an immediate feature of *sign*, made up of four components; (i) prosodic word, (ii) phonological phrase, (iii) intonational phrase, and (iv) phonological utterance. The other layer is intonation, which takes charge of (v) pitch accents, and (vi) boundary tones. Building upon their operation, a schema of focus prominence rules is suggested, mainly concentrating on the top level of prosodic hierarchy (i.e. phonological utterance). Bildhauer's formalism develops from Klein's proposal that the level of syllables does not matter, and instead the prosodic hierarchy is represented by prosodic words (*pwrd*) and leaners (*lnr*). The elementary unit of PHON is *pwrd*, whose skeleton is sketched out in (12) (Bildhauer 2007: 161).[11]

(12)
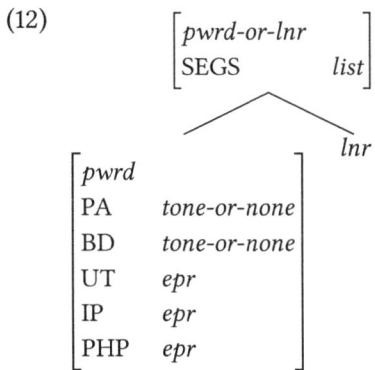

First, the lowest three features within *pwrd* in (12) represent prosodic hierar-

---

[11]In (12), the value of SEGS is a list of segments.

6 Literature review

chical levels above prosodic word; PHP stands for PHonological Phrase, IP is for Intonational Phrase, and UT is the abbreviation for phonological UTterance. Each of them has *epr* meaning Edges and Prominence as its value type, whose typed feature structure is provided in (13); LE stands for Left Edge, RE for Right Edge, and most importantly DTE for Designated Terminal Element. Grounded upon the prosodic rules that Bildhauer (2007: 181) creates, PHP, IP, and UT are defined by a relational constraint, which places a restriction on LE, RE, and DTE values of *pwrd* objects and thereby specifies the relation that a prosodic word has to higher prosodic constituents.

(13) $\quad epr \Rightarrow \begin{bmatrix} LE & bool \\ RE & bool \\ DTE & bool \end{bmatrix}$

Second, pitch accents (PA) and boundary tones (BD), which carry intonational information, take *tone-or-none* as their value type. Bildhauer (2007: 183–184) provides the hierarchy of *tone-or-none* in Spanish as follows, which is to be further revised for better cross-linguistic coverage in the present study. Each type name on the bottom line is an element in the ToBI format. For example, *high* means H, *low* means L, and *low-high-star* means L+H* (i.e. the B-accent in English, Bolinger 1961; Jackendoff 1972).

(14)
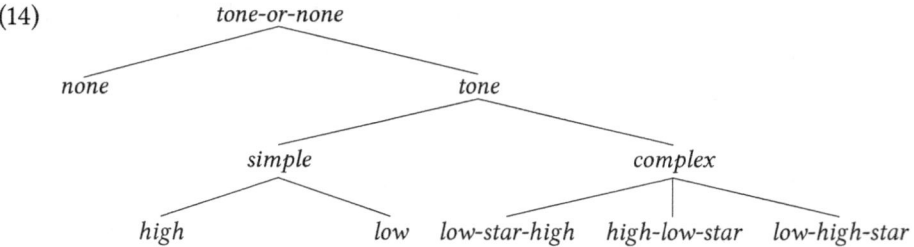

Those pitch accents and boundary tones are related to *pwrd*, whose relationship is ruled as follows. Pitch accents are attached to phonological phrases, and boundary tones are connected to intonational phrases (Steedman 2000).

(15) a. $\begin{bmatrix} \text{PHP} | \text{DTE} & + \end{bmatrix} \rightarrow \begin{bmatrix} \text{PA} & tone \end{bmatrix}$

b. $\begin{bmatrix} \text{PHP} | \text{DTE} & - \end{bmatrix} \rightarrow \begin{bmatrix} \text{PA} & none \end{bmatrix}$

c. $\begin{bmatrix} \text{IP} | \text{RE} & + \end{bmatrix} \rightarrow \begin{bmatrix} \text{BD} & tone \end{bmatrix}$

d. $\begin{bmatrix} \text{IP} | \text{RE} & - \end{bmatrix} \rightarrow \begin{bmatrix} \text{BD} & none \end{bmatrix}$

Given that Bildhauer (2007) provides a cross-linguistically convincing proposal as such, the type hierarchy of *tone* and the typed feature structure for phonological structure are described in matrix.tdl. Although the current work is not deeply concerned with prosodic realizations of information structure, information relevant to those realizations should be included into the system as it's a common structure in human languages. This is highly motivated by the necessity to refer to prosodic patterns for further refinement of meaning representation in future studies.

However, the specific phonological rules given in (15) are only selectively implemented in the current work. For instance, in the following chapters, two hypothetical suffixes are used for indicating the A and B accents in English for ease of processing. The rules for them are in accordance with what Bildhauer (2007) proposes. However, no other rules use that phonological information. There are two reasons for this. First, for many languages, the correlation between prosody and information structure is not fully tested and thereby remains unclear. Thus, I leave it to future users of the current model to create these (potentially language-specific) rules. Second, since the current model does not make use of any acoustic system, it is almost impossible for the current model to implement and test Bildhauer's phonological rules in a comprehensive way.

6.4 Information structure in other frameworks

6.4.1 CCG-based studies

The CCG (Combinatory Categorial Grammar, Steedman 2001) framework, which provides a detailed analysis of the relationship between intonation and other structures (e.g. syntax, semantics, and pragmatics), has addressed information

6 Literature review

structure since the early days of the theory (Steedman 2000).[12] Consequently, one of the main characteristics of CCG is that it is particularly and deeply oriented toward information structure. Moreover, several CCG-based studies have accounted for how categories of information structure in CCG can be of use for practical systems from the standpoint of computational linguistics.

The components of information structure that Steedman (2000) and Traat & Bos (2004) introduce include theme (i.e. topic), and rheme, and focus. There are three structures that coincide with each other: (a) surface structure, (b) information structure, and (c) intonation. Among these, only (c) has significance for combinatory prosody, consisting of (c-1) pitch accents and (c-2) boundary tones. Whereas pitch accents are viewed as properties of words, boundary tones are defined as a boundary between theme and rheme categories. A sequence of one or more pitch accents followed by a boundary is referred to as an intonational phrasal tune.

Pitch accents and boundary tones in CCG are mostly represented in the ToBI format as follows. There are six pitch accents to mark theme and rheme, for example L+H*, L*+H for theme and H*, L*, H*+L, and H+L* for rheme. Boundary tones are what make a clear difference between Steedman's analysis and others in that he considers them to be crucial to specifying phrasal type and thereby configuring information structure. Intermediate phrases consist of one or more pitch accents, followed by either the L or the H boundary, also known as the phrasal tone. Intonational phrase, on the other hand, consists of one or more intermediate phrases followed by an L% of H% boundary tone. Therefore, in Steedman's analysis of information structure in English, the L+H* and LH% tune is associated with the theme, and the H* L and H* LL% tunes are associated with the rheme. For instance, a surface structure *Anna married Manny.* can be analyzed as follows (Traat & Bos 2004: 302).

---

[12] CCG departing from CC (Categorial Grammar) has two versions of formalism, whose history of progress is also deeply related to incorporating information structure into the formalism. The first development of CG theories is called UCG (Unification Categorial Grammar, Zeevat 1987), which employs an HPSG-style typed feature structures (i.e. *sign*). The HPSG-style formalism facilitates more efficient co-operation of interface across grammatical layers (e.g. syntax, semantics, etc.). The second development is UCCG (Unificational Combinatory Categorial Grammar, Traat & Bos 2004), which integrates CCG and UCG, and then adds DRT (Discourse Representation Theory, Kamp & Reyle 1993) into the formalism, in order to facilitate a compositional analysis of information structure. Roughly speaking, those categorial grammars replace phrasal structure rules by lexical categories and general combinatory rules. In other words, the CCG framework associates syntactically potent elements with a syntactic category that identifies them as functors. There are two major rules to combine functional categories and their arguments, which specify directionality such as (i) forward application represented as '>' and (ii) backward application represented as '<'.

6.4 Information structure in other frameworks

(16) a. **Anna** [$_f$ married [$_f$ MANNY]].

b. Anna L+H* LH% married Manny H* LL%

In (16a), **Anna** bears the B-accent (i.e. L+H*), MANNY bears the A-accent (i.e. H*), and the focus can be projected into either the NP MANNY itself or the VP *married Manny*. In (16b), the topic meaning that *ANNA* conveys comes from a pitch accent (L+H* after the word), and the focus meaning that **Manny** delivers comes from another pitch accent (H*). A boundary tone (LH%) forms a border of theme. Finally, *married* without any boundary tone (i.e. an invisible boundary as an edge of an unmarked theme) is included in the rheme, but it creates an ambiguous meaning with respect to the focus domain. Traat & Bos (2004) represent (16b) into the CCG-based formalism, in which three information structure values θ, ρ, and ϕ are used for theme, rheme, and phrase, respectively. Those values are used as the value types of INF (INFormation structure), and focus is independently represented as a boolean type.

The CCG-based studies have several key implications for my work. First, they pay particular attention to the creation of a computational model for information structure with an eye toward implementing applications from the beginning. In particular, Traat & Bos (2004) argue that an information structure-based computational model should be used for both parsing and generation, and conduct an experiment to verify that their model works. The information structure-based model used here was created with the same considerations in mind. This computational model, developed in the context of grammar engineering, can be used not only for parsing human sentences into semantic representations but also for generating sentences using that representation. Second, Traat & Bos make use of prosodically annotated strings as input for their experiment, because current automatic speech recognizers do not provide enriched prosodic information. In the current experiment, I employ two suffixes (e.g. *-a* for the A-accent, *-b* for the B-accent) that hypothetically represent prosodic information (see Section 13.2). Though I am not working with naturally occurring speech, the *-a* and *-b* suffixes are inspired by prosodic annotation. Lastly, the CCG-based studies include prosodic information in their formalism in a fine-grained way and also create linguistic rules in which prosodic information and information structure interact with each other in a systemic way. My model does not yet fully use prosodic information for the reasons discussed in Section 6.3, but future work will look at how to systematize the interaction between prosody and information structure, taking CCG-based work as a starting point and guide. Although the current model is mainly concerned with text processing, it could work through acoustic

6 Literature review

analysis of speech, through pre-tagging of information structure, and/or through mark-up like **boldface** or ALL CAPS.

6.4.2 LFG-based studies

While most HPSG/CCG-based studies on information structure emphasize the interaction between phonological factors and morphosyntactic structures, previous studies based on LFG tend to be more concerned with morphosyntactic operation.[13] Discourse-related information is largely represented in LFG either within an independent structure (i.e. i-structure) (King 1997) or just inside of f-structure (Bresnan 2001).

It is my understanding that the first endeavor to study linguistic phenomena related to information structure within the LFG framework is offered in Bresnan & Mchombo (1987). Grammatical functions in LFG can be roughly divided into discourse functions and non-discourse functions. In their analysis, grammaticalized discourse functions such as TOP(ic) and FOC(us) are captured within f-structure.

The practice of putting information structure elements into f-structure, however, is potentially controversial, because information structure does not always coincide with grammatical functions such as OBJ(ect), COMPL(ement), and so forth (King & Zaenen 2004). In order to overcome potential problems related to this, King (1997) introduces i-structure to represent how information structure units (e.g. focus domain) are constructed. In other words, i-structure can be represented independently of morphosyntactic operation, thereby disentangling information structure forms and meanings. Several subsequent LFG-based studies such as H.-W. Choi (1999) and Man (2007) are in line with King. While King is mainly concerned with Russian, the following studies adapt i-structure to other languages and substantiate its feasibility within the LFG framework. These include, Korean (H.-W. Choi 1999), German (H.-W. Choi 1999), and Cantonese (Man 2007).

---

[13] The Lexical-Functional Grammar framework, as the name itself implies, has two motivations: (i) Lexical items are substantially structured, and (ii) grammatical functions (e.g. subject and object) play an important role. LFG assumes several structural layers in the analysis of language phenomena, which include c-structure (constituent structure), and f-structure (functional structure). C-structure converts overt linear and hierarchical organization of words into phrases with non-configurationally structured information about grammatical functions, which plays a role to form f-structure. F-structure refers to abstract functional organization of the sentence, (e.g. syntactic predicate-argument structure and functional relations), which is of help in explaining universal phenomena in human language. In addition to the two basic structures, several other structures are also hypothesized such as a-structure (argument structure), s-structure (semantic structure), m-structure (morphological structure), p-structure (phonological structure), and i-structure (information structure).

6.4 Information structure in other frameworks

Another characteristic of LFG-based studies for information structure uses two types of boolean features which constrain information status such as new/-given and prominent/non-prominent. This distinction is proposed in H.-W. Choi (1999), who classifies (i) focus into (i-a) completive focus involving new information and (i-b) contrastive focus entailing alternatives in a set, and makes a clear-cut distinction between (ii) topic and (iii) tail using [± prominent]. H.-W. Choi's cross-classification between them is sketched out in (17).[14] H.-W. Choi applies this classification to the representation of information structure in Korean, and Man (2007) applies it to Cantonese in almost the same way.

(17)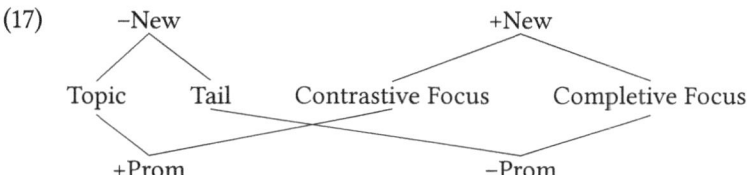

Though the underlying framework is different, these LFG-based studies also have implications for the current model. First of all, Bresnan & Mchombo (1987) provides an analysis of information structure in multiclausal utterances. They delve into how topic relations in English and Chicheŵa can be captured in several types of multiclausal constructions such as embedded clauses, relative clauses, and cleft clauses. This highlights the importance of capturing an information structure relation between a subordinate clause and the main clause that the subordinate clause belongs to. In other words, subordinate clauses constitute their own information structure, but the relation to their main clauses additionally needs to be represented with respect to information structure. This is discussed in more detail in Section 7.2.3 and Section 9.2.1. Second, LFG-based studies deal with a variety of constructions in the study of information structure, whereas a large number of studies based on other frameworks treat only simple declarative sentences. The construction types that LFG-based studies address include interrogatives (*wh*-questions and *yes/no*-questions), negation, clefts (King 1995), scrambling (H.-W. Choi 1999), and so-called topicalization (i.e. focus/topic fronting in the present study) (Man 2007). Third, it is also noteworthy that LFG-based studies tend to apply their formalism directly within a specific language. Studies within other frameworks normally apply their formalisms to English first, and then project them analogously into other languages. As a consequence, the analyses tend to be rather dependent on English-like criteria. LFG-based work,

---

[14]In (17), Prom is short for Prominence.

6 Literature review

on the other hand, straightforwardly looks into how a language configures information structure. LFG-based work on information structure has sometimes been criticized for not treating prosodic factors significantly, but to my understanding this is mainly because they do not start their work from English, and as we have seen, prosody is not heavily responsible for information structure markings in a number of languages (e.g. Chicheŵa, Korean, and Cantonese). Fourth, LFG-based studies take significant notice of the mismatches between meanings and markings of information structure and seek to reflect these discrepancies in their formalism. Lastly, the present model is similar to Bresnan & Mchombo (1987) in that information structure is handled within SYNSEM and an independent structure is therefore not needed.

6.5 Summary

Since the pioneering work of Engdahl & Vallduví (1996), information structure has received attention in HPSG-based research. The main endeavor of these studies is to point out the necessity of viewing sentential form in relation to information structure. This motivation is also importantly applied to my model. Nevertheless, the present study differs from previous studies in several key ways. First, underspecification is not widely used in the previous studies, but the current model emphasizes underspecification as a key to the representation of information structure. Second, while most previous studies do not differentiate information structure marking and information structure meaning, the two are entirely distinct in the current model. Third, information structure is represented only under CONT(ent) (i.e. MRS) in the current model rather than in a separate structure. Fourth, prosodic information is selectively incorporated into the formalism, in accordance with what Bildhauer (2007) suggests from a big picture perspective, but with the direct application of his specific rules. The implementation details are discusses in the following chapters in addition to several interesting points proposed in other frameworks. In particular, inspired by the LFG-based studies, Chapter 9 delves into information structure with special reference to various types of utterances (i.e. multiclausal constructions).

7 Individual CONStraints: fundamentals

The present study suggests the use of ICONS (Individual CONStraints) as the key means of representing information structure within the framework of HPSG (Pollard & Sag 1994) and MRS (Copestake et al. 2005).[1] Section 7.1 goes over the basic skeletons of Minimal Recursion Semantics. Section 7.2 offers the basic necessities for using ICONS in processing information structure. Section 7.3, Section 7.4, and Section 7.5 propose three type hierarchies that place constraints on information structure semantically and morphosyntactically. Section 7.6 presents a simplified version of representation for ease of exposition.

7.1 Minimal Recursion Semantics

MRS (Minimal Recursion Semantics (Copestake et al. 2005), or sometimes called Meaning Representation System) is a framework for computational modeling of semantic representation. The current work represents information structure in MRS via ICONS. That is, representation of information structure is incorporated into MRS (Meaning Representation System, in this context). This is an important departure from previous work in which MRS was conceived as a (possibly underspecified) representation of a truth-condition associated with a sentence.

There are two distinct characteristics of MRS representations: First, MRS introduces a flat representation expressing meanings by feature structures. Second, MRS takes advantage of underspecification (for handling quantifier scopes and other phenomena), which allows for flexibility in representation. In MRS description, it is important to represent the meanings of a sentence in an efficient

---

[1] The feature ICONS was originally proposed by Ann Copestake and Dan Flickinger, for the purpose of capturing semantically relevant connections between individuals which are nonetheless not well modeled as elementary predications, such as those found in intrasentential anaphora, apposition, and nonrestrictive relative clauses. Copestake and Flickinger suggested that the same mechanism can be used to anchor information structure constraints to particular clauses. In a more general system that uses ICONS, the value of ICONS would be a list of items of type *icons*, where *info-str* is a subtype of *icons*. For instance, Song (2016) represents honorification as a binary relation between referential items in dialogue via ICONS.

7 Individual CONStraints: fundamentals

manner for a practical purpose. The main criteria MRS is grounded upon are as follows.

(1) a. Expressive Adequacy: The framework must allow linguistic meanings to be expressed correctly.

b. Grammatical Compatibility: Semantic representations must be linked cleanly to other kinds of grammatical information (most notably syntax).

c. Computational Tractability: It must be possible to process meanings and to check semantic equivalence efficiently and to express relationships between semantic representations straightforwardly.

d. Underspecifiability: Semantic representations should allow underspecification (leaving semantic distinctions unresolved), in such a way as to allow flexible, monotonic resolution of such partial semantic representations. (Copestake et al. 2005: 281–282)

The minimal components of MRS include HOOK, RELS, and HCONS as shown in (2).

(2) a. $\begin{bmatrix} mrs \\ \text{HOOK} & hook \\ \text{RELS} & \textit{diff-list} \\ \text{HCONS} & \textit{diff-list} \end{bmatrix}$

b. $\begin{bmatrix} hook \\ \text{LTOP} & handle \\ \text{INDEX} & individual \\ \text{XARG} & individual \end{bmatrix}$

c. $\left[\text{RELS} \left\langle !\ldots, \begin{bmatrix} relation \\ \text{LBL} & handle \\ \text{PRED} & string \\ \text{ARG0} & individual \end{bmatrix}, \ldots ! \right\rangle \right]$

d. $\left[\text{HCONS} \left\langle !\ldots, \begin{bmatrix} qeq \\ \text{HARG} & handle \\ \text{LARG} & handle \end{bmatrix}, \ldots ! \right\rangle \right]$

7.1 Minimal Recursion Semantics

First of all, note that AVMs in (2), in which a difference list (i.e. *diff-list*) is used as the value of RELS and HCONS, are the grammar-internal representations of MRS as feature structures. When MRSs are used as an interface representation, they use *list* rather than *diff-list*, and do not involve feature structures. Second, HOOK keeps track of the attributes that need to be externally visible upon semantic composition, whose minimal components are included in (2b). The value of LTOP (Local TOP) is the handle of the relation or relations with the widest fixed scope within the constituent. The value of INDEX is the index that a word or phrase combining with this constituent might need access to. The value of ARG (external ARGument) is identified with the index of a semantic argument which serves as the subject in raising and control constructions. Third, REL is a bag of EPs (Elementary Predicates), whose type is a *relation*. Each *relation* has at least three attributes: LBL (Label), PRED (Predicate), and ARG0 (ARGument #0). The value of LBL is a *handle*, which represents the current EP. The value of PRED is normally a string, such as "_dog_n_1_rel", "_bark_v_rel", etc.[2] The value of ARG0 is either *ref-ind* for EPs introduced by nominals or *event-ind* for EPs introduced by verbals, adjectives, adverbs, and adpositions. Depending on the semantic argument structure of an EP, more ARGs can be introduced. For example, intransitive verbs (e.g. *bark*) additionally have ARG1, transitive verbs (e.g. *chase*) have ARG1 and ARG2, and ditransitive verbs (e.g. *give*) have ARG1, ARG2, and ARG3. Finally, HCONS represents partial information about scope. The value of HCONS is a bag of *qeq* (equality modulo quantifier) constraints.

More recently, alternative representations of MRS have been suggested for ease of utilizing the MRS formalism for a variety of language applications, which include RMRS (Robust MRS, Copestake 2007), and DMRS (Dependency MRS, Copestake 2009). RMRS involves the functionality of underspecification of relational information, which facilitates shallow techniques in language processing (e.g. NP chunking). DMRS makes use of a dependency style representation designed to facilitate machine learning algorithms. It mainly aims to remove redundancies that (R)MRS may have. The current work makes use of the conventional version of MRS, but the dependency style representation DMRS deploys is introduced for ease of explication.

---

[2] The PRED value can be a type, particularly for incorporating lexical semantics (i.e. wordnet) into the meaning representation. Besides, even though the PRED value is treated as a string, it is structured.

7 Individual CONStraints: fundamentals

7.2 Motivations

The use of ICONS is motivated by three necessities; (i) resolving discrepancies between forms and meanings in information structure, (ii) facilitating underspecifiability in order to allow for flexible and partial constraints, and (iii) capturing the information structure relations between expressions and particular clauses. To these, I add a working hypothesis to facilitate (iv) informative emptiness in representing information structure.

7.2.1 Morphosyntactic markings vs. Semantic representation

First, the morphosyntactic markings for information structure need to be kept distinct from semantic markings. This is analogous to the linguistic fact that morphological tense can sometimes differ from semantic tense as in counterfactual constructions. Some forms of expressing information structure do indeed directly indicate specific information structure roles such as topic, focus, and contrast. For instance, the contrastive topic marker *thì* in Vietnamese directly assigns contrastive topic meaning to the NP that the marker is attached to, as repeatedly exemplified below.

(3) Nam thì đi Hà Nội
Nam THI go Ha Noi
'Nam goes to Hanoi(, but nobody else).' [vie] (Nguyen 2006: 1)

A specific sentence position can also play the same role. For example, if the word order is not neutral in Russian, the clause-final position assigns the non-contrastive focus meaning, while preposing is responsible for contrastive focus meaning (Neeleman & Titov 2009). Yet, quite a few marking systems do not necessarily reveal which information structure meanings are being conveyed. The typical case of a discrepancy between morphosyntactic marking and semantic representation is the information structure marker *wa* in Japanese and *-(n)un* in Korean as discussed before. Even when a language has a relatively deterministic relation between forms and meanings, the correlation is neither perfect nor perfectly understood. For example, the A-accent in English has been widely evaluated as containing focus meaning, but there are some counterexamples to this generalization as exemplified previously in Section 4.1.2 (i.e. Second Occurrence Focus). Moreover, there has been a debate concerning the function of the B-accent, which could mark (i) just topic (Jackendoff 1972), (ii) contrastive topic (Kadmon 2001; Büring 2003), (iii) theme (Steedman 2000), and (iv) contrast (Hedberg 2006).

7.2 Motivations

7.2.2 Underspecification

Unless there exists a decisive clue to identify the intended information structure meaning, that meaning is most parsimoniously represented as underspecified. This proposal is especially crucial for analyzing sentences which appear in an unmarked word order. Without clues to indicate a particular meaning (e.g. the contrastive topic marker *thì* in Vietnamese), any constituents in the unmarked order are not specified for meaning with respect to information structure. For instance, (4a) presented again below is in the neutral word order in Russian, and the orthography does not represent prosodic patterns related to information structure.

(4) a. Sobaka laet.
    dog   bark
    'The dog barks.' [rus]

   b. Laet sobaka.
      bark dog
      'The DOG barks.' [rus]

When we do not know which element plays which information structure role in text-based processing (as in 4a), it would be better to leave the information structure values underspecified allowing for all meanings that the constituents may potentially have. On the other hand, with in a sentence like (4b) we can say the *sobaka* has focus meaning because the subject is not in situ, and the inversion serves as the clue for determining focus.

As exemplified hitherto, it is not likely that we can precisely determine an information structure role of each constituent in many cases, particularly given that sentence-by-sentence processing usually lacks discourse-related information. Hence, it is highly necessary to represent information structure meanings in a flexible way. For instance, note the following example in Greek.[3]

(5) a. Thelo   kafe.
       want.1SG coffee.ACC
       'I would like coffee.'

---

[3] The subscript in the original example such as []$_{\text{C-Foc}}$, which stands for contrastive focus, is removed in (5) in order to show the difference between the neutral sentence and the marked sentence.

109

7 Individual CONStraints: fundamentals

> b. Kafe   thelo.
>   coffee.ACC want.1SG
>   'Coffee I would like.' [ell] (Gryllia 2009: 44)

Because the postverbal focus *kafe* 'coffee' in (5a) takes the object position in the basic word order and there is no other clue to disclose the information structure role within the single sentence, it does not have to have any specific meanings per se. That means that *kafe* in (5a) can be evaluated as containing (i) non-contrastive focus, (ii) contrastive focus, or even as being (iii) background if the preceding verb *thelo* 'want' plays a focus role. Hence, the semantic representation of *kafe* in (5a) has to cover all those potential meanings simultaneously (i.e. *non-topic* in the present study). On the other hand, the preverbal focus in (5b) (ex situ) presents a clue identifying its information structure meaning. In other words, *kafe* in (5b) is constructionally marked and thereby conveys a more specific meaning than that in (5a) and it can no longer be interpreted as background. Nonetheless, its meaning is still vague allowing for readings as either non-contrastive focus or contrastive focus. Thus, the ideal representation would be able to allow for both meanings while still excluding background as a possible reading (i.e. *focus* as the supertype of both *semantic-focus* and *contrast-focus*).

7.2.3 Binary relations

Third, using ICONS is motivated by the necessity of finding binary relations between a clause and an element used in the construction of MRSs that belongs to the clause. These binary relations are crucial in representing the information structure of various types of utterances. The typed feature structure of ICONS consists of three components to identify which element has which information structure value within which clause.

Information structure roles can be represented not as a property of the constituent itself, but as a relationship that holds between the clause and the constituent it belongs to. For example, in the English sentence *The DOG barks.*, the subject *the DOG* with the A-accent should be viewed as the focus of the clause headed by the predicate *barks*, rather than as simply focused. This approach is in line with Lambrecht (1996) and Engdahl & Vallduví (1996) who regard information structure as a subtype of sentential grammar. That is, whether a constituent is associated with focus or topic should be identified within the sentence that includes the constituent.

Furthermore, a constituent can have multiple relations with different clauses. One element can have two (or more) information structure relations, if it be-

7.2 Motivations

longs to different clauses simultaneously. This notion can be clearly understood if we consider multiclausal utterances such as those which contain relative and embedded clauses. Most previous studies on information structure treat only fairly simple and monoclausal constructions. However, expanding a theory to include embedded clauses introduces the need to allow a single element to have multiple information structure meanings. This is because an embedded clause not only configures its own information structure, but also plays an information structure role in the domain of the main clause that takes the embedded clause as one of the arguments. A typical example of this come from relative clauses where the antecedent of the relative clauses has relations with both (i) the verb in the relative clause and (ii) the other verb in main clause, whose values are not necessarily identical to each other.

Those kinds of relations have been already captured in an LFG-based study on information structure. Bresnan & Mchombo (1987) argue that relative pronouns function as the topic of relative clauses, following the theorem presented in Kuno (1976).[4] In this analysis, then, relative pronouns are assigned an information structure value within the relative clause, as shown in (6).

(6) a. The car [which you don't want ___] is a Renault.
            TOPIC   OBJ

 b. I know [what you want ___].
           FOCUS   OBJ

 c. [It is my car [that you don't want ___]].
          FOCUS TOPIC   OBJ

(Bresnan & Mchombo 1987: 757–758)

The antecedent corresponding to the relative pronoun (e.g. *the car* in 6a) has an additional information structure value within the main clause. Additionally, embedded constructions realized as free relative clauses (e.g. *what you want* in 6b) play yet another information structure role within the main clause. The clefted NP (e.g. *my car* in 6c) is assigned a focus meaning, but its relative pronoun (e.g. *that* in 6c) plays the topic role in the relative. While these analyses do not accord perfectly to the argument presented in the present study, they are still significant and highlight the necessity of treating information structure as a relationship between an element and its clause.

---

[4] The present study does not defer to this argument. Section 5.2 presents the details.

7.2.4 Informative emptiness

In addition to the motivations presented in the previous subsections, I provide a working hypothesis about informatively empty categories. Lambrecht (1996: 156) argues that expressions which cannot be stressed, such as expletives (e.g. *it* in *It is raining.* and *there* in *There is nobody in the room.*), unstressed determiners, and so on, cannot be used as topic in principle. What is to be noted is that they cannot be used for expressing any other information structure meanings, either. For this reason, the present study presents a working hypothesis that semantically empty categories (e.g. complementizers, expletives) and syncategorematic items[5] (e.g. relative pronouns) are informatively empty as well. This means no information structure category can be assigned to them, though they may be required by constructions which serve to mark information structure, such as the cleft construction in English. For example, in (7a), the expletive *it* and the copula *is* are semantically empty and the relative pronoun *that* is syncategorematic; thus, they are informatively vacuous. Likewise, since the copula *was* and the preposition *by* in passive sentences in English are semantically empty, they cannot take part in information structure in principle, as shown in (7b).[6] S̶t̶r̶i̶k̶e̶ in (7) indicates that they are informatively meaningless.

(7) a. I̶t̶ i̶s̶ the book t̶h̶a̶t̶ was torn by Kim.

b. The book w̶a̶s̶ torn b̶y̶ Kim.

Lexical markers to express information structure, such as case-marking adpositions (e.g. nominative *ga* in Japanese) are mostly semantically and informatively empty. Although they participate in forming information structure and behave as a clue for identifying information structure meanings, they do not have their own predicate names, and do not exist in the semantic representation (i.e. MRS as presented here), either. In other words, they assign no information structure values to themselves, but instead identify and assign information structure values to the phrase that they are combined with. Since the information structure

---

[5] Syncategorematic items refer to words that cannot serve as the main syntactic category of human language sentences, such as the subject (in the matrix clause) and the predicate. Lambrecht (1996) does not capture any generalization about them, but I argue that they cannot be used as topic, either.

[6] In colloquial expressions, copular may participate in information structure. For example, if a question is given like *Are you a student?*, then the answer can be *I WAS a student*. In this case, focus is assigned to a specific linguistic feature, such as *tense*, rather than a specific constituent. Admittedly, the current model does not handle such a peculiar focus assignment.

constraints in the representation of the current work are all relative to elements in the RELS list, what is not represented in the RELS list cannot bear any information structure value. In sum, semantically empty lexical items and syncategorematic items are incapable of bearing their own information structure value, but they can assign an information structure value to others.

7.2.5 Summary

The motivations and the working hypothesis presented in this section are rigorously applied within the remaining parts of this book. They can be summarized as follows.

(8) a. The formal markings of information structure should be modeled separately from the semantic representation of information structure.

b. The information structure value should be specified so that it can cover all potential information structures that a given sentence may have.

c. The semantic representation of information structure involves a binary relation identifying which element has which information structure relation to which clause.

d. Semantically empty and syncategorematic items are informatively empty.

These hypotheses are built upon in the following chapters into three type hierarchies: *info-str*, *mkg*, and *sform*.

7.3 Information structure (*info-str*)

The type hierarchy of *info-str* is sketched out in Figure 7.1. The values of information structure are represented as node names (i.e. type names) within the *info-str* type hierarchy. For instance, if a linguistic unit introducing an EP (Elementary Predicate) into RELS is computed as conveying meaning of non-contrastive focus (i.e. *semantic-focus*), it also introduces one *info-str* value whose type name is *semantic-focus* into ICONS. The nodes at the bottom represent the most specific meanings, which cannot be further subdivided with respect to information structure. The nodes in the third line include the major components of information structure. *Focus* and *topic* are mutually exclusive, and *contrast* should be realized with either of them. The nodes in the second line are abstract. Each of them

7 Individual CONStraints: fundamentals

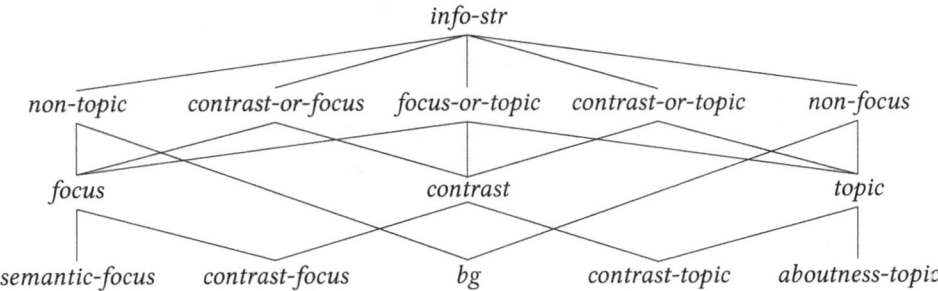

Figure 7.1: Type hierarchy of *Info-str*

stands for a linguistic property that the major components of information structure exhibit: possibility of topicality or focality (*non-topic*, *non-focus*, and *focus-or-topic*), and possibility of contrastiveness (*contrast-or-topic* and *contrast-or-topic*). These are motivated by the need to capture via underspecification exactly the range of information structure meanings associated to particular information structure markings in certain languages, as detailed below.

This *info-str* hierarchy is based on Song & Bender (2011), but is extended with several additional nodes. *Non-topic* means the target cannot be read as topic (e.g. case-marked NPs in Japanese). *Focus-or-topic* is assigned to the fronted NPs in focus/topic fronting constructions. *Contrast-or-topic* is used for *wa* in Japanese and *-(n)un* in Korean, because *wa* or *(n)un*-marked constituents in those languages can convey a meaning of non-contrastive topic, contrastive topic, or even contrastive focus. *Contrast-or-focus* likewise can be used for forms responsible for a meaning of non-contrastive focus, contrastive focus, or even contrastive topic.[7] *Non-focus* similarly indicates that the target cannot be the focus, and would be appropriate for dropped elements in *pro*-drop languages. As discussed thus far, *focus* and *topic* are mutually exclusive because they designate disjoint portions of a sentence. *Focus*, *contrast*, and *topic* multiply inherit from the components in the second row. The types in the bottom line represent the fully specified meaning of each component of information structure. *Semantic-focus* taken from Gundel (1999) means non-contrastive focus, and *aboutness-topic* means non-contrastive topic. Finally, *bg* (background) means the constituent is neither *focus* nor *topic*, which typically does not involve additional marking but may be forced by particular positions in a sentence.

---

[7] Such a marking system has not been observed, but it is included into the hierarchy as a counterpart of *contrast-or-topic*.

7.3 Information structure (info-str)

Compared to the previous version presented in Song & Bender (2011) and other approaches in previous literature, the type hierarchy illustrated in Figure 7.1 allows greater flexibility. First, Figure 7.1 shows us that *contrast*, which is in a sister relation to *non-topic* and *non-focus*, behaves independently of *topic* and *focus*. Second, *focus-or-topic* and *contrast-or-topic* can help in the modeling of the discrepancies between forms and meanings in information structure (e.g. focus/topic fronting, *wa* or *(n)un*-marked focus in Japanese and Korean, etc.), and represent ambiguous meanings involving a classification across *focus*, *topic*, and *contrast*. Third, *non-topic* and *non-focus* also facilitate more flexible representation for informatively undetermined items in some languages. For example, case-marked NPs can convey either focus or background meaning in Japanese (Heycock 1994). That is, since a Japanese case marker (i.e. *ga* for nominatives) can convey two information structure meanings (*focus* and *bg*), the marker itself has to be less specifically represented as *non-topic*. Note that *non-topic* is the supertype of both *focus* and *bg*. Finally, *bg* is made use of as an explicit component of information structure.

Using ICONS involves several fundamental points in operation: First, ICONS represents information structure as a binary relation between two elements. In other words, the current model regards *clause* as the locus where information structure is determined.[8] Second, ICONS behaves analogously to HCONS and RELS in that values of *info-str* are gathered up from daughters to mother up the tree. The value type of ICONS, HCONS, and RELS is *diff-list*, which incrementally collects linguistic information during the formation of parse trees. Additionally, ICONS and HCONS share almost the same format of feature structure. Both are, so to speak, accumulator lists. The value type in the *diff-list* of ICONS is *info-str*, and that of HCONS is *qeq*, both of these include two attributes to represent a binary relation (i.e. TARGET to CLAUSE, and HARG to LARG). Third, despite the similarity in structure, RELS and HCONS are different from ICONS in terms of how they function in the semantics. RELS and HCONS directly engage in the building up of the logical form, and also interact in an intimate manner with each other. Although ICONS also interact with truth-conditions (Partee 1991), this interaction is not implemented in the same way. Fourth, HCONS and ICONS also behave differently in generation. ICONS-based sentence generation is carried out via a subsumption check, using the type hierarchy whose value type is *icons*

---

[8][CLAUSE *individual*] and [CLAUSE-KEY *event*] at first blush might look like an inconsistency. However, *event* is a subtype of *individual* in the current type hierarchy of the LinGO Grammar Matrix system. Roughly speaking, *individual* (an immediate subtype of *index*) is the lowest meaningful supertype of *ref-ind* for nominals and *event* for verbals.

7 Individual CONStraints: fundamentals

or its subtypes (e.g. *info-str*). That is, the generator first creates all potential sentences that logically fit in the input MRS without considering the constraints on ICONS, and then postprocesses the intermediate results to filter out sentences mismatching the values on the ICONS list. Chapter 13 deals with the details of ICONS-based generation.

7.3.1 ICONS

ICONS is newly added to structures of type *mrs* (i.e. under CONT) as shown in (9).

(9) $\begin{bmatrix} mrs \\ \text{HOOK} & \begin{bmatrix} hook \\ \text{GTOP} & handle \\ \text{LTOP} & handle \\ \text{INDEX} & individual \\ \text{XARG} & individual \\ \text{ICONS-KEY} & \textit{info-str} \\ \text{CLAUSE-KEY} & event \end{bmatrix} \\ \text{RELS} & \textit{diff-list} \\ \text{HCONS} & \textit{diff-list} \\ \text{ICONS} & \left\langle !\ldots, \begin{bmatrix} \textit{info-str} \\ \text{CLAUSE} & individual \\ \text{TARGET} & individual \end{bmatrix}, \ldots ! \right\rangle \end{bmatrix}$

An ICONS element has two features, namely TARGET and CLAUSE. When an element is information-structure marked and also is exhibited as an EP, that element's ARG0 value will be structure-shared with the value of TARGET. That is to say, each type name indicates which information structure meaning is associated with the EP, and the connection between them is specified by the co-index between TARGET and ARG0. On the other hand, the value of CLAUSE is structure-shared with the INDEX value of the predicate that functions as the semantic head of the clause.

To take a simple example, (10a) can be represented as the following AVM (10b). Note that in (10a) the subject ***Kim*** is B-accented and the object *the* BOOK is A-accented.

7.3 Information structure (info-str)

(10) a. **Kim** reads the BOOK.

b.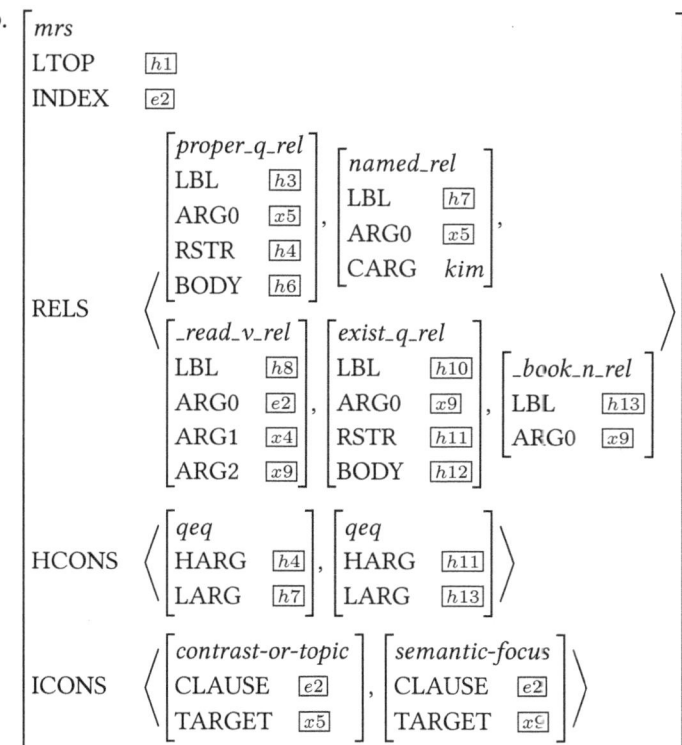

In (10b), the first element in ICONS is specified as *contrast-or-topic*, which stands for the information structure meaning that **Kim** (potentially) delivers. Likewise, the second element in ICONS indicates that *the BOOK* is evaluated as containing *semantic-focus*. The connection between the elements in ICONS and the EPs in RELS is determined by the coreference between TARGET of each ICONS element and ARG0 of EP(s). The first element in ICONS has $x5$ for TARGET, and the first and the second EPs in RELS have the same value. Likewise, the TARGET of the second element in ICONS is co-indexed with the fourth and the fifth EPs' ARG0. The values of CLAUSE indicate which EP is the head in the clause. In this case, the verb *reads* plays the role as indicated by $e2$. The clues to determine information structure meanings are built up incrementally by lexical and phrasal rules with an interaction of the type hierarchies. In this case, the rules for identifying each information structure value are (hypothetical) lexical rules that constrain the A and B accents. When a specific *info-str* value is created by such a rule, this value is gathered up to the tree via *diff-list* (p. 238).

7 Individual CONStraints: fundamentals

What is key in this method of representation is that the intermediate types in the hierarchy allow for underspecified representations. As discussed several times thus far, the grammar of many human languages does not fully pin down the information structure role an element plays even when it does provide partial information about it. Because *contrast-or-topic* on the first ICONS value is not a terminal node in Figure 7.1, **Kim** in (10a) can be interpreted as any of the categories subtypes: *contrast-focus*, *contrastive-topic*, or *aboutness-topic*. The specific choice among them can be determined by the contextual information. This flexible representation is crucial in a robust computational model for processing natural language sentences.

7.3.2 ICONS-KEY and CLAUSE-KEY

In (9), there are two pointers under HOOK; ICONS-KEY and CLAUSE-KEY. They are acquired in an incremental way.

ICONS-KEY makes both the phrase/ lexical structure rules and the lexical entries contribute partial information to the same ICONS element. When an *info-str* element can be inserted into the ICONS list, we may not specifically know which information structure meaning the element carries because information structure markings often provide only partial information. The meaning can be further constrained by multiple sources when the parse tree is further constructed. For example, *wa* in Japanese in itself is assigned *contrast-or-topic*, but this meaning can be further constrained (e.g. as *topic*, *contrast-topic*, or *contrast-focus*) by other syntactic operations such as scrambling. Thus, it is necessary to use a pointer in order to impose a more specific constraint on an *info-str* element already augmented in the ICONS list. ICONS-KEY is used for this purpose.

However, the value of CLAUSE of a constituent cannot be identified until the clause it belongs to is identified. Thus, when an *info-str* element is inserted into the ICONS list, the value of CLAUSE is in most cases not yet specified. This value can be filled in later by using another pointer called CLAUSE-KEY. Each ICONS-KEY|CLAUSE is not lexically bound. The value of CLAUSE is naturally identified at the clausal level. In other words, the CLAUSE values have to remain unbound until each clause an individual is overtly expressed in is chosen.[9] There are two assumptions to be noted. The first is that individuals play an information

---

[9] This strategy is different from the approach presented in Song & Bender (2012), in which *verbal-lex* and *headed-icons-phrase* take the responsibility of linking CLAUSE-KEY to the INDEX of heads. The main reason for the change in strategy is that using *headed-icons-phrase* ends up with introducing too many subtypes of *head-comp-phrase*. This runs against the spirit of the HPSG formalism (i.e. reducing redundancy and using a minimal number of grammatical types).

7.3 Information structure (info-str)

structure role only with respect to overt clauses. That is, if an utterance contains no items that can play a role of the semantic head, the utterance is assumed to have no CLAUSE binding.[10] The second is that clauses in this context do not include non-finite (i.e. tenseless) clauses. That is, whether or not a verbal type has a clausal dependent (subject or complement) is dependent upon whether or not the dependent involves a verb for which a tense is identified. The underlined VPs in (11) are not clausal arguments. In other words, the number of clauses in an utterance is the same as the number of tensed VPs in the utterance.

(11) a. Kim seems to sleep.

b. Kim tried to sleep.

c. Kim saw Fido sleeping.

d. Kim made Fido sleep.

e. Kim promised Lee to leave.

f. Kim believed Lee to have left.

The framework of the LinGO Grammar Matrix employs a type hierarchy representing clausal types, as sketched out in (12). The *clause* hierarchy is already implemented in the core of the LinGO Grammar Matrix system (i.e. matrix.tdl).

(12)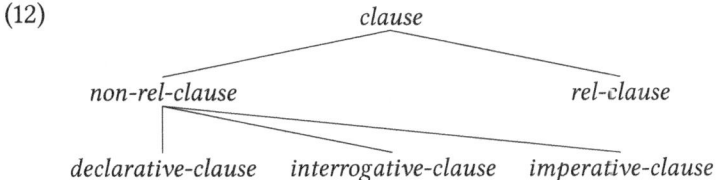

Among the nodes in (12), *non-rel-clause* and *rel-clause* are responsible for constraining the CLAUSE values. The CLAUSE values of the elements on the ICONS list become co-indexed with the INDEX of the semantic head of the CLAUSE (i.e. the value of INDEX being structure-shared with the value of ARG0 of some EP whose label is the value of LTOP). This constraint on *non-rel-clause* is represented in (13), in which CLAUSE-KEY is identified with its INDEX.

---

[10] There are some utterances in which no verbal item is used in human language. First, if an utterance is vocative (e.g. *Madam!*), the information structure value of the entire utterance can be evaluated as *focus*. Second, in languages that do not make use of copula (e.g. Russian) copula constructions include non-verbal predicates. In this case, since the complement plays the semantic head role, the value of CLAUSE is bound to the complement.

7 Individual CONStraints: fundamentals

(13)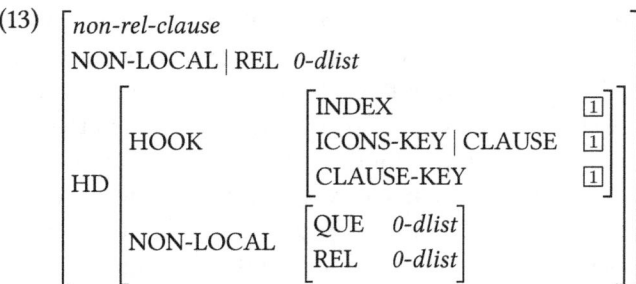

Because every element in a single clause shares the same CLAUSE-KEY, this coreference is also applied to all information structure values' ICONS|CLAUSE in ICONS.[11] For instance, lexical types that have an intransitive argument structure (e.g. an intransitive verb *bark* in English) inherit from the type depicted in AVM (14). The CLAUSE-KEY of the subject is identified with the verb's CLAUSE, but the specific value is not yet given.

$$(14) \begin{bmatrix} \textit{intransitive-lex-item} \\ \text{LKEYS} \mid \text{KEYREL} \mid \text{ARG1} \quad \boxed{1} \\ \text{HOOK} \mid \text{CLAUSE-KEY} \quad \boxed{2} \\ \text{ARG-ST} \left\langle \begin{bmatrix} \text{HOOK} \mid \text{INDEX} & \boxed{1} \\ \text{ICONS-KEY} \mid \text{CLAUSE} & \boxed{2} \end{bmatrix} \right\rangle \end{bmatrix}$$

The CLAUSE values (not yet specified) of the elements on the ICONS list are specified when a clause is constructed by (13). The same goes for adjuncts in a single clause. Adjuncts (e.g. attributive adjectives, adverbs, etc.) and the heads they are modifying share the same value of CLAUSE. That is, the ICONS-KEY|CLAUSE and CLAUSE-KEY of NON-HEAD-DTR is identified with the CLAUSE value of ICONS-KEY of HEAD-DTR. More information about this is given in Section 8.2 (p. 151).

In `matrix.tdl` in the LinGO Grammar Matrix system, the subtypes of *head-subj-phrase* also inherit from the types at the bottom in (12) (e.g. *declarative-clause*, etc.). Hence, the instance types (e.g. *decl-head-subj-phrase* and *decl-head-*

---

[11]The constraint on *non-rel-clause* shown in (13) would be incompatible with some interrogative sentences in Bulgarian: *0-list* in NON-LOCAL|QUE can cause a problem in that Bulgarian employs multiple *wh*-fronting (Grewendorf 2001). Nonetheless, the constraint on *non-rel-clause* is presented as is, because the current proposal focuses on information structure in the LinGO Grammar Matrix. The *wh*-fronting is beyond the scope of the present work, but should be addressed in future work.

opt-subj-phrase) naturally bear the constraint (13). In other words, instances of *head-subj-phrase* are responsible for the binding of CLAUSE-KEY.

7.3.3 Summary

As discussed thus far, in order to see the larger picture of how information is packaged in an utterance, it is necessary to look at (i) which element has (ii) which information structure relation to (iii) which clause. In particular, if an utterance is made up of two or more clauses, a single entity can have an information structure relation (e.g topic, focus, and so on) with each clause, and those relations are not necessarily the same. Leveraging binary relations meets this need specifically TARGET for (i), CLAUSE for (iii), and a value of *info-str* (i.e. a node in the type hierarchy) for (ii). The items on the ICONS list are feature structures of type *info-str*, which indicate which index (the value of TARGET) has a property of information structure and with respect to which clause (the value of CLAUSE). Information structure meanings conveyed by each individual are represented in MRS as an element of the ICONS list, which our infrastructure of machine translation can refer to for both transfer and generation.

7.4 Markings (*mkg*)

The information structure marking itself is recorded via a morphosyntactic feature MKG (MarKinG) inside of SYNSEM|CAT, which places lexical and syntactic constraints on forms expressing information structure meanings. MKG features are exclusively concerned with markings of information structure. They are particularly of use for constraining the scrambling constructions in Korean and Japanese, which will be deeply analyzed in Section 10.3 (p. 196). Before delving into those details, the present subsection presents the basic functionality of the feature structure.

MKG plays two roles in handling information structure; one is theoretically driven, and the other is practical. First, MKG contributes to resolving discrepancies between form and meaning in information structure. As mentioned earlier, the MKG value reflects the morphosyntactic marking, but does not necessarily coincide with the semantic value. For instance, *wa* in Japanese and *-(n)un* in Korean (as discussed in Section 5.1) can sometimes convey a contrastive focus reading as exemplified in (15): *ecey-nun* 'yesterday-NUN' in the answer should be evaluated as conveying a meaning of contrastive focus. In this case, the value of MKG that *ecey-nun* has (under CAT) is *tp*, but the information structure value in semantic representation is *contrast-focus*.

7 Individual CONStraints: fundamentals

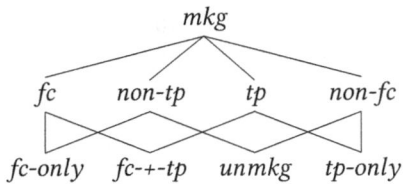

Figure 7.2: Type hierarchy of *Mkg*

(15) Q: Kim-i   onul   o-ass-ni?
       Kim-NOM today come-PST-INT
       'Did Kim come today?'

   A: ani. (Kim-un) ecey-nun   o-ass-e.
      No. Kim-NUN yesterday-NUN come-PST-DECL
      'No. Kim came yesterday.' [kor]

Second, MKG also functions as a flag feature for blocking overgeneration. The typical instantiation that might be overgenerated but for MKG is *topic-comment* constructions, which the next subsection elaborates on.

The type *mkg* is used as the value of the feature MKG, and introduces two further features, FC (FoCus-marked) and TP (ToPic-marked).

(16) $\left[\text{MKG} \begin{bmatrix} \text{FC} & luk \\ \text{TP} & luk \end{bmatrix} \right]$

The value type of TP and FC is *luk*, which is a supertype of *bool* (boolean) and *na* (not-applicable). As shown in (16), *luk* consists of six subtypes including +, –, and *na*, and can therefore capture the marking type of constituents more flexibly than *bool* which, as shown below, only has subtypes for + or –.

(17)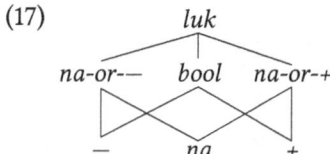

The value of MKG is always a subtype of *mkg*, as sketched out in Figure 7.2, in which *tp* is constrained as [TP +], *non-tp* as [TP na-or-–], *fc* as [FC +], and *non-fc* as [FC na-or-–]. Types at the bottom multiply inherit from the intermediate

122

7.4 Markings (mkg)

supertypes, and thereby both FC and TP are fully specified. Instantiations of the *mkg* values assigned to particular information structure markings are as follows.

Focus and topic markers in some languages have a fairly straightforward MKG value. For instance, the contrastive topic marker in Vietnamese *thì* presented in (3) is [MKG *tp-only*]. The focus clitics *é* and *á* in Rendile exemplified in (p. 49) are [MKG *fc-only*]. The clitic =*m* in Ingush conveys a contrastive focus meaning (p. 68), which also involves [MKG *fc-only*]. The two types of Cantonese particles (p. 50), such as *aa4* for topic and *aa3* for focus, are [MKG *tp-only*] and [MKG *fc-only*], respectively.

The A and B accents in English, in line with the analysis in Hedberg (2006), are also straightforwardly assigned. The A-accent (H*) is responsible for conveying a non-contrastive focus meaning, whereas the B-accent (L+H*) can be used to express topic (irrespective of contrastive or non-contrastive) or contrastive focus. The A-accent exclusively used for marking focus is [MKG *fc-only*], while the B-accent can be left underspecified with a value like [MKG *tp*].

Lexical markers in Japanese and Korean only partially constrain meaning. As is well known, Japanese and Korean employ three types of NP markings; (i) case-marking (e.g. *ga* and *i / ka* for nominatives), (ii) *wa* and *(n)un*-marking, and (iii) null-marking (expressed as ∅ in the examples presented thus far). The distinction among their MKG values is crucially used in handling the interaction between lexical markings and scrambling in these languages (discussed in detail in Section 10.3). Initially, the case markers are [MKG *unmkg*], given that they are not expressly markers of information structure, although they indirectly influence information structure meanings (i.e. *non-topic*, Heycock 1994). Yet, *unmkg* does not necessarily imply a case-marked constituent cannot be used for focus or topic. Note that, in the current analysis, information structure markings are neither a necessary condition nor a sufficient condition for information structure meanings. Second, the MKG value of *wa* and -(*n*)*un* may be either *tp* or a fully specified type such as *tp-only*. The present study supports the former, because contrastively used markers and non-contrastively used ones show different prosodic behavior from each other in Korean and Japanese (Chang 2002; Nakanishi 2007). For example, as already provided in Chapter 6 (p. 90), Chang (2002) argues that non-contrastive ('thematic' in his terminology) topic has [STR < 1 >] while contrastive topic has [STR < 3 >] in Korean. If we can deploy a resolution system distinguishing the difference between them in the future, the value of MKG|FC would not remain underspecified, and thereby the information structure will be more concretely constrained. In other words, non-contrastively topic-marked constituents will have [MKG *tp-only*], whereas contrastively topic-marked ones

7 Individual CONStraints: fundamentals

will have [MKG *fc-+-tp*]. *Fc-+-tp* as shown in Figure 7.2 means both values of MKG|FC and MKG|TP are +. Note that these values do not violate the theorem that focus and topic are mutually exclusive. Since MKG is exclusively concerned with markings, *fc-+-tp* does not imply the constituent is regarded as containing both focus and topic. This value indicates that the constituent is either focused-marked or topic-marked. [MKG|TP +] will come from the lexical information of *-(n)un*, and [MKG|FC +] will be obtained from the prosodic information of the constituent (i.e. [STR < 3 >]). However, a completely reliable system for detecting prosody in Japanese and Korean, to my knowledge, is non-existent for now. The value of MKG|FC of the topic markers, therefore should (and does) remain underspecified in the current work. Finally, null-marked phrases in Japanese and Korean should be evaluated as remaining undetermined with respect to information structure markings (i.e. *unmkg*).

The MKG feature also plays a role in calculating the extent of focus projection. As surveyed in the previous chapter, most previous HPSG-based analyses of information structure assume that prosody expressing focus is responsible for spreading the meaning of focus to larger constituents (Bildhauer 2007). However, focus is projected onto larger phrases not only by means of prosody but also by lexical markers in some cases (Choe 2002). The feature responsible for focus projection in the current proposal is [MKG|FC +].[12]

7.5 Sentential forms (*sform*)

The value of ICONS can be constrained by phrasal types as well as lexical types. In order to capture a generalization about syntactic combination between two phrases with respect to information structure, a type hierarchy representing sentential forms is required. Recall that many previous studies argue that information structure contributes to a sentential grammar (Lambrecht 1996; Engdahl & Vallduví 1996; Paggio 2009; Song & Bender 2011). Building on the previous literature, I propose Figure 7.3 as the classification of phrasal types. The main purpose of *sform* is to arrange information structure components in a sentence. However, this type hierarchy is not concerned with the linear ordering of components, unlike Figure 6.1 given in the previous chapter (p. 86).

Lambrecht (1996) posits that information structure is deeply associated with how a sentence is formed. Engdahl & Vallduví (1996), likewise, regard informa-

---

[12]The A-accent in English and the prosodic pattern of marking focus in Spanish inherently have [MKG|FC +], which originally comes from [UT|DTE +], if we include the phonological structure and related rules suggested by Bildhauer (2007) into the grammars.

7.5 Sentential forms (sform)

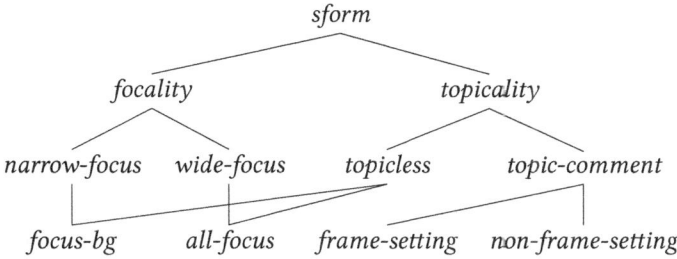

Figure 7.3: Type hierarchy of *Sform*

tion structure (information packaging in their terminology) as a part of sentential grammar. Paggio (2009) provides a hierarchy for representing sentential forms in Danish as shown in Figure 6.1, which is quite similar to Figure 7.3. Paggio's type hierarchy terminates in various phrasal rules that simultaneously inherit from other fundamental phrasal rules. This method is also taken up by Song & Bender (2011). In Song & Bender's analysis of scrambling in Japanese and Korean (i.e. in the OSV order), the combination of scrambled objects and VPs forms an instance whose type inherits from both *head-comp-phrase* and *topic-comment*. The current model follows the same combinatoric strategy for placing constraints on phrase structure types with respect to information structure.

However, there is a methodological difference between what was proposed in previous literature and that in the present study. In previous studies the types representing sentential forms also characterize the linear order of components. For instance, the instruction-types provided in Engdahl & Vallduví (1996), such as *link-focus*, *link-focus-tail*, *all-focus*, and *focus-tail*, and the node names in the hierarchies of Paggio (2009) and Song & Bender (2011), such as *topic-focus* and *topic-bg-focus*, reflect constraints on the ordering of elements. In Figure 7.3, by contrast, only *topic-comment* is constructed based on linear order. All the other types merely represent the components that the construction comprises without respect to the linear order. *Focus-bg* in Figure 7.3, which is normally used for clefts constructions, does not mean that *focus* is necessarily followed by *bg*. For example, focused constituents are postposed in the cleft constructions in Korean (Kim & Yang 2009), but these constructions are nonetheless instances of *focus-bg*. In the current work, the linear order of the components is manipulated by phrase structure rules in each language grammar.

The types of *sform* interact with MKG features to stratify meaning of information structure at the phrase level. The *sform* types are inherited by phrase

125

7 Individual CONStraints: fundamentals

structure rules. Not all phrase structure rules inherit from *sform* types, but if a specific syntactic operation is used for expressing information structure (e.g. scrambling in Japanese and Korean), the rule for the constructions inherits from something in Figure 7.3.

Since sentential forms are basically a matter of how two phrases are combined with each other, *sform* inherits from *binary-headed-phrase* (made up of HEAD-DTR and NON-HEAD-DTR). We may ask why it is necessary to refer to MKG features of daughters in building up parse trees and why *sform* is required to be additionally introduced as a single phrase structure type. Several types of constructions use *sform*. Those include (i) the preverbal/postverbal position of focused constituents, (ii) cleft constructions, (iii) comment markers (e.g. *shì* in Mandarin Chinese and *ba* in Abma) that always entail focus projection, and (iv) scrambling in Japanese and Korean (H.-W. Choi 1999; Ishihara 2001; Song & Bender 2011). These are respectively relevant to (i) *narrow-focus*, (ii) *focus-bg*, (iii) *wide-focus*, and (iv) *topicless* vs. *topic-comment*.

Sform is bipartitely divided into *focality* and *topicality*, which indicates marking (i.e. values of MKG) and/or meaning (i.e. values of ICONS) of components of information structure in the arguments. *Sform* and its subtypes, as presented below, place constraints on MKG, which implies sentences are realized depending on information structure markings of elements. Since *sform* also places constraints on ICONS, it serves to relate the marking to the meaning.

Focality takes *fc-only* as the value of MKG, which indicates the phrase includes a focus-marked constituent. *Focality* is divided into *narrow-focus* and *wide-focus*. The distinction between them, however, is not necessarily equivalent to argument focus vs. predicate focus (Lambrecht 1996; Erteschik-Shir 2007), because verbs can bear *narrow-focus*. As shown in (18), only the MKG value on the mother is restricted in *focality*. The value is used for further composition: Some phrase structure rules prevent focus-marked constituents (i.e. specified as [MKG|FC +]) from being used as the daughter. Some phrase structure rules, on the contrary, require an explicitly focus-marked constituent as the daughter.

(18) $\begin{bmatrix} \textit{focality} \\ \text{MKG} \quad \textit{fc-only} \end{bmatrix}$

Topicality is mainly concerned with how the topic is realized in a sentence. *Topicality* does not have any specific constraint for now, because *topicless* and *topic-comment* are unlikely to share a feature cross-linguistically. Nonetheless, it is introduced into the hierarchy out of consideration for symmetry with *focality*. Subtypes of *topicality* are constrained in the following way.

7.5 Sentential forms (sform)

(19) a. $\begin{bmatrix} \textit{topicless} & \\ \text{HD} \mid \text{MKG} & \textit{non-tp} \\ \text{NHD} \mid \text{MKG} & \textit{non-tp} \end{bmatrix}$ b. $\begin{bmatrix} \textit{topic-comment} & \\ \text{MKG} & \textit{tp} \\ \text{NHD} \mid \text{MKG} & \textit{tp} \end{bmatrix}$

Note that *topic-comment* has a constraint on the MKG value of the mother, just as *focality* above has the constraint [MKG *fc-only*]. In *topic-comment* constructions (e.g. *as for* ... constructions), topics are followed by other constituents. Once a construction is identified as *topic-comment*, there are two options in further composition. If there exists another topic in the left side, and the topic is a frame-setter, then further composition is allowed. Otherwise, the *topic-comment* instance itself cannot be used as a head (i.e. a secondary *comment*) in further composition. The subtypes of *topic-comment* (i.e. *frame-setting* and *non-frame-setting*) details this distinction.

As noted, not all sentences have topics. Cleft constructions are presumably *topicless* in many languages.[13] Accordingly, a constituent with [MKG|TP +] cannot be the non-head-daughter in cleft constructions. For example, cleft clauses in Korean show a strong tendency to be exclusive to (*n*)*un*-marked constituents, as exemplified below.

(20) a. ku chayk-ul/*un ilk-nun salam-i/un Kim-i-ta.
the book-ACC/NUN read-REL person-NOM/NUN Kim-COP-DECL
'It is Kim that reads the book.'

b. Kim-i/*un ilk-nun kes-i/un ku chayk-i-ta.
Kim-NOM/NUN read-REL thing-NOM/NUN the book-COP-DECL
'It is the book that Kim reads.' [kor]

The distinction between *topicless* and *topic-comment* is especially significant in topic-prominent languages, such as Chinese, Japanese, and Korean, in which forms of marking topics play an important role in syntactic configuration (Li & Thompson 1976; Huang 1984). Lambrecht (1996) regards (21), in which *inu* 'dog' is combined with the nominative marker *ga* instead of the so-called topic marker *wa*, as a topicless sentence.[14] This is further evidence that not all subjects are topics.

---

[13] There exists some exception to this generalization. It is reported that some languages (e.g. Spanish) allow for left-dislocated topics in cleft constructions.
[14] Kuroda (1972) regards (21) as a subjectless sentence.

7 Individual CONStraints: fundamentals

(21) inu ga   hasitte iru.
  dog NOM running
  'The dog is running.' [jpn] (Kuroda 1972: 161)

In line with Lambrecht's claim, the present analysis provides for this with the type *topicless*. The difference between *topicless* and *topic-comment* performs a role in constructing Japanese and Korean grammars, which is partially proposed in Song & Bender (2011). For instance, *head-subj-rule* and *head-comp-rule* in these languages need to be divided into several subrules, depending on whether the non-head-daughter of the rules are *wa* or *(n)un*-marked or not. The rules dependent upon the value of MKG in Japanese and Korean are provided in Section 10.3.

There is a need to refine the meaning of *topicless*. On one hand, it indicates that topic is not realized in surface form, not that there is no topic at all in the utterance. For example, *topicless* in Japanese means that the non-head-daughter of the phrase is not *wa*-marked. For example, since *inu ga* 'dog NOM' in (21) is not a *wa*-marked constituent, and it constitutes the sentence with the predicate *hasitte iru* 'running' as a non-head-daughter, the sentence ends up being *topicless*. On the other hand, MKG only reflects overtly expressed items and an utterance might have an implicit topic which is not overtly expressed as is the case in topic-drop, which often occurs in topic-prominent languages (e.g., Chinese, Japanese, Korean). It is true that dropped topics in the current work surely have a representation in the ICONS, but they are irrelevant to MKG.

Narrow-focus and *focus-bg* come under *focality*, but constraints on them are language-specific. This is because they are not reflected in the linearization of components. For example, assume two hypothetical languages Language *A* and *B*, which have a symmetrical property as follows.[15]

(22) a. Language *A* employs SVO as its basic word order.

  b. Focused constituents in Language *A* are realized in the immediate preverbal position.

  c. Additionally, there is an optionally used accent, which expresses focus.

---

[15]Language *A* is hypothetically modeled quite analogously to Hungarian (É. Kiss 1998; Szendrői 1999). Hungarian is known as adopting SVO word order preferentially (Gell-Mann & Ruhlen 2011), though it is sometimes reported that the word order in Hungarian is pragmatically conditioned (i.e. no dominant order, Kiefer 1967).

7.5 Sentential forms (sform)

(23) a. Language *B* employs SOV as its basic word order.

b. Focused constituents in Language *B* are realized in the immediate post-verbal position.

c. The same as (22c)

Based on (22-23), the object in SOV word order in Language *A* and the objects in SVO word order in Language *B* are narrowly focused. They participate in *narrow-focus* as a non-head-daughter. Both [OV] in Language *A* and [VO] in Language *B* are instantiated as *head-comp-phrase*, but the former is constrained by *head-final* in which the head (i.e. the verb) follows its complement, while the latter is constrained by *head-initial* in which the head precedes. Thus, from a cross-linguistic perspective, linear order does not have to be used as a key to constrain *narrow-focus*. On the other hand, a distinction between HEAD-DTR and NON-HEAD-DTR cannot be used for constraining *narrow-focus*, either. For instance, focused constituents in clefts behave as the head of cleft clauses realized as relatives. In other words, while the focused items in [OV/VO] in Language *A* and *B* respectively are NON-HEAD-DTRs, the focused items in cleft are HEAD-DTRs. In a nutshell, it is true that *narrow-focus* and *focus-bg* require some constraints on information structure marking and meaning, but the constraints must be applied on a language by language or construction by construction basis.

There are at least two subtypes of *focus-bg* across languages: One where the HD involves [MKG *fc*] and one where the NHD does. For example, the cleft constructions (as an instance of *focus-bg*) in English basically inherit the following AVM. More specific constraints can be imposed language-specifically.

(24) $\begin{bmatrix} focus\text{-}bg \\ \text{HD} \mid \text{MKG} & fc \\ \text{NHD} \mid \text{MKG} & unmkg \end{bmatrix}$

This AVM serves to prevent constituents with information structure markers from being used in cleft constructions. For instance, -(n)un in Korean is not allowed to be used in cleft clauses, as exemplified in (25).

(25) Kim-i/*un   mek-nun kes-un   sakwa-i-ta.
Kim-NOM/NUN eat-REL thing-NUN apple-COP-DECL
'It is an apple that Kim is eating.' [kor]

7 Individual CONStraints: fundamentals

If a grammar employs a set of phrase structure rules that transmit the MKG value of the subject in the cleft clause to the higher phrase node, then only the nominative marker that involves [MKG *unmkg*] can be chosen. The [MKG *tp*] feature -(*n*)*un* involves prevents the clause from being used in the clefted clause (see Section 8.4.2).

To present another instance, *narrow-focus* in Language A can be constrained as follows. Note that the values on HD and NHD are the reverse of those in (24).

(26) $\begin{bmatrix} \textit{narrow-focus} \\ \text{HD} \mid \text{MKG} \quad \textit{unmkg} \\ \text{NHD} \mid \text{MKG} \quad \textit{fc-only} \end{bmatrix}$

(26) also explains the ungrammaticality of pseudo sentence (27c) in Language A; HD of *narrow-focus* requires a minus value as a value of MKG|FC, which conflicts with a focus accent that falls on the verb. Because presumably there is no other way to construct (27c), a pseudo sentence like (27c) remains ungrammatical.

(27) a. subj verb obj. (in the neutral word order)

b. subj obj verb. (focus on obj)

c. *subj obj VERB. (a focus-marking accent on verb)

A sample derivation for (27b) can be sketched out as (28), showing only information structure markings and sentential forms. Note that MKG is seen only locally, because it is not a head feature. Thus, the value would not be transmitted to the higher nodes if it were not for an extra constraint.

(28)

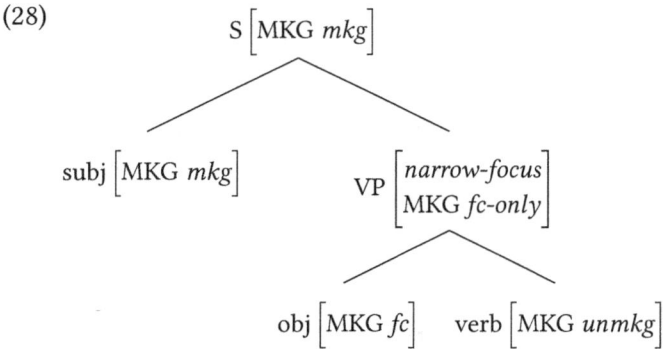

7.5 Sentential forms (sform)

Wide-focus, next, is particularly related to realization of comment markers as mentioned earlier. For instance, Mandarin Chinese employs *shì* as exemplified below, which indicates the remaining part after it is in the focus domain (von Prince 2012).[16] In a similar vein, Li (2009) regards *shì* as a marker responsible for contrastive meanings: The constituents after *shì* are contrastively focused.

(29) Zhāngsān [shì [xuéxí yīxué]].
 Zhangsan SHI study medicine
 'Zhangsan studies medicine.' [cmn] (von Prince 2012: 336)

Thus, the type of construction licensed by *shì* (and comment markers in other languages such as Abma, Schneider 2009) has to inherit (30). Note that this constraint is language-universal, unlike *narrow-focus*. In the context of grammar engineering for the LinGO Grammar Matrix system, (30) is encoded into matrix.tdl, while the AVM for *narrow-focus* could be either empty or encoded in mylang.tdl. In accordance with (30), any constituents after the comment marker should not be topic-marked.

(30) $\begin{bmatrix} \textit{wide-focus} \\ \text{HD} \mid \text{MKG} & fc \\ \text{NHD} \mid \text{MKG} & fc \end{bmatrix}$

All-focus inherits from both *wide-focus* and *topicless*.[17] Finally, it is necessary to discriminate between *frame-setting* and *non-frame-setting*. As noted, this use of the MKG feature aims to pass up appropriate values; in particular, when a topic-marked constituent occurs in the leftmost position. [NHD|L-PERIPH +] in (31a) imposes this constraint. L-PERIPH (Left-PERIPHeral) will be discussed in the next chapter (Section 8.3.1).

(31) a. $\begin{bmatrix} \textit{frame-setting} \\ \text{NHD} \mid \text{L-PERIPH} & + \end{bmatrix}$

 b. $\begin{bmatrix} \textit{non-frame-setting} \\ \text{HD} \mid \text{MKG} & \textit{fc-only} \end{bmatrix}$

---

[16] von Prince (2012) says this *shì* is different from the copula *shì* (i.e. homonym).
[17] Regarding the status of *all-focus*, Lambrecht (1996: 232) argues that there is a clear difference from other types of focused constructions in that the pragmatic core of *all-focus* is "an absence of the relevant presuppositions". The argument sounds convincing, but the present study does not represent such pragmatic information on the AVMs of *sform*.

7 Individual CONStraints: fundamentals

As seen in Chapter 3 (Section 3.3.3.3) topics that function to restrict the frame of what the speaker is speaking about (i.e. so-called frame-setting topics) can appear multiply.

In English, while left-dislocated NPs cannot occur more than once without affecting grammaticality as shown in (32a),[18] frame-setters such as *yesterday* in (32b) can occur multiple times in the sentence-initial position as presented in (32d). In other words, *topic-comment* constructions can be used as another comment, and do not constrain the value of MKG of the head-daughter. However, they cannot be used again for *non-frame-setting*.

(32) a. *Kim, the book, he read it.

 b. Yesterday, Kim read the book.

 c. The book, Kim read it.

 d. Yesterday, the book, Kim read it.

To summarize, *sform* is concerned with syntactic combination between two phrases with respect to information structure. This places constraints on both MKG and ICONS, relating the marking to the meaning. In other words, *sform* makes information structure marking and meaning interact with each other. The type hierarchy here used is adapted from the proposal of Paggio (2009). The current proposal has one method in common with Paggio's: If a phrase structure rule is related to expressing information structure, it can multiply inherit from both a specific type of *sform* and an ordinary phrase structure type, such as *head-subj-phrase*, *head-comp-phrase*, etc. The main difference between Paggio's approach and mine is that my *sform* hierarchy does not directly constrain the linear order of components.

---

[18]This generalization is language-specific, not universal. Some counterexamples have been reported: Vallduví (1993: 123) argues for Catalan that "There is no structural restriction on the number of phrases that may be right or left detached." Left-dislocated NPs in Spanish are also sometimes multiply used (Zagona 2002: 224).

7.6 Graphical representation

Song & Bender (2012) suggest representing constraints on information structure in the style of the dependency graphs of DMRS (Dependency MRS; Copestake 2009) for ease of exposition. Likewise, the remainder of this book makes use of dependency graphs to present information structure relations between individuals and clauses.

In these graphs, the ICONS values are represented as links between informatively contentful elements (introducing the referential index as the value of TARGET) and verbs (introducing the event variable as the value of CLAUSE) and as unary properties of verbs themselves. The direction of a given arrow stands for the binary relation between a TARGET (an entity) and a CLAUSE that the TARGET belongs to. The start point indicates the constituent that occupies the CLAUSE-KEY within the clause. The end point refers to the constituent whose INDEX is shared with the TARGET, and whose ICONS-KEY|CLAUSE is co-indexed with the CLAUSE-KEY. The node name on each arrow indicates the information structure value that the binary relation has, such as *focus*, *topic*, and so forth.

For example, a dependency graph (33b), which stands for the binary relations on the ICONS list, is a shorthand version of the corresponding MRS representation (33a), which stands for ***Kim*** *reads the* BOOK. in which the B-accented ***Kim*** conveys meaning of contrast and/or topic, and the A-accented BOOK bears non-contrastive focus.

7 Individual CONStraints: fundamentals

(33) a.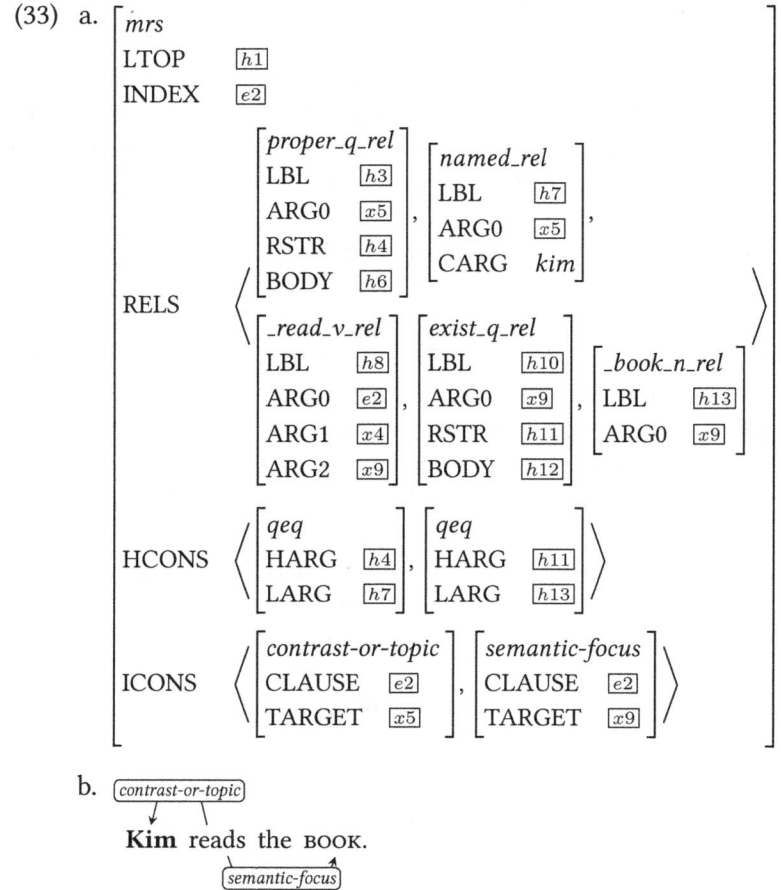

b.
    ⌜contrast-or-topic⌝
        ↙   ↖
  Kim reads the BOOK.
          ↖____↗
      ⌞semantic-focus⌟

The arc from *reads* to **Kim** means that the index of **Kim** has a *contrast-or-topic* relation to the clause represented by READS.[19] The arc from *reads* to BOOK, likewise, means the index of BOOK has a *semantic-focus* relation to the index of READS. The root arrow on READS indicates that the verb is linguistically underspecified with respect to the clause that it heads.

---

[19] The present study, according to the argument of Hedberg (2006), regards the A-accent (i.e. marked as SMALL CAPS) as prosodic means expressing non-contrastive focus (i.e. *semantic-focus*), and the B-accent (i.e. **boldfaced**) as conveying one of the meanings of non-contrastive topic, contrastive topic, or sometimes contrastive focus.

7.7 Summary

This chapter has outlined three considerations motivating the representation of information structure via ICONS: resolving discrepancies between forms and meanings in information structure, facilitating underspecifiability for allowing flexible and partial constraints, and capturing the fact that information structure relations are between expressions and particular clauses. Additionally, the ICONS-based representation reflects the working hypothesis that semantically empty and syncategorematic items are informatively empty. Guided by these considerations, I provide three type hierarchies: *info-str* whose value types stratify information structure meaning, *mkg* indicating morphosyntactic markings of information structure, and *sform* that works with MKG relating to the *info-str* value. ICONS is added into *mrs*, and the value is a *diff-list* of *info-str*. ICONS identifies which element has which information structure relation to which clause. For this purpose, the typed feature structure of *infc-str* includes TARGET and CLAUSE. TARGET is identified with the EP INDEX (i.e. *individual*), and CLAUSE is determined by the subtype(s) of *clause*. In addition, ICONS-KEY and CLAUSE-KEY are used as pointers during the construction of parse trees. MKG has two features; one is FC (FoCus-marked), and the other is TP (ToPic-marked). These features are independent of meanings represented as an *info-str* type. The next chapter will discuss how these elements are used to impose constraints on information structure and represent it in MRS.

8 Individual CONStraints: specifics of the implementation

This chapter dives into the details of implementing ICONS (Individual CONStraints) into MRS (Minimal Recursion Semantics (Copestake et al. 2005), or Meaning Representation System in the current context) by constraining lexical types and phrasal types. Section 8.1 shows how information structure is dealt with in various lexical types. Section 8.2 gives an explanation of information structure constraints on phrasal types. Next, Section 8.3 presents three additional constraints for configuring information structure in a specific way. Building upon the hierarchies and constraints presented thus far, Section 8.4 illustrates how information structure is represented via ICONS in four languages (English, Japanese, Korean, and Russian).

8.1 Lexical types

This section largely addresses which lexical item inherits from which *icons-lex-item* type out of *no-icons-lex-item*, *basic-icons-lex-item*, *one-icons-lex-item*, and *two-icons-lex-item*. They are constrained as presented in the following AVMs.

(1) a. $\begin{bmatrix} \textit{no-icons-lex-item} \\ \text{MKG} \begin{bmatrix} \text{FC} & \textit{na} \\ \text{TP} & \textit{na} \end{bmatrix} \\ \text{ICONS} \langle !\ !\rangle \end{bmatrix}$
   b. $\begin{bmatrix} \textit{basic-icons-lex-item} \\ \text{ICONS} \langle !\ !\rangle \end{bmatrix}$

   c. $\begin{bmatrix} \textit{one-icons-lex-item} \\ \text{ICONS} \langle !\ [\ ]\ !\rangle \end{bmatrix}$
   d. $\begin{bmatrix} \textit{two-icons-lex-item} \\ \text{ICONS} \langle !\ [\ ],\ [\ ]\ !\rangle \end{bmatrix}$

The first two AVMs do not inherently have an *info-str* element on the ICONS list, but information-structure related rules can insert a value into the list for the

8 Individual CONStraints: specifics of the implementation

second type. That is, if there is a clue for identifying its information structure value, a value of *info-str* is introduced into the list of ICONS and its TARGET is co-indexed with the HOOK|INDEX of the word. The last two inherently have non-empty ICONS lists. That means that they lexically have an *info-str* value in ICONS.

Lexical entries that cannot be marked with respect to information structure inherit from *no-icons-lex-item* (1a). In other words, information structure markings are not-applicable to them, a constraint formalized as [MKG [FC *na*, TP *na*]]. For example, relative pronouns and expletives in English are instances of *no-icons-lex-item*. Other contentful items introducing an EP inherit from one of the types in (1b–d). The choice among them depends on how many clauses are subcategorized by the lexical type. The prefixes represent how many clauses are created by the type: *Basic-* means the lexical type does not include any clausal subject or clausal complement in ARG-ST. *One-* means either a clausal subject or a clausal complement is subordinate to the lexical type. *Two-* means there exists a clausal subject and also a clausal complement. If a verbal type forms a monoclausal construction, the *icons-lex-item* type of that verbal item is the basic one (i.e. *basic-icons-lex-item*). If a verbal type has ARG-ST information that includes one or more clausal argument(s) (i.e. multiclausal), its *icons-lex-item* type is either *one-icons-lex-item* (a sentential complement or a sentential subject) or *two-icons-lex-item* (both of them). The extra *info-str* values in (1c–d) are required for this purpose.

8.1.1 Nominal items

Nominal items, including common nouns, proper nouns, and pronouns, inherit from *basic-icons-lex-item*. One exceptional lexical type is that of expletives (e.g. *it* in English), because they cannot be marked with respect to information structure (Lambrecht 1996). Expletives inherit from *no-icons-lex-item*. One question regarding *info-str* of nominal items is whether different types of nominals can participate in information structure in the same way and with the same status. The current work does not recognize any difference in the information structure of nominal items. In other words, other than *basic-icons-lex-item*, there is no further information structure constraint on nominal items.

Pronouns have been regarded as a component associated with information structure in a different way (Lambrecht 1996). Pronouns, roughly speaking, can be divided into two categories, such as (i) unaccented and (ii) accented. Lambrecht argues that the distinction between these two categories can be sufficiently explained in terms of information structure. Across languages, (i) unaccented pronouns preferentially involve topics. This finding is bolstered by the evidence that unaccented pronouns are the most frequently used form of expressing topic in Spoken French (Lambrecht 1986). Besides, unaccented pronouns cannot be used for expressing focus, because they are incompatible with (2).

(2) Focus Prominence: Focus needs to be maximally prominent. (Büring 2010: 277)

On the other hand, (ii) accented pronouns can be divided again into (ii-a) those with a topic-marking accent, and (ii-b) those with a focus-marking accent. Lambrecht illustrates the linguistic distinction between (ii-a) and (ii-b) in Italian as follows.

(3) a. Io PAGO.
    I pay.
    'I'll pay.' [ita]

b. Pago IO.
   pay I
   'I'll pay.' [ita] (Lambrecht 1996: 115)

The preverbal pronoun *Io* in (3a) expresses a topic, with a rising intonation contour. On the other hand, the pronoun conveying a focus meaning in (3b) occurs sentence-finally, and has a falling intonation contour, indicating the end of the assertion.

From a theoretical point of view, it seems clear that pronouns show different behaviors in packaging information.[1] However, the current work, based on text processing, cannot deploy such a division. Phenomena related to (ii) can be modeled with hypothetical suffixes such as *-a* and *-b*, however the responsibility is borne by the hypothetical suffixes or alternatively lexical rules introducing the prosodic information, not the pronouns themselves.

---

[1]The nominal items also differ from each other in discourse status. Kaiser (2009) argues that the use of different kinds of referring expressions is relevant to the salience of the antecedents; the more salient antecedent it refers to, the more reduced a form (e.g. dropped subjects) appears. That is, selecting a type of referential form largely hinges on how salient the antecedent is. The discourse status of nominal categories that take *ref-ind* (a subtype of *individual*) as the value type of HOOK|INDEX is represented as COG-ST (COGnitive-STatus) in the current LinGO Grammar Matrix system (Bender & Goss-Grubbs 2008). Discourse status is related to information status (e.g. given vs. . new); COG-ST covers information status from a higher level. Information status, as discussed in Chapter 3, has often been studied in tandem with information structure, but it is neither a necessary nor a sufficient condition for information structure. In sum, since discourse status is not directly responsible for representing information structure, the current work leaves discourse-related information to future work.

8 Individual CONStraints: specifics of the implementation

8.1.2 Verbal items

The analysis proposed here uses the event variable associated with the head of the clause to stand in for the clause, and as a result, the lexical types for verbs (typical clausal heads) need to be constrained appropriately. Most contentful verbal items inherit from either *basic-icons-lex-item*, *one-icons-lex-item*, or *two-icons-lex-item*. Verbs inherently have lexical information about how many elements exist on the ICONS list and how they are bound with the semantic head in the clause that the elements belong to. That means the number of elements on the ICONS list depends on how many clausal dependents a verbal type has. This information is specified inside the ARG-ST of verbal types. If a verb takes no clausal phrase(s) as its dependent(s), the verb locally constitutes a monoclausal phrase. In this case, no element is required to be included on the ICONS list (i.e. *basic-icons-lex-item*). In some cases, a verb lexically places an information structure constraint on its subordinated clause(s). If the ARG-ST of a verbal type includes either one clausal subject or one clausal complement, the verbal type constitutes a locally embedded constructions in which one clause is subordinate to the main clause (i.e. *one-icons-lex-item*). Sometimes, both the subject and one of the complements can be clausal. In this case, two elements of *info-str* are needed on the ICONS list (i.e. *two-icons-lex-item*).

There is an exception: Some semantically and informatively empty verbal items are not able to be marked with respect to information structure. These verbs inherit from *no-icons-lex-item*. For example, semantically empty copulae (e.g. specificational copulae English) are incapable of contributing an ICONS element.

8.1.2.1 Main verbs

Because main verbs in principle can be marked with respect to information structure, they do not inherit from *no-icons-lex-item*. Excluding *no-icons-lex-item* for this reason, main verbs can be one of these three types of *icons-lex-item*: *basic-icons-lex-item*, *one-icons-lex-item*, or *two-icons-lex-item*.

Common verbs that constitute a monoclausal construction, including intransitives (e.g. *bark* in 4a), transitives (e.g. *read* in 4b), and ditransitives (e.g. *give* in 4c), inherit from *basic-icons-lex-item*. Causative verbs (e.g. *make* in 4d) and perception verbs (e.g. *see* in 4e) also inherit from *basic-icons-lex-item*, because their verbal complements (e.g. *bark* in 4d and *barking* in 4e) are tenseless (i.e. infinite). Thus, all dependents, including the subject and the complements, are bound to the verb that functions as the semantic head in the sentence (i.e. an element that

8.1 Lexical types

takes the INDEX in the finite clause). That means the CLAUSEs of the dependents are co-indexed with the HOOK|INDEX of the main verb by *non-rel-clause* (p. 120) which *decl-head-subj-phrase* inherits from. Note that some relations of information structure are not captured in the following graphs. This is because if there is no specific clue to identify the information structure meaning a constituent conveys, no value is gathered into the list of ICONS. For ease of exposition, in the following examples, the left-most elements (i.e. subjects) are B-accented (conveying *contrast-or-topic*) and the right-most elements are A-accented (conveying *semantic-focus*).

(4)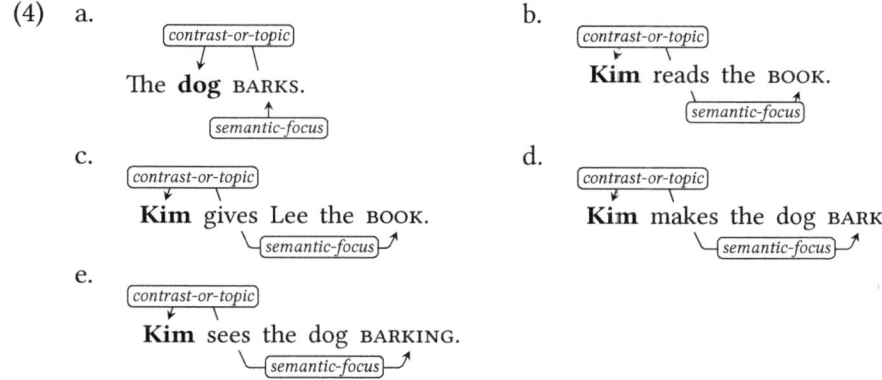

Raising and control verbs have the same mapping type in *info-str*; every dependent marked with respect to information structure within a single clause has a co-index between its CLAUSE and the INDEX of the semantic head in the clause (i.e. matrix clause verb).

(5)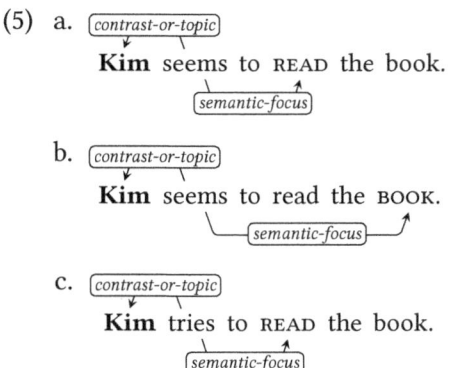

8 Individual CONStraints: specifics of the implementation

d.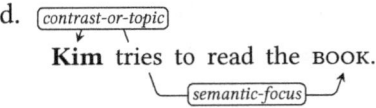

For example, *the* BOOK in (5b) is syntactically a complement of *read*, but is informatively bound to *seems* whose INDEX is connected to the INDEX in the clause. Additionally, it is interesting that *Kim* has an *info-str* role in the matrix finite clause, even though it is not the semantic argument of *seems*. The same goes for a control verb *try* in (5c–d).[2]

Several verbal types take clausal complements as shown in (6a) or clausal subjects as shown in (6b), and these inherit from *one-icons-lex-item*.

(6)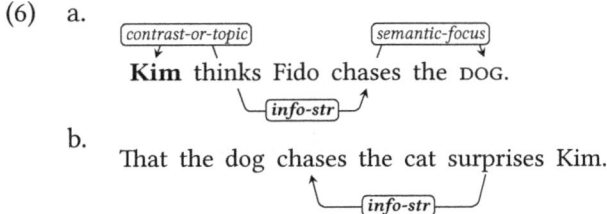

In (6a), the arrow from *chases* and *dog* is locally established within the embedded clause. The binary relation in the embedded clause does not have to do with the main verb *thinks*. The main verb *thinks* also has an arrow to the subject *Kim* in the local domain. The key point of this example is the arrow from the main verb *thinks* to the verb in the embedded clause *chases*. This arrow is introduced by element on the ICONS list of *think* (*one-icons-lex-item*), and shows which information structure relation the embedded clause has to the matrix clause. Likewise, the arrow from *surprises* and *chases* in (6b) represents the inherent *info-str* element on the ICONS list of *surprise*.

Both subjects and complements can be clausal at the same time. In these cases, it is necessary to inherit from *two-icons-lex-item*. A typical example can be found in pseudo-clefts, including *wh*-clefts, and inverted *wh*-clefts as exemplified in (7).[3] In (7), the matrix verb *is* inherently has two elements of *info-str* on the ICONS

---

[2] As is well known, raising verbs (e.g. *seem, appear, happen, believe, expect*, etc.) and control verbs (e.g. *try, hope, persuade, promise*, etc.) display several different properties, such as the semantic role of the subject, expletive subjects, subcategorization, selectional restriction, and meaning preservation (Kim & Sells 2008). Nonetheless, they have *basic-icons-lex-item* in common as their supertypes, because they do not take tensed clauses as complements.

[3] (7) is originally taken from the ICE-GB (Nelson, Wallis & Aarts 2002), and the expressions in angled brackets represent the indices of each sentence in the corpus.

8.1 Lexical types

list: The CLAUSE value of the first element is its INDEX, and the TARGET is co-indexed with the INDEX of the verb in the clausal subject (i.e. *happened*). The CLAUSE of the second is still linked to its INDEX, and the TARGET is co-indexed with the INDEX of the verb in the complement (i.e. *caught*).

(7) [What happened] is [they caught her without a license]. <S1A-078 #30:2:A>

The dependency graph corresponding to (7) is presented in (8). Note that the second arrow in (7) is specified as *focus*. That is, the clausal complement in a *wh*-cleft (e.g. *they caught her without a license* in 7) is focused (J.-B. Kim 2007). Since the other constituents cannot be assigned focus, the clausal subject in (7) is specified as *non-focus*. The verbal entry *is* includes these values as lexical information.

(8)

      non-focus
        ↓
What happened is they caught her without a license.
           focus

8.1.2.2 Adjectives

Predicative adjective items are the same as the verbal items presented thus far. The copula *is* in (10) is assumed to be semantically and informatively empty, with the adjective functioning as the semantic head of such sentences. This constraint is specified in the following AVM, which passes up the CLAUSE-KEY of the second argument (i.e. the adjective).

(9) $\begin{bmatrix} \textit{copula-verb-lex} \\ \text{ARG-ST} \left\langle \begin{bmatrix} \text{ICONS-KEY} \mid \text{CLAUSE } \boxed{1} \end{bmatrix}, \begin{bmatrix} \text{CLAUSE-KEY } \boxed{1} \end{bmatrix} \right\rangle \end{bmatrix}$

Happy in (10a) and *fond of* in (10b), which do not constitute multiclausal constructions, inherit from *basic-icons-lex-item*. Next, *obvious* in (10c–d) takes clausal subjects, and *sure* and *curious* in (10e–f) take clausal complements. These inherit from *one-icons-lex-item*.

(10) a. Kim is happy.

    b. Kim is fond of apples.

    c. That the dog barks is obvious.

8 Individual CONStraints: specifics of the implementation

    d. It is obvious that the dog barks.

    e. Kim is sure that the dog barks.

    f. Kim is curious whether the dog barks.

There are also raising adjectives (e.g. *likely*) and control adjectives (e.g. *eager*), which, like raising and control verbs, inherit from *basic-icons-lex-item*.

Attributive adjectives are different in that they do not introduce the *info-str* value that take their own event variable as the value of CLAUSE. Attributive adjectives and the nouns they are modifying share the value of CLAUSE, which is co-indexed with the INDEX of the verb heading the clause that they are part of. For example, the arrows on *big* in (11) come from the main verb of each sentence. This linking strategy is constructionally constrained by *head-mod-phrase*. Section 8.2 gives an explanation of how this linking is achieved via *head-mod-phrase*.

(11) a.   b.

        [semantic-focus]   [semantic-focus]

    The BIG dog barks.   Kim reads the BIG books.

There is a distinction between attributive and predicative adjectives with respect to building up the list of ICONS, but there is no need to use an extra lexical rule to discriminate them. What is of importance is incrementally gathering *info-str* values into the list of ICONS, and this strategy is achieved by phrase structure rules, such as *head-comp-rule* for predicative adjectives (as specified in the ARG-ST of 9) and *head-mod-rule* for attribute ones.

8.1.2.3 Auxiliaries

As far as ICONS is concerned, auxiliaries in English are divided into two subtypes. One contributes no predicate and no ICONS element, and thereby inherits from *no-icons-lex-item*. The other introduces an EP to RELS, and thereby inherits from *basic-icons-lex-item*. Since complements of auxiliaries are always non-finite, there are no auxiliaries of type *one-icons-lex-item* or *two-icons-lex-item*. An example of the first category, *will* in (12a) is semantically empty, and does not occupy the INDEX of the clause. Such an auxiliary, therefore, does not have any *info-str* element in ICONS, either. Instead, the main verb, *read* in (12a), has arrows to each of its dependents. By contrast, *can* in (12b) introduces an EP to RELS and has arrows to all individuals that introduce *info-str* into the clause.[4]

---

[4] Its LKEYS|KEYREL|PRED is specified as "_can_v_modal_rel" in the ERG.

8.1 Lexical types

(12) a. 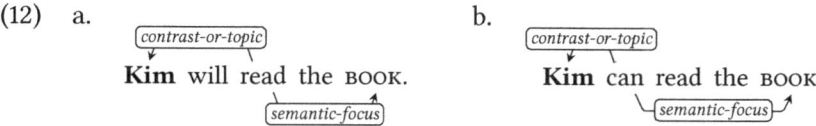 b.

As stated above, these two types of auxiliaries inherit from different lexical types. *Will* is an instance of *no-icons-lex-item*, and therefore does not participate in the articulation of information structure. Second, *can* inherits from *trans-first-arg-raising-lex-item-1* as represented in (13). The CLAUSE value of the subject (i.e. the first element in ARG-ST) is co-linked to its own CLAUSE-KEY, and the second argument (i.e. the VP) also shares the CLAUSE value with its own CLAUSE-KEY.[5]

(13) $\begin{bmatrix} \textit{trans-first-arg-raising-lex-item-1} \\ \text{CLAUSE-KEY } \boxed{1} \\ \text{ARG-ST} \left\langle \begin{bmatrix} \text{ICONS-KEY | CLAUSE } \boxed{1} \end{bmatrix}, \begin{bmatrix} \text{ICONS-KEY | CLAUSE } \boxed{1} \\ \text{CLAUSE-KEY} \quad \boxed{1} \end{bmatrix} \right\rangle \end{bmatrix}$

The main verb which serves as the complement of modal auxiliaries can sometimes take clausal complements. In this case, the CLAUSE-KEY is still occupied by the auxiliary as sketched out in (14): The arrow to the verb in the embedded clause headed by *chases* is lexically introduced by *think*, which inherits from *one-icons-lex-item*. The CLAUSE-KEY of the second *info-str* that *think* introduces is still unbound in the VP *think Fido chases the dog*. Building up *head-subj-phrase*, the CLAUSE-KEY that *chases* has in relation to the matrix clause is finally co-indexed with the INDEX of *can*. Recall that the value of CLAUSE is bound when one clause is identified (Section 7.3.1). *Head-subj-phrase* serves to identify which EP occupies the INDEX of the clause and fills in the value of CLAUSE.

(14) [contrast-or-topic]   [semantic-focs]
     Kim can think Fido chases the DOG.
                  [info-str]

8.1.2.4 Copulae

Copulae, generally speaking, have at least three usages as exemplified in (15). Note that some languages employ lexically different copulae. For example, Korean employs *i* as an ordinary copula and *iss* as a locative verb. To take another

---

[5]Note that (13) actually contains more constraints, such as HCONS.

145

8 Individual CONStraints: specifics of the implementation

example, Mandarin Chinese employs *shì* as an ordinary copula and *zài* as a locative verb. For this reason, I would use the three different names.

(15) a. Kim is the student. (identificational)

b. Kim is happy. (specificational)

c. Kim is in Seattle. (locative)

(15a) can be paraphrased as *Kim is identical to the student.*, while (15b–c) cannot. Traditionally, identificational copulae in many languages are treated as ordinary transitive verbs, whose ARG-ST includes one NP for the subject and the other NP for the complement (i.e. a two-place predicate). Thus, identificational copulae are assumed to be contentful and thereby introduce an EP, whose LKEYS|KEYREL|PRED value would be something like "_be_v_id_rel".

In contrast, the other two copula types are semantically empty items that do not introduce any EP into the list of RELS in MRS. Thus, the semantic heads of (15b–c) are respectively computed as *happy* and *in*. Since the locative verb is not semantically void in such a language, the lexical entry for the locative verb has a PRED value like "_be+located_v_rel".

Identificational copulae inherit from *basic-icons-lex-item*, while the others inherit from *no-icons-lex-item*. That means semantic heads that occupy the INDEX of the clauses in (15b–c) are *happy* and *in*, respectively. In other words, the CLAUSE-KEY in (15b–c) is linked to the INDEX of *happy* and *in*. (16a–c) represent the information structure of (15a–c), respectively.

(16)

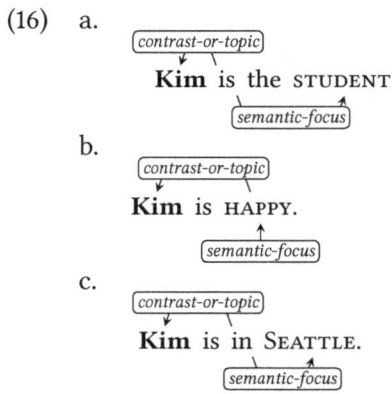

8.1.3 Adpositions

Adpositions normally inherit from either *basic-icons-lex-items* or *one-icons-lex-item*. Every information-structure marking adposition inherits from *one-icons-lex-item*. If an adposition does not contribute to information structure, it inherits from *basic-icons-lex-item*. Adpositions that inherit from *basic-icons-lex-items* can have an ICONS element introduced later when another means of marking information structure (e.g. an accent on *under* in 17b) is used.

(17) Q: Did Kim put the book <u>on</u> the desk?
A: No. Kim put the book <u>under</u> the desk.

Prepositions in English do not inherit from *one-icons-lex-items*, because there is no information-structure marking preposition in English. Japanese has both types. As discussed thus far, information-structure marking postpositions, such as *ga* (nominative) and *o* (accusative) and *wa* (contrast or topic), are instances of *one-icons-lex-item*. That means they introduce one element into the ICONS list. The TARGET of the ICONS element is co-indexed with the INDEX of their complement (i.e. XP that they are attached to), and the ICONS-KEY of each postposition is lexically specified: *non-topic* for *ga* and *o*, *contras-or-topic* for *wa*. Other than these, focus particles syntactically classified as postpositions in Japanese are also instances of *one-icons-lex-item*. These include *dake* 'only', *shika* 'except', *mo* 'also', and so on (Hasegawa 2011; Hasegawa & Koenig 2011). They behave in the same manner as *ga*, *o*, and *wa*, but their *info-str* value is *focus*. Other postpositions that do not mark information structure in Japanese inherit from *basic-icons-lex-item*. These include *made* 'till', *kara* 'from', etc.

8.1.4 Determiners

Determiners inherit from either *one-icons-lex-item* or *basic-icons-lex-item*, depending on whether or not they mark information structure by themselves. English does not have determiners that inherit from *one-icons-lex-item*, because there is no information-structure marking determiner. It is reported that some languages employ information-structure marking determiners. For example, Lakota (a Siouan language spoken in Dakota) uses a definite determiner *k'uŋ* to signal contrastive topic.[6] These determiners inherently include an ICONS element (i.e. *one-icons-lex-item*).

---

[6] Section 12.6.1 provides more explanation about *k'uŋ* in Lakota (p. 254).

8 Individual CONStraints: specifics of the implementation

Determiners in English may bear the A-accent as shown in (18).

(18) a. Kim reads THE book.

b. Kim reads SOME/ALL books.

Notice that *focus* is assigned to the nouns, not the determiners themselves. That is, the focused items in (18) are *book(s)*, not the determiners. Thus, when a determiner has an ICONS element, its TARGET should be co-indexed with the INDEX of the NP. For example, the A-accented ALL in (18b) is constrained as follows.[7]

(19) $\begin{bmatrix} \text{STEM} & \langle all \rangle \\ \text{MKG} & \textit{fc-only} \\ \text{SPEC} & \left\langle \begin{bmatrix} \text{INDEX} & \boxed{1} \\ \text{ICONS-KEY} & \boxed{2} \end{bmatrix} \right\rangle \\ \text{ICONS} & \left\langle ! \boxed{2} \begin{bmatrix} \textit{semantic-focus} \\ \text{TARGET} & \boxed{1} \end{bmatrix} ! \right\rangle \end{bmatrix}$

Notably, the *info-str* value that determiners assign to the specified NPs should be consistent with the ICONS-KEY of the NPs; for example, 'THE **book**' is ill-formed, because the *semantic-focus* that the determiner involves is inconsistent with the *contrast-or-topic* the noun carries.[8]

8.1.5 Adverbs

Adverbs cross-linguistically inherit from *basic-icons-lex-item*. (20) is illustrative of the information structure relation that adverbs have within a clause. Just as with attributive adjectives, the relation is bound to the HOOK|INDEX of the semantic head within the clause.

(20) a. The dog barks LOUDLY. *[semantic-focus]*   b. The dog tries to bark LOUDLY. *[semantic-focus]*

---

[7] The current analysis employs two hypothetical suffixes (-a for the A-accent and -b for the B-accent) and the suffixes are attached by lexical rules. Two lexical rules presented in (37) later take nominal and verbal items as their daughter. In addition to them, there could be one more lexical rule that takes determiners as their daughter. These rules are not presented in the current analysis.

[8] Section 10.1.1 provides more discussion on information structure values of quantifiers (p. 189).

8.1.6 Conjunctions

First of all, all conjunctions that take adverbial clauses as their complement inherit from *one-icons-lex-item*. They have their CLAUSE-KEY linked to the INDEX of the main clause's semantic head. Note that the semantic head of the matrix clause is co-indexed with the element in HEAD|MOD. They also have their TARGET linked to the INDEX of their complement (i.e. the semantic head of the adverbial clause).

(21) $\begin{bmatrix} \textit{subconj-word} \\ \text{HEAD} \mid \text{MOD} \ \langle [\text{INDEX} \ \boxed{1}] \rangle \\ \text{VAL} \mid \text{COMPS} \ \langle [\text{INDEX} \ \boxed{2}] \rangle \\ \text{ICONS} \ \langle \, ! \begin{bmatrix} \text{TARGET} & \boxed{2} \\ \text{CLAUSE} & \boxed{1} \end{bmatrix} ! \, \rangle \end{bmatrix}$

Second, conjunctions that involve temporal adverbial clauses, such as *when*, *before*, and *after*, are related to *topic*, if they appear before the main clause (Haiman 1978). That means that the information structure value between the two semantic heads should be *topic*. This value is assigned by the temporal conjunctions themselves. Third, conditional conjunctions (e.g. *if* and *unless* in English) also assign *topic* to the element in ICONS (Ramsay 1987).[9] Fourth, causal conjunctions, such as *because* in English, and *weil* in German, differ by language with respect to information structure relation to the matrix clause (Heycock 2007). Therefore, their information structure value is language-specifically constrained. That is, causal conjunctions in some languages (e.g. English) have an ICONS element whose value is *info-str*, while similar conjunctions in other language might have an ICONS element whose value is more specific.

Coordinating conjunctions, such as *and* and *or*, are another story. First, each coordinand can have its own information structure relation to the semantic head in the clause if it is marked with respect to information structure. Second, coordinands in a single coordination may have different information structure values from each other. For example, *Kim* and **Sandy** in (22B) have the same status in the syntax of coordination, but **Sandy** is contrastively focused as vetted by the correction test. In this case, while *Kim* introduces no ICONS element, **Sandy** introduces an ICONS element and the element is assigned *contrast-or-topic* by the B-accent.

---

[9] Section 9.3 provides more information about temporal and conditional conjunctions (p. 182).

(22) A: Kim and Lee came.
      B: No. Kim and **Sandy** came.

Third, the coordinate phrase itself also can have an information structure relation to the semantic head. For instance, the fronted constituent in (23) (specified as *focus-or-topic*) is a coordinate phrase.

(23) The book and the magazine, Kim read.

In this case, an ICONS element that indicates the information structure relation between the coordinate phrase *The book and the magazine* and the main verb *read* is added into C-CONT|ICONS.[10]

8.2 Phrasal types

Information structure can also be restricted by phrase structure rules. Phrasal types can be roughly divided into *unary-phrase* and *binary-phrase*. First, ICONS is an accumulator list: ICONS is implemented as a *diff-list*, and the elements are gathered up the tree using *diff-list* append. Second, the information-structure related features (e.g. MKG and L/R-PERIPH) are shared between mother and daughter in a *unary-phrase*, with no further constraint. For instance, *unary-phrase* is defined as in (24). L-PERIPH and R-PERIPH in (24) have not yet been mentioned. They impose an ordering constraint on constituents with respect to expressing information structure. Section 8.3.1 discusses how they contribute to constraining information structure at the phrasal level.

---

[10]Information structure in coordinated phrases would be an interesting research topic. In particular, since the LinGO Grammar Matrix system includes a library of coordination, this idea needs to be implemented and tested though it is left to future work.

8.2 Phrasal types

(24) $\begin{bmatrix} \textit{unary-phrase} \\ \text{MKG} & \boxed{1} \\ \text{LIGHT} & - \\ \text{L-PERIPH} & \boxed{2} \\ \text{R-PERIPH} & \boxed{3} \\ \text{ICONS} & \begin{bmatrix} \text{LIST} & \boxed{4} \\ \text{LAST} & \boxed{6} \end{bmatrix} \\ \text{C-CONT} \mid \text{ICONS} & \begin{bmatrix} \text{LIST} & \boxed{5} \\ \text{LAST} & \boxed{6} \end{bmatrix} \\ \text{HD} & \begin{bmatrix} \text{MKG} & \boxed{1} \\ \text{L-PERIPH} & \boxed{2} \\ \text{R-PERIPH} & \boxed{3} \\ \text{ICONS} & \begin{bmatrix} \text{LIST} & \boxed{4} \\ \text{LAST} & \boxed{5} \end{bmatrix} \end{bmatrix} \end{bmatrix}$

Third, there are five basic subtypes of *binary-headed-phrase*: (i) *basic-head-subj-phrase*, (ii) *basic-head-comp-phrase*, (iii) *basic-head-spec-phrase*, (iv) *basic-head-mod-phrase-simple*, and (v) *basic-head-filler-phrase*. The first three (i-iii) are the same as the previous versions, but with [C-CONT|ICONS <! !>] added. The empty *diff-list* in C-CONT|ICONS means that these rules never contribute ICONS elements. *Basic-head-mod-phrase-simple* is further constrained as follows: The ICONS-KEY|CLAUSE and CLAUSE-KEY of NON-HEAD-DTR has a coreference with the ICONS-KEY|CLAUSE of HEAD-DTR. That means the modifier and the modificand share the same CLAUSE-KEY. The ICONS-KEY and CLAUSE-KEY indicate in which clause the adjunct is focused or topicalized. Additionally, an empty ICONS list is added.

(25) $\begin{bmatrix} \textit{basic-head-mod-phrase-simple} \\ \text{HD} \mid \text{HOOK} \mid \text{ICONS-KEY} \mid \text{CLAUSE} & \boxed{1} \\ \text{NHD} \mid \text{HOOK} & \begin{bmatrix} \text{ICONS-KEY} \mid \text{CLAUSE} & \boxed{1} \\ \text{CLAUSE-KEY} & \boxed{1} \end{bmatrix} \\ \text{C-CONT} \mid \text{ICONS} \langle ! \ ! \rangle \end{bmatrix}$

Finally, *basic-head-filler-phrase* does not include [C-CONT|ICONS <! !>], because this phrase may or may not contribute ICONS elements. Section 12.3.4 provides an explanation of its role in configuring information structure. Re-

8 Individual CONStraints: specifics of the implementation

lated constructions include clause-initial/final focus constructions, focus/topic fronting, and so forth.

8.3 Additional constraints on configuring information structure

Other than the hierarchical constraints presented in the previous chapter, there must be some additional constraints in order to implement information-structure related phenomena within the LinGO Grammar Matrix system. L/R-PERIPH in Section 8.3.1 and LIGHT in Section 8.3.2, as flag features, impose a constraint on the position of components of information structure. The former is newly introduced, while the latter had already been implemented in the system. PHON in Section 8.3.3, newly introduced, is adapted from Bildhauer (2007).

8.3.1 Periphery

As surveyed in Chapter 4, syntactic positioning is one method of expressing information structure. The positions associated with focus include (i) clause-initial (e.g. in Akan, Ingush, Yiddish, etc.), (ii) clause-final (e.g. in Russian, Bosnian Croatian Serbian, etc.), (iii) preverbal (e.g. in Hungarian, Basque, Turkish, etc.), and (iv) postverbal (e.g. in Portuguese, Chicheŵa, etc.). The common position for topics is sentence-initial though some languages (e.g. Danish) do not use the initial positions to signal topic.

In order to implement constraints on periphery, the present study suggests the use of two flag features that constrain the first two focus positions (i.e. (i) L-PERIPH for clause(sentence)-initial focus and (ii) R-PERIPH for clause-final focus). The remaining two positions, including (iii) preverbal and (iv) postverbal, are constrained by the feature called LIGHT, discussed in Section 8.3.2. Even though flag features are related to syntax and semantics, they take part in syntactic configuration and semantic computing only in an indirect way. They are traditionally located directly under SYNSEM. This tradition holds L/R-PERIPH. Additionally, although their value type is *luk*, they are usually constrained as + or − (i.e. *bool*).

[L-PERIPH +] indicates that a constituent with this feature value cannot be combined with another constituent leftward. [R-PERIPH +] likewise indicates there must be no other constituent to the right of a constituent marked as such. In other words, a constituent marked as [L/R-PERIPH +] has to be peripheral in word order unless there is an exceptional rule. A constituent with [L-PERIPH +]

8.3 Additional constraints on configuring information structure

should be in the left-most position within a given clause (i.e. clause-initial). A constituent that is [R-PERIPH +] should be in the right-most position, in other words clause-final.

One of the representative cases in which both features are required can be found in Russian, which places contrastively focused constituents in the clause-initial position and non-contrastively focused ones in the clause-final position (Neeleman & Titov 2009). Thus, the clause-initial constituent (*contrast-focus*) is [L-PERIPH +], and the clause-final constituent (*semantic-focus*) is [R-PERIPH +]. Russian has several more examples that clearly interact with periphery: Russian employs a clitic *li*, which should appear in the second position of an utterance (Gracheva 2013).[11] This clitic modifies the immediately preceding constituent (i.e. the most left-peripheral item), and sometimes assigns *contrast-focus* to it, depending on the part of speech of the constituent it attaches to and context. Notably, *li* imposes the [L-PERIPH +] constraint on left-located constituents. For example, the emphasized constituents in (26) can be evaluated as containing *contrast-focus*.

(26) a. **Na rynke**   li Ivan   kupil   popugaya?
    On market-PREP li Ivan-NOM buy-PST.SG.M parrot-ACC
    'Was it **in the market** that Ivan bought a parrot?'

  b. **Govoriashego**   li popugaja kupil   Ivan?
    Talking-SG.MASC.ACC li parrot-ACC buy-PST.SG.M Ivan-NOM
    'Did Ivan buy a **talking** parrot?' [rus]

Gracheva (2013) provides other clitics that potentially signal information structure meanings in Russian, of these *-to, že,* and *ved'* also interact with the periphery of their modificands in a similar way.[12] These findings indicate that L-PERIPH and R-PERIPH play an important role in configuring information structure in Russian-like languages.

L-PERIPH can also be used for imposing a restriction on the position of topics in topic-first languages (e.g. Japanese and Korean). The left-most (i.e. sentence-initial) and probably topic-marked constituent in topic-first languages should be [L-PERIPH +] disallowing the appearance of any constituents to its left. One exceptional case to this restriction is *frame-setting*, because a series of constituents

---

[11] According to Gracheva (2013), there is one more constraint on *li*: The sentence should be interrogative. That is, the sentential force of the utterance is conditioned as [SF *ques*] by *li*.

[12] Russian has been known to employ pragmatically conditioned word order (Rodionova 2001). In that case, the pragmatic condition largely refers to information structure. For the reason, it seems that a variety of means are used for expressing information structure in Russian.

8 Individual CONStraints: specifics of the implementation

functioning as frame-setters can show up in the sentence-initial position. This is a phenomenon which seems language-universal (Li & Thompson 1976; Chafe 1976; Lambrecht 1996). Now that *topic-comment* and its subtypes have an additional constraint on L-PERIPH, the AVMs offered in Section 7.5 (p. 131) are extended as follows. The more specific rules that inherit from these will be presented in Section 10.3 (p. 198) with specific examples of articulating the scrambling constructions in Japanese and Korean.

(27) a. $\begin{bmatrix} \textit{topic-comment} \\ \text{L-PERIPH} & + \\ \text{MKG} & tp \\ \text{NHD} & \begin{bmatrix} \text{MKG} & tp \\ \text{L-PERIPH} & + \end{bmatrix} \end{bmatrix}$

b. $\begin{bmatrix} \textit{non-frame-setting} \\ \text{HD} & \begin{bmatrix} \text{MKG} & \textit{fc-only} \\ \text{L-PERIPH} & - \end{bmatrix} \end{bmatrix}$

L-PERIPH also plays a role in focus/topic fronting constructions. If a language places focused constituents in the clause-initial position and also has the topic-first restriction, the fronted constituents are associated with *focus-or-topic*, as suggested before. Yiddish typically exhibits such a behavior as in (28). Yiddish is a V2 language with a neutral word order of SVO, in which the verb (i.e. the syntactic head in a sentence) should occur in the second position of the linear order (N. G. Jacobs 2005). Therefore, if the object is focused in Yiddish, the linear order, as exemplified (28b), should be OVS, not OSV. The same goes for sentences in which adverbials are fronted as shown in (28c–d).[13]

(28) a. Der lerər šrajbt di zacn mit krajd afn tovl.
The teacher writes the sentences with chalk on the blackboard (neutral)

b. Di zacn šrajbt der lerər mit krajd afn tovl.
the sentences writes the teacher with chalk on the blackboard
'It's the sentence (not mathematical equations) that the teacher is writing with chalk on the blackboard.'

---

[13] In fact, the translations in (28) provided by N. G. Jacobs (2005) follow the notion that the focused XPs in cleft constructions exhibit exhaustive inferences (i.e. contrastive meaning). Chapter 10 addresses this interpretation in detail (Section 10.4).

8.3 Additional constraints on configuring information structure

    c. mit krajd šrajbt der lerər di zacn afn tovl.
       with chalk writes the teacher the sentences on the blackboard
       'It's with chalk (not with a crayon) that that the teacher is writing the sentence on the blackboard.'

    d. afn tovl šrajbt der lerər di zacn mit krajd.
       on the blackboard writes the teacher the sentences with chalk
       'It's on the blackboard (not the notepad) that that the teacher is writing the sentence with chalk.' [ydd] (N. G. Jacobs 2005: 224)

Note that (28a) is ambiguous (See Section 4.3). This is like ordinary focus/topic fronting constructions in other languages. However, in either case the focused or topicalized constituent should be first, and is constrained as [L-PERIPH +].

8.3.2 Lightness

Preverbal and postverbal focus positions are constrained by LIGHT, which already existed in the LinGO Grammar Matrix core (i.e. matrix.tdl) in order to distinguish words from phrases. Using LIGHT for discriminating words and phrases is inspired by the "Lite" feature Abeillé & Godard (2001) suggest.[14] LIGHT is located directly under SYNSEM because it is a flag feature.

[LIGHT +] is attached to words, while [LIGHT –] is attached to phrases. The value of LIGHT, whose type is *luk*, is sometimes co-indexed with that of HC-LIGHT originally taken from the ERG. HC stands for Head-Complement. The purpose of using HC-LIGHT is to indicate whether a *head-comp-phrase* projected from a head is regarded as light or heavy. If an element in a parse tree has [LIGHT +], it indicates the element has not yet been converted into an instance of a phrasal type. As for verbal nodes in parse trees, the distinction between V and VP is naturally made by the value of LIGHT.

Preverbal and postverbal foci are always realized as *narrow-focus* presented in the previous chapter (p. 130). In addition to this constraint, I argue that preverbal and postverbal focus can be combined only with Vs that are [LIGHT +]. Basque, for instance, is known for the preverbal focus position. In the Basque sentence below, *Jonek* 'Jon' is signaled as *focus*, which is immediately followed by *irakurri du* 'read has'.

---

[14] Crowgey & Bender (2011: 54) also make use of this feature to impose a constraint on negation in Basque: "The feature LIGHT is defined on synsems with a value *luk*. Lexical items are [LIGHT +], while phrases are [LIGHT –]. This stipulation ensures that the verbal complex rule applies before the auxiliary picks up any arguments in any successful parse."

8 Individual CONStraints: specifics of the implementation

(29) Eskutitza, Jonek irakurri du
 letter Jon read has
 'JON has read the letter.' [eus] (Ortiz de Urbina 1999: 312)

My analysis of the sentence is as follows: The auxiliary verbal item *du* 'has' takes *irakurri* 'read' as its complement, but combination is still regarded as a word rather than a phrase. That is, *irakurri du* is [HC-LIGHT +], and shares a coreference with LIGHT. *Jonek* then combines with *irakurri du* (which is still [LIGHT +]), constituting a *head-subj-phrase*. Because the *head-subj-phrase* (i.e. *Jonek irakurri du*) is now [LIGHT −], no more preverbal foci can take place. Crowgey & Bender (2011) provide a similar analysis. They argue that Basque has a constraint like (30) with respect to the variation of word order.

(30) If the lexical verb is to the left of the auxiliary, then the lexical verb must be left-adjacent to the auxiliary. (Crowgey & Bender 2011: 49)

This constraint explains the ungrammaticality of (31), in which the main verb and the auxiliary are not adjacent to each other. This is further evidence that a main verb plus an auxiliary (e.g. *irakurri du*) behave as a single [LIGHT +] (in other words non-phrasal) verbal constituent.

(31) *Liburu irakurri Mirenek du
 book.ABS.SG read.PERF Mary.ERG.SG 3SGO.PRES.3SGA
 'Mary has read a book.' [eus] (Crowgey & Bender 2011: 48)

For more explanation about constraints on preverbal and postverbal foci, two pseudo sentences in Language *A* (presented in Section 7.5) can be instantiated as shown in (33). If Language *A*, whose word-order properties are repeated in (32), has ditransitive verbs, and the ordinary order between objects is [indirect object (*iobj*) + direct object (*dobj*)], then (33a) is in the basic word order.

(32) a. Language *A* employs SVO as its basic word order.

 b. Focused constituents in Language *A* are realized in the immediate preverbal position.

 c. Additionally, there is an optionally used accent, which expresses focus.

(33) a. subj verb iobj dobj. (neutral)

 b. subj dobj verb iobj. (focus on dobj)

8.3 Additional constraints on configuring information structure

A sample derivation for (33b) in which the direct object is focused and preverbal is illustrated below.

(34)

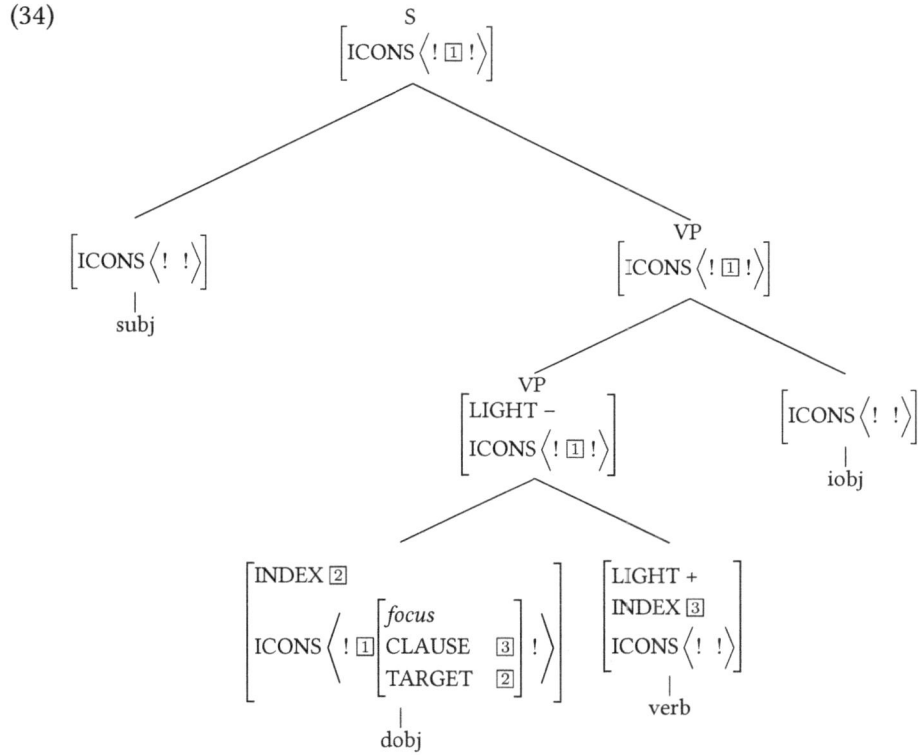

The focused item *dobj*, which is not in situ, is combined with a [LIGHT +] verb before anything else. They constitutes a *head-comp-phrase*, which is now [LIGHT −]. Next, the VP takes *iobj*, which is in situ, as the second complement, and forms another VP as *head-comp-phrase*. Finally, the subject is combined with the second VP into a *head-subj-phrase*. In this case, the first and the second *head-comp-phrase* are realized as two different rules. The first one puts constraints on both the NON-HEAD-DTR (e.g. *dobj* in 33b) and the HEAD-DTR (e.g. *verb*); an information structure value *focus* is assigned to the NON-HEAD-DTR and the HEAD-DTR required to be [LIGHT +]. The second one does not signal any specific values of information structure, but requires the HEAD-DTR to be [LIGHT −]. Notably, this analysis is not applied to sentences in the neutral word order. For example, *subj* in (33a) is in the immediately preverbal position, but it is in situ in the neutral word order. Thus, it is not necessarily analyzed as containing *focus*.

8 Individual CONStraints: specifics of the implementation

8.3.3 Phonological structure

The phonological structure proposed by Bildhauer (2007) is not completely applied to the customization system as is, because the phonological behaviors in many languages remain hitherto unknown. As far as the LinGO Grammar Matrix system is concerned, the phonological structure itself is implemented into `matrix.tdl` in TDL, but no further rules are implemented. Crucially a set of phonology-related features are now implemented in `matrix.tdl` and available for use by future developers of Matrix-derived grammars.

Bildhauer (2007) proposes four levels of phonological structure, consisting of (i) prosodic word, (ii) phonological phrase, (iii) intonational phrase, and (iv) phonological utterance, and two intonational typed feature structures, including (v) pitch accents, and (vi) boundary tones. Among them, the present study is not concerned with the first three structures, because it is difficult to obtain an acoustic system to resolve the prosodic levels reliably. In other words, the rules presented in Chapter 6 (p. 99) are tentatively disregarded in the current work. The last three are largely related to focus projection, but the rules for them are also altered to be suitable for implementation. The altered rules, such as the focus-prominence rule and focus-projection rule, are presented in Chapter 11 which is especially concerned with how to calculate the spreading of focus.

Prosodic patterns in Japanese and Korean, with respect to information structure, have been substantially revealed by phonetic experiments (Jun et al. 2007; Ueyama & Jun 1998; Jun & Lee 1998). Prosodic behaviors of information structure in Spanish are well-summarized in Bildhauer (2007) as well. Yet, the present study has little interest in them, because the main purpose of the current work is to create a grammar library for information structure in the LinGO Grammar Matrix system. The system is built for text-based processing, and has not yet reflected phonological information in a significant manner. It is left to the future research to implement prosodic rules in Japanese, Korean, Spanish, and other languages.

8.4 Sample derivations

This section provides sample derivations, which briefly show how information structure works with ICONS in several different types of languages. The languages that this section presents are English, Japanese, Korean, and Russian. The type of the ICONS-KEY value of a constituent, which points to an element of the ICONS list, can be constrained by (i) accents responsible for information

8.4 Sample derivations

structure meanings, (ii) lexical rules attaching information structure marking morphemes, (iii) particles like Japanese *wa* combining as heads or modifiers with NPs, and/or (iv) phrase structure rules corresponding to distinguished positions.

8.4.1 English

Pitch accents primarily serve to express information structure meanings in English as shown in (35).

(35) a. The DOG barks.
      b. The **dog** barks.

In other words, English imposes a constraint on the A and B accents. In the current work, they are hypothetically realized as suffixes (e.g. *-a*, *-b*), whose lexical rules are provided in (37a–b). That is, (35a–b) are actually encoded into *The dog-a barks.* and *The dog-b barks.* respectively as an input string for parsing and an output string from generation.

UT|DTE, adapted from Bildhauer (2007), aims to calculate focus projection in Chapter 11 (Section 11.2). The current work gives the value of UT|DTE a coreference with that of MKG|FC, because focus projection is not always licensed by prosodic means across languages (Choe 2002). This means that MKG|FC is responsible for spreading the focus domain to larger phrases, and the value should be the same value as the value of UT|DTE in English.

(36) *lex-rule* →
$$\begin{bmatrix} \text{UT} \mid \text{DTE} & \boxed{1} \\ \text{MKG} \mid \text{FC} & \boxed{1} \end{bmatrix}$$

Next, (37a–b) are the lexical rules for A and B accents. Each of their PA values, taken from Bildhauer's hierarchy (14), stands for H* and L+H* in the ToBI format, respectively. MKG for the A-accent is valued as *fc-only* and accordingly UT|DTE is also valued as +. MKG for the B-accent has *tp*, whose FC remains underspecified and has a structure-sharing with UT|DTE. Because A and B accents indicate which information structure meaning is being conveyed in a fairly direct way, they add *semantic-focus* and *contrast-or-topic* into the list of ICONS. Note that the value of MKG|FC and its co-indexed value of DTE are only related to the marking of information structure, and that a plus value does not necessarily indicate a focused meaning. In other words, [MKG|FC +] indicates only F(ocus)-marking, not focus-meaning.[15]

---

[15] A head type *+nv* in (37a) refers to a disjunctive head type for nouns and verbs.

8 Individual CONStraints: specifics of the implementation

(37) a. *fc-lex-rule* →
$$\begin{bmatrix} \text{UT} \mid \text{DTE} & + \\ \text{PA} & \textit{high-star} \\ \text{MKG} & \textit{fc-only} \\ \text{INDEX} & \boxed{1} \\ \text{ICONS-KEY} & \boxed{2} \\ \text{C-CONT} \mid \text{ICONS} & \left\langle ! \boxed{2} \begin{bmatrix} \textit{semantic-focus} \\ \text{TARGET } \boxed{1} \end{bmatrix} ! \right\rangle \\ \text{DTR} & \begin{bmatrix} \text{HEAD} +nv \end{bmatrix} \end{bmatrix}$$

b. *tp-lex-rule* →
$$\begin{bmatrix} \text{UT} \mid \text{DTE} & \textit{luk} \\ \text{PA} & \textit{low-high-star} \\ \text{MKG} & \textit{tp} \\ \text{INDEX} & \boxed{1} \\ \text{ICONS-KEY} & \boxed{2} \\ \text{C-CONT} \mid \text{ICONS} & \left\langle ! \boxed{2} \begin{bmatrix} \textit{contrast-or-topic} \\ \text{TARGET } \boxed{1} \end{bmatrix} ! \right\rangle \\ \text{DTR} & \begin{bmatrix} \text{HEAD } \textit{noun} \end{bmatrix} \end{bmatrix}$$

Building upon these rules, (35a) in which DOG bears the A-accent for expressing *semantic-focus* is constructed as (38). The corresponding MRS and dependency graph are presented in (39). The utterance forms a clause, and the clausal type (i.e. *declarative-clause* imposing [SF *prop-or-ques*]) is inherited by the phrase structure type (i.e. *head-subj-phrase*). Applying the constraint on *clause* presented before, the CLAUSE-KEY of the NP *the dog* points to the INDEX of the HEAD-DTR (i.e. the verb *barks*). The TARGET of the NP is co-indexed with its INDEX, and the CLAUSE is co-indexed with the INDEX of the verb. The TARGET and CLAUSE of *barks* is recursively linked. Each value in the *diff-list* of ICONS is collected into higher phrases.

8.4 Sample derivations

(38)
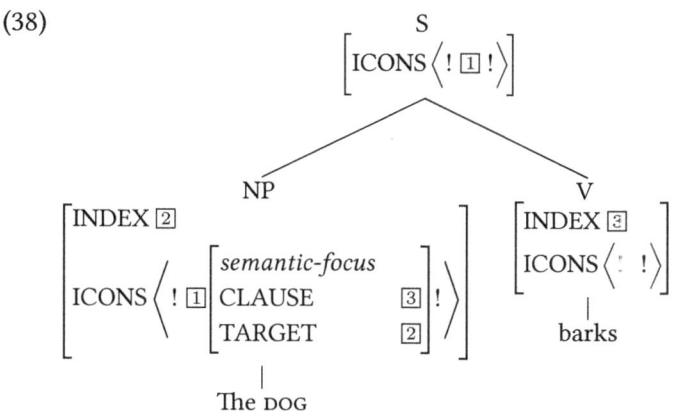

(39) a.
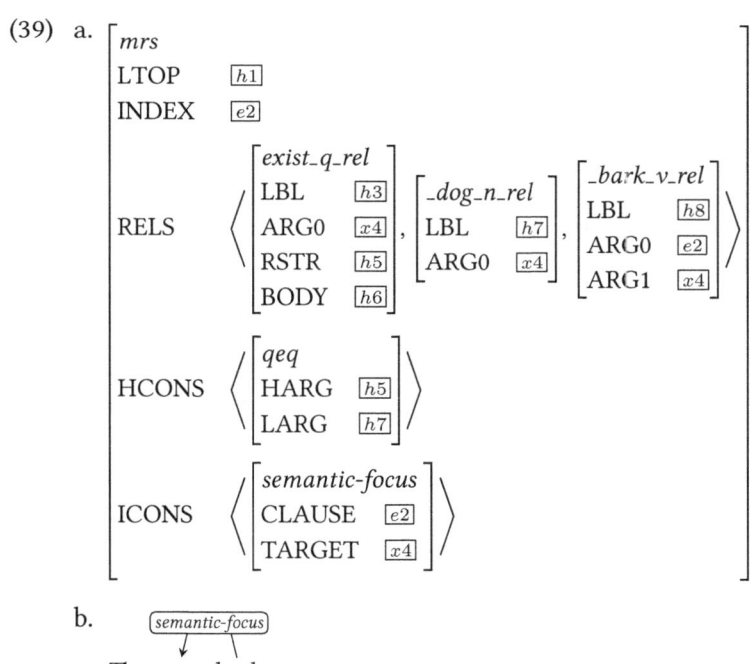

b. The DOG barks.
(with semantic-focus arrow pointing to DOG)

8.4.2 Japanese and Korean

In Japanese and Korean, the distinction between lexical markers (i.e. *ga* vs. *wa* in Japanese and *i / ka* vs. *-(n)un* in Korean) is responsible for delivering several different meanings with respect to information structure. Note that case-marking NPs in Japanese and Korean do not always correspond to A-accented NPs in

8 Individual CONStraints: specifics of the implementation

English: NPs with *ga* in Japanese or *i* / *ka* in Korean basically involve *non-topic*. On the other hand, A-accented NPs in English are straightforwardly interpreted as possessing semantic (i.e. non-contrastive) focus.

(40) a. inu ga hoeru.
   dog NOM bark
  b. inu wa hoeru.
   dog WA bark
   'The dog barks.' [jpn]

(41) a. kay-ka cic-ta.
   dog-NOM bark-DECL
  b. kay-nun cic-ta.
   dog-NUN bark-DECL
   'The dog barks.' [kor]

In Japanese, *ga* and *wa* are treated as adpositions, following the convention in Jacy (Siegel, Bender & Bond 2016). The information structure value that the null marker assigns to constituents is in line with Yatabe (1999). As for the null marker ∅, the grammar developed here uses a lexical rule (in `lrules.tdl` of the core of LinGO Grammar Matrix).[16] Although this is different from Yatabe's proposal (the null marking system as particle ellipsis), I agree with Yatabe's argument regarding the information structure meaning of null-marked constituents in Japanese (and Korean). Yatabe claims that *ga* cannot be dropped when the *ga*-marked expression is focused, which implies that null-marked phrases (mostly NPs) should be evaluated as containing *non-focus*. The AVMs for them are provided in (42). Note that the values of MKG are not coreferenced with anything, and the element of ICONS specifies the relation of the complement, not of the adposition itself.

---

[16] This instance can be a daughter of a unary rule (i.e. *bare-np-phrase*) which promotes the word to a phrase.

8.4 Sample derivations

(42) a. nom-marker →
$$\begin{bmatrix} \text{STEM} & \langle ga \rangle \\ \text{CASE} & nom \\ \text{ICONS-KEY} & \boxed{2} \\ \text{MKG} & unmkg \\ \text{COMPS} & \langle [\text{INDEX } \boxed{1}] \rangle \\ \text{ICONS} & \langle ! \boxed{2} \begin{bmatrix} non\text{-}topic \\ \text{TARGET } \boxed{1} \end{bmatrix} ! \rangle \end{bmatrix}$$

b. wa-marker →
$$\begin{bmatrix} \text{STEM} & \langle wa \rangle \\ \text{ICONS-KEY} & \boxed{2} \\ \text{MKG} & tp \\ \text{COMPS} & \langle [\text{INDEX } \boxed{1}] \rangle \\ \text{ICONS} & \langle ! \boxed{2} \begin{bmatrix} contrast\text{-}or\text{-}topic \\ \text{TARGET } \boxed{1} \end{bmatrix} ! \rangle \end{bmatrix}$$

c. null-lex-rule →
$$\begin{bmatrix} \text{INDEX} & \boxed{1} \\ \text{ICONS-KEY} & \boxed{2} \\ \text{MKG} & unmkg \\ \text{C-CONT | ICONS} & \langle ! \boxed{2} \begin{bmatrix} non\text{-}focus \\ \text{TARGET } \boxed{1} \end{bmatrix} ! \rangle \end{bmatrix}$$

The sample derivation for (40a), in which *inu* 'dog' is combined with *ga* to indicate *non-topic*, is illustrated in (43).[17] The corresponding MRS representation is given in (44a), and the graphical version is in (44b).

---

[17] In HPSG-based analyses for syntactic configuration in Japanese, PPs are important. That means the case markers (e.g. *ga* for nominatives), the *wa* marker, and a null-marker are adpositions that take the NPs that they are attached to as the complement, and constitute PPs. The reason why the combination between NPs and the markers should be PPs in Japanese has been already explained in several previous HPSG-based studies (Gunji 1987; Siegel 1999; Yatabe 1999).

8 Individual CONStraints: specifics of the implementation

(43)

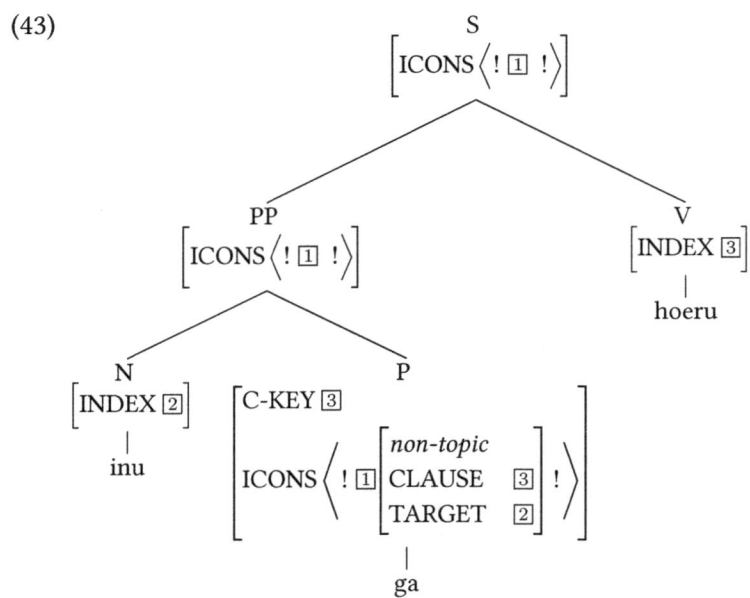

(44) a.

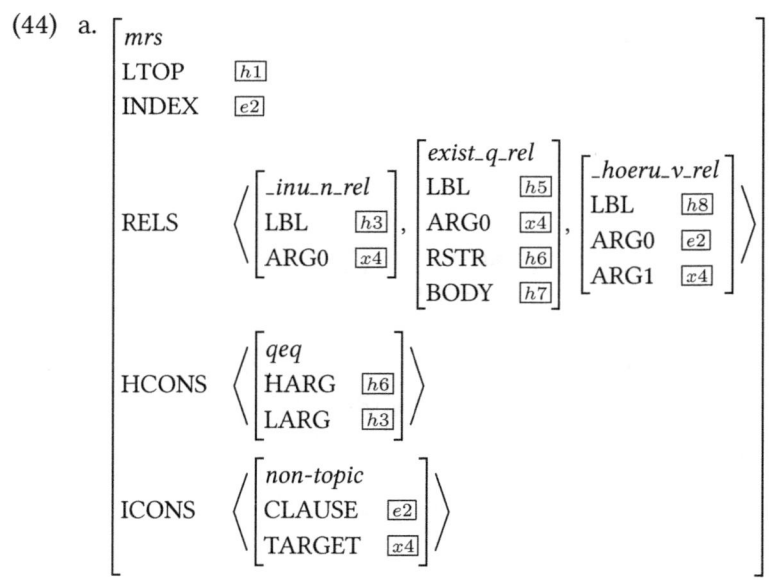

b. inu ga hoeru.
   dog NOM bark

   (non-topic scope over inu ga)

8.4 Sample derivations

The CLAUSE-KEY of the nominative marker *ga* is identified with its own ICONS-KEY|CLAUSE. Second, when the *head-comp-phrase* combines *inu* and *ga*, the ICONS-KEY|CLAUSE of *inu* is identified with the CLAUSE-KEY of *ga*. The ICONS-KEY of *ga* is passed up to the mother (Semantic Inheritance Principle).[18] When the *head-subj-phrase* combines *inu ga* and *hoeru*, the ICONS-KEY|CLAUSE of the subject *inu ga* is identified with the INDEX of *hoeru*.

With respect to Korean, the present study basically assumes that the marking systems (e.g. *wa* or *(n)un*-marking, case-marking, and null-marking) in Japanese and Korean share the same properties in terms of information structure, given that counterexamples to this assumption are very rare.[19] Despite similarity the resulting phrase structures in Korean have been analyzed differently from those in Japanese. In a nutshell, *ga* and *wa* in Japanese are dealt with as words, whereas *i / ka* and *-(n)un* in Korean are treated as suffixes. Because postpositions are crucially employed in the building blocks of a clause in most analyses of Japanese syntax (Sato & Tam 2012), the combination between nouns and these markers (e.g. *ga, wa,* etc.) forms a PP, rather than an NP. Kim & Yang (2004), in contrast, regard the lexical markers in Korean (e.g. *i / ka, -(n)un*, etc.) as affixes, rather than adpositions.[20] That means that the combination between nouns and their markers still remains as an NP. The present analysis respects the two different analyses of these languages. Technically speaking in the context of grammar engineering, the adpositions *ga* and *wa* in Japanese are treated as independent lexical entries, while the morphemes *i / ka* and *-(n)un* in Korean are dealt with by lexical rules. Accordingly, the derivation of an NP plus *i / ka* or *-(n)un* is created at the lexical level. The inflectional rules are as follows.

---

[18] "The CONTENT value of a phrase is token-identical to that of the head daughter." (Pollard & Sag 1994: 48)

[19] One counterexample in which *wa* and *-(n)un* show different behavior is reported in some Japanese dialects. For example, the Tokyo dialect does not show any difference from Korean with respect to using topic markers, but the Kansai dialect sometimes makes a subtle difference in *wa*-marking from *(n)un*-marking in Korean.

[20] Another approach to Korean postpositions is given in Ko (2008), who insists that Korean postpositions should be analyzed as clitics attaching to either the preceding lexical item or weak syntactic heads sharing syntactic feature values of the complement phrase.

8 Individual CONStraints: specifics of the implementation

(45) a. *nom-lex-rule* →
$$\begin{bmatrix} \text{INFOSTR-FLAG} & + \\ \text{CASE} & \textit{nom} \\ \text{MKG} & \textit{unmkg} \\ \text{INDEX} & \boxed{1} \\ \text{ICONS-KEY} & \boxed{2} \\ \text{C-CONT} \mid \text{ICONS} & \left\langle !\,\boxed{2}\begin{bmatrix} \textit{non-topic} \\ \text{TARGET}\,\boxed{1} \end{bmatrix}!\right\rangle \\ \text{DTR} & \begin{bmatrix} \text{INFOSTR-FLAG} & - \end{bmatrix} \end{bmatrix}$$

b. *nun-lex-rule* →
$$\begin{bmatrix} \text{INFOSTR-FLAG} & + \\ \text{CASE} & \textit{case} \\ \text{MKG} & \textit{tp} \\ \text{INDEX} & \boxed{1} \\ \text{ICONS-KEY} & \boxed{2} \\ \text{C-CONT} \mid \text{ICONS} & \left\langle !\,\boxed{2}\begin{bmatrix} \textit{contrast-or-topic} \\ \text{TARGET}\,\boxed{1} \end{bmatrix}!\right\rangle \\ \text{DTR} & \begin{bmatrix} \text{INFOSTR-FLAG} & - \end{bmatrix} \end{bmatrix}$$

c. *null-lex-rule* →
$$\begin{bmatrix} \text{INDEX} & \boxed{1} \\ \text{ICONS-KEY} & \boxed{2} \\ \text{MKG} & \textit{unmkg} \\ \text{C-CONT} \mid \text{ICONS} & \left\langle !\,\boxed{2}\begin{bmatrix} \textit{non-focus} \\ \text{TARGET}\,\boxed{1} \end{bmatrix}!\right\rangle \end{bmatrix}$$

Note that they are in complementary distribution. They share the same slot in the morphological paradigm. Additionally, *null-lex-rule* is required to constrain information structure of null-marked constituents.[21] Though the markers represented in (45) are realized as inflectional rules in the morphological paradigm, the values of MKGs in Korean are identical to those in Japanese, and the elements on the ICONS lists are the same as the values of COMPS|ICONS-KEY in Japanese. Altogether, the analysis of Korean sentences is syntactically similar to those in English, and informatively similar to those in Japanese. The sample derivation

---
[21]Note, incidentally, that (45c) for Korean is the same as (42c) for Japanese.

for (41b), in which the (n)un-marked *kay* 'dog' is associated with *contrast-or-topic*, is sketched out in (46a). The graphical representation is also shown in (46b).

(46) a.

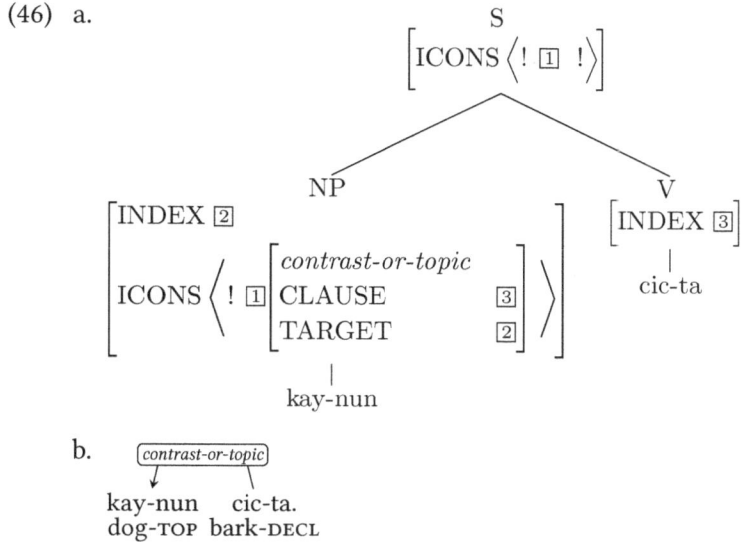

b. kay-nun cic-ta.
    dog-TOP bark-DECL
    [contrast-or-topic]

8.4.3 Russian

Russian employs its relatively free word order to mark focus with clause-final constituents bearing non-contrastive focus (Neeleman & Titov 2009). Notably, constituents in situ can also convey focus meaning, if they involve a specific prosody for expressing focus. Thus, in (47a) in the basic word order, the focus can fall on either the subject *sobaka* or the verb *laet*, or both (i.e. *all-focus*). This is because Russian also employs prosody to signal focus. This could be modeled by methods similar to those we have use for English. Nonetheless, for ease of explanation, we will limit our current focus to syntactic position.

(47) a. Sobaka laet.
        dog   bark
        'The dog barks.'
    b. Laet sobaka.
        bark dog
        'The DOG barks.' [rus]

Headed rules can have subtypes which handle information structure differently, resolving the type of an ICONS element or leaving it underspecified. For example, the Russian allosentences of (47) are instances of *head-subj-phrase*, but the first one (*sobaka laet*), in which the subject is in situ, is licensed by a subtype that does not resolve the ICONS value, while the second one (*laet sobaka*), in which the subject is marked through being postposed, is licensed by a different one which does. Hence, the subject *in-situ* is specified as *info-str* (i.e. underspecified), whereas the postposed subject is specified as *focus*. Consequently, (47a–b) are graphically represented as follows.

(48)   a.   sobaka laet.   b.   *focus*
             dog   bark   laet sobaka.
                                 bark dog

In order to construct a derivation tree for (47b) whose word order is not neutral, it is necessary to implement several additional devices: an additional flag feature [INFOSTR-FLAG *luk*], a unary phrase structure rule *narrow-focused-phrase*, and *head-subj-phrase* (i.e. a counterpart of the ordinary one *subj-head-phrase*). First, the flag feature INFOSTR-FLAG is immediately under SYNSEM like L/R-PERIPH and LIGHT.[22] This feature serves to indicate whether the current phrase is information structure-marked and includes an ICONS element. *Narrow-focused-phrase* takes only a constituent with [INFOSTR-FLAG −] as its daughter, assigns [INFOSTR-FLAG +] to itself, and introduces an *focus* element into the C-CONT|ICONS.[23] Finally, *head-subj-phrase* in Russian inherits from both *basic-head-subj-phrase* and *head-initial*. It takes a constituent that has both [INFOSTR-FLAG +] and [R-PERIPH +] as its non-head-daughter. These indicate that the subject is marked for information structure and that no constituent can be further attached to the right. Recall that L-PERIPH and R-PERIPH are outside of SYNSEM. Thus, the R-PERIPH value of *head-subj-phrase* is still underspecified (i.e. *luk*), which allows the phrase to serve as the head-daughter when combined with a peripheral frame-setter.

---

[22] Although they are housed in the same position, not all languages use INFOSTR-FLAG, while L/R-PERIPH and LIGHT are commonly used in human language. Thus, this flag feature is not included in the basic *synsem*.

[23] Using C-CONT|ICONS for further constraining information structure values may raise one question. Given that ICONS is an accumulator list, like RELS and HCONS, some lexical rules and phrase structure rules that contribute a new *info-str* object can end up with more than one *info-str* object for the same CLAUSE/TARGET combination. This can be instantiated with Korean examples, although the rules are irrelevant to C-CONT. In Korean, there are some lexical markers in Korean that participate in information structure; for example, *kay-man-un* 'dog-ONLY-NUN'. In this NP, *man* adds one value into the ICONS list, and then *un* adds another. This latent problem in the functionality of using the ICONS list needs to be resolved in further study.

8.4 Sample derivations

Narrow-focused-phrase and *head-subj-phrase* are represented in the following AVMs. The derivation tree for (47b) is sketched out in (50).

(49) a.
$$\begin{bmatrix} \textit{narrow-focused-phrase} \\ \text{INFOSTR-FLAG} & + \\ \text{INDEX} & \boxed{1} \\ \text{ICONS-KEY} & \boxed{2} \\ \text{HD} \mid \text{INFOSTR-FLAG} & - \\ \text{C-CONT} \mid \text{ICONS} & \left\langle ! \boxed{2} \begin{bmatrix} \textit{focus} \\ \text{TARGET} \boxed{1} \end{bmatrix} ! \right\rangle \end{bmatrix}$$

b.
$$\begin{bmatrix} \textit{head-subj-phrase} \\ \text{NHD} \begin{bmatrix} \text{INFOSTR-FLAG} + \\ \text{R-PERIPH} + \end{bmatrix} \end{bmatrix}$$

(50)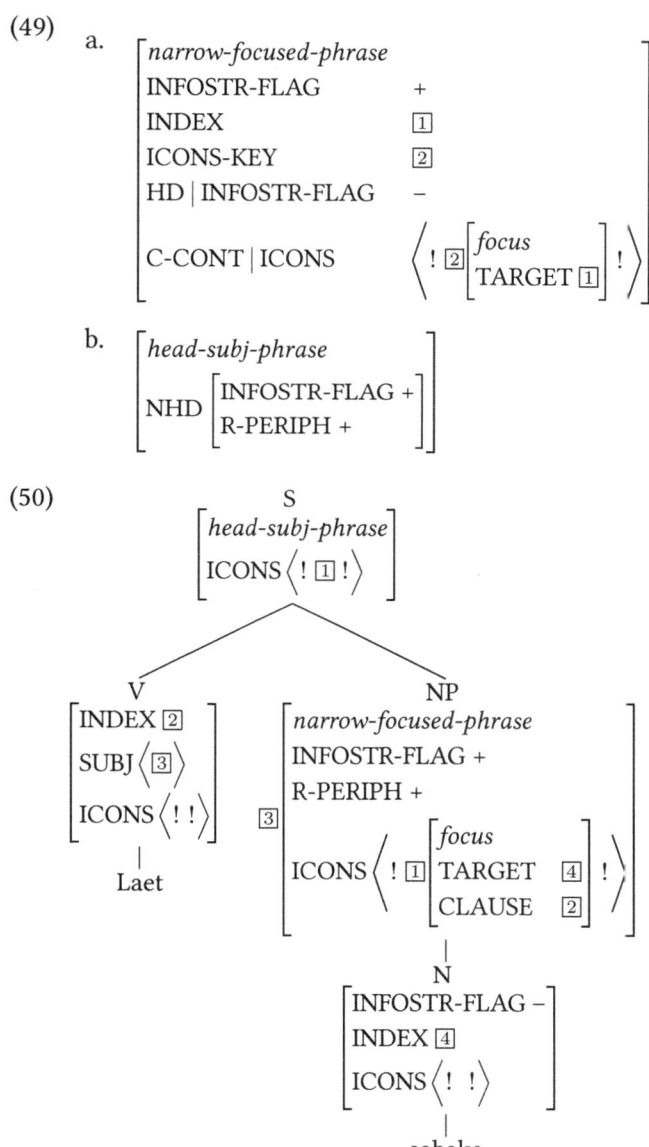

8 Individual CONStraints: specifics of the implementation

8.5 Summary

This chapter has discussed specifics of implementing ICONS into lexical and phrasal types for constraining information structure. Lexical types inherit from one of four potential types of *icons-lex-item*: *no-icons-lex-item*, *basic-icons-lex-item*, *one-icons-lex-item*, and *two-icons-lex-item*. Both *no-icons-lex-item* and *basic-icons-lex-item* have an empty ICONS list, and *no-icons-lex-item* is additionally [MKG [FC *na*, TP *na*]]. This constraint indicates that lexical entries which inherit from *no-icons-lex-item* cannot be marked with respect to information structure; for instance, relative pronouns, expletives, etc. Nominal items normally inherit from *basic-icons-lex-item*, while inheritance for verbal items is determined by how many clauses are subordinated to the verbal item. Adpositions and determiners inherit from either *basic-icons-lex-item* or *one-icons-lex-item*, adverbs inherit from *basic-icons-lex-item*, and syncategorematic items inherit from *no-icons-lex-item*. Conjunctions may or may not introduce a *topic* value into ICONS depending on which type of adverbial clauses they involve. The values of CLAUSE are identified when *basic-head-subj-phrase* is constructed. *Basic-head-mod-phrase-simple* and *head-filler-phrase* have some extra constraints to specify which element is linked to which clause. There are three additional constraints for elaborating on properties of information structure: L/R-PERIPH, LIGHT, and PHON. L/R-PERIPH constrain the clause-initial/final positioning of constituents, and likewise LIGHT is used for constraining preverbal and postverbal constituents. PHON is included in `matrix.tdl` of the core of LinGO Grammar Matrix for use in future work with acoustic resolution systems.

9 Multiclausal constructions

As discussed previously, one of the main motivations for using ICONS (Individual CONstraints) is to capture binary relations across clauses. This chapter looks into how the relations between matrix clauses and non-matrix clauses are represented via ICONS. Since ICONS is a way of representing a relation between an individual and a clause that the individual belongs to, it is necessary to identify the relation between two clauses in a single sentence. This chapter also looks at the restrictions non-matrix clauses have with respect to information structure. Many previous studies argue that information structure in non-matrix clauses is differently formed from that in matrix clauses. For example, according to Kuno (1973), *wa* in Japanese is seldom used in relative clauses. Similarly, (1a) indicates that English normally disallows left dislocation in relative clauses.

(1) a. *A man who your book$_i$ could buy it$_i$.

 b. Un uomo che, il tuo libro$_i$, lo$_i$ potrebbe comprare.
 A man who, your book, could buy it. [ita] (Rizzi 1997: 306)

However, this restriction is language-specific. Embedded clauses in some languages exhibit properties of root clauses as shown in (1b). Furthermore, Haegeman (2004) argues that topic fronting can occur in non-root clauses even in English under certain circumstances, such as adversative clauses, *because* clauses, and sometimes conditional clauses. This restriction is related to so-called embedded root phenomena (Heycock 2007). While a root clause is most simply defined as a clause that is not embedded, there exist some counterexamples to such a definition. It is known that root phenomena have an effect on the appearance of topics in embedded clauses. For instance, Portner & Yabushita (1998) insist that topic should only be interpretable with the wide scope on the root clause. OSV word order constructions in English and *wa*-marking in Japanese typically exhibit a root effect in that they tend not to appear in non-root clauses.

Non-matrix clauses can be roughly classified into at least three types. These are complement clauses (Section 9.1), relative clauses (Section 9.2), and adverbial clauses (Section 9.3). Each section in this chapter looks into linguistic factors that

9 Multiclausal constructions

have an influence on information structure in each clausal type, and provides an HPSG/MRS-based analysis of the clausal type.

9.1 Complement clauses

The issues that this section addresses include how components of information structure are constituted in complement clauses, and how assignment of information structure values is conditioned in different complement clauses. Dependency graphs in (2) show the basic mechanism of indexing between TARGETs and CLAUSEs in multiclausal constructions. In accordance with the AVMs presented hitherto, (2a–c) are the representations of a sentence *Kim thinks that the dog barks*. In (2a), the subject in the matrix clause is B-accented, and the subject in the embedded clause is A-accented. Hence, they are assigned *contrast-or-topic* and *semantic-focus*, respectively (p. 160). The arc from the main verb *thinks* to the verb in the embedded clause *barks* comes from the lexical information of the main verb, which inherits from *one-icons-lex-item*. That is, *thinks* has one inherent element on its ICONS list, which links its own INDEX to INDEX of *barks*.[1]

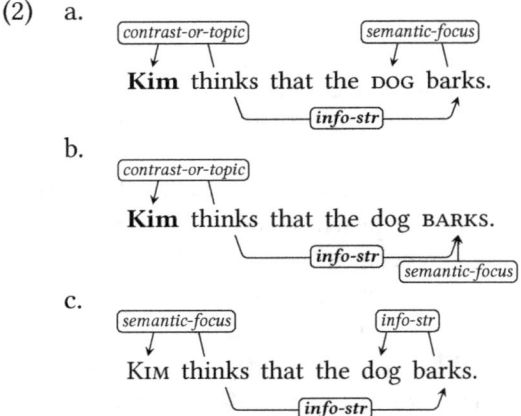

9.1.1 Background

Topic can sometimes occur in complement clauses, largely depending on the characteristics of the predicate in the main clause. The properties that license top-

---

[1]These underspecified *info-str* elements are not fully desirable. An analysis that allows specific ICONS elements relating the two clauses but does not entail inserting these underspecified ones is left for future work.

9.1 Complement clauses

ics to appear in complement clauses include speech acts, semi-factives, and quasi-evidentials (Roberts 2011). Maki, Kaiser & Ochi (1999) argue that topic fronting in embedded clauses in English and appearance of *wa* in embedded clauses in Japanese commonly exhibit four characteristics as given in (3).[2]

(3) a. Embedded topicalization is possible in complement clauses of bridge verbs (e.g. *believe*, *sinziteiru* 'believe').

 b. Embedded topicalization is possible in interrogative clauses.

 c. Embedded topicalization is impossible in complement clauses of factive verbs (e.g. *regret*, *kookaisiteiru* 'regret') and noun-complement clauses.

 d. Embedded topicalization is impossible in an adjunct clause and in a sentential subject. (Maki, Kaiser & Ochi 1999: 8–10)

Heycock (2007), in a similar vein, elaborates on cases in which embedded clauses have a root function. According to Heycock's analysis, the main criterion to distinguish whether sentential subjects/complements exhibit root phenomena or not is assertion. In other words, whether a topic can occur in subordinate clauses is influenced by whether the subordinate clause is asserted. A five-way division of predicates is offered as follows.

(4) a. Class A predicates (e.g. "say", "report", "be true", "be obvious"). The verbs in this group are all verbs of saying. Both the verbs and the adjectives in this group can function parenthetically, in which case the subordinate clause constitutes the main assertion of the sentence. It is claimed however that if the subordinate clause occurs in subject position (as in, e.g. "*That German beer is better than American beer is true*") it is not asserted.

 b. Class B predicates (e.g. "suppose", "expect", "it seems", "it appears"). In this group also the predicates can function parenthetically, and in this case the subordinate clause is asserted. The distinction between this group and Group A is not made entirely clear, although it is noted that Class B predicates allow "Neg raising" and tag questions based on the subordinate clause.

---

[2]In the previous studies, topic-marking (also known as topicalization) and meaning of topic seem to be used without distinction. Nonetheless, we can say that topic can be marked even in embedded clauses and the topic-marked constituents can be potentially interpreted as conveying topic meaning.

9 Multiclausal constructions

   c. Class C predicates (e.g. "be (un)likely", "be (im)possible", "doubt", "deny") have complements which are not asserted.

   d. Class D predicates (e.g. "resent", "regret", "be odd", "be strange"); these factive predicates have complements which are argued to be presupposed, and hence not asserted.

   e. Class E predicates (e.g. "realize", "know"); these semifactives (factives that lose their factivity in questions and conditionals) have a reading on which the subordinate clause is asserted. (Heycock 2007: 189)

Based on the division presented in (4), complement clauses may or may not contain a topicalized phrase, depending upon whether the predicate of the matrix clause belongs to Class A, B, or E.

Moreover, contrastive topic can relatively freely appear in embedded clauses. Bianchi & Frascarelli (2010) examine embedded topicalization in English. In short, their conclusion is that a contrastive topic (C-Topics in their terminology) interpretation is readily available within complement clauses. In other words, although the complement clauses are not endowed with assertive force, an interpretation of contrastive topic is acceptable by native speakers. This claim shows a similarity to the analysis of (n)un-marked phrases in Korean relative clauses (Section 3.3.3.2). If -(n)un appears in relative clauses as presented below, the (n)un-marked constituent is evaluated as containing a contrastive meaning (Lim 2012).

   (5) hyangki-nun coh-un   kkoch-i   phi-n-ta.
       scent-NUN   good-REL flower-NOM bloom-PRES-DECL
       'A flower with a good scent blooms.' [kor] (Lim 2012: 229)

9.1.2 Analysis

Two restrictions are factored into constraining information structure in complement clauses.

First, topic fronting can happen even in embedded clauses. Some languages, such as Italian, do not impose any restriction on topic fronting in embedded clauses (Roberts 2011). Even in languages which have such a restriction (e.g. English, Japanese, and Korean), constituents can be topicalized in embedded clauses if the constituents carry a contrastive meaning as shown in (5). The topicalized constituents in complement clauses would have to be evaluated as containing *contrast-topic* in my intuition. At least in English, Japanese, and Korean, the clear-cut distinction between contrastive topics and non-contrastive topics does not matter in generating sentences, because the meaning difference between them is not marked in surface forms. One potential problem can be found in languages which employ different marking systems for contrastive topics and non-contrastive topics. Recall that Vietnamese uses *thì* for expressing contrastive topics but not for marking non-contrastive topic (Nguyen 2006).[3]

Second, if the main verb is one of the members of verbs of saying (*say*), semi-factive verbs (*realize*), and quasi-evidential verbs (*it appears*), the complement clause can be asserted, and thereby the structural relation between main and complement clauses is normally (but not always) specified as *focus*. Otherwise, the complement clause has an underspecified relation (i.e. *info-str*) to its matrix clause(s).

For instance, since the main verb *appears* in (6) is quasi-evidential, it has an arrow to *read* in complement clauses, whose value is specified as *focus*. Note that the syntactic subject *it* is an expletive (i.e. semantically and informatively vacuous), and does not have any information structure relation to the clause.[4]

(6) It appears that Kim read the books.
    _____focus_____/

Appears in (6), accordingly, has the following structure.

(7) $\begin{bmatrix} \text{STEM} & \langle appears \rangle \\ \text{CLAUSE-KEY} & \boxed{1} \\ \text{COMPS} & \langle [\text{INDEX} \ \boxed{2}] \rangle \\ \text{ICONS} & \langle \begin{bmatrix} focus \\ \text{TARGET} \ \boxed{2} \\ \text{CLAUSE} \ \boxed{1} \end{bmatrix} \rangle \end{bmatrix}$

9.2 Relative clauses

Which information structure value is assigned to the head noun modified by relative clauses? The behaviors of information structure shown by relative clauses

---

[3] Topic-marking systems in embedded clauses in Vietnamese-like languages need to be further examined in future work.
[4] There could be some counterexamples to this analysis. Further work will examine the full range of information structure relations that complement clauses have to their main clauses.

9 Multiclausal constructions

have been analyzed from three points of view in previous literature: (i) Relative clauses assign topic to their modificands or the relative pronouns (Kuno 1976; Bresnan & Mchombo 1987; Jiang 1991; Bjerre 2011). (ii) Relative clauses do not always give a topic meaning to the head NPs (Ning 1993; Huang, Li & Li 2009). (iii) Relative clauses signal focus on the head nouns (Schachter 1973; Schafer et al. 1996). This subsection examines each perspective, and offers a new approach to the information structure properties that relative clauses have in relation to their relativized constituents.[5]

9.2.1 Background

First, Bresnan & Mchombo (1987) and Bjerre (2011) claim that relative pronouns indicate a topic function, as stated before. For convenience sake, the analysis that Bresnan & Mchombo provide is shown again below.

(8) The car [which you don't want ___] is a Renault.
            TOPIC   OBJ

                                        (Bresnan & Mchombo 1987: 757)

Bjerre (2011) provides a similar analysis to (8). This analysis is presented in an example (9) in Danish. Bjerre, making use of clefting as a tool to diagnose focus, claims that (9b), which has a clefted relative pronoun *den*, is of dubious acceptability. Whereas (9a), in which an interrogative pronoun *hvem* is clefted, sounds normal. Recall that focus and topic are mutually exclusive in the present study.

(9) a. Som   komponist   er   det   naturligvis   vigtigt,
        as   composer   is   it   of course   important
        at   lytterne   ved,
        that listeners.DEF know
        hvem det er der har skrevet den musik,
        who   it   is   there has written   that music
        de   lytter   til.
        they listen to
    'As a composer it is of course important that the listeners know who it is that has written the music they are listening to.'

---

[5] A deeper details of analyzing information structure of relative clauses is provided in Song (2014).

b. | ???Som | komponist | er | det | naturligvis | vigtigt,
   | as | composer | is | it | of course | important
   | at | lytterne | kender
   | that | listeners.DEF | know
   | **den** | musik | hvilken | det | er | der | lyttes | til.
   | **that** | music | which | it | is | there | listen.PRS.PAS | to
   'As a composer it is of course important that the listeners know that music which it is that is listened to.' [dan] (Bjerre 2011: 279)

However, attempts to apply their approach to the current work are blocked by three key issues. Two of them are related to distributional properties of relative pronouns, and the other is related to system-internal factors. The first and the most important problem is that relative pronouns do not necessarily exist in all human languages. Japanese and Korean, for example, do not have relative pronouns, and relative clauses in these languages are constructed in a different way (Baldwin 1998; Kim & Park 2000). If relative pronouns were universally to be evaluated as bearing the topic function, all relative clauses in Korean and Japanese would be topicless constructions. A second issue is that relative pronouns can be missing in some circumstances even in English (e.g. those corresponding to object nouns in restrictive readings). Since English is not a topic dropping language (e.g. Chinese, Japanese, Korean, etc.), the dropped relative pronouns would therefore be rather difficult to explain with respect to information structure. Lastly, as hypothesized in Section 7.2.4, relative pronouns are syncategorematic and their lexical type inherits from *no-icons-lex-items* which has an empty list of ICONS. Hence, relative pronouns within the current work cannot participate in building up the list of ICONS, though they can perform a role in signaling information structure values on their heads and/or dependents.

The first two problems posed above may be (partially) resolved by the following constraint (Bresnan & Mchombo 1987: 19f). That is to say, when there is no relative pronoun, relativized constituents would play the same role.

(10) The thematic constraint on relative clauses: A relative clause must be a statement about its head noun. (Kuno 1976: 420)

Kuno provides several examples in Japanese and English to verify (10). First of all, Kuno argues (11a) is derived from not (11b) but (11c), in which *sono hon* 'the book' occurs sentence-initially with the topic marker *wa* to signal the theme (i.e. topic in the present study). Recall that the constituent associated with aboutness

9 Multiclausal constructions

topic usually shows up in the initial position in Japanese (Maki, Kaiser & Ochi 1999; Vermeulen 2009).

(11) a. [Hanko-ga yonda] hon
Hanako-NOM read book
'The book that Hanako read'

b. [Hanko-ga sono hon-o yonda] hon
Hanako-NOM the book-ACC read book

c. [[sono hon-wa]theme Hanko-ga yonda] hon
the book-WA Hanako-NOM read book [jpn] (Kuno 1976: 419)

At first glance, the explanation about the linguistic phenomena presented above sounds reasonable. It seems clear that relative clauses present certain constraints on information structure. Yet, it is still necessary to verify whether the head nouns modified by relative clauses always and cross-linguistically carry the meaning of topic. Several previous studies present counterarguments to (10).

Huang, Li & Li (2009), from a movement-based standpoint, basically accepts that topics and relative clauses share some characteristics with *wh*-constructions as A'-movement structures. The common properties notwithstanding, they argue that relative clause structures are not derived from topic structures for two reasons, contra Kuno (1976). First, a topic relation does not license a relative construction in Chinese. For instance, if a topic structure were sufficient for relativization in Chinese, (12b) and its relativized counterpart (12c) would be equally acceptable.

(12) a. yiwai fasheng-le
accident happen-LE
'An accident happened.'

b. tamen, yiwai fasheng-le
they accident happen-LE
'(As for) them, an accident happened.'

c. *[[yiwai fasheng-le de] neixie ren]
accident happen-LE
textscde those person
'the people such that an accident happened' [cmn] (Huang, Li & Li 2009: 212–213)

9.2 Relative clauses

In other words, Kuno's claim (10) is not cross-linguistically true. Second, Ning (1993) reveals that a relativized construction may be well-formed even though its corresponding topic structure is ill-formed. Thus, the well-formedness of a topic structure is neither necessary nor sufficient for the acceptability of a corresponding relative structure at least in Mandarin Chinese.

Schachter (1973) probes into the relationship between focus constructions (e.g. clefts) and restrictive relative constructions, and concludes that they bear a striking likeness to each other. On the basis of the findings from four languages including English, Akan, Hausa, and Ilonggo (an Austronesian language spoken in the Philippines), Schachter sets up a hypothesis: both constructions syntactically necessitate the promotion of a linguistic item from an embedded clause into the main clause, and semantically involve foregrounding (i.e. making a specific part of a sentence conspicuous at the expense of the rest). The following examples in Akan [aka] and Ilonggo [hil] show that constructions involving relative clauses and focus constructions are structurally quite similar to each other.

(13) a. àbòfrá áà   míhúù nó
       child that I.saw him
       'a child that I saw'

   b. àbòfrá nà   míhúù nó
      child that I.saw him
      'It's a child that I saw.' [aka] (Croft 2002: 108)

   c. babayi nga nag-   dala sang   bata
      woman that AG.TOP- bring NONTOP child
      'the woman that brought a child'

   d. ang babayi and nag-   dala sang   bata
      TOP woman TOP AG.TOP- bring NONTOP child
      'It was the woman who brought a child' [hil] (Croft 2002: 108)

One difference between (13a) and (13b) is which marker (i.e. a relative marker vs. a focus marker) is used. As exemplified earlier in Section 4.2, *nà* in (13b) behaves as a focus marker in Akan, and is in complementary distribution with a relative marker *áà* in (13a). The same goes for (13c) and (13d) in Ilonggo. The relative marker *nga* and the second topic marker *ang* share the same position to draw a boundary between the promoted NP and the relative clause or the cleft clause.

The structural similarity notwithstanding, we cannot conclude from the given examples that the head nouns of relative clauses always bear the focus function.

9 Multiclausal constructions

We cannot even say that a structural likeness is equal to likeness of information structure meaning. There are certainly formal similarities between cleft constructions and relative clauses, but these do not necessarily imply a corresponding similarity in information structure meanings.

9.2.2 Analysis

In sum, there are opposing arguments about the information structure properties assigned to the head nouns of relative clauses. Thus, it is my understanding that it is still an open question whether relative clauses assign their head nouns a focus meaning or a topic meaning. Moreover, previous studies show that the relation could ultimately be language-specific. The present study does not rush to create a generalization and instead allows a flexible representation: The information structure values of the constituents modified by relative clauses should be *focus-or-topic*, which is the supertype of both *focus* and *topic* within the hierarchy of *info-str* (Figure 7.1). This means that the relativized constituents can be evaluated as delivering either focus in some cases or topic. In the present framework then, information structure in constructions involving relative clauses is analyzed analogously to focus/topic fronting constructions (Section 10.6). The preposed constituents in focus/topic fronting constructions carry ambiguous meanings but for the help of contextual information, and because of this they have to be flexibly specified as *focus-or-topic*. The same motivation goes for relativized constituents.

The present analysis also highlights the difference between restrictive readings and non-restrictive readings of relative clauses with respect to the *info-str* values they assign.

First, restrictive relative clauses and non-restrictive relative clauses have been regarded as having different linguistic behaviors in most previous work. To begin with, there is an orthographic convention in English of setting off non-restrictive relatives with commas, and not using commas for ordinary restrictive relatives.[6] Syntactically, it has been stated that the distinction between restrictive readings vs. non-restrictive ones yields different bracketing as presented in (14). The restrictive relative clause in (14a) modifies the head noun *dog* itself, and then the entire NP *dog which Kim chases* is combined with the determiner as *head-spec-phrase*. In contrast, the non-restrictive relative clause in (14b) modifies the NP

---

[6]The use of comma is just a convention in writing style, rather than a mandatory requirement for a non-restrictive reading. That is, even though the comma does not appear before (and after) a relative clause, we cannot say that the relative is necessarily restrictive until the contextual information is clearly given. In the present study, commas are inserted just for ease of comparison.

9.2 Relative clauses

in which the noun *dog* takes the determiner beforehand. They also show contrastive syntactic behavior in binding of anaphora (Emonds 1979), co-occurrence with NPIs (e.g. *any*), and focus sensitive items (e.g. *only*) (Fabb 1990).

(14) a. [[The [dog that Kim chases]] barks.]

b. [[[The dog,] which Kim chases,] barks.]

Semantically, they may not share the same truth-conditions.

(15) a. Kim has two children that study linguistics.

b. Kim has two children, who study linguistics.

(15b) implies that Kim has two and only two children, while (15a) does not. For example, if Kim has three children, the proposition of (15b) would not be felicitously used, whereas that of (15a) may or may not be true depending on how many children among them study linguistics. Given that restrictive and non-restrictive relative clauses exhibit different properties in semantics as well as syntax, it is a natural assumption that they behave differently with respect to information structure as well.

Beyond the general properties that restrictive relative clauses and non-restrictive relative clauses have, there is a distributional reason for viewing them differently with regard to their information structure.

(16) a. Kim chases the dog that likes Lee.

b. Kim chases the dog, which likes Lee.

c. Kim chases the dog, and it likes Lee.

d. Kim chases the dog, and as for the dog, it likes Lee.

e. Kim chases the dog, and speaking of the dog, it likes Lee.

Unlike restrictive relative constructions such as (16a), non-restrictive constructions such as (16b) can be paraphrased into (16c–e). (16c) reveals that non-restrictive relatives are almost equivalent to coordinated clauses which clearly involve root phenomena (Heycock 2007: 177). In (16c), a pronoun *it* is used as referring to *the dog* in the previous clause, which means *the dog* cannot receive *focus* from

9 Multiclausal constructions

the non-restrictive clause in (16b). The focused constituents in the non-restrictive clause should be either the object *Lee* or the VP *likes Lee*. Finally, the relative clauses in (16d–e) conclusively pass the test for aboutness topic.

In sum, the semantic head of relative clauses (i.e. the verb in relative clauses) basically has a *focus-or-topic* relation with relativized dependents. Non-restrictive relatives additionally have a more specific constraint; *aboutness-topic*. The schema of those constraints is exemplified in the following dependency diagrams. The information structure relations between *dog* and the verb in the main clause *barks* are underspecified in these diagrams, because for now there is no additional clue for identifying the relations (e.g. through the A/B-accents).

(17) a. The dog that Kim chases barks. *[focus-or-topic]*

b. The dog, which Kim chases, barks. *[aboutness-topic]*

Because *aboutness-topic* is a subtype of *focus-or-topic* all relative clauses can be understood as inheriting from rel-clause as defined in (18).

(18) $\begin{bmatrix} \text{rel-clause} \\ \text{HD} \mid \text{INDEX} \; \boxed{1} \\ \text{NHD} \mid \text{CLAUSE-KEY} \; \boxed{2} \\ \text{C-CONT} \mid \text{ICONS} \begin{bmatrix} \text{focus-or-topic} \\ \text{TARGET} & \boxed{1} \\ \text{CLAUSE} & \boxed{2} \end{bmatrix} \end{bmatrix}$

Note that the information structure relation that the relativized NPs have to the relative clauses should be constructionally added using C-CONT, because the meaning is specified at the phrasal level. The phrase structure type responsible for non-restrictive relative clauses requires us to impose a more specific value (i.e. *aboutness-topic*). This is left to future work.

9.3 Adverbial clauses

Adverbial clauses in the current analysis may be evaluated as having a relation of either *topic* or just the underspecified value *info-str* with respect to the main

9.3 Adverbial clauses

clauses. The choice depends on the type of subordinating conjunction and the details are elaborated in the subsections below.[7]

9.3.1 Background

Several previous studies investigate conditional *if*-clauses and temporal *when*-clauses with respect to topichood. Haiman (1978) argues that conditionals are topics, and Ramsay (1987) also argues that *if/when* clauses are endowed with topichood when they precede the main clauses. Implicit in these claims is the argument that *if/when* clauses differ in their information structure depending on whether they are at the beginning, at the end, and in the middle of an utterance. Traditional movement-based studies account for variation in conditional and temporal clauses in terms of the so-called Adjunct Island Constraint (Huang 1982): Postposed conditional and temporal clauses are adjoined to VPs forming an adjunct island, while preposed ones are moved into IP's specifier position (Iatridou 1991) or generated in situ (Taylor 2007). In other words, preposed adverbial clauses modify the main sentence, while postposed ones modify the VP.

Consequently, conditional and temporal clauses have a topic feature when they are sentence-initial. Following this line of reasoning, the present work assumes that topic is associated with preposed conditional and temporal clauses with respect to the main clauses. Syntactically, because they appear in the sentence-initial position and their function is to restrict the domain of what the speaker is talking about, they are understood as *frame-setting* as presented in Figure 7.3 (p. 125). With respect to sentence-final/internal conditional and temporal clauses, their information structure relation to the main clause parsimoniously remains underspecified.

9.3.2 Analysis

Before analyzing adverbial clauses, it is necessary to look at the information structure relationship between adverbs and their clauses. Frame-setters, as discussed previously, have several restrictions: (i) they normally appear initially, (ii) they can multiply occur in a single clause, and (iii) they should play a role in restricting the domain of what the speaker is talking about (e.g. spatial, temporal, manner, or conditional). First, the clause-initial constraint can be conditioned by

---

[7]Using this strategy, subordinating conjunctions sometimes introduce an underspecified *infostr* element into ICONS like verbal items that take clausal complements (Section 9.1).These underspecified elements are disadvantageous as mentioned in the first footnote of the current chapter, and a revised analysis in future work will suppress this problem.

9 Multiclausal constructions

[L-PERIPH +], which renders the constituents left-peripheral. The second constraint can be enforced by *sform*, as presented in Chapter 7, namely *frame-setting* vs. *non-frame-setting*. The third constraint is potentially controversial, because information about lexical semantics has not yet been included into the DELPH-IN reference formalism. Future work would then reference lexical semantic information to identify whether a given adverb conveys a spatial, temporal, or manner meaning.[8]

The combination of a frame-setting adverb with the rest of sentence should be carried out using a specific subtype of *head-mod-phrase*, meaning that *head-mod-phrase* needs to be divided into at least two subtypes; one requiring [L-PERIPH +] of its NON-HEAD-DTR, and the other requiring [L-PERIPH −] of both daughters. The former imposes an *info-str* constraint on the NON-HEAD-DTR. Thereby, the sentence-initial adverb *today* in (19) has a *topic* relation to the main verb *barks*.

(19) Today the dog barks.
     ↖──[topic]──↗

Note that the mother node of *frame-setting* has an underspecified value for L-PERIPH (i.e. [L-PERIPH *luk*]). Thus, *today the dog barks* with the frame-setter *today* can serve as the head-daughter of another *frame-setting* construction, such as *At home today the dog barks*. In this analysis, each frame-setter (e.g. *at home* and *today*) has its own *topic* relation to the verb.

In Japanese and Korean, *wa* and *-(n)un* can be attached to adjuncts. If they are adjacent to adjuncts, the constituents are normally evaluated as bearing contrastiveness. If an adjunct is combined with *wa* or *-(n)un*, the adjunct should be associated with *contrast*, even when it appears in the leftmost position. Consequently, *kyoo* 'today' in the left-peripheral position has a plain *topic* relation, while *kyoo-wa* 'today-wa' has a *contrast-topic* relation to the verb *hoeru* 'bark'.

(20) kyoo (wa) inu ga hoeru.
     today (WA) dog NOM bark
     'Today, the dog barks.' [jpn]

(21) a.   b.

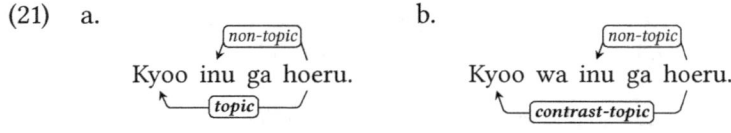

---

[8]There is some on-going research which seeks to incorporate lexical semantic information within DELPH-IN grammars using WordNets (Bond et al. 2009; Pozen 2013).

9.3 Adverbial clauses

Regarding adverbial clauses, my argument is that subordinating conjunctions are responsible for the information structure relation between adverbial clauses and main clauses. First of all, subordinating conjunctions that entail temporal and conditional clauses signal *topic* (Haiman 1978; Ramsay 1987), as discussed above. Other subordinating conjunctions assign an underspecified *info-str* value, because there seems to be no clear distinction of information structure status. Causal conjunctions, such as *because* in English and *weil* in German, do not show consistency in information structure (Heycock 2007), which means there is no lexical and phrasal clue to identify the information structure relations.[9] It is even less clear how concessive conjunctions, such as *(al)though*, configure information structure, though they are known to be partially related to information structure (Chung & Kim 2009). They are also provisionally treated as underspecified in this analysis. Some conjunctions with multiple meanings, such as *as*, are also assumed to assign an underspecified value, because we cannot clearly identify the associated information structure meanings in the absence of contextual information.

(22) when-subord →
$$\begin{bmatrix} \text{STEM} & \langle when \rangle \\ \text{ICONS-KEY} & topic \end{bmatrix}$$

All subordinate conjunctions have one *info-str* value on their ICONS list. However, they do not inherit from any *icons-lex-item* presented in Chapter 7. This is because in this case TARGET should point to the semantic head (usually a verb) of the adverbial clause, rather than the conjunction itself, and also because the CLAUSE is readily and lexically identified to be the INDEX of the main clause. The following AVM presents this co-indexation.

(23)
$$\begin{bmatrix} \textit{subconj-word} \\ \text{HEAD} \mid \text{MOD} & \langle [\text{INDEX} \; \boxed{1}] \rangle \\ \text{VAL} \mid \text{COMPS} & \langle [\text{INDEX} \; \boxed{2}] \rangle \\ \text{ICONS} & \langle !\, \begin{bmatrix} \text{TARGET} & \boxed{2} \\ \text{CLAUSE} & \boxed{1} \end{bmatrix} \,! \rangle \end{bmatrix}$$

---

[9] The meaning could be clear by a specific prosodic pattern, like intonation.

9 Multiclausal constructions

As a consequence, adverbial clauses have the information structure relation to the main clauses exemplified in (24). The arrows from *reads* to *barks* at the bottom are created by (23). The value *topic* on the arrow of (24a) is specified in (22). In addition, the arrow of (24b) is specified as merely *info-str*, since the subordinate conjunction is devoid of any similar constraint.

(24) a. When the dog barks, Kim reads the book.
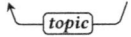

b. Because the dog barks, Kim reads the book.
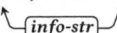

9.4 Summary

This chapter has addressed how information structure in multiclausal utterances is represented via ICONS and what kinds of constraints are imposed on non-matrix clauses. There are three types of non-matrix clauses that this chapter explores: complement clauses, relative clauses, and adverbial clauses. First, the information structure relation between matrix clauses and their complement clauses largely depends on the verbal type of the main predicate. In particular, if the predicate serves to invoke an assertion regarding the complement clause, the complement clause has a *focus* relation to the main clause. Second, information structure relations between head nouns and associated relative clauses depend on the reading of the particular relative clauses. If the relative is restrictive, the head nouns are assigned a *focus-or-topic* interpretation by the relative clauses. Otherwise, they are assigned the more specific type *aboutness-topic*. Third, information structure in adverbial clauses is influenced by the position of the clauses and the type of conjunction. If the adverbial clause is temporal or conditional and appears sentence-initially, it is assigned a *topic* interpretation. Other adverbial clauses are preferentially underspecified.

10 Forms of expressing information structure

This chapter looks into specific forms of expressing information structure in human language. Every language presumably has one or more operations for articulating information structure. The operations are strategized sometimes at the lexical level by employing specific lexical items or rules, and sometimes at the phrasal level by using special constructions. Section 10.1 goes over focus sensitive items, and presents how they are represented in the articulation of information structure via ICONS (Individual CONStraints). Section 10.2 deals with argument optionality from the perspective that focus is defined in terms of whether or not a constituent is omissible (i.e. optionality). The remaining portion of the chapter addresses specific constructions related to forming information structure. Section 10.3 probes scrambling behaviors in Japanese and Korean, which are deeply related to the arrangement of information structure components. Section 10.4 delves into cleft constructions, which are the most well known operation for expressing focus in an overt way. Section 10.5 explores passive constructions which play a role in structuring of information in some languages. Lastly, Section 10.6 and Section 10.7 investigate two types of syntactic operations which are seemingly similar to each other, but are constructed differently: focus/topic fronting and dislocation.

10.1 Focus sensitive items

Lambrecht (1996) provides several intriguing explanations concerning the lexical properties of focus sensitive items. First, emphatic reflexives cannot involve a topic interpretation, because they are usually focused in the sentence. Second, NPIs (e.g. *any* in English) and negative words (e.g. *not, never, no, nobody, nothing*, and so forth in English) cannot play a topic role, for the same reason, either. This means that some lexical categories, such as reflexives, NPIs, and negative words, are inherently incompatible with the topic role. Nonetheless, focus sensitive items do not all share the same properties. Rather, there are two subtypes of words with an inherent focus meaning. The nominal elements, such as *anybody*, *nobody*, and *nothing*, are focus-sensitive by themselves. In contrast, negative modifiers such as *any*, *not*, *never*, and *no* assign a focus relation not to themselves, but to the constituent they modify. Henceforth, I call the former Type I, and the latter Type II.

(1) a. Focus Sensitive Type I assigns an information structure role (either *non-topic* or *focus*) to itself.

b. Focus Sensitive Type II assigns such a role to its adjacent constituent.

Type I includes *nothing*, *nobody*, etc. These lexical items are contentful, introducing an EP into the list of RELS. Their lexical constraint is inherited from *one-icons-lex-item*, and additionally the TARGET of the element on their ICONS list is co-indexed with their INDEX. Lexical items under Type II also inherit from *one-icons-lex-item*, but their TARGET is co-indexed with the INDEX of their modificands. For instance, a lexical entry for *only* (Type II) can be described as (2).

(2) *only* →

$$\begin{bmatrix} \text{STEM} \langle only \rangle \\ \text{HEAD} \mid \text{MOD} \left\langle \begin{bmatrix} \text{INDEX} & \boxed{1} \\ \text{ICONS-KEY} & \boxed{2} \end{bmatrix} \right\rangle \\ \text{CONT} \mid \text{ICONS} \left\langle ! \boxed{2} \begin{bmatrix} \textit{contrast-focus} \\ \text{TARGET} & \boxed{1} \end{bmatrix} ! \right\rangle \end{bmatrix}$$

Regarding the *info-str* value that *only* assigns to its modificands, it is specified as *contrast-focus* in that *only* has an exhaustive effect (Velleman et al. 2012).

The current analysis of the focus sensitive particle *only* leaves one central issue, which has to be left to further research. *Only* in English needs not be adjacent to the focused item that it is associated with. For example, in the following sentence, *only* has an information structure relation to KIM inside of the VP (A-accented).

(3) He only introduced KIM to Lee.

The current constraint presented in (2) cannot handle this particular relation. I leave it it to a future study to find a way to link two non-adjacent individuals with respect to information structure.

10.1 Focus sensitive items

10.1.1 Quantifiers

Quantifiers exhibit focus-sensitivity. In particular, Lambrecht (1996) argues that universally quantified NPs can be used as topics, whereas other quantified NPs cannot, as exemplified in (4).

(4) a. As for all his friends, they ...

 b. *As for some people, they ... (Lambrecht 1996: 156)

That implies that non-universally quantifying determiners, such as *some*, assign *non-topic* to the head as represented in (5).

(5) *some* →
$$\begin{bmatrix} \text{STEM} & \langle some \rangle \\ \text{VAL} \mid \text{SPEC} & \langle [\text{ICONS-KEY} \quad non\text{-}topic] \rangle \end{bmatrix}$$

In (4b), what is responsible for putting an *info-str* element into the ICONS list is *as for* when we are not using the hypothetical suffixes *-a* and *-b*. In this case, the *info-str* value of the element is *topic*, the TARGET of the element is co-indexed with the INDEX of *people*, and the element itself is co-indexed with the ICONS-KEY of *people*. However, the ICONS-KEY of *people* is already constrained as *non-topic* by (5). Because this value is inconsistent with the *topic* value introduced by *as for*, *as for some people* is ruled out.

10.1.2 *Wh*-words

Wh-questions, as has been stated many times so far, have been employed as a tool to probe the meaning and markings of focus: a technique which looks quite reliable from a cross-linguistic stance. *Wh*-words have often been regarded as inherently containing a focus meaning. That is to say, in almost all human languages, *wh*-words share nearly the same distributional characteristics with focused words or phrases in non-interrogative sentences.

A typological implication is provided in Drubig (2003: 5): In a language with *wh*-phrases ex situ, the *wh*-phrase usually appears in focus position. This typological argument is convincingly supported by several previous studies in which the linguistic similarity of *wh*-words to meaning and marking of focus is addressed. According to Comrie (1984) and Büring (2010), Armenian is a language with strict focus position: Focused constituents should appear in the immediately

10 Forms of expressing information structure

preverbal position (as exemplified earlier in Section 4.3.1.3). Tamrazian (1991) and Megerdoomian (2011) argue that focused elements and *wh*-words in Armenian show a striking similarity to each other from various points of view. Tellingly, *wh*-words and focused constituents cannot co-occur, because they occupy the same syntactic position. In other words, *wh*-words should occur in the focus position in Armenian (i.e., in complementary distribution).

(6) a. ov   a   Ara-in həravir-el?
        who AUX/3SG.PR Ara-DAT invite-PERF
        'Who has invited Ara'

   b. *ov Ara-in   a   həravir-el?
        who Ara-DAT AUX/3SG.PR invite-PERF [hye]

   c. *Ara-in a   ov həravir-el?
        Ara-DAT AUX/3SG.PR who invite-PERF [hye] (Megerdoomian 2011)

According to the analysis of Ortiz de Urbina (1999), *wh*-words in Basque are also in complementary distribution with focused constituents in that both of them occupy the immediately preverbal position, optionally preceded by a constituent with topic meaning, and seldom occur in embedded clauses. Recall that the canonical position of focused items in Basque is preverbal as exemplified in Section 4.3.1.3 (p. 61). From a transformational perspective, Ortiz de Urbina (1999) argues that *wh*-words and focused items are able to undergo cyclic movement with bridge verbs.

From these linguistic facts and analyses, the present study assumes that *wh*-words are inherently focused items which always have a *focus* relation with the clause that they belong to. The linguistic constraint on *wh*-words is represented as the following AVM. Note that *wh*-words are focus sensitive items under Type I (*one-icons-lex-item*). The TARGET is co-indexed with its INDEX.

(7) $\begin{bmatrix} \textit{wh-words} \\ \text{INDEX} & \boxed{1} \\ \text{ICONS-KEY} & \boxed{2} \\ \text{ICONS} & \left\langle !\boxed{2}\begin{bmatrix} \textit{semantic-focus} \\ \text{TARGET} & \boxed{1} \end{bmatrix}! \right\rangle \end{bmatrix}$

(7) illustrates two more features of *wh*-words. First, as investigated in Gryllia (2009) *wh*-questions are incompatible with contrastive focus. The value of ICONS

10.1 Focus sensitive items

should therefore be specified as *semantic-focus*. However, this does not necessarily imply that the answer to a given *wh*-question will itself have *semantic-focus*. As discussed in Chapter 3 (Section 3.4.4), the answerers may alter information structure in a solicited question as they want, because contrastiveness is heavily speaker-oriented (Chang 2002). The (*n*)*un*-marked *Kim-un* in (44) delivers a contrastive meaning, but the answer does not directly correspond to the question's information structure. Instead, the replier manipulates information structure in order to attract a special attention to *Kim*. In other words, *wh*-words themselves are still assigned *semantic-focus* irrespective of the information structure of the subsequent response.

(8) Q: nwuka o-ass-ni?
    who   come-PST-INT
    'Who came?'

A: Kim-un   o-ass-e.
   Kim-NUN come-PST-DECL
   'Kim came.'
   (conveying "I know that at least Kim came, but I'm not sure whether or not others came.") [kor]

On the other hand, functionally speaking, there are two types of interrogatives; informational questions and rhetorical questions. The former explicitly solicits the hearer's reply, while the latter does not. Since rhetorical questions perform a function of expressing an assertion in a strong and paradoxical manner, their interpretation naturally hinges on the context. For example, (9a) can be ambiguously read as either an informational question or a rhetorical question, and each reading can be paraphrased as (9b–c), respectively. That means the *wh*-elements in rhetorical questions function like a trigger to derive the form of interrogative sentences, but they can also convey quantificational readings as implied by *nobody* in (9c). In other words, it is true that *wh*-words convey focus meaning in *wh*-questions, but not in all the sentential forms in which they might appear.

(9) a. Who comes?

   b. I'm wondering which person comes.

   c. Nobody comes.

10 Forms of expressing information structure

Do all *wh*-questions sound ambiguous (at least in English)?[1] We know that in actual speech they do not. This is because the meaning becomes unambiguous depending on where the accent is assigned as illustrated in (10), in which the A-accent falls on different words.

(10) a. WHO comes?
 ≈ I'm wondering which person comes.

b. Who COMES?
 ≈ Nobody comes.

Informational questions, in order to clarify the meaning of an assertion, employ an ordinary intonation pattern (i.e. rise-fall), whereas rhetorical questions involve pitch accent within the intonation contour (Gunlogson 2001). In other words, the prosodic marking for information structure (i.e. intonation contour driven by pitch accent) has an influence on the interpretation of *wh*-questions. Note that *comes* in (10a) can be eliminated, while both *who* and COMES are inomissible in (10b). The focus in (10b) comes from the accented verb COMES and spreads to the whole sentence (i.e. all-focus), whereby it forms a different information structure from that of (10a).

If a *wh*-question is rhetorically used, the entire sentence is in the focus domain. For example, if *Who comes?* is not asked rhetorically, its information structure can be represented as (11a). The verb *comes* in (11a) has *bg*, which implies that *Who* exclusively bears a focus relation in the sentence. In contrast, if the question is rhetorically used, the sentence should be informatively structured as (11b), in which the verb *comes* also has a *focus* relation within the clause (i.e. *all-focus*). Since the choice between them is only contextually conditioned, in an approach to grammar engineering that represents ambiguity via underspecification wherever possible, the MRS (Copestake et al. 2005) representing *Who comes?* has to be able to subsume (11a–b). Given that the lowest supertype of *bg* and *focus* is *non-topic*, *wh*-questions should be analyzed as (11c).[2]

---

[1] At the level of compositional semantics, rhetorical questions may not have to be considered in linguistic modeling, because they are basically a pragmatic phenomenon. What I want to say here is that other sentential constituents in *wh*-questions can be focused, and this needs to be taken into account in modeling *wh*-questions in a flexible way.

[2] *Non-topic* on *comes* in (11c) should be introduced by a specific phrase structure rule to constrain *wh*-questions with respect to information structure. A creation of phrase structure rules for interrogative sentences is left to future work.

10.2 Argument optionality

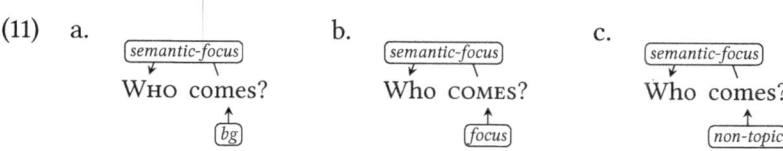

10.1.3 Negative expressions

Negation is sensitive to focus (Partee 1991; Krifka 2008). For example, negative quantifiers (e.g. *no*), replacing sentential negation (e.g. *not ..., but ...*), and some other constructions including negation such as *neither ...* are associated with focus almost invariably. However, we cannot say negative verbs are assigned *focus* all the time. For example, in the following Q/A pair, the focused element should be the subject KIM. The rest of the reply can be elided in the context.

(12) Q: Who didn't read the book?

    A: KIM (didn't read the book).

For this reason, the present analysis argues that the value that negative operators assign to operands is that of *non-topic*, which can be further resolved to *focus* or *bg* depending on context.

10.2 Argument optionality

Argument-optionality (also known as *pro*-drop, including subject-drop and topic-drop) has been assumed to be related to information structure. A basic explanation of the relationship between dropped elements and articulation of information structure is provided in Alonso-Ovalle et al. (2002), with special reference to subject-dropping in Spanish. Additionally, the distinction between subject-drop and topic-drop has also been studied in Li & Thompson (1976), Huang (1984) and Yang (2002) (as discussed in Section 3.2.3.1). Argument-optionality is also crucial in computational linguistics; in multilingual processing, such as (multilingual) anaphora resolution and machine translation (Mitkov, Choi & Sharp 1995; Mitkov 1999), as well as in monolingual processing, such as syntactic parsing and semantic interpretation. Just as with other subfields of language processing, there are two approaches to resolve dropped elements within language applications: First, several rule-based algorithms have been designed to resolve zero anaphora in *pro*-drop languages.[3] Second, there are several (semi-)machine-learning methods

---

[3] These are provided in Han (2006), Byron, Gegg-Harrison & Lee (2006), and so on.

to compute zero anaphora in topic-drop languages for the purpose of machine translation.[4]

In the present study, I use optionality and omissibility as synonyms. Whether an argument can be elided or not needs to be augmented into an analysis of argument optionality with respect to focality. As discussed thus far, the most noteworthy feature of focused constituents is their inomissibility. If a constituent is omitted then the constituent is not focused. This restriction can be defined as (13). Note that (13a) entails (13b).

(13) a. C is inomissible iff C is focused.

b. If C is omitted then C is not focused.

For example, Spanish is a subject-drop language. The pronouns are often missing as shown in (14). However, if they have a meaning of *focus*, they have to appear with an accent (Cinque 1977; Lambrecht 1996). Therefore, the dropped subject in (14) should be regarded as *non-focus*.

(14) Ø Habla.
    speaks
    '(He/She/It) speaks.' [spa]

In the Argument Optionality library in the customization system (Saleem 2010; Saleem & Bender 2010), both subject dropping and object dropping are described and modeled. The questionnaire requires that users answer several questions, namely: (i) whether or not subjects/objects can be dropped in the user's language, (ii) whether or not the verb needs to have a marker when the subjects/objects are dropped, (iii) whether or not subject-drop only happens in particular contexts, and (iv) whether or not object-drop is lexically licensed. To these potential constraints, I add one more: Dropped elements are informatively constrained as *non-focus*. This constraint should be written into *basic-head-opt-subj-phrase* and *basic-head-opt-comp-phrase*. These two phrasal types now include some additional constraints on their subjects and complements as follows.

---

[4]These can be found in Zhao & Ng (2007), Yeh & Chen (2004), Kong & Ng (2013), and Chen & Ng (2013) for Chinese, Nakaiwa & Shirai (1996) and Matsui (1999) and Hangyo, Kawahara & Kurohashi (2013) for Japanese, and Roh & Lee (2003) for Korean.

10.2 Argument optionality

(15) a.
$$\begin{bmatrix} \textit{basic-head-opt-subj-phrase} \\ \text{HD} \mid \text{VAL} \mid \text{SUBJ} \quad \left\langle \begin{bmatrix} \text{INDEX} & \boxed{1} \\ \text{ICONS-KEY} & \boxed{2} \\ \text{CLAUSE-KEY} & \boxed{3} \end{bmatrix} \right\rangle \\ \text{C-CONT} \mid \text{ICONS} \quad \left\langle !\boxed{2} \begin{bmatrix} \textit{non-focus} \\ \text{TARGET} & \boxed{1} \\ \text{CLAUSE} & \boxed{3} \end{bmatrix} ! \right\rangle \end{bmatrix}$$

b.
$$\begin{bmatrix} \textit{basic-head-opt-comp-phrase} \\ \text{HD} \mid \text{VAL} \mid \text{COMPS} \quad \left\langle ..., \begin{bmatrix} \text{INDEX} & \boxed{1} \\ \text{ICONS-KEY} & \boxed{2} \\ \text{CLAUSE-KEY} & \boxed{3} \end{bmatrix} \right\rangle \\ \text{C-CONT} \mid \text{ICONS} \quad \left\langle !\boxed{2} \begin{bmatrix} \textit{non-focus} \\ \text{TARGET} & \boxed{1} \\ \text{CLAUSE} & \boxed{3} \end{bmatrix} ! \right\rangle \end{bmatrix}$$

Building upon (15a), the derivation tree for (14) is sketched out in (16).

(16)
$$\begin{array}{c} \text{S} \\ \begin{bmatrix} \textit{head-opt-subj-phrase} \\ \text{SUBJ} \; \langle \, \rangle \\ \text{ICONS} \left\langle ! \begin{bmatrix} \textit{non-focus} \\ \text{TARGET} & \boxed{1} \\ \text{CLAUSE} & \boxed{2} \end{bmatrix} ! \right\rangle \end{bmatrix} \\ | \\ \text{V} \\ \begin{bmatrix} \text{SUBJ} \quad \left\langle \begin{bmatrix} \textit{unexpressed-reg} \\ \text{INDEX} \; \boxed{1} \end{bmatrix} \right\rangle \\ \text{INDEX} \quad \boxed{2} \\ \text{ICONS} \quad \langle !\,! \rangle \end{bmatrix} \\ | \\ \text{Habla} \end{array}$$

195

10 Forms of expressing information structure

10.3 Scrambling

The typical case in which forms of expressing information structure do not coincide with information structure meanings can be found in the use of *wa* in Japanese and *-(n)un* in Korean. NPs in Japanese and Korean, as presented several times, can have three types of marking; case-marking, *wa* or *(n)un*-marking, and null-marking (also known as case ellipsis). These are in complementary distribution with each other, and the choice among them is largely conditioned by information structure.

(17) Kim-ga/wa/Ø   kita.
Kim-NOM/WA/NULL came
'Kim came. [jpn]'

As stated before, *wa* and *-(n)un* can convey meaning of aboutness topic, contrastive topic, or even contrastive focus (H.-W. Choi 1999; Song & Bender 2011).[5] Case markers are also ambiguously interpreted. They have sometimes been assumed to be associated with focus, but there are quite a few counterexamples which show that all case-marked NPs do not necessarily convey focus meaning in all languages (Heycock 1994). Null-marking is also conditioned by information structure in some languages: The markers are not omissible if an NP is associated with *focus*, which means that the null-marked NPs receive an interpretation of either topic or background (i.e. *non-focus*).

Nevertheless, this does not mean that NPs in Japanese and Korean deliver an informatively knotty meaning all the time. The meanings can be disentangled at the phrasal level, mainly via different word orders, such as basic vs. scrambling. Scrambling refers to constructions in which one or two objects are followed by the subject. This construction is productively used in Japanese and Korean (i.e. SOV in the basic order vs. OSV in the scrambled order). Scrambling has been rather discounted as a dummy operation in syntax and semantics, but H.-W. Choi (1999) and Ishihara (2001) argue that scrambling has a strong effect on information structure. The contrast between orders with respect to *wa* is exhibited in the following examples.[6]

---

[5] In this vein, *wa* and *-(n)un* perform the same role as the B-accent in English, which can also be used to express non-contrastive topic, contrastive topic, or sometimes contrastive focus (Hedberg 2006).

[6] There can be one more sentence from this paradigm though Maki, Kaiser & Ochi (1999) do not include it in their source; *Kono hon-o John-wa yonda*, which is completely grammatical, but the *wa*-marked *John* is interpreted as indicating contrastiveness. In order to show the authors' example as is, this sentence is not included in (18).

(18) a. John-wa kono hon-o   yonda.
       John-WA this book-ACC read
       'As for John, he read this book.'

   b. Kono hon-wa John-ga   yonda.
      this book-WA John-NOM read
      'As for this book, John read it.'

   c. John-ga   kono hon-wa yonda.
      John-NOM this book-WA read
      'John read this book, as opposed to some other book.'
      '*As for this book, he read this it.' [jpn] (Maki, Kaiser & Ochi 1999: 7–8)

The first sentence is in the basic word order, in which the subject is topicalized. The second sentence is scrambled, and the fronted object carries a topic meaning (i.e. *contrast-topic*). The third sentence is in the basic word order, but *wa* is attached to the object, not the subject. In that case, the topicalized object should be interpreted as containing contrastiveness (i.e. *contrast-focus*). Regarding the relationship between *wa* or *(n)un*-marking and word-order in Japanese and Korean, Song & Bender (2011) provide Table 10.1, adapted from H.-W. Choi (1999).

Table 10.1: Information structure of *(n)un*-marked NP

	in-situ	scrambling
subject	*topic*	*contrast-focus*
non-subject	*contrast-focus*	*contrast-topic*

According to Table 10.1, the set of allosentences given in (19) have different information structure. In other words, the default meaning of *wa* and -*(n)un* (i.e. *contrast-or-topic*) can be narrowed down, through interaction with word order (e.g. scrambling).

(19) a. Kim wa sono hon o   yomu.
        Kim WA DET book ACC read (*topic*)

   b. sono hon o   Kim wa yomu.
      DET book ACC Kim WA read (*contrast-focus*)

   c. Kim ga   sono hon wa yomu.
      Kim NOM DET book WA read (*contrast-focus*)

10 Forms of expressing information structure

    d. sono hon wa Kim ga yomu.
       DET book WA Kim NOM read (*contrast-topic*) [jpn]

There is one additional property that *wa* and *-(n)un* display: They cannot appear in an *all-focus* construction that allows only *semantic-focus* lacking contrastive meanings, as exemplified in (20).

(20) Q: doushita nano
       what   INT
      'What happened?'

    A: Kim ga/#wa sono hon o/#wa yabut-ta.
       Kim NOM/WA DET book ACC/WA tear-PST
      'Kim tore the book.' [jpn]

In syntactic derivation, *topic-comment* presented below plays an important role in creating grammatical rules. The construction itself is [MKG *tp*] so that constituents which have picked up a topic cannot serve as the head daughter of another *topic-comment* phrase.

(21) $\begin{bmatrix} \textit{topic-comment} \\ \text{L-PEPIPH} & + \\ \text{MKG} & \textit{tp} \\ \text{HD}\,|\,\text{MKG}\,|\,\text{TP} & - \\ \text{NHD} & \begin{bmatrix} \text{MKG} & \textit{tp} \\ \text{L-PERIPH} & + \end{bmatrix} \end{bmatrix}$

The phrasal rules, such as *subj-head-rule* and *comp-head-rule*, are classified into subrules, which inherit from two types of head-phrases (i.e. *subj-head-phrase* and *comp-head-phrase*) and optionally *topic-comment*. This type hierarchy is presented in Figure 10.1, in which there are two factors that have an influence on branching nodes; *wa* or *(n)un*-marking (i.e. *top-*) and scrambling (i.e. *scr-*).

    This tripartite strategy is potentially controversial in that several types of headed rules are introduced. In the spirit of HPSG, reducing the number of rules should be considered in order to avoid redundancy. From this point of view, the six grammatical rules presented in Figure 10.1 might look rather superfluous. Nevertheless, the present model pursues this strategy for several reasons. First, Japanese and Korean are typical topic-prominent languages in which expressing topics plays an important role in configuring sentences (Li & Thompson 1976;

10.3 Scrambling

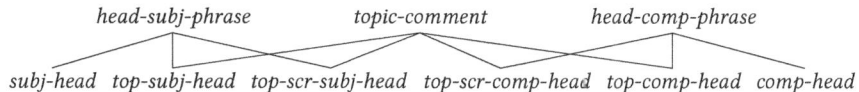

Figure 10.1: Phrase structure rules of scrambling in Japanese and Korean

Sohn 2001). Accordingly, it is my belief that the use of *topic-comment* as one of the major phrase structure types is never ill-conceived in creating Japanese and Korean grammars. Second, if we did not refer to the marking system (i.e. MKG), we would allow too wide an interpretation of scrambled constructions. That is, it would be almost impossible to narrow down the information structure meaning that *wa* and *-(n)un* inherently carry (i.e. *contrast-or-topic*), if it were not for such discrimination. One alternative analysis would be to treat topicalized and scrambled constituents as a *head-filler-phrase*. However, this is poorly suited to handling scrambling. Such a *head-filler*-based analysis predicts the creation of a long-distance dependency (i.e. scrambling across clause boundaries), but such a dependency is unlikely to occur. Furthermore, the basic *head-comp* and *head-subj* properties are still encoded in single types, and these types are cross-classified with others to give the more specific rules. That means that there are no missing generalizations. It seems clear that the tripartite strategy is well-motivated and is the most effective way to manipulate information structure in Japanese and Korean.

More specific information structure values are assigned by each grammatical rule, adding constraints to both HEAD-DTR and NON-HEAD-DTR. For example, *top-scr-subj-head* and *top-scr-comp-head* impose a value on NON-HEAD-DTR as shown in (22).[7]

(22) a. $\begin{bmatrix} \textit{top-scr-subj-head} \\ \text{HD} \mid \text{VAL} \mid \text{COMPS} \langle [\ ] \rangle \\ \text{NHD} \mid \text{ICONS-KEY } \textit{contrast-focus} \end{bmatrix}$

b. $\begin{bmatrix} \textit{top-scr-comp-head} \\ \text{HD} \mid \text{VAL} \mid \text{COMPS} \langle \rangle \\ \text{NHD} \mid \text{ICONS-KEY } \textit{contrast-topic} \end{bmatrix}$

---

[7]ICONS-KEY is doing some valuable work here, because it lets both the phrase structure rules and the lexical rules/entries contribute partial information to the same ICONS element.

10 Forms of expressing information structure

On the other hand, grammatical rules whose NON-HEAD-DTR is non-topicalized (e.g. *subj-head* and *comp-head*) constrain the NON-HEAD-DTR to be [MKG| TP *na-or--*], and the information structure values (i.e. ICONS-KEY) comes from the lexical information provided by case markers (i.e. *non-topic*) and the null marker (i.e. *non-focus*). Consequently, the parse trees and dependency graphs for (19b) and (19d) are illustrated in (23) and (24), respectively.

(23) a.

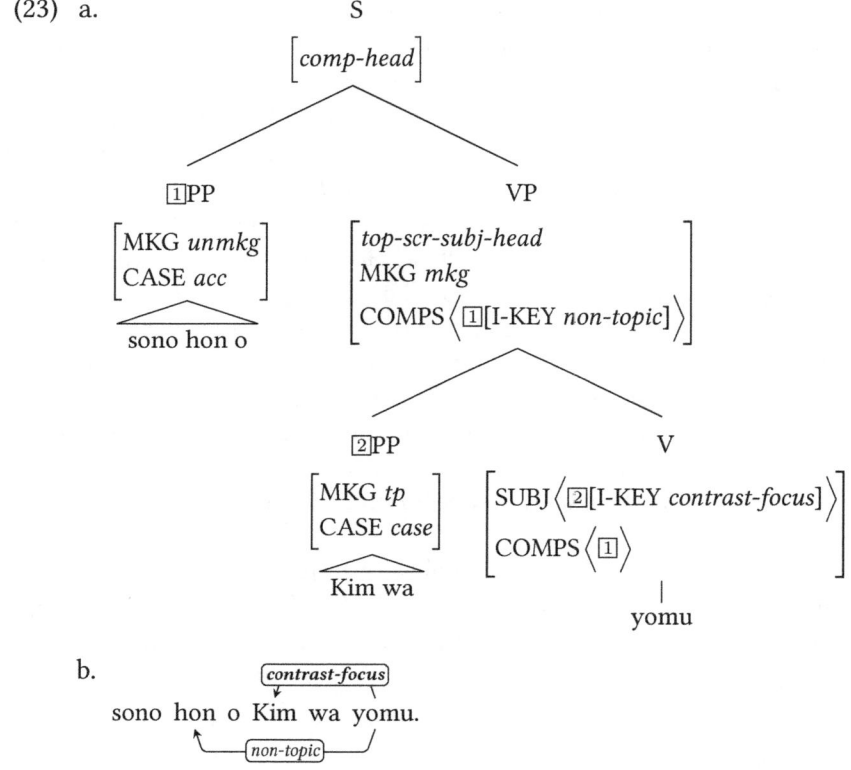

b.

In (23a), the *wa*-marked subject *Kim* is combined with the verb *yomu* 'read'.[8] This combination is an instance of *top-scr-subj-head* which requires [MKG *tp*] of the NON-HEAD-DTR (i.e. *Kim wa*) and assigns *contrast-focus* to the ICONS-KEY of the NON-HEAD-DTR. Since there is no specific constraint on MKG in this phrase structure, the value of MKG remains underspecified (i.e. *mkg*). Next, the VP takes *sono hon o* 'the book' as its complement. Because the fronted object

---

[8] The reason why *sono hon o/wa* and *Kim ga/wa* are labeled as PPs, not NPs is given in Yatabe (1999) and Siegel (1999).

10.3 Scrambling

is not *wa*-marked, its information structure meaning is still represented as *non-topic*, which comes from the case-marking adposition *o* 'ACC'.

(24) a.
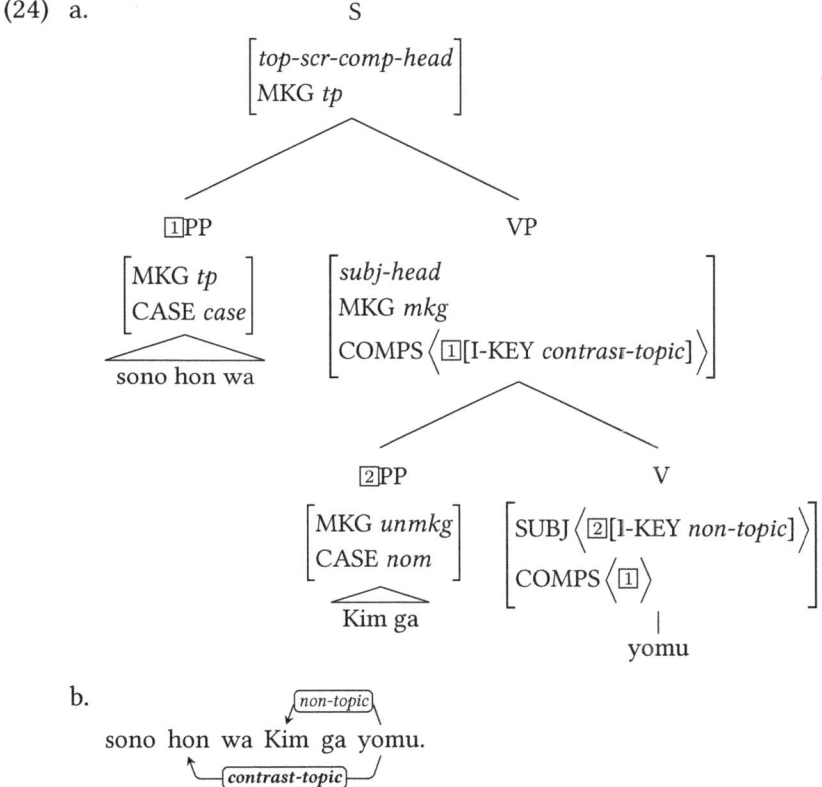

b. sono hon wa Kim ga yomu.

On the other hand, since the scrambled object in (24a) is *wa*-marked, the top node is an instance of *top-scr-comp-head*, which assigns *contrast-topic* to the complement. Thus, topic falls on the object, while the case-marked subject conveys *non-topic*.

To summarize, scrambling in Japanese and Korean has to do with both lexical markers (e.g. *wa* and *-(n)un*) and constraints on *topic-comment*. In order to systematize the different values that scrambled arguments and non-scrambled arguments have with respect to information structure, the present study proposes a tripartite strategy using cross-classification of three phrase structure types: *head-subj-phrase*, *head-comp-phrase*, and *topic-comment*. [MKG tp] is used to control the combination of the different phrase structure rules (and lexical markers) so that the scrambled and non-scrambled versions can be detected and related to their appropriate *info-str* values.

201

10 Forms of expressing information structure

10.4 Cleft constructions

Clefting is a special syntactic operation expressing focus in a marked way. Quite a few languages, including English, have the focus-related syntactic device called cleft constructions. All languages have at least one way to express focus, but it is unlikely that all languages have cleft constructions.

Cleft constructions normally involve relative clauses, which are not yet implemented in the LinGO Grammar Matrix system. For these reasons, clefts are not included within the information structure grammar library for the customization system (Chapter 12). This section, instead, deals with how cleft constructions are analyzed within the HPSG/MRS formalism on a theoretical basis with special reference to ERG (English Resource Grammar, Flickinger 2000).

10.4.1 Properties

Cleft constructions are regarded as showing different behaviors from ordinary focused constructions in syntax as well as semantics. In a nutshell, clefts are associated with exhaustive focus, which renders (25b) infelicitous.

(25) a. JOHN laughed, and so did MARY.

b. #It was JOHN who laughed, and so did MARY. (Velleman et al. 2012: 444)

J.-B. Kim (2012), in a similar vein, argues clefts cannot coincide with lexical items that conflict with exhaustive focus. For example, *even* cannot be used in the focused XPs of cleft constructions as exemplified below.

(26) *It was even the advanced textbook that the student read. (J.-B. Kim 2012: 48)

However, not all identificational foci are always realized as cleft constructions. Identificational foci can be conveyed in some languages using marked word order, as exemplified in the examples in Hungarian (27a) and Standard Arabic (28a). That is, clefting is a sufficient condition for expressing identificational focus, but not a necessary one.

(27) Mari EGY KALAPOT nézett ki magának.
Mary a hat.ACC picked out herself.ACC
'It was A HAT that Mary picked for herself.' [hun] (É. Kiss 1998: 249)

(28) RIWAAYAT-AN ʔallat-at   Zaynab-u
     novel-ACC   wrote-she Zaynab-NOM
     'It was a NOVEL that Zaynab wrote.' [arb] (Ouhalla 1999: 337)

In addition to the semantic differences, Hungarian clefts also exhibit distinct prosodic patterns as shown in (27). Gussenhoven (2007) offers an analysis of cleft constructions in English with respect to information status. The clefted and non-clefted constituents are optionally accented. If the non-clefted constituent is accented, then clefts cause the non-clefted constituent to be interpreted as reactivated information (as presented in the first pair of 42).[9] On the other hand, if the non-clefted constituent is unaccented, and the clefted one bears the accent as given in the second pair of (29), the clefted and non-clefted part denote new/old information, respectively. It is impossible to have both clefted and non-clefted constituents deliver new information at the same time.

(29) Q: Does Helen know JOHN?

   A: It is John/JOHN she DISLIKES.

   Q: I wonder who she dislikes.

   A: It is JOHN she dislikes. (Gussenhoven 2007: 96)

10.4.2 Subtypes

Clefts can be classified into subtypes.[10] These include *it*-clefts, *wh*-clefts (also known as pseudo clefts), and inverted *wh*-clefts (J.-B. Kim 2007). Each of them is exemplified in (30), whose skeletons are represented in (31) in turn.[11]

(30) a. *It*-clefts: In fact it's their teaching material that we're using... <S1A-024 #68:1:B>

---

[9] Gussenhoven (2007) argues that the first reply in (29) implies Helen's disfavor to somebody had been discussed recently.

[10] From a functional perspective, Kim & Yang (2009) classify cleft constructions into predicational, identificational, and eventual types. Similarly Clech-Darbon, Rebuschi & Rialland (1999) classify cleft constructions in French (basically realized in the form as *C'est ... que/qui ...*) into four types: basic, broad event-related focus, broad presentational focus, exclamatory comment. This taxonomy is not used in the current analysis.

[11] (30a) is originally taken from the ICE-GB corpus (Nelson, Wallis & Aarts 2002), and the bracketed expression after the sentence stands for the indexing number. (30a) is paraphrased into (30b–c) by J.-B. Kim (2007).

b. *Wh*-clefts: What we're using is their teaching material.

c. Inverted *wh*-clefts: Their teaching material is what we are using. (J.-B. Kim 2007: 217)

(31) a. *It*-clefts: It + be + XP$_i$ + cleft clause

b. *Wh*-clefts: Cleft clause + be + XP$_i$

c. Inverted *wh*-clefts: XP$_i$ + be + cleft clause (J.-B. Kim 2007: 218)

J.-B. Kim (2007), building upon this taxonomy, provides a corpus study with reference to ICE-GB (a syntactically annotated corpus of British English, Nelson, Wallis & Aarts 2002). Out of 88,357 sentences in the corpus, *it*-clefts occur 422 times (0.47%), *wh*-clefts occur 544 times (0.61%), and inverted *wh*-clefts occur 537 times (0.60%). In addition to NPs, various phrasal categories can be focused in cleft constructions. These include APs, AdvPs, PPs, VPs, and even CPs. For example, *it*-clefts can take various types of XPs as the focused constituent.

(32) a. NP: It was [the gauge] that was the killer in the first place. <S1A-010 #126:1:B>

b. AdvP: And it was [then] that he felt a sharp pain. <S2A-067 #68:1:A>

c. Subordinate Clause: It wasn't [till I was perhaps twenty-five or thirty] that I read them and enjoyed them <S1A-013 #238:1:E> (J.-B. Kim 2007: 220)

One interesting point is that there is a restriction on categorical choice. J.-B. Kim (2007: 220–223) presents the frequency as shown in Table 10.2.

Table 10.2: Frequency of the three types of clefts (J.-B. Kim 2007)

Types of XP	NP	AP	AdvP	PP	VP	CP
it-cleft	324	0	18	65	0	16
wh-cleft	136	19	3	14	19	275
inverted *wh*-cleft	518	0	0	0	0	19

Table 10.2 shows the following: *It*-clefts seldom take verbal items as the pivot XP, while *wh*-clefts do not show such a restriction. Inverted *wh*-clefts exclusively

10.4 Cleft constructions

put focus on NPs, but there are some exceptional cases in which the focused constituent is clausal as exemplified below.

(33) a. [To feel something you have written has reached someone] is what matters. <S1A-044 #096>

b. [What one wonders] is what went on in his mind. <S1A-044 #096> (J.-B. Kim 2007: 222)

Though various types of phrases can be focused in clefts, Velleman et al. (2012) argues that only a portion of the pivot is assigned genuine focus. This implies that clefts involve narrowly focused items inside of the pivot XP as Beaver & Clark (2008) argue that the clefts raise an exhaustive reading as a focus sensitive operator.

The present analysis is exclusively concerned with *it*-clefts, basically following the analysis provided by the ERG. Implementing *it*-clefts in TDL (Type Description Language) requires a categorical constraint indicated in Table 10.2: non-clausal verbal items are not used as the pivot XPs. Pseudo cleft constructions, such as *wh*-clefts and inverted *wh*-clefts, are left to future work, because free relative clauses need to be separately implemented in relation to ICONS.

10.4.3 Components

Cleft constructions across languages are made up of four components (Gundel 2002; Kim & Yang 2009; J.-B. Kim 2012); placeholder, copula, pivot XP, and cleft clause.

(34) [It]   [is]   [the dog] [that barks].
     placeholder copula pivot XP cleft clause

Some languages constitute cleft constructions in the same way as English. For instance, a basic cleft sentence (35) in Norwegian is comprised of all the four components.

(35) Det var Nielsen som vant.
     It was Nielsen that won [nor] (Gundel 2002: 113)

However, the first two components are not necessarily used in all languages that employ clefts. The following subsections explore these four components in turn.

10 Forms of expressing information structure

10.4.3.1 Placeholders

For English, placeholders in cleft constructions are usually realized as expletives (i.e. *it* in English) (Pollard & Sag 1994), but some counterexamples to this generalization exist. J.-B. Kim (2012) presents a dialogue in which *it* in a cleft construction is made use of as a referential pronoun, rather than an expletive. Han & Hedberg (2008) exemplify a specific context in which demonstrative pronouns (e.g. *this* and *that*) can be substituted for *it*. Moreover, some languages do not employ any placeholder. For example, clefts in Arabic languages and in Wolof (a Niger-Congo language, spoken in Senegal) have no counterpart to *it*. In the following examples (Standard Arabic in (36a), Moroccan Arabic in (36b), and Wolof in 36c), the focused constituents occupy the first position of the sentence, followed by pronominal copulae, such as *hiyya* in (36a) and *huma* in (36b) or an ordinary copula *la* in (36c), and then followed by cleft clauses.

(36) a. ZAYNAB-u hiyya llatii ʔallaf-at l-riwaayat-a.
 Zaynab-NOM PRON.she RM wrote-she the-novel-ACC
 'It was ZAYNAB who wrote the novel.' [arb]

 b. L-WLAD huma lli sarrd-at (-hum) Nadia.
 the-children PRON.they RM sent-she (-them) Nadia
 'It was the CHILDREN that Nadia sent.' [ary] (Ouhalla 1999: 341)

 c. Fas wi la jaakat bi jënd
 horse the COP.3SG merchant the buy
 'It is the horse (that) the merchant bought.' [wol] (Kihm 1999: 256)

This current model assumes that the placeholder for clefts is conditioned language-specifically. As for the placeholder *it* in English clefts, it is assumed to be a semantically vacuous pronoun (i.e. an expletive) that introduces no EP and involves an empty ICONS list (i.e. *no-icons-lex-item*).

10.4.3.2 Copulae

Copulae participate in cleft constructions. However, not all languages employ copulae, and the use of copulae is language-specific. For example, Russian does not use any copula in clefts, as exemplified below.

(37) Eto [Boris] vypil vodku.
 it Boris drank vodka
 'It is Boris-FOC (who) drank the vodka.' [rus] (King 1995: 80)

10.4 Cleft constructions

Thus, (ii) the use of a copula is not a mandatory cross-linguistic component for constructing clefts.

On the other hand, it is necessary to determine the grammatical status of the copulae in clefts. J.-B. Kim (2012) surveys two traditional approaches to cleft constructions: (a) extraposition (Gundel 1977) and (b) expletive (É. Kiss 1999; Lambrecht 2001). First, the extraposition analysis assumes *it*-clefts stem from *wh*-clefts; a free relative clause in a *wh*-cleft construction is first extraposed (i.e. right-dislocated) leaving *it* in the basic position, and then *what* in the extraposed clause turns into an ordinary relative pronoun such as *that*. Second, the expletive analysis assumes that the pronoun *it* is a genuine expletive (i.e. generated in situ), and the cleft clause is directly associated with the pivot XP. For example, a simple cleft sentence *It is the dog that barks.* can be parsed into (38a–b) respectively. In (38a), the copula *is* takes two complements; one is the pivot XP *the dog*, and the other is the cleft clause *that barks*. In contrast, the copula in (38b) takes only one complement, and the pivot XP and the cleft clause are combined with each other before being dominated by the copula.

(38) a. [It [[$_{\text{HEAD-DTR}}$ is the dog] [$_{\text{NON-HEAD-DTR}}$ that barks]]].

b. [It [is [[$_{\text{HEAD-DTR}}$ the dog] [$_{\text{NON-HEAD-DTR}}$ that barks]]]].

J.-B. Kim provides a hybrid approach between the extraposition analysis and the expletive analysis. For him, the focused XP constitutes a *cleft-cx* with the following cleft clause first, and then the copula takes the *cleft-cx* as a single complement. That is, his analysis takes (38b) as the proper derivation of the cleft sentence.

The ERG parses a cleft sentence similarly to the extraposition analysis; along the lines of the parse in (38a). That is, in the ERG analysis of *it*-clefts the focused XP complements the copula, and the construction introduces a constructional content structure (i.e. C-CONT) whose EP is "_be_v_itclefts_rel", and then the VP (i.e. [copula + XP]) is complemented once again by cleft clauses. This follows the traditional approach in which the copula in clefts takes two complements; one for the focused constituent, and the other for the cleft clause.

On one hand, the two HPSG-based analyses both treat the copula in clefts as a single entry, lexically different from ordinary copulae. On the other hand, they differ with respect to the ARG-ST values of the cleft copula. J.-B. Kim (2012) argues that the focused XP and the cleft clause is a syntactic unit (as presented in 38b), which means the cleft clause does not directly complement the copula. That is, the cleft copula has only one element (*cleft-cx*) in its VAL|COMPS list. In contrast, the cleft copula in the ERG is syntactically a ditransitive verb that takes

10 Forms of expressing information structure

two complements, the second of which is clausal.[12] The ARG-ST of the *it*-cleft copula is <*it*, XP, CP>.

10.4.3.3 Pivot XPs

Cleft constructions are expected to exhibit an exhaustive (i.e. contrastive) effect (É. Kiss 1998; J.-B. Kim 2012). This means that the focused XPs in clefts deliver a contrastive focus meaning across languages, and this is supported by the fact that clefts pass the correction test (Gryllia 2009). Gracheva (2013) provides a corpus study with reference to the Russian National Corpus (Grishina 2006), and substantiates that cleft constructions in Russian are compatible with *contrast-focus* using the correction test as shown in (39).

(39) Q: Eto Ivan vypil vodku?
     It Ivan drank vodka
     '(Was) it Ivan (that) drank vodka?'

   A: (Net.) Eto [Boris] vypil vodku.
      (No.) It Boris   drank vodka
      '(No). It (was) Boris (that) drank vodka.' [rus] (Gracheva 2013: 118)

Her analysis is also applicable to other languages, such as French in (40) and Mandarin Chinese in (41). Li (2009), especially, regards the *shì ... de* constructions exemplified (41) as the canonical syntactic means of expressing contrastive focus in Mandarin Chinese.

(40) Q: Ta fille est tombée dans l'escalier?
        Did your daughter fall down the stairs?
     A: Non. c'est le petit qui est tombé dans l'escalier.
        No, it's the youngest one [+masc.] that fell down the stairs.
        [fra] (Clech-Darbon, Rebuschi & Rialland 1999: 84)

(41) Ta shi zai Beijing xue   yuyanxue de, bu shi zai Shanghai learn   de.
     3SG be at Beijing learn linguistics DE NEG be at Shanghai learn DE
     'It's in Beijing that he studied linguistics, not in Shanghai. [cmn] (Paul & Whitman 2008: 414)

Hence, the present study takes up the position that the focused XPs in clefts are assigned *contrast-focus*.

---

[12] For example, *tell* in *Kim told Sandy that Pat slept.* is an instance of *clausal-third-arg-ditrans-lex-item* in the current matrix.tdl of the LinGO Grammar Matrix system. The cleft copula should be a subtype of the lexical type with some additional constraints on the complements.

10.4.3.4 Cleft clauses

The semantic head of cleft clauses (i.e. the verbs) could be assigned *bg* in line with previous studies which analyze cleft constructions as a *focus-bg* realization (Paggio 2009). The principle motivation for this comes from the fact that cleft clauses can be freely omitted (J.-B. Kim 2012). However, the first reply in (42), in which the verb in cleft clauses bears the A-accent (i.e. focused), serves as a counterexample to this generalization. Because our formalism should account for all possible meanings of a form, the verbs in cleft clauses are not specified with respect to information structure meanings.

(42) Q: Does Helen know JOHN?

    A: It is John/JOHN she DISLIKES.

    Q: I wonder who she dislikes.

    A: It is JOHN she dislikes. (Gussenhoven 2007: 96)

There are some additional properties of cleft clauses to be considered. J.-B. Kim (2012) claims that cleft clauses show a kind of ambivalent behavior between restrictive relatives and non-restrictive relatives: the focused XP and the cleft clause are basically combined with each other in the restrictive way, but the combined phrase does not look like a canonical restrictive relative in that proper nouns and pronouns can be used for the focused XP. Though his argument sounds intriguing, the present study does not take this ambivalence into account in revising the implementation of cleft constructions in the ERG, because the basic approach to clefts is different (i.e. *cleft-cx* vs. two complements of the cleft copula).

10.4.4 *It*-clefts in the ERG

It-clefts in the ERG are constrained by only the specific type of copulae *itcleft-verb*. Building upon the analyses discussed hitherto, I present a revised version of *itcleft-verb* tested in the ERG (*ver.* 1111). The original constraints in the ERG are represented in (43).

10 Forms of expressing information structure

(43) *itcleft-verb* →

$$\begin{bmatrix} \text{VAL} \begin{bmatrix} \text{SUBJ} & \langle [\textit{it-expl}] \rangle \\ \text{COMPS} & \left\langle \begin{bmatrix} \text{HOOK} | \text{LTOP} \; \boxed{1} \\ \text{VAL} \begin{bmatrix} \text{SUBJ } *\textit{olist}* \\ \text{COMPS} \langle \rangle \end{bmatrix} \end{bmatrix}, \begin{bmatrix} \text{HEAD} & \textit{verb} \\ \text{HOOK} | \text{LTOP} & \boxed{1} \end{bmatrix} \right\rangle \end{bmatrix} \\ \text{LKEYS} | \text{KEYREL} \begin{bmatrix} \text{PRED} & \_be\_v\_itcleft\_rel \\ \text{ARG2} & \boxed{1} \end{bmatrix} \end{bmatrix}$$

(44) is my version which places several constraints on *it*-clefts in accordance with my analysis presented hitherto.

(44) *itcleft-verb* →

$$\begin{bmatrix} \text{VAL} \begin{bmatrix} \text{SUBJ} & \langle [\textit{it-expl}] \rangle \\ \text{COMPS} & \left\langle \begin{bmatrix} \text{HOOK} \begin{bmatrix} \text{LTOP} & \boxed{1} \\ \text{INDEX} & \boxed{2} \end{bmatrix} \\ \text{VAL} \begin{bmatrix} \text{SUBJ } *\textit{olist}* \\ \text{COMPS} \langle \rangle \end{bmatrix} \end{bmatrix}, \begin{bmatrix} \text{HEAD} & \textit{verb} \\ \text{HOOK} \begin{bmatrix} \text{LTOP} & \boxed{1} \\ \text{INDEX} & \boxed{3} \\ \text{CLAUSE-KEY} & \boxed{3} \end{bmatrix} \end{bmatrix} \right\rangle \end{bmatrix} \\ \text{C-CONT} | \text{ICONS} \left\langle ! \begin{bmatrix} \textit{contrast-focus} \\ \text{TARGET} & \boxed{2} \\ \text{CLAUSE} & \boxed{3} \end{bmatrix} ! \right\rangle \\ \text{LKEYS} | \text{KEYREL} | \text{ARG2} \; \boxed{1} \end{bmatrix}$$

The most significant difference between these two analyses is that ICONS replaces the representation using the 'discourse relation' realized as "_be_v_itcleft_p_rel" in (43). The focused XPs are assigned *contrast-focus* within ICONS, whose CLAUSE value is linked to the cleft clauses. (43) and (44) have the categorical restriction on the focused XPs in common. This restriction is specified in VAL of the first complement. According to the corpus study J.-B. Kim (2007) provides, APs and VPs cannot be focused in *it*-clefts as indicated in Table 10.2, while CPs can be used as the focused XP. Other phrasal types, such as NPs, AdvP, and PPs, can freely become the first complement of *itcleft-verb*. This restriction is specified using *olist* in VAL|SUBJ and an empty list of VAL|COMPS.

Building on the AVM in (44), (45) exemplifies how cleft constructions are represented via ICONS. The information structure relation that the focused item has

10.5 Passive constructions

to the cleft clause is analyzed as contrastive focus at least in English due to the fact that (25b) and (26) sound unacceptable, though it may not hold true cross-linguistically. Therefore, the focused element DOG has a *contrast-focus* relation to the cleft clause, the element *barks* in the cleft clause remains underspecified. Note that the expletive *it* and the copula *is* are semantically empty, and thereby they cannot participate in ICONS.

(45)   ~~It is~~ the DOG ~~that~~ barks.   [contrast-focus]

10.5 Passive constructions

This section is exclusively concerned with passive constructions in English, in order to revise the related types in the ERG with respect to information structure. Nonetheless, a similar version of revision can be applied to other languages.

Passive constructions relate to the current model of information structure in terms of two aspects; information structure and semantics-based machine translation.

First, passivization is (partially) relevant to information structure. It has been reported that some languages, such as Spanish (Casielles-Suárez 2003), exhibit a relationship between passivization and the articulation of information structure. Though such a straightforward relationship between these concepts does not hold for all human languages, there seems to be at least some connection. What is the motivation for using passive forms? For this question, it is necessary to look at promoted arguments and demoted arguments differently. One might think that one function of a passive is to place a different argument in subject position so that it can be the topic (given the general tendency to align topic with subject). However, the promoted arguments in passives are not always assigned *topic*. For example, the promoted argument in the following sentence conveys a focus meaning, which is exclusive from a topic meaning in that the promoted argument *the book* corresponds to the *wh*-word in the question.

(46) Q: What was found by Sandy?
      A: The book was found by Sandy.

Neither are promoted arguments always interpreted as *focus*, because some aspect of passivization is clearly motivated by the desire to put something other than the agent into the canonical topic position (i.e a subject position).

(47) They were looking all over for the book. Finally, it was found by Sandy.

10 Forms of expressing information structure

As a result, the best we can say about the promoted arguments is that they are not background (i.e. *focus-or-topic*). At the same time, the demoted arguments, if they appear overtly, have to be marked as *non-topic*. Particularly in English, the demoted arguments can hardly serve as a topic of a sentence, because NPs with *topic* are preferentially in sentence-initial position.[13]

Second, active/passive pairs are relevant to machine translation as well as monolingual paraphrasing. Presumably they share the same truth-conditions monolingually, and exhibit structural divergence multilingually. For example, in English, passives are used productively and constraints on passivization are relatively weak. In contrast, Japanese and Korean, which tend to downplay the role of passives, have stronger constraints on passivization.[14] In the ERG (*ver.* 1111), the passive constructions constructionally introduce an EP (i.e. using C-CONT), whose predicate is "_parg_d_rel". The original constraint using the 'discourse relation' is represented as follows.

(48) *passive-verb-lex-rule* →

$$\begin{bmatrix} \text{VAL} & \begin{bmatrix} \text{SUBJ} & \langle [\text{INDEX } \boxed{2}] \rangle \\ \text{COMPS} & \langle ..., [\text{INDEX } \boxed{1}] \rangle \end{bmatrix} \\ \text{C-CONT} & \begin{bmatrix} \text{RELS} & \langle ! \begin{bmatrix} \text{PRED} & \textit{parg\_d\_rel} \\ \text{ARG1} & \boxed{1} \\ \text{ARG2} & \boxed{2} \end{bmatrix} ! \rangle \\ \text{HCONS} & \langle ! ! \rangle \end{bmatrix} \end{bmatrix}$$

This method cannot capture the generalization that active/passive pairs are semantically equivalent, and does not allow them to be paraphrased into each other monolingually. This analysis also disregards the fact that active/passive pairs are truth-conditionally equivalent, provided that the demoted argument is overt in the passive. Consequently it causes a problem in that passive sentences in English sometimes need to be translated into active sentences in other languages, such as Japanese and Korean. Moreover, using a discourse relation such as "_parg_d_rel" is redundant in that this information can be provided by an information structure value.

---

[13] It is reported that topicalizing the demoted argument in passives works well in German.

[14] Song & Bender (2011) look at translation of active/passive pairs to confirm how information structure can be used to improve transfer-based machine translation.

10.5 Passive constructions

My alternative method is as follows. The information structure of promoted/demoted arguments is still articulated in the lexical rule which passivizes main verbs. However, the EP involving the discourse predicate (i.e. "parg_d_rel") is removed from the lexical rule, and instead two *info-str* values are inserted into C-CONT. The TARGET value of the first element is coreferenced with ARG2, and that of the second one is co-indexed with ARG1. In addition, the preposition *by* is specified as a semantically empty item. An AVM of the type responsible for passivization is presented as (49). Note that the first element in SUBJ and the last element in COMPS specify their *info-str* values as *focus-or-topic* and *non-topic* respectively.

(49) *passive-verb-lex-rule* →

$$\begin{bmatrix} \text{VAL} & \begin{bmatrix} \text{SUBJ} & \left\langle \begin{bmatrix} \text{INDEX} & \boxed{2} \\ \text{ICONS-KEY} & \boxed{3}[\textit{focus-or-topic}] \end{bmatrix} \right\rangle \\ \text{COMPS} & \left\langle ..., \begin{bmatrix} \text{INDEX} & \boxed{1} \\ \text{ICONS-KEY} & \boxed{4}[\textit{non-topic}] \end{bmatrix} \right\rangle \end{bmatrix} \\ \text{C-CONT} & \begin{bmatrix} \text{RELS} & \left\langle !\begin{bmatrix} \text{ARG1} & \boxed{1} \\ \text{ARG2} & \boxed{2} \end{bmatrix}! \right\rangle \\ \text{HCONS} & \langle ! ! \rangle \\ \text{ICONS} & \left\langle ! \boxed{3}[\text{TARGET}\boxed{2}], \boxed{4}[\text{TARGET}\boxed{1}] ! \right\rangle \end{bmatrix} \end{bmatrix}$$

A sample representation of a passive construction is accordingly sketched out in (50), in which the auxiliary copula *is* and the preposition *by* are semantically and informatively empty.

(50)   [focus-or-topic]
    The dog is chased by Kim.
          [non-topic]

In the future when prosody information is modeled in the ERG and thereby accents for marking focus and topic are employed in the grammar, the constraints on C-CONT|ICONS in (49) should be changed. If rules for dealing with prosody are used, the rules will be responsible for introducing the ICONS elements for constraining information structure values on promoted and demoted arguments.

10 Forms of expressing information structure

In this case, *passive-verb-lex-rule* will have an empty C-CONT|ICONS, but it still will assign specific values to the ICONS-KEYs of the promoted arguments (*focus-or-topic* on the first element of SUBJ) and demoted arguments (*non-topic* on the last element of COMPS). Because prosodic information has not yet been used in the current ERG, tentatively (49) puts the ICONS elements into C-CONT herein.

10.6 Fronting

(51) exemplifies a focus/topic fronting construction in English: (51a) is the unmarked sentential form which is devoid of any specific information structure markings. On the other hand, the object *the book* in (51b) occupies the sentence-initial position, and the remaining part of the sentence has a syntactic gap for the preposed object.

(51) a. Kim reads the book.

b. The book Kim reads.

The point at issue in analyzing focus/topic fronting constructions is to determine which information structure meaning(s) the preposed argument gives. (51b) in itself sounds ambiguous between two possible readings: One assigns a topic reading to *the book*, and bears a likeness to an *'as for ...'* construction. The other, similarly to *it*-clefts, has a focus reading on the preposed argument. The choice between them is largely conditioned by the contextual situation that utterances prior to the current sentence create, which is infeasible to measure in sentence-based language processing (Kuhn 1996). Thus, as long as we do not deploy an extra device to resolve the meaning with respect to the context, the information structure value on *the book* should be underspecified so that it can cover both meanings. The lowest supertype of both *focus* and *topic* in Figure 7.1 is *focus-or-topic*, which implies the associated constituents (e.g. *the book* in 51b) are informatively interpreted as either focus or topic. (52) is illustrative of the schema that (51b) has.

(52) [*focus-or-topic*]
     The book Kim reads.

10.7 Dislocation

Unlike focus/topic fronting constructions, dislocation constructions do not have any syntactic gap irrespective of whether the peripheral topic is sentence-initial (i.e. left dislocation) or sentence-final (i.e. right dislocation). The example structurally similar to (51b) is provided in (53),[15] in which (i) an intonational break at the phonological level intervenes between the left-peripheral NP *the book* and the rest of the utterance, and (ii) a resumptive pronoun *it* corresponding to *the book* satisfies the object of *reads*.

(53) a. The book, Kim reads it.

   b. Kim reads it, the book.

The book in this case is an external topic that is not inside the sentence. It is regarded as containing *frame-setting* information according to the cross-linguistic study offered in the previous chapters. In other words, its pragmatic role is to narrow the domain of what is being referred to.

In the analysis of dislocation, there is one more factor to be considered; agreement between the topicalized NP and the corresponding pronoun inside the head sentence. For example, in (53) only the third singular pronoun *it* which agrees with *the book* can be resumptive. In languages which exhibit rich morphology (e.g. Italian (Cinque 1977; Rizzi 1997), Spanish (Rivero 1980; Zagona 2002; Bildhauer 2008), German (Grohmann 2001), Modern Greek (Alexopoulou & Kolliakou 2002), Czech (Sturgeon 2010), etc.) the choice of resumptive pronouns matters. The options are: (i) (clitic) left dislocations and (ii) hanging topics. The resumptive pronouns in left dislocation constructions have to agree perfectly with the dislocated NP in person, number, gender, case, etc., whereas a hanging topic and its corresponding pronoun do not agree with each other. This implies that hanging topics have a looser relationship with the remaining part of the sentence than left dislocations (Frascarelli 2000).

(54) a. [Seinen$_i$ Vater], den   mag jeder$_i$.
    his-ACC father RP-ACC likes everyone
    'His father, everyone likes.'

---

[15]Commas after topicalized NPs are not obligatorily used, and are mainly attached just as a preferable writing style for the reader's convenience. On the other hand, there should be a phonetic pause between the topicalized NPs and the main sentence in speech. The pause information should be included in the typed feature structure of PHON, because information structure-based TTS (Text-To-Speech) and ASR (Automatic Speech Recognition) systems can use it to improve performance.

b. [Sein$_i$ Vater], jeder$_{*i/k}$ mag den/ihn.
his-NOM father everyone likes RP/him-ACC
'His father, everyone likes him.' [ger] (Grohmann 2001: 92)

c. Honzu, toho ještě neznám.
Honza.ACC that.ACC still NEG-know.1SG
'Honza, I still don't know him.'

d. Anička? Té se nic nestalo.
Anička.NOM that.DAT REFL-CL nothing NEG-happened
'Anička? Nothing happened to her.' [cse] (Sturgeon 2010: 288)

(54a–b) are examples of left dislocation and hanging topics in German, respectively. In (54a), the accusative on the dislocated NP *Seinen Vater* agrees with that on the resumptive pronoun *den*. By contrast, a hanging topic *Sein Vater* in (54b) is in nominative, which does not agree with the resumptive pronoun in accusative. The same holds for (54c–d) in Czech; both *Honza* and its resumptive pronoun *toho* in (54c) are in accusative, while there is no agreement between the lefthand NP *Anička* and *Té* in (54d).

In movement-based analyses, (clitic) left dislocations and hanging topics are regarded as being configured via two different syntactic operations: Dislocated NPs in (clitic) left dislocations are originally realized inside the sentence, and move forward leaving resumptive pronouns with the same features. Hanging topics, by contrast, are base-generated *ab initio* without any agreement with their corresponding pronoun. Hanging topics in transformation-based studies are also assumed to have several additional characteristics (Frascarelli 2000): (i) Only one hanging topic can show up in a sentence, (ii) hanging topics can appear only sentence-initially, (iii) if a hanging topic co-occurs with other topics in a sentence, it should be followed by the other topics (i.e. hanging topic first).[16] From this point of view, Cinque (1977) distinguishes English-like languages from Italian-like languages. The former employ only hanging topics, whereas the latter have both left dislocation and hanging topics.

In HPSG-based studies, agreement between a dislocated NP and its resumptive pronoun is modeled. For instance, in the following AVM taken from Bildhauer (2008: 350), a coreference 3 means the HEAD-values should be consistent in order to capture case-agreement, and another coreference 4 indicates that they share the same INDEX.

---

[16]Frascarelli (2000), exploiting a corpus, provides some counterexamples to these properties that hanging topics presumably possess, which implies they are tendencies, rather than strict rules.

(55) $\text{clld-phrase} \Rightarrow \begin{bmatrix} \text{COMPS} & \langle\rangle \\ \text{CLITICS} & \boxed{1} \oplus \boxed{2} \\ \text{HEAD-DTR} & \begin{bmatrix} \text{COMPS} & \langle\rangle \\ \text{CLITICS} & \boxed{1} \oplus \left\langle \begin{bmatrix} \text{HEAD} & \boxed{3} \\ \text{INDEX} & \boxed{4} \end{bmatrix} \right\rangle \oplus \boxed{2} \end{bmatrix} \\ \text{NON-HD-DTR} & \left\langle \begin{bmatrix} \text{HEAD} & \boxed{3} \\ \text{INDEX} & \boxed{4} \\ \text{SPR} & \langle\rangle \\ \text{COMPS} & \langle\rangle \end{bmatrix} \right\rangle \end{bmatrix}$

Because the present study does not employ a rigid distinction between (clitic) left dislocations and hanging topics, all these constraints can be fully covered in the current proposal. That is, they can be merged into just one single type that assigns *contrast-topic* to the fronted constituent.

(56) a.
          [contrast-topic]
          The book, Kim reads it.

b.
          [contrast-topic]
          Kim reads it, the book.

As mentioned earlier, the present work does not fully implement focus/topic fronting and dislocation in terms of how to build up this representation compositionally. In Section 12.3.4, several types of dislocated constituents are partially implemented using *head-filler-phrase* in order to constrain clause-initial and clause-final foci. Future work needs to look into how the *contrast-topic* element can be added into the ICONS list.

10.8 Summary

This chapter has delved into the specific forms of expressing information structure. First, focus sensitive items are classified into two subtypes; one assigns an information structure value to itself, and the other assigns a value to its adjacent item. Second, in terms of argument optionality, unexpressed arguments always bear *non-focus* because focused items cannot be elided. Third, scrambling in Japanese and Korean was addressed. The present study proposes a cross-classification of three phrase structure types, which refer to an MKG value for looking at which lexical marker is used. Fourth, an AVM responsible for cleft

10 Forms of expressing information structure

constructions in the ERG was revised to signal *focus* (i.e. a plain focus) to the pivot XP in cleft constructions. Fifth, promoted and demoted arguments in passive constructions also have a specific *info-str* value: *focus-or-topic* for the former, and *non-topic* for the latter. Lastly, focus/topic fronting constructions and two types of dislocations (i.e. left dislocation and hanging topics) were examined. The fronted elements in OSV sentences in English have a value of *focus-or-topic*, because they can be interpreted as either *focus* or *topic*. On the other hand, dislocated NPs are assigned *contrast-topic* in line with the analyses of previous studies.

11 Focus projection

Focus projection occurs when the meaning of focus that is associated with specifically marked words is spread over a larger phrase to which the word belongs. In previous research, it has been said that a typical focus domain in a sentence must contain at least one accented word, which functions as the core of focus meaning. That implies that focus projection can be seen to be related to how F(ocus)-marking (normally realized with a specific pattern of prosody, such as the A-accent in English) co-operates with information structure meanings. The fundamentals of focus projection, suggested by Selkirk (1984; 1995) and Büring (2006), are summarized as follows. These definitions remain true when observing English in which prosody is mainly responsible for expressing focus.

(1) a. Basic Focus Rule: An accented word is F-marked.

   b. Focus of a sentence: An F-marked constituent is not dominated by any other F-marked constituent.

   c. Focus Projection: either (i) F-marking of the head of a phrase licenses F-marking of the phrase, or (or both) (ii) F-marking of an internal argument of a head licenses the F-marking of the head. (Büring 2006: 322–323)

This chapter lays the groundwork for how an analysis based on ICONS (Individual CONStraints) and MKG (MarKinG) could eventually support a deeper study of focus projection. A large number of HPSG-based studies on information structure are particularly concerned with focus projection, mostly based on the Focus Projection Principle as presented in (1). The previous studies have three points in common, and these points need to be taken into account in the context of creating a computational model: First, they provide multiple parse trees for a single sentence in which focus projection may occur. The first section (Section 11.1) provides a counterargument to this strategy in representation. Second, previous studies claim that assignment of focus-marking accent plays an important role in calculating the extent of focus domain (Section 11.2). Third, distinctions between grammatical relations, such as peripheral vs. non-peripheral, head vs.

11 Focus projection

non-head, are critically used in constraining focus projection (Section 11.3). The last section (Section 11.4) formulates an illustrative analysis of a single sentence in which we find that focus projection occurs.

11.1 Parse trees

Most previous approaches in the HPSG-based study on information structure provide multiple parse trees. In fact, a sentence that potentially involves focus projection sounds ambiguous in and of itself. For example, (2) may have at least three parse trees following the previous approaches.

(2) [$_f$ Kim [$_f$ gives Lee [$_f$ a BOOK]]].

From the perspective that a single sentence may have multiple readings, following this method may not seem so odd. However, this kind of approach does not work well in the context of computational processing. The issue baring the most concern would be when multiple parse trees for a single sentence can have an adverse effect on system performance. A large number of parse trees decreases speed while an increase in ambiguity decreases accuracy, both detrimental to the system's goals. That is, several external modules that enhance feasibility of computational grammars (e.g. reranking model) do not perform actively with such a large number of intermediate results. Thus, I argue that a single parse tree that potentially transmits the complete meanings that the sentence may convey should necessarily be provided. The main mechanism to facilitate this flexibility is underspecification.

11.2 F(ocus)-marking

F-marking, which crucially contributes to formation of focus projection, has been presumed to be closely associated with prosody, as shown in (1a). That is to say, in previous literature, a set of specific accents (e.g. the A-accent in English) has been considered tantamount to F-marking. However, it is my position that bearing a specific accent is not a necessary condition, but a sufficient condition for F-marking: F-marking does not necessarily depend on whether the word is accented or not. Across languages, there are several examples in which focus projection is triggered by non-prosodic features.

Building on the phonological rules provided in (3) (already presented in Section 6.3), the focus prominence rule that Bildhauer (2007) derives is constrained

11.2 F(ocus)-marking

as represented in (3). The constraints signify that the focused constituent has to contain the Designated Terminal Element (DTE) on the level of phonological UTterance (UT). (In the following rules, PHP is short for PHonological Phrase, IP for Intonational Phrase, RE for Right Edge, PA for Pitch Accent, and BD for BounDary tone.)

(3) a. $\left[\text{PHP} \mid \text{DTE} \quad +\right] \rightarrow \left[\text{PA} \quad tone\right]$

b. $\left[\text{PHP} \mid \text{DTE} \quad -\right] \rightarrow \left[\text{PA} \quad none\right]$

c. $\left[\text{IP} \mid \text{RE} \quad +\right] \rightarrow \left[\text{BD} \quad tone\right]$

d. $\left[\text{IP} \mid \text{RE} \quad -\right] \rightarrow \left[\text{BD} \quad none\right]$

(4) $\begin{bmatrix} sign \\ \text{SYNSEM} \mid \text{CONT} \begin{bmatrix} mrs \\ \text{RELS} \; \boxed{1} \end{bmatrix} \\ \text{IS} \mid \text{FOC} \quad \langle \boxed{1} \rangle \end{bmatrix} \rightarrow \begin{bmatrix} \text{PHON} \; \langle ... [\text{UT} \mid \text{DTE} \quad +] ... \rangle \end{bmatrix}$

Bildhauer claims that the schematic AVM (4) can be presumably applied to most human languages in which focus in marked by means of prosody. Furthermore, it may have a subtype which places a more precise constraint. For instance, given that focus prominence in Spanish has a strong tendency to fall on the last prosodic word in the PHON list of a focused sign, (4) can be altered into (5) in Spanish (Bildhauer 2007: 191).

(5) $\begin{bmatrix} sign \\ \text{SYNSEM} \mid \text{CONT} \begin{bmatrix} mrs \\ \text{RELS} \; \boxed{1} \end{bmatrix} \\ \text{IS} \mid \text{FOC} \quad \langle \boxed{1} \rangle \end{bmatrix} \rightarrow \begin{bmatrix} \text{PHON} \quad list \oplus \langle [\text{UT} \mid \text{DTE} \quad +] \rangle \end{bmatrix}$

One of the more important strengths that this formalism provides may very well be that the relation between focus and prosodic prominence is restricted in a fairly straightforward manner as shown in (4). In addition, it is a significant endeavor to the HPSG framework to look into how various phonological layers interact with each other in phases and end up with focus projection.

11 Focus projection

However, these AVMs are viewed differently with the current model. I propose to argue that F-marking is most relevant to marking information structure. In English, prosody has a relatively straightforward relationship to information structure marking. However, this does not necessarily hold true in other languages. Instead, I argue that F-marking needs to be represented as MKG|FC in the current formalistic framework. In other words, [MKG|FC +] indicates that the word (or the phrase) is F(ocus)-marked. As the name itself implies, F-marking is a matter of markedness, rather than a meaning. In brief, F-marking, which triggers the spread of focus, has to be specified as a feature of MKG under CAT. There several reasons for this argument, which are discussed in Sections 11.2.1 to 11.2.3.

11.2.1 Usage of MRS

First of all, the two AVMs (4) and (5) proposed by Bildhauer (2007) have an inconsistency with the DELPH-IN formalism that the present study relies on. In the DELPH-IN formalism of HPSG, we cannot search a specific element included in a list unless we create pointers into RELS (like ICONS-KEY in the present work).

11.2.2 Languages without focus prosody

Second, as presented in Section 4.1, some languages do not use prosody in expressing focus (e.g. Yucatec Maya, Kügler, Skopeteas & Verhoeven 2007, Akan, Drubig 2003, and Catalan, Engdahl & Vallduví 1996). Besides, in Hausa, prosodic prominence is disallowed for focus in situ (Hartmann & Zimmermann 2007; Büring 2010) (p. 79). If focus projection always occurred by means of prosody, there could be no focus projection in these languages. Yet, it can be understood that focus projection seems to be a universal phenomenon in human language (Büring 2006).

11.2.3 Lexical markers

Finally and most importantly, some languages make use of lexical markers to invoke focus projection. Some previous studies regard these lexical items as comment markers or scope markers. For instance, Korean employs *man* 'only', and this lexical item contributes to extension of focus meaning, although a specific pattern of prosody may or may not occur when an element is focused (Choe 2002). Similarly, *ba* in Abma (Schneider 2009) and *shì* in Mandarin Chinese (von Prince 2012) function to extend focus meaning into the larger constituents. Thus, the main component responsible for the spreading of focus meaning in these specific types of languages is not necessarily prosody.

11.3 Grammatical relations

In previous HPSG-based studies, ARG-ST or a linear arrangement of dependents of verbs play a crucial role in identifying which phrases are projected from a F(ocus)-marked word. Engdahl & Vallduví (1996) claim that focus projection can be licensed if and only if the most oblique argument of the phrase's head is F-marked. Their INFO-STRUCT instantiation principles (for English) are as follows.

(6) a. Either if a DAUGHTER's INFO-STRUCT is instantiated, then the mother inherits this instantiation (for narrow foci, links and tails),

b. or if the most oblique DAUGHTER's FOCUS is instantiated, then the FOCUS of the mother is the sign itself (wide focus). (Engdahl & Vallduví 1996: 12)

De Kuthy (2000) provides a different argument with reference to the linear order of constituents; focus projection can happen if and only if the rightmost daughter is accented. Since the rightmost daughter is not always an oblique argument, De Kuthy's focus projection rules are not concurrent with the claim made by Engdahl & Vallduví. The main point that Chung, Kim & Sells (2003) propose is that ARG-ST is the locus in which focus projection occurs, which is largely in line with Engdahl & Vallduví, but there are some differences. They add two more factors into the formation of focus projection. One includes modification and coordination. The focus that a modifier bears can hardly spread into its modificand and the larger phrase, and none of the operands in coordination (i.e. non-headed phrases) can project focus.[1] The other is agentivity. If the focus value of the non-agentive lowest ranking argument is instantiated in its local position, then focus projection can take place. Bildhauer (2007) is another endeavor to show how focus projection can be dealt with within HPSG formalism. Bildhauer points out various problems with previous studies: First, looking at obliqueness

---

[1] A counterexample to this generalization is provided in Büring (2006: 326f.): "I know that John drove Mary's red convertible. But what did Bill drive? – He drove her [$_f$BLUE convertible]." To my understanding, this counterexample is relevant to contrastive focus, given that the correction test is applied (see Section 3.4.4). The distinction between contrastive focus and non-contrastive focus with respect to focus projection is one of the major further topics.

11 Focus projection

would sometimes be too rigorous or sometimes too loose to identify how the focus domain is built up. Second, the previous approaches are language-specific, and thereby may not be straightforwardly applied to other languages.

There are potentially (at least) six possibilities in spreading of focus meaning in English. For instance, a ditransitive sentence *Kim sent Lee a big book yesterday.* consists of six components as shown in (7).

(7) Kim sent Lee
    (i) subject (ii) verb (iii) non-peripheral argument
    a big book yesterday.
    (iv) NP modification (v) peripheral argument (vi) VP modification

First, focus associated with subjects cannot be projected into the larger phrase (Chung, Kim & Sells 2003). Although the subject in (7) bears the A-accent (i.e. KIM), the whole sentence cannot be in the focus domain. In other words, a Q/A pair (8Q2-A2) sounds infelicitous, whereas (8A1) sounds good as an appropriate reply to (8Q1).

(8) Q1: Who sent Lee a big book yesterday?
    A1: [$_f$KIM] sent Lee a big book yesterday.
    Q2: What happened?
    A2: #[$_f$KIM sent Lee a big book yesterday.].

This is in accordance with the proposal of Selkirk (1984; 1995). The subject is neither the head of the sentence nor an internal argument of the main verb. However, when the subject is an internal argument, the focus on subjects can be projected. The subjects of unaccusative verbs (e.g. *die*) have been analyzed as not an external argument of the verbs, but an internal argument. Chung, Kim & Sells (2003) argue that whether the subject is an internal argument of the verb or not assists in identifying focus projection. Since unergative verbs, such as *ran* in (9b), take their subject as an external argument, the focus cannot be projected from the subject. In contrast, *Tom* in (9a) may act as the core of focus projection, due to the fact that the verb *died* takes it as an internal argument.

(9) a. [$_f$ TOM died].
    b. #[$_f$ TOM ran]. (Chung, Kim & Sells 2003: 395)

Second, it has been said that focus on verbs can be projected into the larger phrases (e.g. VP and S), but Gussenhoven (1999) argues that such a projection is incompatible with intuition. That is, the following Q/A pair does not sound natural to Gussenhoven. That is to say, the focus associated with SENT cannot be projected into the VP.

(10) Q: What did she do?
    A: #She SENT a book to Mary.

Third, distinction between non-peripheral argument and peripheral argument with respect to focus projection has already been the subject of in-depth research. Bresnan (1971) argues that focus projection in English happens if and only if the A-accented word is the peripheral argument.

(11) a. The butler [$_f$ offered the president some COFFEE].
    b. *The butler [$_f$ offered the PRESIDENT some coffee].
    c. The butler offered [$_f$ the PRESIDENT some coffee].
                                    (Chung, Kim & Sells 2003: 388)

Fourth, modifiers (e.g. *big* and *yesterday* in 7) are less capable of extending the focus that they are associated with to their head phrases. Thus, any head can hardly inherit a focus value from its adjunct.

In the following section, I narrow down the scope of analysis to the distinction between non-peripheral argument and peripheral argument, and will address the full range of focus projection in future research with deeper analysis.

11.4 An analysis

My investigation makes use of ICONS and MKG. They are used to place a restriction on possibility of focus projection and to represent the meaning of a sentence in which focus projection can occur into a single parse tree.

11.4.1 Basic data

A set of allosentences (i.e. close paraphrases which share truth-conditions, Lambrecht 1996) is presented in (12), and the principle difference among them is the position of the A-accent (marked as SMALL CAPS). In other words, what is focused upon is different in the different allosentences.

(12) a. KIM sent Lee the book.
    b. Kim SENT Lee the book.
    c. Kim sent LEE the book.
    d. Kim sent Lee the BOOK.

225

11 Focus projection

According to Bresnan (1971), focus projection can happen only in (12d) among these allosentences. Simply put, only the most peripheral argument can be the starting point of focus projection. For example, if a *wh*-question requires an answer of *all-focus* ("an absence of the relevant presuppositions", Lambrecht 1996: 232), only the sentence in which the most peripheral argument bears an focus-marking (e.g. the A-accent) sounds felicitous, as exemplified in (13).[2]

(13) Q: What happened?
     A1: #[$_f$ KIM sent Lee the book].
     A2: #[$_f$ Kim SENT Lee the book].
     A3: #[$_f$ Kim sent LEE the book].
     A4: [$_f$ Kim sent Lee the BOOK].
     A5: #Kim sent [$_f$ Lee the BOOK].

In addition, there are two more restrictions on the occurrence of focus projection: First, focus projection takes place only when the syntactic head dominates the focus-marked element. For instance, focus cannot be projected in the way presented in (13A5) in which the verb *sent* is not in the focus domain. Second, the focus-marked element should be included in the focus domain. For instance, the followings in which the focus-marked BOOK is out of the bracket are ill-formed.

(14) a. *[$_f$Kim] sent Lee the BOOK.
     b. *[$_f$Kim sent] Lee the BOOK.
     c. *[$_f$Kim sent Lee] the BOOK.
     d. *Kim [$_f$ sent] Lee the BOOK.
     e. *Kim [$_f$ sent Lee] the BOOK.
     f. *Kim sent [$_f$ Lee] the BOOK.

11.4.2 Rules

The present study follows the idea Chung, Kim & Sells (2003) propose: ARG-ST is the locus where focus projection takes place. That means that the main constraint on the range of spreading focus should be specified in the lexical structure of the verb (i.e. *sent* in 13A4). I introduce extra lexical rules to manipulate the feature structure(s) under VAL for constraining such a possibility of focus projection. That is, each verbal entry has its own ARG-ST independent of focus marking, and one extra verbal node is introduced at the lexical level when constructing a

---

[2] I would rather say "focus-marked" rather than "accented", because F(ocus)-marking does not necessarily mean prosodic marking as discussed before.

11.4 An analysis

parse tree. On the other hand, the lexical rules for calculating focus projection refer to F-marking specified as a value of MKG|FC of the dependents specified in the list of VAL|COMPS (and VAL|SUBJ).

I propose that a ditransitive verbal entry *send* as used in 13A4) takes <NP(NOM), NP(ACC), NP(ACC)> (i.e. two elements in COMPS) as its ARG-ST.[3] The basic entry is conjugated into *sent* by inflectional rules, and the inflected element can be the daughter of the lexical rules that I employ for computing focus projection. There are two rules to look at the values in VAL|COMPS, as presented below.

(15) a. $\begin{bmatrix} \textit{no-focus-projection-rule} \\ \text{INDEX } \boxed{1} \\ \text{ICONS-KEY } \boxed{2} \\ \text{VAL} \begin{bmatrix} \text{SUBJ} & \langle [\text{ICONS-KEY } \textit{non-focus}] \rangle \\ \text{COMPS} & \langle [\text{MKG} | \text{FC } +], \begin{bmatrix} \text{MKG} | \text{FC } - \\ \text{ICONS} & \langle ! ! \rangle \end{bmatrix} \rangle \end{bmatrix} \\ \text{C-CONT} | \text{ICONS} \langle ! \boxed{2} \begin{bmatrix} \textit{non-focus} \\ \text{TARGET } \boxed{1} \end{bmatrix} ! \rangle \\ \text{DTR } \textit{lex\_rule\_infl\_affixed} \end{bmatrix}$

b. $\begin{bmatrix} \textit{focus-projection-rule} \\ \text{CLAUSE-KEY } \boxed{1} \\ \text{VAL} | \text{COMPS} \langle \begin{bmatrix} \text{MKG} | \text{FC } - \\ \text{INDEX } \boxed{2} \end{bmatrix}, \begin{bmatrix} \text{MKG} | \text{FC } + \\ \text{ICONS} \langle ! [\textit{semantic-focus}] ! \rangle \end{bmatrix} \rangle \\ \text{C-CONT} | \text{ICONS} \langle ! \begin{bmatrix} \textit{non-focus} \\ \text{TARGET } \boxed{2} \\ \text{CLAUSE } \boxed{1} \end{bmatrix} ! \rangle \\ \text{DTR } \textit{lex\_rule\_infl\_affixed} \end{bmatrix}$

No-focus-projection-rule shown in (15a) takes a non-focus-marked element as the last component, while *focus-projection-rule* shown in (15b) takes a focus-marked one. Focus projection in a sentence whose main verb stems from *send* can happen by using only *focus-projection-rule*, and *no-focus-projection-rule* predicts other

---

[3] In the ERG (English Resource Grammar, Flickinger 2000), a default form of *send* is divided into several different types, mainly depending on specification of ARG-ST, such as "send_v1", "send_v2", etc. I follow this strategy of enumerating verbal entries.

11 Focus projection

sentences in which the most peripheral argument (i.e. *the book* in this case) introduces no *info-str* value into ICONS. Note that *focus-projection-rule* requires one information structure value (specified as *semantic-focus*) from the last element in VAL|COMPS.

For example, (16a–b) are not compatible with each other. When *Lee* is A-accented (i.e. LEE with [FC +]), (15b) cannot take it as its complement. (15a) can take LEE as its complement, but (15a) prevents the A-accented BOOK with [FC +] from being the second complement. In other words, *sent* in (16a) is constrained by (15a), while that in (16b) is constrained by (15b).

(16)   a.   Kim sent LEE the book.
       b.   Kim sent Lee the BOOK.

11.4.3 Representation

The primary motivation to use ICONS with respect to focus projection is to provide only one single parse tree that covers all potential meanings of focus projection. The parse tree of (16b) is sketched out in Figure 11.1. The corresponding dependency graph is provided in (17).

(17)   *semantic-focus*
      Kim sent Lee the BOOK.
         non-focus

In (17), there are four information structure relations. Two of them are visible in (17): One is *non-focus* between *Lee* (unmarked) and the semantic head *sent*, and the other is the *semantic-focus* between BOOK (A-accented) and *sent*. In addition to them, there are two other potential relations, left underspecified in the dependency graph. One is between *Kim* and *sent*, and the other is *sent* to itself. These can be monotonically specified in further processing. That is, further constraints can be added, but only if they are consistent with what is there. This underspecified ICONS representation gets further specified to VP focus or S focus. According to the graph in (17), *Lee* should not be focused, *book* should be focused, and *Kim* and *sent* may or may not be focused. When *sent* is focused, the ICONS list in the output includes three ICONS elements (i.e. VP focus). When both *sent* and *sent* are focused, the ICONS list in the output includes four ICONS elements (i.e. S focus). When they are associated with focus, the representations are sketched out in (18a–b), respectively. Note that the input representation provided in (17) subsumes (18a–b), but not *vice versa*.

11.4 An analysis

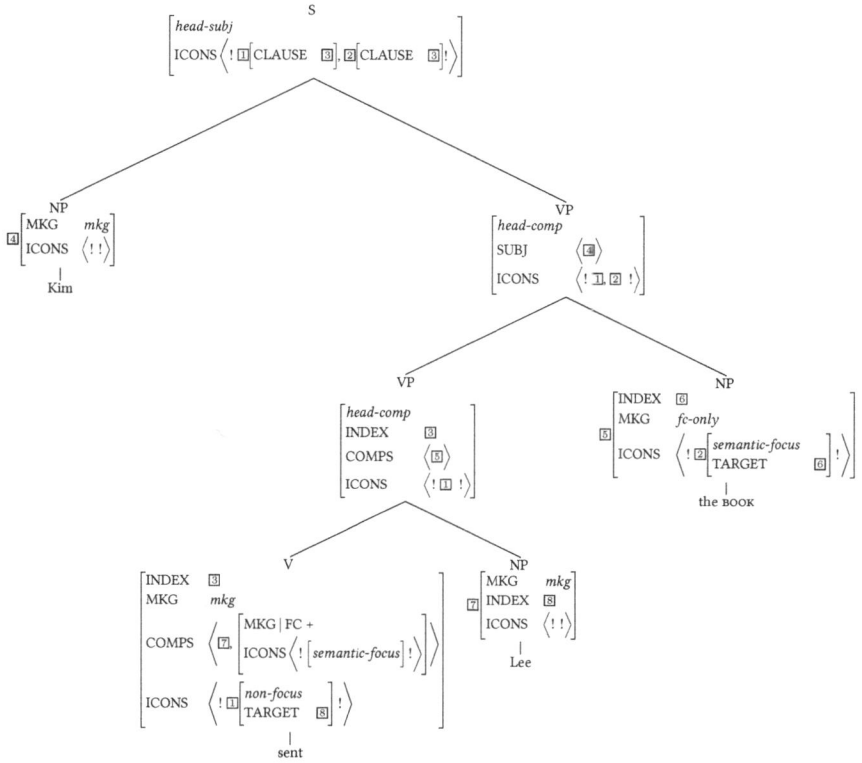

Figure 11.1: Parse tree of (16b)

(18) a.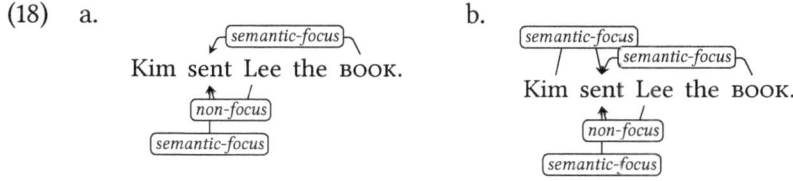

This representation works especially well in terms of generation. First, the first element in the final ICONS list given in (11.1) assigns *non-focus* to *Lee*, an A-accented LEE is ruled out in the generation output. Second, the second element in the final ICONS list assigns *semantic-focus* to *the book*, *the book* must be focus-marked in the generation output (i.e. *the* BOOK). Third, *Kim* and *sent* in the underspecified relations can be associated with *semantic-focus*, and thereby *-a* can be attached to them. Consequently, the following three outputs can be

229

11 Focus projection

generated when using *Kim sent Lee the book-a.* as the input string. (19a–c) hypothetically represent NP focus, VP focus, and S focus, respectively.[4]

(19) a. Kim sent Lee the book-a.
     b. Kim sent-a Lee the book-a.
     c. Kim-a sent-a Lee the book-a.

Lastly, it is noteworthy that a sentence built with (15a), such as (16a), cannot be further specified in the same way. (15a) introduces an element whose value is *non-focus* into the ICONS list. Since this constraint prevents the verb *sent* from being focused, neither VP focus nor S focus can happen in the sentence. Additionally, since the subject is constrained as [ICONS-KEY *non-focus*] in (15a), an A-accented KIM cannot be the subject. In an actual processing, (20a) cannot be paraphrased as sentences in (20b–d).

(20) a. Kim sent Lee-a the book.
     b. Kim sent-a Lee-a the book.
     c. Kim-a sent-a Lee-a the book.
     d. Kim-a sent Lee-a the book.

11.4.4 Further question

My analysis presented thus far leaves an interesting question for future work. The EP that *sent* introduces into the RELS list is represented as (21). In the sentences given in (16), the INDEXes of *Kim*, *Lee*, and *book* have coreferences with ARG1, ARG2, and ARG3, respectively.

(21) $\begin{bmatrix} \text{RELS} \left\langle \begin{bmatrix} \_send\_v\_rel \\ \text{ARG0} \; \boxed{1} \\ \text{ARG1} \; \boxed{2} \\ \text{ARG2} \; \boxed{3} \\ \text{ARG3} \; \boxed{4} \end{bmatrix} \right\rangle \end{bmatrix}$

In accordance with (21), the ICONS lists for (16a–b) are constructed as (22a–b). They explicitly specify the information structure values on ARG2 and ARG3, but ARG1 is not included in them.

---

[4]For ease of comparison, the other hypothetical suffix *-b* is not considered here.

(22) a. Kim sent LEE the book.

$$\left[\text{ICONS} \left\langle \begin{bmatrix} \textit{semantic-focus} \\ \text{TARGET } \boxed{3} \\ \text{CLAUSE } \boxed{1} \end{bmatrix} \right\rangle \right]$$

b. Kim sent Lee the BOOK.

$$\left[\text{ICONS} \left\langle \begin{bmatrix} \textit{non-focus} \\ \text{TARGET } \boxed{3} \\ \text{CLAUSE } \boxed{1} \end{bmatrix}, \begin{bmatrix} \textit{semantic-focus} \\ \text{TARGET } \boxed{4} \\ \text{CLAUSE } \boxed{1} \end{bmatrix} \right\rangle \right]$$

The current assumption is that focus cannot spread to the role associated with the subject (here ARG1) without including the verb. For instance, (22b) cannot be interpreted in the same way as (23) via focus projection, because the ICONS in (23) does not contain an element for the verb. Note that the first ICONS element in (23) is introduced by the A-accent rule for KIM.

(23) KIM sent Lee the BOOK.

$$\left[\text{ICONS} \left\langle \begin{bmatrix} \textit{semantic-focus} \\ \text{TARGET } \boxed{2} \\ \text{CLAUSE } \boxed{1} \end{bmatrix}, \begin{bmatrix} \textit{non-focus} \\ \text{TARGET } \boxed{3} \\ \text{CLAUSE } \boxed{1} \end{bmatrix}, \begin{bmatrix} \textit{semantic-focus} \\ \text{TARGET } \boxed{4} \\ \text{CLAUSE } \boxed{1} \end{bmatrix} \right\rangle \right]$$

This assumption seems linguistically true in that the sentence in (23) is not an instance of S focus. The question is which mechanism technically blocks such specialization. This mechanism for focus projection has to play two functions. First, it allows the subject (here ARG1) to be associated with focus if and only if the verb is also associated with focus. Second, it serves to prevents the ICONS list in (22a) from being further specified. My further research will delve into how the mechanism works.

11.5 Summary

This chapter has offered a new approach of computing focus projection in terms of sentence generation. First, the present study argues that a single parse tree of a sentence with focus projection is enough to represent the meaning of information structure and also more effective in the context of grammar engineering. Second, F-marking is not necessarily encoded by prosody. In some languages (e.g. Mandarin Chinese and Korean), some lexical markers play a role to extend

11 Focus projection

the domain of focus. Thus, F-marking in the present study is dealt with [MKG|FC +]. Third, (at least in English), focus projection happens normally when the most peripheral item is focus-marked though there are some exceptional cases. Fourth, there are two more constraints on focus projection. One is that the focus-marked element should be included in the focus domain. The other is that focus-marked elements are preferred to be headed.[5] In other words, the focus meaning is seldom extended to any non-head phrases. Building upon these arguments, the last section in this chapter showed how a simple ditransitive sentence can be analyzed with respect to focus projection. Two lexical rules are introduced to discriminate a sentence in which focus projection happens. This is a piece of evidence to support my argument in this chapter, but a more thorough study is required in future research.

---

[5] There are some exceptional cases to this: In the sense of entrenched, non-canonical structures, "languages can contain numerous offbeat pieces of syntax with idiosyncratic interpretations" (Jackendoff 2008); for example, "Off with his head!", "Into the house with you!", etc.

12 Customizing information structure

The LinGO Grammar Matrix is an open-source starter kit for the rapid development of HPSG/MRS-based grammars (Bender et al. 2010). The main idea behind the system is that the common architecture simplifies exchange of analyses among groups of developers, and a common semantic representation speeds up implementation of multilingual processing systems such as machine translation.

Roughly speaking, this system is made up of two components. The first one is a core grammar written in matrix.tdl. This contains types and constraints that are useful for modeling phenomena in all human languages The typed feature structure of *sign* defined in matrix.tdl is represented in Figure 12.1, to which the current work adds several more attributes.

The second one includes linguistic libraries for widespread, but non-universal language phenomena (Bender & Flickinger 2005; Drellishak 2009). The libraries work with a customization system (http://www.delph-in.net/matrix/customize). Figure 12.2, reproduced from Bender et al. (2010), shows how the LinGO Grammar Matrix customization system operates on the basis of user input.

Grammar customization with the LinGO Grammar Matrix is provided via a web-based questionnaire which has subpages for a series of language phenomena. The screenshot of the current version's main page is shown in Figure 12.3. For each phenomenon, the questionnaire gives a basic explanation and questions designed to help the user describe an analysis of the phenomenon. After the questionnaire has been answered, the user can press a button to customize a grammar. This button invokes the customization script, which takes the user's answers stored in a choices file, and first validates them for consistency, then articulates grammar fragments into a complete grammar for the user's language. The output is an HPSG/MRS-based grammar built automatically on the basis of specifications the user has given. If the automatic construction is successful, a compressed file (zip or tar.gz) is made available for download. The downloadable file includes all required components for HPSG/MRS-based grammar engineering within the DELPH-IN formalism, so once decompressed, the user can try out the grammar with processors such as LKB (Copestake 2002), PET (Callmeier 2000), *agree* (Slayden 2012), ACE (http://sweaglesw.org/linguistics/ace), and other DELPH-IN software such as [incr tsdb()] (Oepen 2001).

12 Customizing information structure

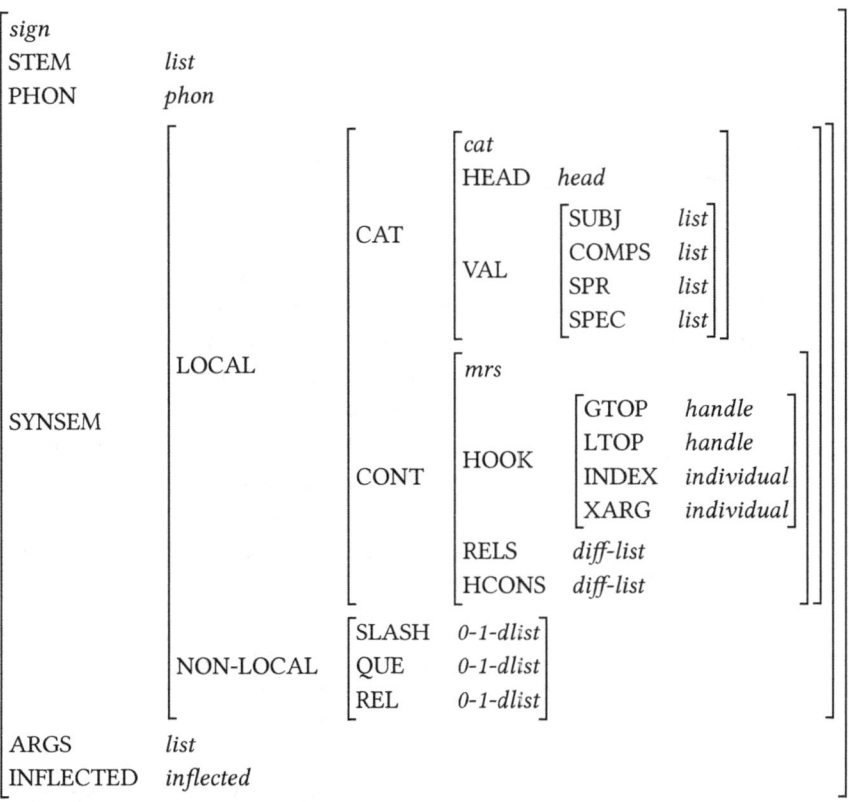

Figure 12.1: Typed feature structure of *sign* defined in matrix.tdl

The grammatical categories covered in the current version are listed in (1). The pages sometimes work independently, and sometimes co-operate with choices given in other subpages. For example, users can add some additional features when there is a need (e.g. animacy) on the "Other Features" page, which will then appear as an option of syntactic or semantic features in other subpages such as "Lexicon" and "Morphology". To take another example, the "Sentential Negation" page elicits information about morphosyntactic strategies of negation in the user's language, and specific forms of negation operators can be inserted in "Lexicon" and/or "Morphology" (Crowgey 2012). The "Information Structure" page works in a similar way.

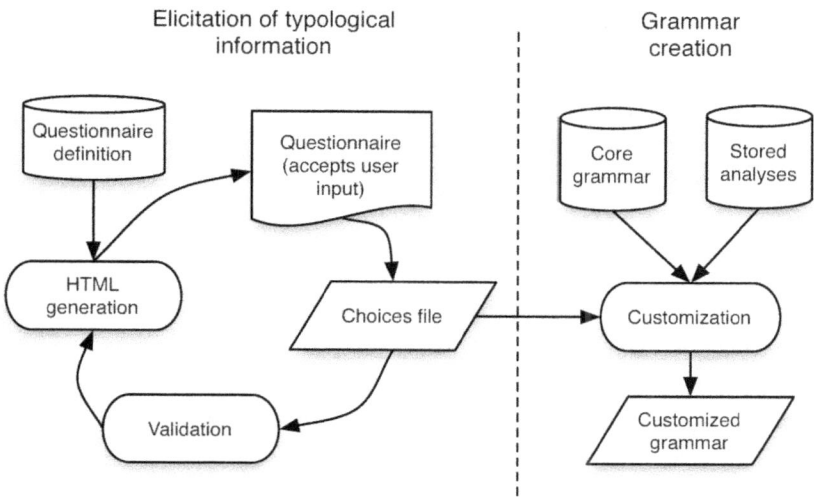

Figure 12.2: The LinGO Grammar Matrix customization system

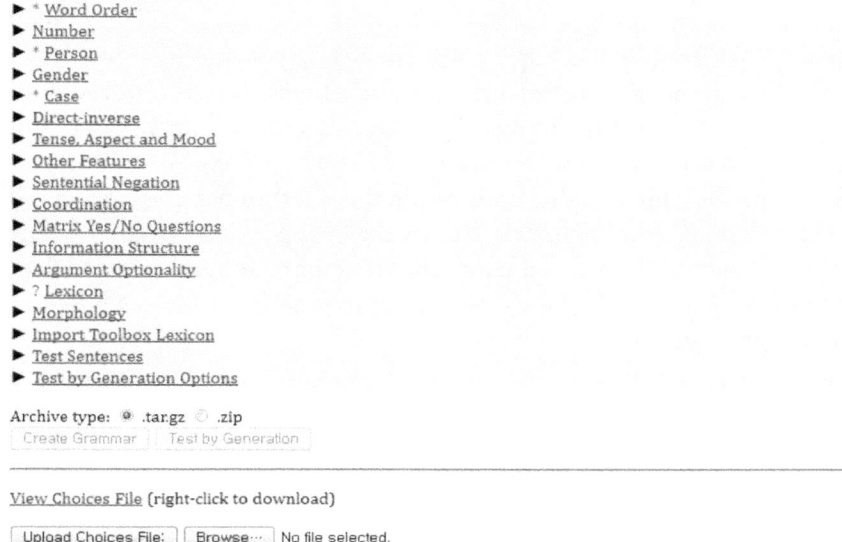

Figure 12.3: Screenshot of the questionnaire (main page)

12 *Customizing information structure*

(1)   a.   Word Order (Fokkens 2010)
       b.   Number (Drellishak 2009)
       c.   Person (Drellishak 2009)
       d.   Gender (Drellishak 2009)
       e.   Case (Drellishak 2009)
       f.   Direct-inverse (Drellishak 2009)
       g.   Tense, Aspect and Mood (Poulson 2011)
       h.   Other Features (Drellishak 2009; Poulson 2011)
       i.   Sentential Negation (Crowgey 2012)
       j.   Coordination (Drellishak & Bender 2005)
       k.   Matrix Yes/No Questions (Bender & Flickinger 2005)
       l.   Information Structure (the present study)
       m.   Argument Optionality (Saleem 2010; Saleem & Bender 2010)
       n.   Lexicon (Drellishak 2009)
       o.   Morphology (Goodman 2013)

Four more pages not directly related to grammar creation but necessary for ease of development are presented in (2). In the "General Information" page, users input supplementary information, such as the ISO 639-3 code of the language, delimiters in the languages, etc. The "Import Toolbox Lexicon" page provides an interface to the Field Linguist's Toolbox, which is provided by SIL (Summer Institute of Linguistics, http://www.sil.org). Users can input test sentences in the "Test Sentences" page, which are included with the customized grammar for basic evaluation of the grammar's parsing coverage. The last one provides several options for fine-tuning the results of "Test by Generation". The users can check out the feasibility of their choices on the questionnaire beforehand by using "Test by Generation", which performs the customization in the background and displays sentences realized using the grammar for generation with predefined semantic templates. The users can then refine their choices based on the quality of the results.

(2)   a.   General Information
       b.   Import Toolbox Lexicon
       c.   Test Sentences
       d.   Test by Generation Options

The grammars created by the LinGO Grammar Matrix customization system are rule-based, scalable to broad-coverage, and cross-linguistically comparable. The starter grammars make two contributions to grammar engineering. First, the starter-grammar is useful to those who have an interest in testing linguistic hypotheses within the context of a small implemented grammar (Bender, Flickinger & Oepen 2011). Second, starter grammars serve as a departure point to those who want to construct broad-coverage implemented grammars, and sometimes presents directions for improvement to an existing grammar. Thus far, the LinGO Grammar Matrix has been used to construct new HPSG/MRS-based grammars (e.g. BURGER, BUlgarian Resource Grammar – Efficient and Realistic, Osenova 2011), and to improve existing grammars (e.g. KRG2, Korean Resource Grammar ver. 2, Song et al. 2010).

12.1 Type description language

The grammatical fragments the current work creates are written in TDL. To facilitate an understanding of the syntax, this subsection provides a summary of TDL.

TDL describes feature structures within constraint-based grammars.[1] TDL has been partially simplified and partially extended in the reference formalism of DELPH-IN. Thus, all processors in the DELPH-IN collection: LKB, PET, ACE, and *agree*, are fully compatible with TDL. The syntax of TDL in the DELPH-IN formalism has three components: (i) multiple type inheritance, (ii) attribute-value constraints, and (iii) coreference. For example, (3) indicates that the current type inherits from two supertypes and that the value of an attribute SYNSEM|HEAD should be consistent with the value of the head daughter's SYNSEM|HEAD.

```
(3) type-name := supertype-name-1 & supertype-name-2 &
      [ SYNSEM.CAT.HEAD #head,
        HEAD-DTR.SYNSEM.CAT.HEAD #head ].
```

One of the frequently used data structures in TDL is list. For instance, a list <a,b,c> can be represented as follows.

```
(4) [ FIRST a,
      REST [ FIRST b,
             REST [ FIRST c,
                    REST e-list ] ] ]
```

Lists sometimes need to work more flexibly to allow concatenation, append, removal, etc. For these operations, the DELPH-IN formalism utilizes difference lists (*diff-list*). This structure maintains a pointer to the last element of the list. Analogously to (4), a difference list <! a,b,c !> can be represented as in (5).

---
[1] http://moin.delph-in.net/DelphinTutorial/Formalisms

12 Customizing information structure

(5) [LIST [FIRST a,
            REST [FIRST b,
                   REST [FIRST c,
                          REST #last]]],
     LAST #last]

12.2 The questionnaire

The first task of implementing the customization system's information structure library centers around adding an HTML-based page to the web-based questionnaire. The "Information Structure" page is comprised of four sections, namely "Focus", "Topic", "Contrastive Focus", and "Contrastive Topic". Each section, except the last one, consists of two subparts: one for syntactic positioning and the other for lexical marking(s).

12.2.1 Focus

First, in the "Focus" section, users can specify the canonical position of focus in the user's language. A screenshot is shown in Figure 12.4. According to the cross-linguistic survey given in Chapter 4 (p. 57), there are four options: clause-initial, clause-final, preverbal, and postverbal. A sentence in the neutral word order is a default form in the language, which can be interpreted as conveying a range of information structure values. For example, if SVO is the default order in a language, we cannot look at postverbal or clause-final [O] as being marked for *focus*.

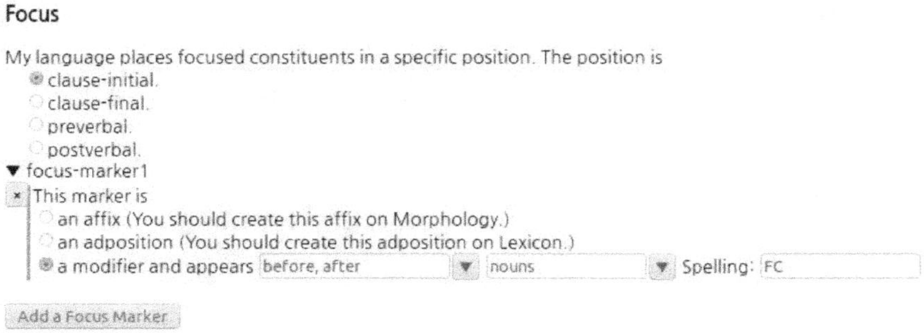

Figure 12.4: Screenshot of editing focus position/markers in the questionnaire

12.2 The questionnaire

Users can add one or more focus markers. The type of a focus marker is either an affix, an adposition, or a modifier as surveyed in Section 4.2 (p. 49). Affixes are treated in the morphological paradigm (i.e. irules.tdl), while the other two are treated like a word (i.e. lexicon.tdl). The distinction between the last two is also discussed in Section 4.2: If a language employs case-marking adpositions and a lexical marker to express focus and/or topic is in complementary distribution with the case-marking adpositions, the marker is categorized as an adposition in principle. Otherwise, the marker is treated as just a modifier.[2] Specific forms for information-structure marking affixes and adpositions are not specified in the "Information Structure" page, and instead they should be defined in the "Morphology" and "Lexicon" pages, respectively. If users select that their language has an affix or an adposition of expressing focus in the "Information Structure" page, but an affix or an adposition that involves *focus* or super/subtypes of *focus* as a value of "information-structural meaning" is not added in the "Morphology" or "Lexicon" pages, a validation error is produced. The spelling of information-structure marking modifier(s) is directly specified on the "Information Structure" page, because there is no room for such an expression (e.g. particles, clitics, etc.) in "Morphology" and "Lexicon". Users can specify more constraints on information-structure marking modifier(s), such as before and/or after nouns and/or verbs.

For instance, Figure 12.4 is illustrative of users' choices on "Focus". As mentioned earlier in Section 4.2.3 (p. 53), one lexical marker may be used to signal focus to both nominal and verbal items. One lexical marker may occur sometimes before focused constituents and sometimes after them. Thus, the users can take multiple options for the constraints, as presented as [before, after] in Figure 12.4.

12.2.2 Topic

Second, the "Topic" section has two choices for constraints. As for the constraint on positioning, an option for the topic-first restriction is provided for the languages in which topic always occupies the sentence-initial position. Next, one or more topic markers can be added, which operate in the same way as the "Add a Focus Marker" button discussed above. As shown in Section 3.3.3.4 (p. 30), verbal items can be topicalized in some languages (e.g. Paumarí, Chapman 1981). Thus, [verbs] in Figure 12.5 is selected for illustrating the language-specific constraint.

---

[2]Nonetheless, the users of the LinGO Grammar Matrix system may have the flexibility to describe what the users see in their language following the meta-modeling idea of Poulson (2011).

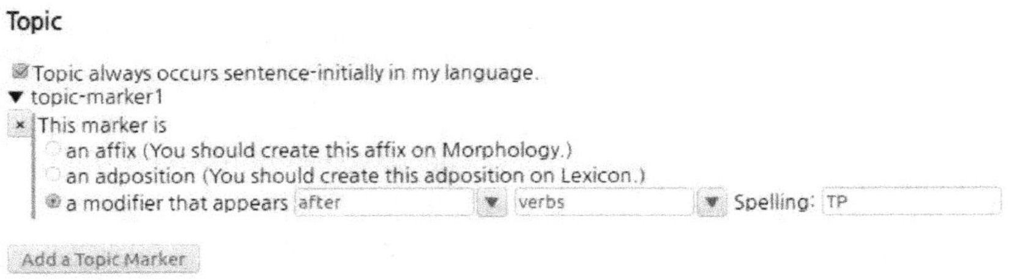

12 Customizing information structure

Topic

☑ Topic always occurs sentence-initially in my language.
▼ topic-marker1
　× This marker is
　　○ an affix (You should create this affix on Morphology.)
　　○ an adposition (You should create this adposition on Lexicon.)
　　⦿ a modifier that appears [after] [▼] [verbs] [▼] Spelling: [TP]

[Add a Topic Marker]

Figure 12.5: Screenshot of editing topic position/markers in the questionnaire

Contrastive Focus

☑ My language uses the same position to express contrastive focus as non-contrastive focus.

My language places contrastively focused constituents in a specific position. The position is
　○ clause-initial.
　○ clause-final.
　○ preverbal.
　○ postverbal.
▼ c-focus-marker1
　× This marker is
　　⦿ an affix (You should create this affix on Morphology.)
　　○ an adposition (You should create this adposition on Lexicon.)
　　○ a modifier that appears [   ] [▼] [   ] [▼] Spelling: [   ]

[Add a Contrastive Focus Marker]

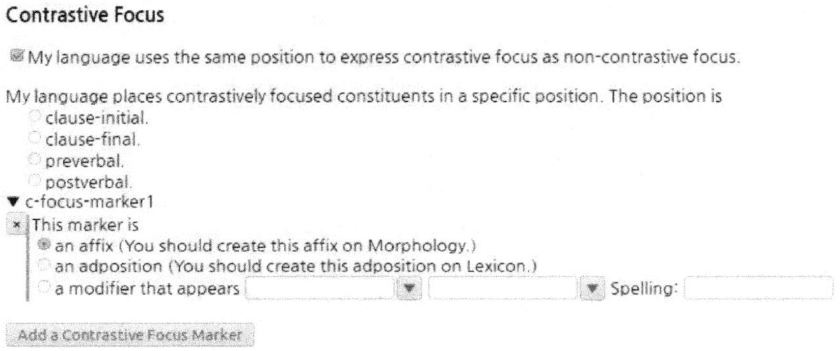

Figure 12.6: Screenshot of editing contrastive focus position/markers in the questionnaire

12.2.3 Contrastive focus

Third, contrastive focus may or may not be marked differently from non-contrastive focus, which is language-specific. If the first checkbox in Figure 12.6 (just under the title "Contrastive Focus") is not selected, there can be two types of foci: one is *semantic-focus* for non-contrastive focus, and the other is *contrast-focus* for contrastive focus. In the latter case, users have to choose a specific position for contrastive focus, such as clause-initial, clause-final, preverbal, or postverbal. If users do not choose one of them, the validation script gives an error message. Contrastive focus markers are added using the same tools and selectors as other markers.

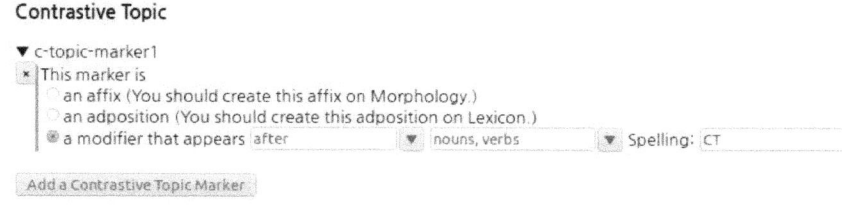

Figure 12.7: Screenshot of editing contrastive topic markers in the questionnaire

12.2.4 Contrastive topic

Finally, there is an option for "Contrastive Topic". According to the cross-linguistic survey the present study has conducted, there seems to be no language in which contrastive topics have a constraint on positioning, and this is also supported by several previous analyses (H.-W. Choi 1999; Erteschik-Shir 2007; Bianchi & Frascarelli 2010). Accordingly, there is no checkbox for adding a position constraint. On the other hand, some languages employ a contrastive topic marker (e.g. *thì* in Vietnamese, Nguyen 2006). These can also be specified using the button "Add a Contrastive Topic Marker".

12.3 The Matrix core

The next task was to incorporate the analysis based on ICONS (Individual CONStraints) into the Matrix core. The core TDL fragments written in `matrix.tdl` define universally useful types in widespread linguistic phenomena. Notably, integrating ICONS into the grammar requires editing lots of previously implemented types as well as adding several new types. This is because I am concerned not merely with the representations (implemented via changes to MRS and the addition of the actual type for ICONS), but also with their composition at the syntactic level. Thus, I had to revise many lexical rules and types inherited by almost all phrase structure rules and lexical rules. The details are as follows.

12.3.1 Fundamentals

First of all, three type hierarchies presented in Chapter 7, such as *info-str*, *mkg*, and *sform*, were added. Then, [MKG *mkg*] was added into CAT, and CONT values were also edited as containing ICONS-related features, such as [ICONS-KEY *icons*] and [CLAUSE-KEY *event*] under *hook*, and [ICONS *diff-list*] under *mrs*. The TDL statements for representing *info-str* is presented in (6) (cf. Figure 7.1).

```
(6)  icons := avm.
     info-str := icons &
        [ CLAUSE individual,
          TARGET individual ].
     non-topic := info-str.
     contrast-or-focus := info-str.
     focus-or-topic := info-str.
     contrast-or-topic := info-str.
     non-focus := info-str.
     focus := non-topic & contrast-or-focus & focus-or-topic.
     contrast := focus-or-topic & contrast-or-focus & contrast-or-topic.
     topic := non-focus & focus-or-topic & contrast-or-topic.
     bg := non-topic & non-focus.
     semantic-focus := focus.
     contrast-focus := contrast & focus.
     contrast-topic := contrast & topic.
     aboutness-topic := topic.
```

ICONS were added into the basic lexical and phrasal types in matrix.tdl (e.g. *unary-phrase, binary-phrase, ternary-phrase,* etc.). Next, I specifically inserted [C-CONT|ICONS <! !>] into phrase structure rules and lexical rules: when a lexical or phrasal type has nothing to do with information structure, C-CONT|ICONS is specified as an empty list.

12.3.2 Lexical types

Regarding lexical types, the set of types used for marking *icons* within a lexical item, such as *no-icons-lex-item, basic-icons-lex-item, one-icons-lex-item,* and *two-icons-lex-item* (Section 8.1), were written as TDL statements. Lexical types for constraining ARG-ST (ARGument-STructure) inherit from one of them and impose some additional constraints on CLAUSE-KEY. For example, *intransitive-lex-item*, which places a constraint on ARG-ST of intransitive verbs, is defined as in (8). Note that this type inherits from *basic-icons-lex-item* that has an empty ICONS list as shown in (7). There is a coreference tag #clause in (8), which indicates that every argument shares the value of CLAUSE-KEY with the semantic head within a single clause.

```
(7)  basic-icons-lex-item := lex-item &
        [ SYNSEM.LOCAL.CONT.ICONS <! !> ] ].
```

12.3 The Matrix core

(8) intransitive-lex-item := basic-one-arg-no-hcons &
```
                          basic-icons-lex-item &
 [ ARG-ST < [ LOCAL.CONT.HOOK [ INDEX ref-ind & #ind,
                                ICONS-KEY.CLAUSE #clause ] ] >,
     SYNSEM [ LKEYS.KEYREL.ARG1 #ind,
              LOCAL.CONT.HOOK.CLAUSE-KEY #clause ] ].
```

Some lexical types inherently include an *info-str* value. In this case, lexical types for ARG-ST impose a constraint on the element of *info-str*. For instance, the type *clausal-second-arg-trans-lex-item*, which is responsible for the AGT-ST of verb classes which take a clausal complement (e.g. *think, ask*), is defined as shown in (10) (see Section 9.1). Note that the INDEX of the second argument (i.e. a clausal complement) and the TARGET of the element in the ICONS list are co-indexed (#target).

(9) one-icons-lex-item := lex-item &
```
    [ SYNSEM.LOCAL.CONT.ICONS <! [ ] !> ] ].
```

(10) clausal-second-arg-trans-lex-item := basic-two-arg &
```
                                  one-icons-lex-item &
 [ ARG-ST < [ LOCAL.CONT.HOOK [ INDEX ref-ind & #ind,
                                ICONS-KEY.CLAUSE #clause ] ],
            [ LOCAL.CONT.HOOK [ LTOP #larg,
                                INDEX #target ] ] >,
   SYNSEM [ LOCAL.CONT [ HOOK.CLAUSE-KEY #clause,
                         HCONS <! qeq & [ HARG #harg,
                                          LARG #larg ] !>,
                         ICONS <! [ CLAUSE #clause,
                                    TARGET #target ] !> ],
            LKEYS.KEYREL [ ARG1 #ind, ARG2 #harg ] ] ].
```

12.3.3 Lexical rules

There are two types of lexical rules. One introduces an element of *info-str* into C-CONT|ICONS, and the other does not. In order to support these types, I needed to change *no-ccont-rule* to include [C-CONT|ICONS <! !>] and to add a type that allows for a non-empty ICONS list. This type is called *no-rels-hcons-rule*, and constrains RELS and HCONS to be empty while leaving ICONS underspecified. These rules are also used for phrase structure rules as well.

12.3.4 Phrase structure rules

First, *basic-head-subj-phrase*, *basic-head-comp-phrase*, *basic-head-spec-phrase* as well as *basic-bare-np-phrase* inherit from *no-ccont-rule*. Therefore, they have an

12 Customizing information structure

empty ICONS list. Second, I edited two phrase structure rules for argument optionality, namely *basic-head-opt-subj-phrase* and *basic-head-opt-comp-phrase*. They introduce an ICONS element that indicates the value of information structure the dropped argument has (i.e. *non-focus*) into C-CONT|ICONS. This constraint is in line with my analysis presented in Section 10.2 (p. 194). Third, I modified *basic-head-mod-phrase-simple* (a subtype of *head-mod-phrase*) in accordance with the AVM presented in Section 8.2 (p. 151): now it has an empty list in C-CONT|ICONS, and the CLAUSE-KEY of modifiers (NON-HEAD-DTR) and that of their modificands are co-indexed with each other. Finally, *head-filler-phrase* does not include [C-CONT|ICONS <! !>]. This is because its subtypes sometimes constructionally introduce an element of *info-str*. For example, clause-initial and clause-final focus in languages with a fixed word order are instances of *head-filler-phrase*, and introduce an element into C-CONT|ICONS. The remaining part of a sentence which has a syntactic gap is constrained by *basic-head-subj-nmc-phrase* or *basic-head-comp-nmc-phrase*, in which *nmc* stands for non-matrix-clause. These rules work for *head-subj-phrase* and *head-comp-phrase* that cannot be root nodes by themselves (i.e. specified as [MC –]). These phrases are supposed to be combined only with a *filler-phrase*. There is one more phrase structure rule related to *filler-phrase*: *nc-filler-phrase*. This rule handles a non-canonical *filler-phrase*; for example, detached constituents in right dislocation.

12.4 Customized grammar creation

The third task is to implement the Python code to customize the users' choices. The code first validates the content in the choices file to check for inconsistencies and missing inputs. If no error occurs, then the code converts the content in the choices file into TDL statements.

(11) ```
section=info-str
  focus-pos=clause-final
    focus-marker1_type=modifier
    focus-marker1_pos=after
    focus-marker1_cat=nouns, verbs
    focus-marker1_orth=FC
  topic-first=on
  c-focus-pos=preverbal
  c-topic-marker1_type=affix
```

The users' answers about information structure are stored in a choices file as shown in (11). The choices shown in (11) specify that the language places a focused constituent in the clause-final position, and employs a focus marker, which
```

12.4 Customized grammar creation

is a single word spelled as 'FC' appearing after nouns or verbs. The language is a topic-first language as indicated by 'topic-first=on'. The language uses a different place for signaling contrastive focus. In this case, it is the preverbal position. Finally, the language has an affix responsible for conveying a meaning of contrastive topic, which should be defined in the "Morphology" page. Those choices are transmitted into the customization script for information structure.

12.4.1 Lexical markers

There are three types of lexical markers: (i) affixes, (ii) adpositions, and (iii) modifiers. Among them, the first one and the second one are specified in the "Morphology" and "Lexicon" pages respectively. They are handled by existing customization code, which works seamlessly with the information-structure related features and values enabled by the information structure library. I edited two existing customization libraries for the first two options and the script for information structure (i.e. information_structure.py) creates only the last type of marker.

(i) Affixes are customized by morphotactics.py. If a lexical rule imposes a constraint on information structure meaning, the lexical rule inherits from *no-rels-hcons-rule* (explained before in (Section 12.3.3) and introduces an element of *info-str* into C-CONT|ICONS. Otherwise, it inherits just from *add-only-no-ccont-rule* (or other lexical rules with an empty C-CONT|ICONS). For instance, the TDL statements presented in (12) are responsible for a focus-marking suffix, and introduces a value of *info-str* into ICONS. Note the two coreference tags in *add-icons-rule*, namely #icons and #target.

```
(12) add-icons-rule := phrase-or-lexrule & word-or-lexrule &
        [ SYNSEM.LOCAL.CONT.HOOK [ INDEX #target,
                                  ICONS-KEY #icons ],
          C-CONT.ICONS <! info-str & #icons & [ TARGET #target] !> ].

    p1-lex-rule-super := add-only-no-rels-hcons-rule & infl-lex-rule &
        [ DTR noun-lex ].

    r1-lex-rule := add-icons-rule & p1-lex-rule-super &
        [ SYNSEM.LOCAL [ CAT.MKG fc,
                         CONT.HOOK.ICONS-KEY focus ] ].
```

(ii) Adpositions are dealt with by lexical_items.py. Likewise, an ICONS list of an adposition is constructed depending on whether an adposition has a feature that constrains the semantics related to information structure. An instance

12 Customizing information structure

is provided in (13). In this case, the adposition lexically includes a value of *info-str* in CONT|ICONS, and the TARGET is co-indexed with the INDEX of the complement. This works in the same manner as *ga* and *wa* in Japanese as presented previously in Section 8.4.2 (p. 162).

```
(13) infostr-marking-adp-lex := basic-one-arg & raise-sem-lex-item &
                                one-icons-lex-item &
     [ SYNSEM.LOCAL [ CAT [ HEAD adp & [ MOD < > ],
                            VAL [ SPR < >,
                                  SUBJ < >,
                                  COMPS
                                    < #comps &
                                      [ LOCAL.CONT.HOOK.INDEX
                                            #target ] >,
                                  SPEC < > ] ],
                      CONT [ HOOK.ICONS-KEY #icons,
                             ICONS <! #icons &
                                      [ TARGET #target ] !> ] ],
       ARG-ST < #comps &
                [ LOCAL.CAT [ HEAD noun,
                              VAL.SPR < > ] ] > ].
```

(iii) Finally, information_structure.py creates TDL statements for information-structure marking modifiers, and depending on the specific choices, the lexical types are also elaborated. For example, the choices in (11) yield the following TDL statements given in (14-15). The TDL statements presented in (14-15) define the lexical type of modifiers that mark information structure. Like the information-structure marking adpositions shown above, a value for *info-str* is lexically included in CONT|ICONS, but the TARGET is co-indexed with the INDEX of its modificand.

```
(14) infostr-marking-mod-lex := no-rels-hcons-lex-item &
                                one-icons-lex-item &
     [ SYNSEM.LOCAL [ CAT [ HEAD adv &
                            [ MOD
                              < [ LIGHT -,
                                  LOCAL.CONT.HOOK
                                    [ INDEX #target,
                                      ICONS-KEY #icons ] ] > ],
                            VAL [ SUBJ < >,
                                  COMPS < >,
                                  SPR < >,
                                  SPEC < > ] ],
                      CONT.ICONS
                        <! #icons & [ TARGET #target ] !> ] ].
```

12.4 Customized grammar creation

(15) ```
    focus-marking-mod-lex := infostr-marking-mod-lex &
      [SYNSEM.LOCAL.CAT [MKG fc,
                          HEAD.MOD
                            < [L-PERIPH luk,
                                LOCAL
                                  [CAT.HEAD noun,
                                    CONT.HOOK.ICONS-KEY
                                      focus]] >]].
```

Since a modifier and its modificand are combined with each other by a phrase structure rule, the customization script additionally creates some TDL statements related to *head-mod-phrase*. For example, if the language employs an information-structure marking modifier and the modifier appears after its modificand, *head-adj-int-phrase* (a subtype of *basic-head-mod-phrase-simple*) and *head-adj-int* are inserted into mylang.tdl and rules.tdl, respectively. Additionally, an entry for the information-structure marking modifier is specified in lexicon.tdl.

### 12.4.2 Syntactic positioning

The customization script information_structure.py also creates grammatical fragments in TDL for constraining focus or topic in a specific position. As an initial step, the script merges the users' choices into a single type. For example, if a language places focused constituents in the clause-initial position and the language has the topic-first restriction, clause-initial constituents ex situ are specified as *focus-or-topic* in the language.

As mentioned in Section 12.3.4, languages with a fixed word order (e.g. SVO, SOV, VSO, VOS, OSV, and OVS) employ a specific type of *head-filler-phrase* for clause-initial and clause-final focus and clause-initial topic. In other words, the focused and topicalized constituents fill out the syntactic gap of the remaining part of a sentence. The remaining part of the sentence is realized as non-main-clausal constituents (e.g. *head-nmc-subj-phrase* and *head-nmc-comp-phrase*), which (i) have a nonempty list in NON-LOCAL|SLASH, and flag features indicating (ii) the phrase cannot be a main clause (i.e. [MC –]), and (iii) the phrase is not peripheral (i.e. [L-PERIPH –, R-PERIPH –]). Such a phrasal type with the *nmc* prefix should be combined with phrases with [L-PERIPH +] or [R-PERIPH +] to constitute a *infostr-filler-head-phrase*. The assignment of an *info-str* value is carried out by *infostr-dislocated-phrase* presented in (16). The gap is filled in by *infostr-filler-head-phrase* presented in (17).[3] Since this type specifies [L-PERIPH –] on itself, no further combination to the left side is allowed.

---

[3] In the case of right dislocation, *infostr-head-filler-phrase* which inherits from *nc-filler-phrase* instead of *basic-head-filler-phrase* is used.
```

12 Customizing information structure

(16) infostr-dislocated-phrase := no-rels-hcons-rule & narrow-focus &
```
  [ SYNSEM.LOCAL.CAT.MC +,
    C-CONT.ICONS <! info-str & #icons &
                    [ TARGET #index, CLAUSE #clause ] !>,
    HEAD-DTR.SYNSEM.LOCAL
      [ CAT [ MC -,
              HEAD verb ],
        CONT.HOOK [ INDEX #clause,
                    CLAUSE-KEY #clause ] ],
    NON-HEAD-DTR.SYNSEM
      [ LIGHT -,
        LOCAL [ CAT.HEAD +np,
                CONT.HOOK [ INDEX #index,
                            ICONS-KEY #icons ] ] ] ].
```

(17) infostr-filler-head-phrase := basic-head-filler-phrase &
                                   infostr-dislocated-phrase &
                                   head-final &
```
  [ SYNSEM.L-PERIPH +,
    HEAD-DTR.SYNSEM [ L-PERIPH -, LOCAL.CAT.VAL.SUBJ < > ],
    NON-HEAD-DTR.SYNSEM.LOCAL.CONT.HOOK.ICONS-KEY
      semantic-focus ].
```

If the user's language employs a fixed word order, preverbal and postverbal focus is constrained not by *head-filler-phrase*, but by specific types of *head-subj-phrase* and *head-comp-phrase*. Since preverbal/postverbal foci are immediately adjoined to the verb or the verb cluster,[4] they do not behave as a syntactic filler. Such a specific phrasal type imposes [LIGHT +] on the HEAD-DTR and [ICONS-KEY *focus*] (or a subtype of *focus*) on the NON-HEAD-DTR. What is significant here is using a flag feature, namely INFOSTR-FLAG. This feature indicates whether a constituent can be used as the preverbal and postverbal focus. *Narrow-focused-phrase*, presented in (18), is a unary phrase structure rule that specifies the plus value of INFOSTR-FLAG and introduces an element into ICONS. Only constituents with [INFOSTR-FLAG +] can be narrowly focused as constrained by *head-nf-comp-phrase-super* given in (19) (or *head-nf-subj-phrase-super*). The specific value of *info-str* (e.g. *focus*) is assigned by *nf-comp-head-phrase* (or its siblings) presented in (20).

---

[4]See the Basque example presented in Section 8.3.2 (p. 156), in which the subject is combined with a verb plus an auxiliary.

12.4 Customized grammar creation

(18) narrow-focused-phrase := head-only & no-rels-hcons-rule &
```
    [ C-CONT [ HOOK #hook,
              ICONS <! focus-or-topic & #icons &
                     [ TARGET #target ] !> ],
      SYNSEM [ LIGHT -,
               INFOSTR-FLAG +,
               LOCAL [ CAT.VAL [ SPR < >,
                                 SUBJ < >,
                                 COMPS < >,
                                 SPEC < > ],
                       CONT.HOOK [ INDEX #target,
                                   ICONS-KEY #icons ] ] ],
      HEAD-DTR.SYNSEM [ LIGHT -,
                        INFOSTR-FLAG -,
                        LOCAL [ CAT.HEAD noun,
                                CONT [ HOOK #hook,
                                       ICONS <! !> ] ] ] ].
```

(19) head-nf-comp-phrase-super := basic-head-comp-phrase &
```
                                  narrow-focus &
    [ SYNSEM.LOCAL.CAT [ MC -, VAL.COMPS #comps ],
      HEAD-DTR.SYNSEM.LOCAL.CAT.VAL.COMPS < #synsem . #comps >,
      NON-HEAD-DTR.SYNSEM #synsem & [ INFOSTR-FLAG + ] ].
```

(20) nf-comp-head-phrase := head-nf-comp-phrase-super &
```
                             head-final &
    [ SYNSEM.LOCAL.CAT.MC -,
      HEAD-DTR.SYNSEM [ LIGHT +,
                        LOCAL.CAT.MC - ],
      NON-HEAD-DTR.SYNSEM.LOCAL [ CAT.HEAD +np,
                                  CONT.HOOK.ICONS-KEY focus ] ].
```

When these constraints are included in users' grammar, other ordinary phrase structure rules have an additional constraint: [INFOSTR-FLAG +] on themselves and their daughter(s).

If the word order is flexible (e.g. v-final and v-initial), no subtype of *head-filler-phrase* is introduced. Instead, *head-subj-phrase* and/or *head-comp-phrase* become twofold, depending on the positioning constraint(s). Such a twofold strategy is the same as how scrambling in Japanese and Korean is constrained with respect to information structure roles (Section 10.3). In this case, the flag feature INFOSTR-FLAG is also used, because arguments ex situ introduce an *info-str* element into ICONS while arguments in situ do not. INFOSTR-FLAG serves to make a distinction between them. That is, this strategy is almost the same as that in languages that employ a fixed word order and place focused constituents in the preverbal or postverbal position. The same goes for V2 languages. If a

12 Customizing information structure

language employs the V2 word order (e.g. Yiddish), all information structure-marked constituents are dealt with in the same way as in (18-20). Section 12.6 shows how information structure in V2 languages is customized with reference to two particular V2 languages: Frisian and Yiddish.

There is still room for refinement, which should be studied in future work. First, the treatment of free word order languages (e.g. Russian) could be improved. It is reported that word ordering variation in in such languages largely depends on information structure (Rodionova 2001). Grammatical modules for constraining positions of information structure components in free word order languages should be designed in tandem with a study of the full range of word order possibilities. Second, *head-filler* also predicts the possibility of long-distance dependencies, which are not fully tested in the present work. Whether or not using *head-filler* for constraining information structure causes unforeseen side effects should be thoroughly investigated in future work.

12.5 Regression testing

When developing a grammar library, regression testing using testsuites (a collection of sentences intended to demonstrate the capabilities of the implementation, Bender et al. 2007) is crucial. Using a set of testsuites, regression testing checks if a new implementation works well with all the previous functionality in the development of software. That is to say, regression testing ensures that the newly adapted development is not detrimental to the previous implementation. I ran the regression tests from all previous libraries in order to confirm that my library did not break anything, and then added regression tests to document the current library for information structure.

12.5.1 Testsuites

The first step is to develop pseudo languages, picking up hypothetical types of languages that that show the full range of information structure marking systems and to write down sentences for each pseudo language. The testsuites represent abstract language types in the space defined by "Information Structure" library.

Testsuites for pseudo languages consist of pseudo words that stand for sentential configurations. Each pseudo word indicates its linguistic category, similar to glosses in interlinear annotation. For example, CN in the string stands for 'Common Noun', IV for 'Intransitive Verb', TV for 'Transitive Verb', and so on. The linear order of the elements within strings simulates the word order. For instance,

"CN IV" is an instance of an intransitive sentence like *Dogs bark*. In the pseudo languages that I created for testing this library, there are several specific strings that simulate an *info-str* role. For instance, a morpheme '-FC' or a separate word (i.e. an adposition and a modifier) 'FC' (FoCus), can be used in languages that employ lexical markers to yield focus meaning. For example, "CN-FC IN" carries an information structure meaning similar to what DOGS *bark* conveys. Each testsuite includes both grammatical pseudo sentences and ungrammatical ones. For example, "IV CN" in which the verb (IN) is inversed may or may not be grammatical depending on whether the grammar allows clause-final or postverbal focus.

The pseudo languages are created according to several factors that have an influence on information structure marking. These include (a) components of information structure (i.e. focus, topic, contrast), (b) word order, and (c) means of expression (i.e. prosody, lexical markers, syntactic positioning). For example, a pseudo language *infostr-foc-svo-initial* is a SVO language and places focused constituents in the clause-initial position.

12.5.2 Pseudo grammars

The second step is to customize each grammar for each testsuite. After a language phenomenon in the testsuites is analyzed and implemented into a library, the library should be verified via regression testing. This checks out if the current system works right using regression tests. Grammatical sentences should be parsed and generated, while ungrammatical ones should not. A parse tree and its MRS representation should indicate information structure roles correctly. This step also includes checking the resulting semantic representations by hand, which then become the gold standard for future runs to check against.

I created 46 pseudo grammars (i.e. 46 choices files) for regression tests of the "Information Structure" library. These grammars are representative of a range of information structure marking in human language.

First, I referred to the choices of word order and focus position. There are nine options of word order, excluding free word order, namely SVO, SOV, VSO, VOS, OSV, OVS, v-final, v-initial, and v2. On the other hand, there are four options of focus positions, namely clause-initial, clause-final, preverbal, and postverbal. Thus, using these two factors, logically we can have 36 grammars (9×4). Among them, I excluded four grammars which I doubted if such types authentically exist in natural languages. For instance, if NPs canonically appear in the clause-final or postverbal position, we cannot say that the language is a genuine v-final language. All human languages presumably have right dislocation constructions (Lambrecht 1996), but they are non-canonical at least in v-final and v-initial lan-

12 Customizing information structure

guages. Note that the present work does not use *head-filler-phrase* for these languages. For example, Korean is a v-final language and employs right dislocation (T. Kim 2011), but the constructions do not seem to be *head-filler-phrases*. The excluded ones include `infostr-foc-vf-final`, `infostr-foc-vf-postv`, `infostr-foc-vi-initial`, and `infostr-foc-vi-prev`. Thus, I developed 32 grammars. This subgroup is called TYPE A. Second, three grammars in which multiple positions are used for different components of information structure were added. This subgroup is called TYPE B. The other subgroups in which lexical markers are chosen are TYPE C. Third, three types of lexical markers (affixes, adpositions, and modifiers) that express focus are separately chosen in the creation of pseudo grammars (TYPE C-1). Fourth, the other three components (topic, contrastive focus, contrastive topic) are selected with an option of modifiers (TYPE C-2). Fifth, the categorical choices (e.g. nouns, verbs, and both) and positioning choices are also considered. This provided five more grammars (TYPE C-3).

12.5.3 Processing

The third step is running the regression tests.[5] I ran a series of regression tests with the `choices` files which were previously created without considering ICONS. After getting 100% of matches using the previous testsuites, then I created new gold profiles with ICONS using ACE (http://sweaglesw.org/linguistics/ace). The newly created profiles were manually checked to make sure the ICONS were properly computed.

12.6 Testing with Language CoLLAGE

Language CoLLAGE (Collection of Language Lore Amassed through Grammar Engineering) is a repository of student-created grammars built on the LinGO Grammar Matrix system (Bender 2014). This collection of grammars covers a variety of language types in different language families, and a linguistic survey of them could offer valuable insights into language phenomena in human language. Language CoLLAGE provides a set of grammars, `choices` files, and testsuites for five languages, and there are many other languages to be curated later.[6]

---

[5] The processor for the regression test was LKB previously, but I modified the script to run with ACE. Because there were some minor mismatches in representation between LKB and ACE, some gold profiles used in the regression test were altered.

[6] This language resource is readily available under the MIT license.

12.6 Testing with Language CoLLAGE

Table 12.1: Customized grammars with information structure in 2013

name	ISO 639-3	language family
Classical Chinese	[lzh]	Sino-Tibetan
(Northern) Frisian†	[frr]	Indo-European
Halkomelem	[hur]	Salish
Lakota†	[lkt]	Siouan
Miyako†	[mvi]	Japonic
Penobscot	[aaq-pen]	Algic
Yiddish†	[ydd]	Indo-European

The grammars were created in fulfillment of a grammar engineering course in the Department of Linguistics at the University of Washington, Linguistics 567 (http://courses.washington.edu/ling567, Bender 2007). In 2013, information structure in seven languages was explored and customized using the initial version of the information structure library in this course. These seven languages are listed in Table 12.1. Of these, there are four languages for which the respective grammar's author gave full permission for the grammar to be used in Language CoLLAGE. They are marked with † in Table 12.1: (Northern) Frisian, Lakota, Miyako, and Yiddish.

After the course concluded, I refined the grammar library for information structure based on the results of the customized grammars and the feedback of their authors. Thus, in the spirit of regression testing, it was necessary to check if the updated library still worked with the students' grammars. I tested whether the newer version provided a better representation of information structure, and whether there was an adverse effect on grammar configuration. Moreover, it is necessary to examine how information structure in these languages is articulated and represented. Saleem (2010) makes use of three types of languages for evaluating her "Argument Optionality" library, namely pseudo languages, illustrative languages, and held-out languages. Pseudo languages are hypothetical languages (i.e. not human languages) that indicate the major properties of language phenomenon that the library developer has a keen interest in. Illustrative languages are actual languages whose analysis was considered during the development of the Grammar Matrix library. This contrasts with held-out languages (i.e. natural languages used in the evaluation of the library only). Thus, the four languages (Frisian, Lakota, Miyako, and Yiddish) in this testing play a similar role to illustrative languages. One difference is that the four grammars used here were already

12 Customizing information structure

constructed with specifications on information structure properties by the initial library. I used their `choices` files in order to compare the two results produced by the initial library and the newer library.

12.6.1 Languages

The four languages differ typologically and employ different strategies of marking information structure. (i) Northern Frisian (spoken in Schleswig-Holstein, Germany) is a V2 language. That is, verbs in Frisian have to appear in the second position in the word order, and the first position can be occupied by subjects or objects. According to the `choices` file created by the developers, Frisian makes use of the preverbal position to indicate focus, and contrastive and non-contrastive focus share this position. Accordingly, the preverbal objects in Frisian are assigned a plain *focus* (a supertype of both *semantic-focus* and *contrast-focus*). (ii) Yiddish is also a V2 language, and employs focus/topic-fronting. That is, focused and topicalized constituents occur sentence-initially.[7] Thus, fronted constituents in Yiddish are assigned *focus-or-topic*. (iii) Miyako (a Ryukyuan language spoken in Okinawa, Japan) is very similar to Japanese. It makes use of information-structure marking adpositions. There are three adpositions of expressing information structure. Two of them signal topic, but they are different in case assignment (i.e. *a* for nominatives vs. *baa* for accusatives). The other one, spelled as *du*, signals focus, and can be used for both nominatives and accusatives. (iv) Lakota (a Siouan language spoken around North and South Dakota) uses a specific definite determiner *k'uŋ* to signal contrastive topic. The information-structure related fragments taken from the `choices` files are presented in (21).

(21) a. (Northern) Frisian
```
section=info-str
focus-pos=preverbal
c-focus=on
```
b. Yiddish
```
section=info-str
focus-pos=clause-initial
topic-first=on
```

---

[7] As surveyed before in Section 5.2 (p. 74), if focus and topic contest for the sentence-initial position, topic normally wins. However, I have not yet verified if this generalization is straightforwardly applied to V2 languages.

12.6 Testing with Language CoLLAGE

c. Miyako
```
section=info-str
  focus-marker1_type=adp
  topic-marker1_type=adp
...
  adp6_orth=a
  adp6_order=after
    adp6_feat1_name=information-structure marking
    adp6_feat1_value=tp
    adp6_feat2_name=information-structure meaning
    adp6_feat2_value=topic
    adp6_feat3_name=case
    adp6_feat3_value=nom
  adp7_orth=du
  adp7_order=after
    adp7_feat1_name=information-structure marking
    adp7_feat1_value=fc
    adp7_feat2_name=information-structure meaning
    adp7_feat2_value=focus
  adp8_orth=baa
  adp8_order=after
    adp8_feat1_name=information-structure marking
    adp8_feat1_value=tp
    adp8_feat2_name=information-structure meaning
    adp8_feat2_value=topic
    adp8_feat3_name=case
    adp8_feat3_value=acc
```
d. Lakota
```
det11_name=def-pst
  det11_stem1_orth=k'uŋ
  det11_stem1_pred=_def-pst_q_rel
  det11_feat1_name=information-structure meaning
  det11_feat1_value=contrast-topic
```

12.6.2 Testsuites

The numbers of sentences in each testsuite for the four languages are shown in Table 12.2. Note that testsuites consist of both grammatical sentences and ungrammatical sentences. Each testsuite also includes test items that represent how information structure is configured for the language.

12.6.3 Comparison

The data set of Language CoLLAGE includes the final grammar and the choices file, in addition to the testsuite. Using the choices file, I created two different ver-

12 Customizing information structure

Table 12.2: # of test items

language	# of total items	# of grammatical items	# of information-structure related items
Frisian	164	109	6
Yiddish	228	150	6
Miyako	102	71	6
Lakota	168	100	2

sions. One was customized by the previous library, and the other was customized by the new library. These two versions of grammars are represented as 'old' and 'new' respectively hereafter. I ran these two grammars plus the final grammar ('final') provided by each developer to see the coverage and the number of parse trees. Using the LKB and [incr tsdb()], I parsed all test items in the testsuites for each language, and then examined how many sentences were covered by each grammar (i.e. coverage) and how many readings were produced (i.e. number of parse trees).

First, coverage of these three types of grammars are compared. The grammars created only using the choices file include the main linguistic modules that can be fully created on the LinGO Grammar Matrix customization system, while the final grammars ('final') contain more elaborated types and rules that developers manually edited. Accordingly, the final grammars always yield better coverage than the other two versions of each grammar. Regarding 'old', and 'new', ideally, the coverage between the grammars created by the old library and those created by the new library should be the same. That is to say, the distinction between handling grammatical sentences and ungrammatical sentences should not have changed. The coverage that each grammar produced were calculated as shown in Table 12.3. As indicated in the third and fourth columns of Table 12.3, there was no difference in coverage between the two versions of the grammars.

Second, the number of parse trees (i.e. readings) may or may not have changed. This is because I elaborated phrase structure rules that place constraints on syntactic positioning of marking information structure. In particular, one of the main components that I refined in the newer version is a routine that deals with narrow foci in V2 languages. In fact, the old version had a vulnerability in constraining narrow foci in V2 languages, and syntactic composition did not work well. As shown in the third and fourth column of Table 12.4, the numbers of parse trees produced by the grammars in Miyako and Lakota are the same, while those

12.6 Testing with Language CoLLAGE

Table 12.3: Coverage (%)

language	final	old	new
Frisian	70.6	45.0	45.0
Yiddish	60.0	32.0	32.0
Miyako	77.5	38.0	38.0
Lakota	91.0	60.0	60.0

Table 12.4: # of readings

language	final	old	new
Frisian	178	195	209
Yiddish	118	97	98
Miyako	80	34	34
Lakota	103	62	62

in V2 languages increase in the new versions. I manually checked whether the newly produced parse trees were properly constructed and their semantic representations were correct. That implies that the newer version performs better.

12.6.4 Information structure in the four languages

Finally, I checked out how information-structure related test items, whose numbers are given in the last column of Table 12.2, were parsed and represented in the ICONS list. I found that the customized grammars had complete coverage over these items and returned correct analyses.

Frisian, a V2 language, is specified as placing focused constituents in the preverbal position irrespective of contrastiveness. As discussed before in Section 12.4.2, this language includes *head-nf-comp-phrase-super*, *nf-comp-head-phrase*, and *narrow-focused-phrase*. The value of *info-str* that preverbal foci have is *focus* which can be used for both *semantic-focus* and *contrast-focus*.

Yiddish employs focus/topic-fronting. The grammar for Yiddish also includes *head-nf-comp-phrase-super*, *nf-comp-head-phrase*, and *narrow-focused-phrase* like Frisian, and the value of *info-str* that fronted constituents involve is constrained as *focus-or-topic*.

Three adpositions that mark information structure in Miyako were also inspected. For example, the nominative topic marker *a* in Miyako is customized as follows.

```
(22) top-marker := case-marking-adp-lex &
       [ STEM < "a" >,
         SYNSEM.LOCAL [ CAT [ VAL.COMPS
                              < [ LOCAL.CONT.HOOK.INDEX #target ] >,
                              HEAD.CASE nom,
                              MKG tp ],
                        CONT [ ICONS <! #icons & info-str &
                                        [ TARGET #target ] !>,
                              HOOK.ICONS-KEY #icons & topic ] ] ].
```

12 Customizing information structure

The adpositions introduce an *info-str* element into ICONS, and the value is successfully copied up the trees.

The topic-marking determiner *k'uŋ* in Lakota is an instance of *def-pst-determiner-lex* in the grammar, and the type is described as follows.

```
(23) infostr-marking-determiner-lex := basic-determiner-lex &
                                       one-icons-lex-item &
     [ SYNSEM.LOCAL [ CAT.VAL.SPEC.FIRST.LOCAL.CONT.HOOK
                        [ INDEX #target,
                          ICONS-KEY #icons ],
                      CONT.ICONS
                        <! info-str & #icons & [ TARGET #target] !> ] ].

     def-pst-determiner-lex := determiner-lex &
                               infostr-marking-determiner-lex &
     [ SYNSEM.LOCAL.CAT.VAL.SPEC.FIRST.LOCAL.CONT.HOOK.ICONS-KEY
         contrast-topic ].
```

The *infostr-marking-determiner-lex* type includes an element in CONT|ICONS (i.e. *one-icons-lex-item*), and *def-pst-determiner-lex* constrains the value as *contrast-topic*. This value comes from the user's choice given in (21d).

12.6.5 Summary

This section substantiates whether my newer version of the information structure library works well using four grammars and choices provided in Language CoLLAGE (Frisian, Lakota, Miyako, and Yiddish). I customized four old versions of grammars as well as four new versions of grammars using the choices files. Exploiting the testsuites also included in Language CoLLAGE, I ran the grammars to see if there was no change in coverage, and how many parse trees were produced. Notably, I recognized that the newer version yielded better performance in manipulating information structure in V2 languages (Frisian and Yiddish). Additionally, I verified that information structure values were properly constrained and the values were incrementally augmented in the ICONS list. In summary, I confirmed that the newer version correctly operated at least with these four languages.

12.7 Live-site

All the components of the information structure library (e.g. web-based questionnaire, the Matrix-core in TDL, and the Python code for validation and customization) were successfully implemented in the LinGO Grammar Matrix system. The library for information structure was added in the live site of the customization system, whose url is presented below.

(24) http://www.delph-in.net/matrix/customize

Thereby, the functionality of the information structure library is now available for all users of the Grammar Matrix customization system.

12.8 Download

The source code is downloadable in the subversion repository of the LinGO Grammar Matrix system (25a). The specific version that the present study describes is separately provided, and can be obtained from (25b). This version is also independently served in another web page, whose url is (25c).

(25) a. svn://lemur.ling.washington.edu/shared/matrix/trunk

   b. svn://lemur.ling.washington.edu/shared/matrix/branches/sanghoun

   c. http://depts.washington.edu/uwcl/sanghoun/matrix.cgi

13 Multilingual machine translation

Using information structure can improve multilingual machine translation. A machine translation system informed by information structure is capable of reducing the number of infelicitous translations dramatically. This reduction has two effects on the performance of transfer-based machine translation (Song & Bender 2011): First, the processing burden of the machine translation component which ranks the translations and selects only suitable results can be greatly lightened, which should improve translation speed. Second, although it is still necessary to employ a re-ranking model for choosing translations, we can start from a refined set of translations, which should improve translation accuracy.

Section 13.1 goes over the basis of transfer-based machine translation. Section 13.2 offers an explanation of how ICONS (Individual CONStraints) operate in transfer-based machine translation. Section 13.3 addresses the processor the current work employs for testing machine translation. Section 13.4 conducts an evaluation to examine how many infelicitous translations are filtered out by means of ICONS.

13.1 Transfer-based machine translation

The basic method I employ for testing machine translation herein is built on the symbolic approach to machine translation, which normally consists of three stages: (i) parsing, (ii) transfer, and (iii) generation. Since MRS is not an interlingua (a meaning representation language in which the representations are identical for all languages), using MRS for machine translation requires an independent stage to convert one MRS into another MRS. This stage is called transfer, and is carried out between parsing and generation.

Figure 13.1, adapted from Oepen et al. (2007) and Song et al. (2010), is illustrative of the MRS-based architecture of machine translation. The first step (i.e. parsing) analyses a sentence with a computational grammar for the source language, whose output is a form of semantic representation such as a (near) logical form. The output of the first step serves as the source of the next step (i.e. transfer), which is called MRS_s (i.e. an input MRS). The transfer module converts the

13 Multilingual machine translation

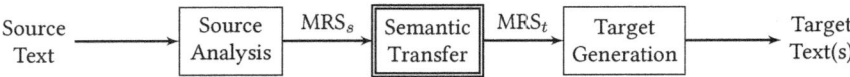

Figure 13.1: HPSG/MRS-based MT architecture

source representation obtained from the parsing process into another type of representation compatible with the target language, which is called MRS_t (i.e. an output MRS). MRS_t is used as the source for the final step (i.e. generation), which constructs one or more surface forms built from the semantic representation. As a consequence, the two surface forms in the source language and the target language are compatible with a common meaning representation.

13.2 Basic machinery

A graph presented in (1a) represents an English sentence in which the subject *the DOG* bears the A-accent, thereby plays the role of *semantic-focus*. The second graph in (1b) represents the Japanese translation, in which the subject *inu* 'dog' is combined with the nominative marker *ga* that signals *non-topic*. That is to say, although the two sentences provided in (1a–b) are proper translations of each other, information is differently structured.

(1) a. 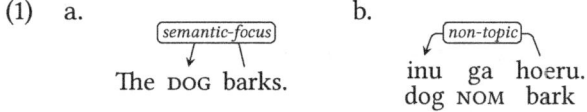 b.

        inu ga hoeru.
        dog NOM bark

Note that *non-topic* is a supertype of *semantic-focus* in the type hierarchy of *info-str* given in Figure 7.1 (p. 114). This ability to partially specify information structure allows us to reduce the range of outputs in translation while still capturing all legitimate possibilities.

Two hypothetical suffixes *-a* and *-b* are employed for testing hereafter, and they represent the A and B accents in English (Bolinger 1961; Jackendoff 1972) respectively. Note that the *-b* suffix cannot be attached to the verb *barks*, because verbs presumably cannot be marked via B-accent for the information structure role of *topic* in English. *The dog barks* without any information structure marking logically can be interpreted as six types of sentences (3×2).

(2) dog   dog: [ICONS: < >]
            dog-a: [ICONS: < e2 **semantic-focus** x4 >]
            dog-b: [ICONS: < e2 **contrast-or-topic** x4 >]
     bark   barks: [ICONS: < >]
            barks-a: [ICONS: < e2 **semantic-focus** e2 >]

However, if we apply ICONS to generation, we can filter out sentences which are not equivalent to the input sentence with respect to information structure. For example, if the input sentences are *The DOG barks* and *The **dog** barks* in which the subject bears the A and B accents respectively, they can be monolingually paraphrased as (3). That is, four infelicitous sentences from each set of sentences can be removed. Two sentences in (3a-i) and (3a-iii) cannot be generated because the subject does not include any value in ICONS. In other words, information structure-marked constituents in the source cannot be generated as an unmarked constituent in the target. Two sentences in (3a-v) and (3a-vi) cannot be generated, either. This is because the B-accented subject conveys *contrast-or-topic* which is incompatible with *semantic-focus*. The same goes for (3b): Since only the last two sentences are compatible with the information structure meaning that the input sentence conveys, the others cannot be paraphrased with respect to information structure.

(3) a. The dog-a barks [ICONS: < e2 **semantic-focus** x4 >]
         (i) ~~The dog barks~~
         (ii) The dog-a barks
         (iii) ~~The dog barks-a~~
         (iv) The dog-a barks-a
         (v) ~~The dog-b barks~~
         (vi) ~~The dog-b barks-a~~

     b. The dog-b barks [ICONS: < e2 **contrast-or-topic** x4 >]
         (i) ~~The dog barks~~
         (ii) ~~The dog-a barks~~
         (iii) ~~The dog barks-a~~
         (iv) ~~The dog-a barks-a~~
         (v) The dog-b barks
         (vi) The dog-b barks-a

The same goes for Japanese in which lexical markers signal information structure. There are at least three Japanese translations (i.e. case-marking, *wa*-marking,

13 Multilingual machine translation

and null-marking) corresponding to *The dog barks*, but case-marked NPs cannot be paraphrased into *wa*-marked NPs within our *info-str* hierarchy given in Figure 7.1, and vice versa. Note that null-marked items in Japanese (e.g. *inu* in 4a-iii and 4b-iii) are assigned *non-focus* (Yatabe 1999), which is compatible with both *non-topic* in (4a) and *contrast-or-topic* (4b). Thus, both *inu ga hoeru* and *inu wa hoeru* can be paraphrased into *inu hoeru*.

(4) a. inu **ga** hoeru [ICONS: < e2 **non-topic** x4 >]
   (i) inu ga hoeru
   (ii) ~~inu wa hoeru~~
   (iii) inu hoeru
  b. inu **wa** hoeru [ICONS: < e2 **contrast-or-topic** x4 >]
   (i) ~~inu ga hoeru~~
   (ii) inu wa hoeru
   (iii) inu hoeru

Translating across languages is constrained in the same manner. An English sentence (5a) cannot be translated into (5a-ii) and (5a-iii), because the *semantic-focus* role that DOG involves is incompatible with the *contrast-or-topic* role that *wa* assigns and the *non-focus* role that the null marker (indicated by ∅) involves. On the other hand, a Japanese sentence (5b) can be translated into only (5b-ii) and (5b-iv). First, because *non-topic*, which comes from the nominative marker *ga*, is contradictory to *contrast-or-topic* that the B-accent signals in English, (5b-v) and (5b-vi) are filtered out. Second, because the constituent corresponding to the *ga*-marked subject should introduce an *info-str* element into ICONS, (5b-i) and (5b-iii) are ruled out.

(5) a. The dog-a barks [ICONS: < e2 **semantic-focus** x4 >]
   (i) inu ga hoeru
   (ii) ~~inu wa hoeru~~
   (iii) ~~inu hoeru~~
  b. inu **ga** hoeru [ICONS: < e2 **non-topic** x4 >]
   (i) ~~The dog barks~~
   (ii) The dog-a barks
   (iii) ~~The dog barks-a~~
   (iv) The dog-a barks-a
   (v) ~~The dog-b barks~~
   (vi) ~~The dog-b barks-a~~

13.3 Processor

The processor the present work uses for the purpose of evaluation is ACE.[1] ACE parses the sentences of natural languages, and generates sentences based on the MRS (Minimal Recursion Semantics, Copestake et al. 2005) representation that the parser creates. As the data ACE uses DELPH-IN grammars, including LinGO Grammar Matrix grammars created by the customization system (Bender & Flickinger 2005; Drellishak 2009; Bender et al. 2010) and resource grammars (e.g. the ERG (English Resource Grammar, Flickinger 2000).

When creating the data file of ACE, ACE refers to parameters described in *ace/-config.tdl*. In the configuration file, grammar users can choose whether or not ICONS is used in MRS representation. The snippet that enables ICONS to be included in MRS representation is as follows.

(6) ```
enable-icons := yes.
   mrs-icons-list := ICONS LIST.
   icons-left := CLAUSE.
   icons-right := TARGET.
```

ACE carries out ICONS-based generation via subsumption check, using the type hierarchy *info-str* (presented in Figure 7.1). ACE generates all potential sentences that logically fit in the input MRS not considering the constraints on ICONS beforehand. After that, if the data file of the grammar for generation is compiled with the parameters given in (6), ACE starts postprocessing the intermediate results. Depending on the subsumption relationship of information structure meanings, sentences mismatching the values in the ICONS list are filtered out in this step. For example, if *semantic-focus* is assigned to a specific individual in the source MRS, only outputs that provide an ICONS element for that individual can be produced. The *info-str* value an individual has in the output should be the same as that in the input (i.e. *semantic-focus*) or its supertypes (e.g. *focus*, *non-topic*, etc.). For instance, an A-accented constituent in English (e.g. DOG) contributes an ICONS element whose value is *semantic-focus*, and this element is translated as a *ga*-marked constituent (e.g. *inu ga*) whose value is monolingually *non-topic* in Japanese. Note that *non-topic* subsumes *semantic-focus* in the type hierarchy presented in Figure 7.1. A completely underspecified output for each ICONS element is not acceptable in generation. For instance, an A-accented DOG that introduces an ICONS element cannot be paraphrased as an unaccented *dog*

---

[1] ACE (http://sweaglesw.org/linguistics/ace) is the first DELPH-IN processor to specifically handle ICONS as part of the MRS, and then *agree* (Slayden 2012) also uses ICONS for constraining information structure in parsing and generation.
```

13 Multilingual machine translation

that does not contribute any ICONS element. By contrast, the opposite direction is acceptable. If a constituent introduces no ICONS element in the input, the output can include an information-structure marked constituent. For instance, an unaccented *dog* can be paraphrased as an A-accented DOG in generation.

13.4 Evaluation

13.4.1 Illustrative grammars

In order to verify a linguistic hypothesis with reference to a computational grammar, it is a good strategy to use a compact grammar presenting the fundamental rules in a precise manner. Illustrative grammars are constructed for this purpose. The illustrative languages used here are English, Japanese, and Korean. These languages are chosen, because the resource grammars for each of the language will be the main concern in my further study.[2] The information structure properties each language has are summarized in the following subsections.

13.4.1.1 English

As is well known, English employs prosody for expressing information structure. Without consideration of the prosodic patterns, we could not draw the basic picture of information-structure related phenomena in English.[3] There are quite a few previous studies on how prosody is realized with respect to information structure (Jackendoff 1972; Steedman 2000; Kadmon 2001; Büring 2003; Hedberg 2006), but there seems to be no clear consensus (as surveyed earlier in Section 4.1). The illustrative grammar for English makes use of just the traditional distinction of the A and B accents (Bolinger 1958). In order to articulate them as a string for ease of exposition, the two hypothetical suffixes *-a* and *-b* are used. However, the meanings that the accents take charge of are represented differently from the traditional approach. The information structure meanings that *-a* and *-b* convey are marked following Hedberg's argument: *-a* for *semantic-focus*

---

[2]The computational grammars include ERG Flickinger (2000), Jacy (Siegel, Bender & Bond 2016), and KRG (Kim et al. 2011).

[3]English also makes use of some constructional means to configure focus and topic. These include focus/topic fronting, clefting, etc. Nonetheless, these have to do with various grammatical components. For example, implementing grammatical modules for cleft constructions necessitates many TDL statements for relative clauses as an essential prerequisite. This involves too much complexity for an illustrative grammar to cover. For this reason, the illustrative grammar for English in this evaluation is exclusively concerned with prosody.

and *-b* for *contrast-or-topic*. The AVMs are already presented in Section 8.4.1 (p. 160).

13.4.1.2 Korean

The illustrative grammar for Korean includes two kinds of grammatical sets of constraints for expressing information structure. The first one employs lexical markers, such as *i / ka* and *(l)ul* for case marking, *-(n)un* for topic marking, and ∅ for null marking. The AVMs for these markers are presented in Section 8.4.2 (p. 165). The second fragment aims to handle scrambling. The AVMs for constraining scrambling constructions are provided in Section 10.3 (p. 199). These AVMs use different rules instantiating *head-subj-phrase* and *head-comp-phrase* with reference to lexical markings of daughters (i.e. MKG).

13.4.1.3 Japanese

As mentioned before, the present study respects the traditional ways of dealing with lexical markers in Japanese and Korean from different points of view. While lexical markers in Korean are dealt with as suffixes (Kim & Yang 2004), those in Japanese are treated as adpositions (Siegel 1999). Other than this difference, the illustrative grammar for Japanese has the same configuration as that for Korean explained above. Notably, the null marker in Japanese is constrained by a lexical rule in the current work (p. 162), which is different from previous HPSG-based suggestion about so-called case-ellipsis (Yatabe 1999; Sato & Tam 2012).

13.4.2 Testsuites

The testsuites (a collection of sentence to be modeled) for this multilingual machine translation testing are provided in (7-9); English, Japanese, and Korean, respectively. There is one intransitive sentence and one transitive sentence in English, and they are encoded with two hypothetical suffixes and differentiated as allosentences.

13 Multilingual machine translation

(7) [1] The dog barks
[2] The dog-a barks
[3] The dog barks-a
[4] The dog-b barks
[5] The dog-b barks-a
[6] The dog-a barks-a
[7] Kim reads the book
[8] Kim-a reads the book
[9] Kim reads-a the book
[10] Kim reads the book-a
[11] Kim-b reads-a the book
[12] Kim-b reads the book-a

(8) [1] 犬 吠える
[2] 犬 が 吠える
[3] 犬 吠える
[4] 犬 は 吠える
[5] 犬 は 吠える
[6] 犬 が 吠える
[7] キム 本 読む
[8] キム が 本 読む
[9] キム 本 読む
[10] キム 本 を 読む
[11] キム は 本 読む
[12] キム は 本 を 読む

(9) [1] 개 짖다
[2] 개가 짖다
[3] 개 짖다
[4] 개는 짖다
[5] 개는 짖다
[6] 개가 짖다
[7] 김 책 읽다
[8] 김이 책 읽다
[9] 김 책 읽다
[10] 김 책을 읽다
[11] 김은 책 읽다
[12] 김은 책을 읽다

13.4.3 An experiment

All test items presented in (7) and their translations in Japanese and Korean are parsed, transferred, and generated. Table 13.1 and Table 13.2 show the number of translation results in each translation pair. The first column in each table indicates the source language, and the first row indicates the target language. For example, [English → Japanese] produces 126 translations when not using ICONS, and 39 translations when using ICONS.

13.4 Evaluation

Table 13.1: # of outputs without ICONS

	eng	jpn	kor
eng	144	126	126
jpn	990	180	180
kor	1080	198	198

Table 13.2: # of outputs with ICONS

	eng	jpn	kor
eng	53	39	39
jpn	150	120	150
kor	140	115	154

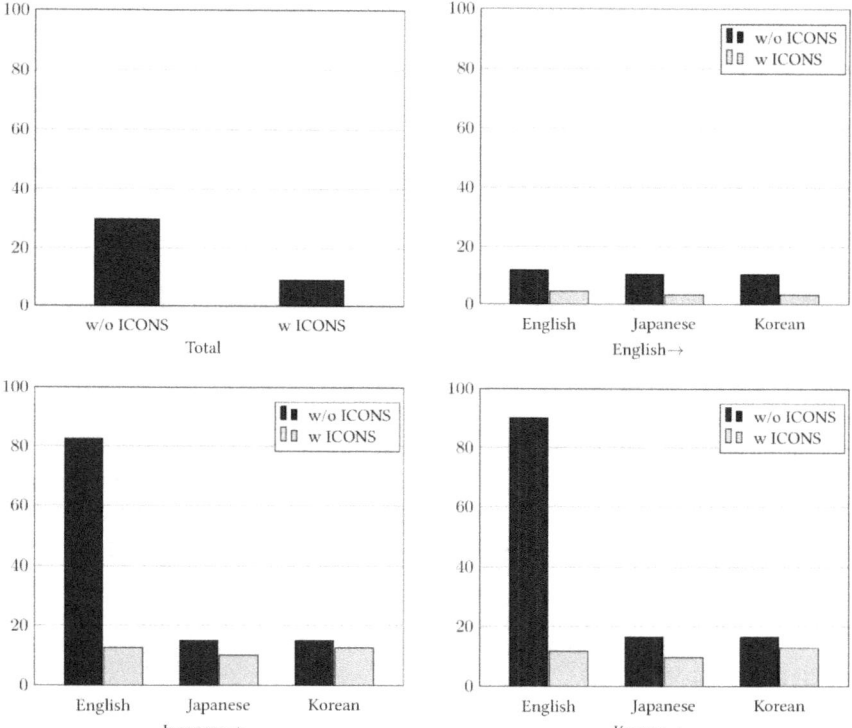

Figure 13.2: Average # of outputs

As indicated in the tables, the number of generated sentences dramatically decreases when using ICONS. The total number of translation outputs in Table 15.1 is 3,222, while that in Table 15.2 is merely 960.[4] That means approximately 70% of the translations are filtered out in total when using ICONS.

---

[4] When the source language is not English and the target language is English, the numbers are rather big in Table 15.1. This is because English employs number and COG-ST features, while Japanese and Korean do not. For example, *inu* in Japanese can be translated into at least four NP types in English: *a dog, the dog, the dogs,* and *dogs*.

13 Multilingual machine translation

The four charts in Figure 13.2 compare the average number of outputs in total and in each translation pair. The decrease indicated in each bar chart shows that information structure can be used to filter out inappropriate sentences from the translation result.

These charts show that when translating Japanese and Korean to English many outputs are filtered out. The main reason for the dramatic decrease in [Japanese → English] and [Korean → English] is that the illustrative grammar for English includes a lexical rule to mark focus on verbal items, while the illustrative grammars for Japanese and Korean do not. When a verb is focused in the English grammar, the lexical rule introduces a *focus* element into ICONS. In contrast, verbs cannot involve any *info-str* value in the current illustrative grammars for Japanese and Korean. Thus, the huge difference in [Japanese → English] and [Korean → English] is largely caused by the different marking system for verbal items.

Finally, I verified 108 sets of translation outputs (9 directions × 12 test items) by hand. The same problem was also found. When an English item includes an A-accented verb (e.g. *barks-a* and *reads-a*), the item cannot be translated into Japanese and Korean. This suggest that there might be a problem with the strategy of requiring some information structure marking in the output for an item if there is some in the input. Other than this difference, the translation outputs were legitimate and felicitous. I also sampled the filtered translations to verify that they were all infelicitous ones, and found that this information structure-based model works for them, too.

13.5 Summary

It is my firm opinion that translating should mean reshaping the ways in which information is conveyed, not simply changing words and reordering phrases. In almost all human languages, articulation of sentential constituents is conditioned by information structure. Because the means of expressing information structure differs across languages, identifying how information is structured in a given set of languages plays a key role in achieving felicity in a machine translation between them. Hence, information structure is of great help to multilingual machine translation in that information structure facilitates more felicitous translations. This chapter conducted a small experiment to support this hypothesis. I created three illustrative grammars for English, Japanese, and Korean following my ICONS-based analyses presented thus far. In the test of transfer-based machine translation, I found that using information structure served to filter out infelicitous translations dramatically. This testing should be further elaborated in future work using resource grammars, such as the ERG (Flickinger 2000), Jacy (Siegel, Bender & Bond 2016), and the KRG (Kim et al. 2011).

14 Conclusion

14.1 Summary

The present study began with key motivations laid out Chapter 1 for the creation of a computational model of information structure. Chapter 2 offered preliminary notes for understanding the current work.

The first part (Chapters 3 to 5) scrutinized meanings and markings of information structure from a cross-linguistic standpoint. Information structure is composed of four components: focus, topic, contrast, and background. Focus identifies that which is important and/or new in an utterance, which cannot be removed from the sentence. Topic can be understood as what the speaker is speaking about, and does not necessarily appear in a sentence (unlike focus). Contrast applies to a set of alternatives, which can be realized as either focus or topic. Lastly, background is defined as that which is neither focus nor topic. There are three means of expressing information structure: prosody, lexical markers, and syntactic positioning. Among them, the current work has been largely concerned with the last two means, leaving room for improvement in modeling the interaction between prosody and information structure as further work. There are three lexical types responsible for marking information structure: affixes, adpositions, and modifiers (e.g. clitics). Canonical positions of focus include clause-initial, clause-final, preverbal, and postverbal. Building upon these fundamental notions, Chapter 5 looked into several cases in which discrepancies in form-meaning mapping of information structure happen.

The second part (Chapters 6 to 11) proposed using ICONS (Individual CONStraints) for representing information structure in MRS (Copestake et al. 2005). This was motivated by three factors. First, information structure markings should be distinguished from information structure meanings in order to solve the apparent mismatches between them. Second, the representation of information structure should be underspecifiable, because there are many sentences whose information structure cannot be conclusively identified in the context of sentence-level, text-based processing. Third, information structure should be represented as a binary relation between an individual and a clause. In other words, informa-

14 Conclusion

tion structure roles should be filled out as being in a relationship with the clause a constituent belongs to, rather than as a property of a constituent itself. In order to meet these requirements, three type hierarchies were suggested; *mkg*, *sform*, and most importantly *info-str*. In addition to them, two types of flag features, such as L/R-PERIPH and LIGHT, were suggested for configuring focus and topic. Using hierarchies and features, the remaining chapters addressed multiclausal utterances and specific forms of expressing information structure. Furthermore, Chapter 11 calculated focus projection via ICONS.

The third part (Chapters 12 to 13) created a customization system for implementing information structure within the LinGO Grammar Matrix (Bender et al. 2010) and examined how information structure improved transfer-based multilingual machine translation. Building on cross-linguistic and corpus-based findings, a large part of HPSG/MRS-based constraints presented thus far was implemented in TDL. A web-based questionnaire was designed in order to allow users to implement information structure constraints within the `choices` file. Common constraints across languages were added into the Matrix core (`matrix.tdl`), and language-specific constraints were processed by Python scripts and stored into the customized grammar. Evaluations of this library using regression tests and Language CoLLAGE (Bender 2014) showed that this library worked well with various types of languages. Finally, an experiment of multilingual machine translation verified that using information structure reduced the number of infelicitous translations dramatically.

14.2 Contributions

The present study holds particular significance for general theoretic studies of the grammar of information structure. Quite a few languages are surveyed to capture cross-linguistic generalizations about information structure meanings and markings, which can serve as an important milestone for typological research on information structure.

The present study also makes a contribution to HPSG/MRS-based studies by enumerating strategies for representing meanings and markings of information structure within the formalism in a comprehensive and fine-grained way. Notably, the present study establishes a single formalism for representation and applies this formalism to various types of forms in a straightforward and cohesive manner. Moreover, the current model addresses how information structure can be articulated within the HPSG/MRS framework and implemented within a computational system in the context of grammar engineering.

The present study also shows that information structure can be used to produce better performance in natural language processing systems. My firm opinion is that information structure contributes to multilingual processing; languages differ from each other not merely in the words and phrases employed but in the structuring of information. It is my expectation that this study will inspire future studies in computational linguistics to pay more attention to information structure.

Last but most importantly, the present model makes a contribution to the LinGO Grammar Matrix library. The actual library makes it easy for other developers to adopt and build on my analyses of information structure. Moreover, the methodology of creating libraries I employ in this study can be used for other libraries in the system. In order to construct the model in a fine-grained way, I collected cross-linguistic findings about information structure markings and exploited a multilingual parallel text in four languages. These two methods are essential in further advancements in the LinGO framework.

14.3 Future Work

First, it is necessary to examine other types of particles responsible for marking information structure. Not all focus sensitive items are entirely implemented in TDL in the current model even for English. Japanese and Korean employ a variety of lexical markers for expressing focus and topic, which are presented in Hasegawa (2011) and Lee (2004). A few focus markers in some languages have positional restrictions. For example, as shown in Section 4.2, the clitic *tvv* in Cherokee signals focus and the focused constituent with *tvv* should be followed by other constituents in the sentence. That is, two means of marking information structure operate at the same time. It would be interesting to investigate these kinds of additional constraints in the future.

Second, a few more types of constructions related to information structure will be studied in future work. The constructions include echo questions, Yes/No-questions (King 1995), coordinated clauses (Heycock 2007), double nominative constructions (Kim & Sells 2007; I. Choi 2012), floating quantifiers (Yoshimoto et al. 2006; J.-B. Kim 2011), pseudo clefts (J.-B. Kim 2007), and *it*-clefts in other languages in the DELPH-IN grammars.

Third, the method for computing focus projection in the present study also needs to be more thoroughly examined. There are various constraints on how focus can be spread to larger constituents. These are not addressed in the present study, which looks at the focus projection of only simple sentences in English.

14 Conclusion

The method the present study employs for handling focus projection could be much reinforced in further studies.

Fourth, it would be interesting for future work to delve into how scopal interpretation can be dealt with within the framework that the present study proposes. Topic has an influence on scopal interpretation in that topic has the widest scope in a sentence (Büring 1997; Portner & Yabushita 1998; Erteschik-Shir 2007). MRS employs HCONS (Handle CONStraints) in order to resolve scope ambiguity. Further work can confirm whether HCONS+ICONS is able to handle the relationship between topic and scope resolution.

Finally, the evaluation of multilingual machine translation will be extended with a large number of test suites. More grammatical fragments related to ICONS will be incorporated into the DELPH-IN resource grammars, such as ERG (English Resource Grammar, Flickinger 2000), Jacy (Siegel, Bender & Bond 2016), KRG (Korean Resource Grammar, Kim et al. 2011), ZHONG (for the Chinese languages, Fan, Song & Bond 2015a,b), INDRA (for Indonesian, Moeljadi, Bond & Song 2015), and so forth.

Bibliography

Abeillé, Anne & Daniele Godard. 2001. A class of "lite" adverbs in French. In Joaquim Camps & Caroline R. Wiltshire (eds.), *Romance syntax, semantics and l2 acquisition: selected papers from the 30th linguistic symposium on romance languages, gainesville, florida, february 2000*, 9–26. Amsterdam: John Benjamins Publishing Company.

Alexopoulou, Theodora & Dimitra Kolliakou. 2002. On linkhood, topicalization and clitic left dislocation. *Journal of Linguistics* 38(2). 193–245.

Alonso-Ovalle, Luis, Susana Fernández-Solera, Lyn Frazier & Charles Jr. Clifton. 2002. Null vs. overt pronouns and the topic-focus articulation in Spanish. *Italian Journal of Linguistics* 14. 151–170.

Ambar, Manuela. 1999. Aspects of the syntax of focus in Portuguese. In Georges Rebuschi & Laurice Tuller (eds.), *The grammar of focus*, 23–54. Amsterdam: John Benjamins Publishing Company.

Arregi, Karlos. 2000. *Tense in Basque (Ms.)*

Arregi, Karlos. 2003. Clitic left dislocation is contrastive topicalization. *U. Penn Working Papers in Linguistics* 9(1). 31–44.

Baldwin, Timothy. 1998. *The analysis of Japanese relative clauses*. Tokyo Institute of Technology dissertation.

Baldwin, Timothy, John Beavers, Emily M. Bender, Dan Flickinger, Ara Kim & Stephan Oepen. 2005. Beauty and the beast: what running a broad-coverage precision grammar over the BNC taught us about the grammar — and the corpus. In Stephan Kepser & Marga Reis (eds.), *Linguistic evidence: empirical, theoretical, and computational perspectives*, 49–70. Berlin: Mouton de Gruyter.

Beaver, David I. & Brady Z. Clark. 2008. *Sense and sensitivity: how focus determines meaning*. Malden, MA: Wiley-Blackwell.

Beaver, David I., Brady Zack Clark, Edward Flemming, T Florian Jaeger & Maria Wolters. 2007. When semantics meets phonetics: acoustical studies of second-occurrence focus. *Language* 83(2). 245–276.

Bender, Emily M. 2007. Combining research and pedagogy in the development of a crosslinguistic grammar resource. In *Proceedings of the workshop on grammar engineering across frameworks (GEAF07)*. Stanford, CA.

Bibliography

Bender, Emily M. 2008. Grammar engineering for linguistic hypothesis testing. In Nicholas Gaylord, Stephen Hilderbrand, Heeyoung Lyu, Alexis Palmer & Elias Ponvert (eds.), *Proceedings of the Texas linguistics society x conference: computational linguistics for less-studied languages*, 16–36. Stanford, CA: CSLI Publications.

Bender, Emily M. 2011. On achieving and evaluating language-independence in nlp. *Linguistic Issues in Language Technology. Special Issue on Interaction of Linguistics and Computational Linguistics* 6(3). 1–26.

Bender, Emily M. 2014. Language collage: grammatical description with the LinGO Grammar Matrix. In *Proceedings of the ninth international conference on language resources and evaluation (LREC'14)*, 2447–2451. Reykjavik, Iceland.

Bender, Emily M., Scott Drellishak, Antske Fokkens, Laurie Poulson & Safiyyah Saleem. 2010. Grammar customization. *Research on Language & Computation* 8(1). 23–72.

Bender, Emily M. & Dan Flickinger. 2005. Rapid prototyping of scalable grammars: towards modularity in extensions to a language-independent core. In *Proceedings of the 2nd international joint conference on natural language processing ijcnlp-05: posters/demos*. Jeju Island, Korea.

Bender, Emily M., Dan Flickinger & Stephan Oepen. 2011. Grammar engineering and linguistic hypothesis testing: computational support for complexity in syntactic analysis. In Emily M. Bender & Jennifer E. Arnold (eds.), *Language from a cognitive perspective: grammar, usage and processing*, 5–29. Stanford,CA: CSLI Publications.

Bender, Emily M. & David Goss-Grubbs. 2008. Semantic representations of syntactically marked discourse status in crosslinguistic perspective. In *Proceedings of the 2008 conference on semantics in text processing*, 17–29.

Bender, Emily M., Laurie Poulson, Scott Drellishak & Chris Evans. 2007. Validation and regression testing for a cross-linguistic grammar resource. In *Acl 2007 workshop on deep linguistic processing*, 136–143. Prague, Czech Republic: Association for Computational Linguistics.

Bianchi, Valentina & Mara Frascarelli. 2010. Is topic a root phenomenon? *Iberia* 2(1). 43–88.

Bildhauer, Felix. 2007. *Representing information structure in an HPSG grammar of Spanish*. Universität Bremen dissertation.

Bildhauer, Felix. 2008. Clitic left dislocation and focus projection in Spanish. In Stefan Müller (ed.), *Proceedings of the 15th international conference on Head-driven Phrase Structure Grammar*, 346–357. Stanford, CA: CSLI Publications.

Bildhauer, Felix & Philippa Cook. 2010. German multiple fronting and expected topichood. In Stefan Müller (ed.), *Proceedings of the 17th international conference on Head-driven Phrase Structure Grammar*, 68–79. Stanford, CA: CSLI Publications.

Bjerre, Anne. 2011. Topic and focus in local subject extractions in Danish. In Stefan Müller (ed.), *Proceedings of the 18th international conference on Head-driven Phrase Structure Grammar*, 270–288. Stanford, CA: CSLI Publications.

Bolinger, Dwight Le Merton. 1958. A theory of pitch accent in English. *Word* 14. 109–149.

Bolinger, Dwight Le Merton. 1961. Contrastive accent and contrastive stress. *Language* 37(1). 83–96.

Bolinger, Dwight Le Merton. 1977. *Meaning and form*. London: Longman.

Bonami, Olivier & Elisabeth Delais-Roussarie. 2006. Metrical phonology in HPSG. In Stefan Müller (ed.), *Proceedings of the 13th international conference on Head-driven Phrase Structure Grammar*, 39–59. Stanford, CA: CSLI Publications.

Bond, Francis, Sanae Fujita & Takaaki Tanaka. 2006. The Hinoki syntactic and semantic treebank of Japanese. *Language Resources and Evaluation* 40(3–4). 253–261.

Bond, Francis, Hitoshi Isahara, Sanae Fujita, Kiyotaka Uchimoto, Takayuki Kuribayashi & Kyoko Kanzaki. 2009. Enhancing the Japanese WordNet. In *Proceedings of the 7th workshop on asian language resources*. Singapore.

Bouma, Gerlof, Lilja Øvrelid & Jonas Kuhn. 2010. Towards a large parallel corpus of cleft constructions. In *Proceedings of the 7th conference on international language resources and evaluation (LREC10)*, 3585–3592. Valletta, Malta.

Branco, António & Francisco Costa. 2010. A deep linguistic processing grammar for Portuguese. In *Computational processing of the Portuguese language*, vol. LNAI6001 (Lecture Notes in Artificial Intelligence), 86–89. Berlin: Springer.

Bresnan, Joan. 1971. Sentence stress and syntactic transformations. *Language* 47(2). 257–281.

Bresnan, Joan. 2001. *Lexical-functional syntax*. Malden, MA: Blackwell Publisher Inc.

Bresnan, Joan & Sam A Mchombo. 1987. Topic, pronoun, and agreement in Chicheŵa. *Language* 63(4). 741–782.

Büring, Daniel. 1997. The great scope inversion conspiracy. *Linguistics and Philosophy* 20(2). 175–194.

Büring, Daniel. 1999. Topic. In Peter Bosch & Rob van der Sandt (eds.), *Focus: linguistic, cognitive, and computational perspectives*, 142–165. Cambridge, UK: Cambridge University Press.

Büring, Daniel. 2003. On d-trees, beans, and b-accents. *Linguistics and Philosophy* 26(5). 511–545.

Büring, Daniel. 2006. Focus projection and default prominence. In Valéria Molnár & Susanne Winkler (eds.), *The architecture of focus*, 321–346. Berlin: Mouton de Gruyter.

Büring, Daniel. 2010. Towards a typology of focus realization. In Malte Zimmermann abd Caroline Féry (ed.), *Information structure*, 177–205. Oxford, UK: Oxford University Press.

Burnard, Lou. 2000. *User Reference Guide for the British National Corpus*. Tech. rep. Oxford University Computing Services.

Byron, Donna K., Whitney Gegg-Harrison & Sun-Hee Lee. 2006. Resolving zero anaphors and pronouns in Korean. *Traitement Automatique des Langues* 46(1). 91–114.

Callmeier, Ulrich. 2000. PET – a platform for experimentation with efficient HPSG processing techniques. *Natural Language Engineering* 6(1). 99–107.

Casielles-Suárez, Eugenia. 2003. On the interaction between syntactic and information structures in Spanish. *Bulletin of Hispanic Studies* 80(1). 1–20.

Casielles-Suárez, Eugenia. 2004. *The syntax-information structure interface: evidence from Spanish and English*. New York & London: Routledge.

Cecchetto, Carlo. 1999. A comparative analysis of left and right dislocation in Romance. *Studia Linguistica* 53(1). 40–67.

Chafe, Wallace L. 1976. Givenness, contrastiveness, definiteness, subjects, topics, and point of view in subject and topic. In Charles N. Li (ed.), *Subject and topic*, 25–55. New York, NY: Academic Press.

Chang, Suk-Jin. 2002. Information unpackaging: a constraint-based grammar approach to topic-focus articulation. *Japanese/Korean Linguistics* 10. 451–464.

Chapman, Shirley. 1981. *Prominence in Paumarí* (Archivo Linguistico). Brasilia: Summer Institute of Linguistics.

Chen, Aoju. 2012. The prosodic investigation of information structure. In Manfred Krifka & Renate Manfred (eds.), *The expression of information structure*, 249–286. Berlin/Boston: Walter de Gruyter GmbH & Co. KG.

Chen, Chen & Vincent Ng. 2013. Chinese zero pronoun resolution: some recent advances. In *Proceedings of the 2013 conference on empirical methods in natural language processing*, 1360–1365. Seattle, WA, USA: Association for Computational Linguistics.

Choe, Jae-Woong. 2002. Extended focus: Korean delimiter *man*. *Language Research* 38(4). 1131–1149.

Choi, Hye-Won. 1999. *Optimizing structure in context: scrambling and information structure*. Stanford, CA: CSLI Publications.

Choi, Incheol. 2012. Sentential specifiers in the Korean clause structure. In Stefan Müller (ed.), *Proceedings of the 19th international conference on Head-driven Phrase Structure Grammar*, 75–85. Stanford, CA: CSLI Publications.

Chung, Chan & Jong-Bok Kim. 2009. Inverted English concessive constructions: a construction-based approach. *Studies in Modern Grammar* 58. 39–58.

Chung, Chan, Jong-Bok Kim & Peter Sells. 2003. On the role of argument structure in focus projections. In *Proceedings from the annual meeting of the Chicago linguistic society*, vol. 39, 386–404.

Churng, Sarah. 2007. The prosody of topic and focus: explained away in phases. *UW Working Papers in Linguistics* 26.

Cinque, Guglielmo. 1977. The movement nature of left dislocation. *Linguistic Inquiry* 8(2). 397–412.

Clech-Darbon, Anne, Georges Rebuschi & Annie Rialland. 1999. Are there cleft sentences in French. In Georges Rebuschi & Laurice Tuller (eds.), *The grammar of focus*, 83–118. John Benjamins Publishing Company.

Comrie, Bernard. 1984. Some formal properties of focus in Modern Eastern Armenian. *Annual of Armenian Linguistics* 5. 1–21.

Constant, Noah. 2012. English rise-fall-rise: a study in the semantics and pragmatics of intonation. *Linguistics and Philosophy* 35(5). 407–442.

Copestake, Ann. 2002. *Implementing typed feature structure grammars*. Stanford, CA: CSLI Publications.

Copestake, Ann. 2007. Semantic composition with (robust) Minimal Recursion Semantics. In *Proceedings of the workshop on deep linguistic processing*, 73–80.

Copestake, Ann. 2009. Slacker semantics: why superficiality, dependency and avoidance of commitment can be the right way to go. In *Proceedings of the 12th conference of the European chapter of the ACL (EACL 2009)*, 1–9. Athens, Greece: Association for Computational Linguistics.

Copestake, Ann, Dan Flickinger, Carl Pollard & Ivan A. Sag. 2005. Minimal Recursion Semantics: an introduction. *Research on Language & Computation* 3(4). 281–332.

Croft, William. 2002. *Typology and universals*. Cambridge, UK: Cambridge University Press.

Crowgey, Joshua. 2012. *The syntactic exponence of negation: a model for the LinGO Grammar Matrix*. University of Washington MA thesis.

Bibliography

Crowgey, Joshua & Emily M. Bender. 2011. Analyzing interacting phenomena: word order and negation in Basque. In Stefan Müller (ed.), *Proceedings of the international conference on Head-driven Phrase Structure Grammar*, 46–59. Stanford, CA: CSLI Publications.

Crysmann, Berthold. 2003. On the efficient implementation of German verb placement in HPSG. In *Proceedings of RANLP 2003*, 112–116. Borovets, Bulgaria.

Crysmann, Berthold. 2005a. Relative clause extraposition in German: an efficient and portable implementation. *Research on Language & Computation* 3(1). 61–82.

Crysmann, Berthold. 2005b. Syncretism in German: a unified approach to underspecification, indeterminacy, and likeness of case. In *Proceedings of the 12th international conference on Head-driven Phrase Structure Grammar*, 91–107. Stanford, CA: CSLI Publications.

De Kuthy, Kordula. 2000. *Discontinuous NPs in German – a case study of the interaction of syntax, semantics and pragmatics*. Stanford, CA: CSLI publications.

De Kuthy, Kordula & Detmar Meurers. 2011. Integrating GIVENness into a structured meaning approach in HPSG. In Stefan Müller (ed.), *Proceedings of the 18th international conference on Head-driven Phrase Structure Grammar*, 289–301. Stanford, CA: CSLI Publications.

Drellishak, Scott. 2009. *Widespread but not universal: improving the typological coverage of the Grammar Matrix*. University of Washington dissertation.

Drellishak, Scott & Emily M. Bender. 2005. A coordination module for a crosslinguistic grammar resource. In Stefan Müller (ed.), *The proceedings of the 12th international conference on Head-driven Phrase Structure Grammar*, 108–128. Stanford, CA: CSLI Publications.

Drubig, Hans Bernhard. 2003. Toward a typology of focus and focus constructions. *Linguistics* 41(1). 1–50.

É. Kiss, Katalin. 1998. Identificational focus versus information focus. *Language* 74(2). 245–273.

É. Kiss, Katalin. 1999. The English cleft construction as a focus phrase. In Lunella Mereu (ed.), *Boundaries of morphology and syntax*, 217–229. Amsterdam: John Benjamins Publishing Company.

Emonds, Joseph. 1979. Appositive relatives have no properties. *Linguistic Inquiry* 10(2). 211–243.

Emonds, Joseph. 2004. Unspecified categories as the key to root constructions. In David Adger, Cécile de Cat & Georges Tsoulas (eds.), *Peripheries: syntactic edges and their effects*, 75–120. Dordrecht: Kluwer Academic Publishers.

Engdahl, Elisabet & Enric Vallduví. 1996. Information packaging in HPSG. *Edinburgh Working Papers in Cognitive Science* 12. 1–32.

Erteschik-Shir, Nomi. 1999. Focus structure and scope. In Georges Rebuschi & Laurice Tuller (eds.), *The grammar of focus*, 119–150. Amsterdam: John Benjamins Publishing Company.

Erteschik-Shir, Nomi. 2007. *Information structure: the syntax-discourse interface.* Oxford, UK: Oxford University Press.

Fabb, Nigel. 1990. The difference between English restrictive and nonrestrictive relative clauses. *Journal of Linguistics* 26(1). 57–77.

Fan, Zhenzhen, Sanghoun Song & Francis Bond. 2015a. An HPSG-based shared-grammar for the chinese languages: ZHONG [|. In *Grammar engineering across frameworks 2015 (in conjunction with ACL 2015)*, 17–24. Beijing, China.

Fan, Zhenzhen, Sanghoun Song & Francis Bond. 2015b. Building ZHONG, a chinese HPSG shared-grammar. In *Proceedings of the 22nd international conference on Head-driven Phrase Structure Grammar*, 96–109. Singapore.

Fanselow, Gisbert. 2007. The restricted access of information structure to syntax. a minority report. *Interdisciplinary Studies on Information Structure, Working Papers of the SFB 632* 6. 205–220.

Fanselow, Gisbert. 2008. In need of mediation: the relation between syntax and information structure. *Acta Linguistica Hungarica* 55(3–4). 397–413.

Féry, Caroline & Shinichiro Ishihara. 2009. The phonology of second occurrence focus. *Journal of Linguistics* 45(2). 285–313.

Féry, Caroline & Manfred Krifka. 2008. Information structure: notional distinctions, ways of expression. In Piet van Sterkenburg (ed.), *Unity and diversity of languages*, 123–136. Amsterdam: John Benjamins Publishing Company.

Firbas, Jan. 1992. *Functional sentence perspective in written and spoken communication.* Cambridge, UK: Cambridge University Press.

Flickinger, Dan. 2000. On building a more efficient grammar by exploiting types. *Natural Language Engineering* 6(1). 15–28.

Fokkens, Antske. 2010. *Documentation for the Grammar Matrix Word Order Library.* Tech. rep. Saarland University.

Frascarelli, Mare. 2000. *The syntax-phonology interface in focus and topic constructions in Italian.* Dordrecht/Boston: Kluwer Academic Publishers.

Frota, Sónia. 2000. *Prosody and focus in European Portuguese: phonological phrasing and intonation.* New York, NY: Garland Publishing Inc.

Gell-Mann, Murray & Merritt Ruhlen. 2011. The origin and evolution of word order. In *Proceedings of the national academy of sciences of the united states of america*, vol. 108, 17290–17295. National Acad Sciences.

Bibliography

Givón, Talmy. 1991. Isomorphism in the grammatical code: cognitive and biological considerations. *Studies in Language* 15(1). 85–114.

Goodman, Michael Wayne. 2013. Generation of machine-readable morphological rules with human readable input. *UW Working Papers in Linguistics* 30.

Götze, Michael, Stephanie Dipper & Stavros Skopeteas (eds.). 2007. *Information Structure in Cross-Linguistic Corpora: Annotation Guidelines for Phonology, Morphology, Syntax, Semantics, and Information Structure.*

Gracheva, Varvara. 2013. *Markers of contrast in Russian: a corpus-based study.* University of Washington MA thesis.

Grewendorf, Günther. 2001. Multiple *Wh*-fronting. *Linguistic Inquiry* 32(1). 87–122.

Grishina, Elena. 2006. Spoken Russian in the Russian National Corpus (RNC). In *Proceedings of the 5th international conference on language resources and evaluation*, 121–124.

Grohmann, Kleanthes K. 2001. On predication, derivation and anti-locality. *ZAS Papers in Linguistics* 26. 87–112.

Gryllia, Styliani. 2009. *On the nature of preverbal focus in Greek: a theoretical and experimental approach.* Leiden University dissertation.

Gundel, Jeanette K. 1977. Where do cleft sentences come from? *Language* 53(3). 543–559.

Gundel, Jeanette K. 1983. *The role of topic and comment in linguistic theory.* New York, NY: Garland.

Gundel, Jeanette K. 1985. Shared knowledge and topicality. *Journal of Pragmatics* 9. 83–107.

Gundel, Jeanette K. 1988. Universals of topic-comment structure. *Studies in Syntactic Typology* 17. 209–239.

Gundel, Jeanette K. 1999. On different kinds of focus. In Peter Bosch & Rob van der Sandt (eds.), *Focus: linguistic, cognitive, and computational perspectives*, 293–305. Cambridge, UK: Cambridge University Press.

Gundel, Jeanette K. 2002. Information structure and the use of cleft sentences in English and Norwegian. In H. Hasselgrd, S. Johansson, B. Behrens & C. Fabricius-Hansen (eds.), *Information structure in a cross-linguistic perspective*, 113–128. Amsterdam: Rodopi.

Gundel, Jeanette K. 2003. Information structure and referential givenness/newness: how much belongs in the grammar? In Stefan Müller (ed.), *Proceedings of the 10th international conference on Head-driven Phrase Structure Grammar*, 122–142. Stanford, CA: CSLI Publications.

Gunji, Takao. 1987. *Japanese phrase structure grammar: a unification-based approach.* Dordrecht: D. Reidel Publishing Company.

Gunlogson, Christine. 2001. *True to form: rising and falling declaratives as questions in English.* University of California at Santa Cruz dissertation.

Gussenhoven, Carlos. 1999. On the limits of focus projection in English. In Peter Bosch & Rob van der Sandt (eds.), *Focus: linguistic, cognitive, and computational perspectives*, 43–55. Cambridge, UK: Cambridge University Press.

Gussenhoven, Carlos. 2007. Types of focus in English. In Chungmin Lee, Matthew Gordon & Daniel Búring (eds.), *Topic and focus: cross-linguistic perspectives on meaning and intonation*, 83–100. Dordrecht: Kluwer Academic Publishers.

Haegeman, Liliane. 2004. Topicalization, CLLD and the left periphery. In *ZAS papers in linguistics 35: proceedings of the dislocated elements workshop*, 157–192.

Haiman, John. 1978. Conditionals are topics. *Language* 54(3). 564–589.

Haji-Abdolhosseini, Mohammad. 2003. A constraint-based approach to information structure and prosody correspondence. In Stefan Müller (ed.), *Proceedings of the 10th international conference on Head-driven Phrase Structure Grammar*, 143–162. Stanford, CA: CSLI Publications.

Halliday, Michael Alexander Kirkwood. 1967. Notes on transitivity and theme in English: part 2. *Journal of Linguistics* 3(2). 199–244.

Halliday, Michael Alexander Kirkwood. 1970. *A course in spoken English: intonation.* Oxford: Oxford University Press.

Han, Chung-Hye & Nancy Hedberg. 2008. Syntax and semantics of *it*-clefts: a Tree Adjoining Grammar analysis. *Journal of Semantics* 25(4). 345–380.

Han, Na-Rae. 2006. *Korean zero pronouns: analysis and resolution.* University of Pennsylvania dissertation.

Hangyo, Masatsugu, Daisuke Kawahara & Sadao Kurohashi. 2013. Japanese zero reference resolution considering exophora and author/reader mentions. In *Proceedings of the 2013 conference on empirical methods in natural language processing*, 9241–934. Seattle, WA, USA: Association for Computational Linguistics.

Hartmann, Katharina & Malte Zimmermann. 2007. Exhaustivity marking in Hausa: a reanalysis of the particle *nee/cee*. In Enoch Oladé Aboh, Katharina Hartmann & Malte Zimmermann (eds.), *Focus strategies in African languages: the interaction of focus and grammar in Niger-Congo and Afro-Asiatic*, 241–263. Berlin: Moutin de Gruyter.

Hasegawa, Akio. 2011. *The semantics and pragmatics of Japanese focus particles.* State University of New York at Buffalo dissertation.

Bibliography

Hasegawa, Akio & Jean-Pierre Koenig. 2011. Focus particles, secondary meanings, and lexical resource semantics: the case of Japanese *shika*. In Stefan Müller (ed.), *Proceedings of the 18th international conference on Head-driven Phrase Structure Grammar*, 81–101. Stanford, CA: CSLI Publications.

Hedberg, Nancy. 2006. Topic-focus controversies. In Susanne Winkler Valéria Molnár (ed.), *The architecture of focus*, 373–397. Berlin: Walter de Gruyter.

Hedberg, Nancy & Juan M. Sosa. 2007. The prosody of topic and focus in spontaneous English dialogue. In Chungmin Lee, Matthew Gordon & Daniel Búring (eds.), *Topic and focus: cross-linguistic perspectives on meaning and intonation*, 101–120. Dordrecht: Kluwer Academic Publishers.

Hellan, Lars. 2005. Implementing Norwegian reflexives in an HPSG grammar. In *Proceedings of the 12th international conference on Head-driven Phrase Structure Grammar*, 519–539. Stanford, CA: CSLI Publications.

Heycock, Caroline. 1994. Focus projection in Japanese. In *Proceedings of north east linguistic society*, 157–171.

Heycock, Caroline. 2007. Embedded root phenomena. In Martin Everaert & Henk van Riemsdijk (eds.), *The blackwell companion to syntax*, 174–209. Wiley Online Library.

Hooper, Joan & Sandra Thompson. 1973. On the applicability of root transformations. *Linguistic Inquiry* 4(4). 465–497.

Horvath, Julia. 2007. Separating focus movement from focus. In Simin Karimi, Vida Samiian & Wendy K. Wilkins (eds.), *Phrasal and clausal architecture*, 108–145. Amsterdam: John Benjamins Publishing Company.

Huang, C.-T. James. 1982. *Logical relations in Chinese and the theory of grammar*. Massachusetts Institute of Technology dissertation.

Huang, C.-T. James. 1984. On the distribution and reference of empty pronouns. *Linguistic Inquiry* 15(4). 531–574.

Huang, C.-T. James, Y.-H. Audrey Li & Yafei Li. 2009. *The syntax of Chinese*. Cambridge, UK: Cambridge University Press.

Iatridou, Sabine. 1991. *Topics in conditionals*. Massachusetts Institute of Technology dissertation.

Iatridou, Sabine. 2000. The grammatical ingredients of counterfactuality. *Linguistic Inquiry* 31(2). 231–270.

Ishihara, Shinichiro. 2001. Stress, focus, and scrambling in Japanese. *MIT Working Papers in Linguistics* 39. 142–175.

İşsever, Selçuk. 2003. Information structure in Turkish: the word order-prosody interface. *Lingua* 113(11). 1025–1053.

Jackendoff, Ray S. 1972. *Semantic interpretation in generative grammar.* Cambridge, MA: The MIT Press.

Jackendoff, Ray S. 2008. Construction after construction and its theoretical challanges. *Language* 81(1). 9–28.

Jacobs, Joachim. 2001. The dimensions of topic-comment. *Linguistics* 39(4). 641–681.

Jacobs, Neil G. 2005. *Yiddish: a linguistic introduction.* New York, NY: Cambridge University Press.

Jiang, Zixin. 1991. *Some aspects of the syntax of topic and subject in Chinese.* University of Chicago dissertation.

Johansson, Mats. 2001. Clefts in contrast: a contrastive study of it clefts and wh clefts in English and Swedish texts and translations. *Linguistics* 39(3). 547–582.

Joshi, Aravind K. & Yves Schabes. 1997. Tree-adjoining grammars. In Grzegorz Rozenberg & Arto Salomaa (eds.), *Handbook of formal languages,* 69–123. Berlin: Springer.

Jun, Sun-Ah, Hee-Sun Kim, Hyuck-Joon Lee & Jong-Bok Kim. 2007. An experimental study on the effect of argument structure on VP focus. *UCLA Working Papers in Phonetics* 105. 66–84.

Jun, Sun-Ah & Hyuck-Joon Lee. 1998. The phonetics and phonology of Korean prosody in Korean. In *International conference on spoken language processing,* 1295–1298. Sydney, Australia.

Kadmon, Nirit. 2001. *Formal pragmatics.* Malden, MA: Blackwell Publisher Inc.

Kaiser, Elsi. 2009. Investigating effects of structural and information-structural factors on pronoun resolution. In Malte Zimmermann & Caroline Féry (eds.), *Information structure: theoretical, typological, and experimental perspectives,* 332–354. Oxford, UK: Oxford University Press.

Kamp, Hans & Uwe Reyle. 1993. *From discourse to logic.* London: Kluwer Academic Publishers.

Kiefer, Ferenc. 1967. *On emphasis and word order in Hungarian.* Bloomington: Indiana University Press.

Kihm, Alain. 1999. Focus in Wolof. In Georges Rebuschi & Laurice Tuller (eds.), *The grammar of focus,* 245–273. John Benjamins Publishing Company.

Kim, Jieun. 2012. How is 'contrast' imposed on -*Nun*? *Language and Information* 16(1). 1–24.

Kim, Jong-Bok. 2007. Syntax and semantics of English it-cleft constructions: a constraint-based analysis. *Studies in Modern Grammar* 48. 217–235.

Kim, Jong-Bok. 2011. Floating numeral classifiers in Korean: a thematic-structure perspective. In Stefan Müller (ed.), *Proceedings of the 18th international confer-*

Bibliography

ence on *Head-driven Phrase Structure Grammar*, 302–313. Stanford, CA: CSLI Publications.

Kim, Jong-Bok. 2012. On the syntax of the it-cleft construction: a construction-based perspective. *Linguistic Research* 29(1). 45–68.

Kim, Jong-Bok & Byung-Soo Park. 2000. Grammatical interfaces in Korean relatives. In Ronnie Cann, Claire Grover & Philip Miller (eds.), *Grammatical interfaces in HPSG*, 153–168. Stanford, CA: CSLI Publications.

Kim, Jong-Bok & Peter Sells. 2007. Two types of multiple nominative construction: a constructional approach. In Stefan Müller (ed.), *Proceedings of the 14th international conference on Head-driven Phrase Structure Grammar*, 364–372. Stanford, CA: CSLI Publications.

Kim, Jong-Bok & Peter Sells. 2008. *English syntax: an introduction*. Stanford, CA: CSLI publications.

Kim, Jong-Bok & Jaehyung Yang. 2004. Projections from morphology to syntax in the Korean Resource Grammar: implementing typed feature structures. *Lecture Notes in Computer Science* 2945. 13–24.

Kim, Jong-Bok & Jaehyung Yang. 2009. Processing three types of Korean cleft constructions in a typed feature structure grammar. *Korean Journal of Cognitive Science* 20(1). 1–28.

Kim, Jong-Bok, Jaehyung Yang, Sanghoun Song & Francis Bond. 2011. Deep processing of Korean and the development of the Korean resource grammar. *Linguistic Research* 28(3). 635–672.

Kim, Taeho. 2011. An empirical study of postposing constructions in Korean. *Linguistic Research* 28(1). 223–238.

King, Tracy Holloway. 1995. *Configuring topic and focus in Russian*. Stanford, CA: CSLI publications.

King, Tracy Holloway. 1997. Focus domains and information-structure. In Butt Miriam & Tracy Holloway King (eds.), *Proceedings of the LFG97 conference*. University of California, San Diego.

King, Tracy Holloway & Annie Zaenen. 2004. F-structures, information structure, and discourse structure. In Butt Miriam & Tracy Holloway King (eds.), *Proceedings of the LFG04 conference*. University of Canterbury, New Zealand.

Klein, Ewan. 2000. Prosodic constituency in HPSG. In Ronnie Cann, Claire Grover & Philip Miller (eds.), *Grammatical interfaces in HPSG*, 169–200. Stanford, CA: CSLI Publications.

Ko, Kil Soo. 2008. Korean postpositions as weak syntactic heads. In Stefan Müller (ed.), *Proceedings of the 15th international conference on Head-driven Phrase Structure Grammar*, 131–151. Stanford, CA: CSLI Publications.

Komagata, Nobo N. 1999. *A computational analysis of information structure using parallel expository texts in English and Japanese*. University of Pennsylvania dissertation.

Kong, Fang & Hwee Tou Ng. 2013. Exploiting zero pronouns to improve Chinese coreference resolution. In *Proceedings of the 2013 conference on empirical methods in natural language processing*, 278–288. Seattle, WA, USA: Association for Computational Linguistics.

Krifka, Manfred. 2008. Basic notions of information structure. *Acta Linguistica Hungarica* 55(3). 243–276.

Kügler, Frank, Stavros Skopeteas & Elisabeth Verhoeven. 2007. Encoding information structure in Yucatec Maya: on the interplay of prosody and syntax. *Interdisciplinary Studies on Information Structure* 8. 187–208.

Kuhn, Jonas. 1996. An underspecified HPSG representation for information structure. In *Proceedings of the 16th conference on computational linguistics*, vol. 2, 670–675.

Kuno, Susumu. 1973. *The structure of the Japanese language*. Cambridge, MA: The MIT Press.

Kuno, Susumu. 1976. Subject, theme and speaker's empathy: a reexamination of relativization phenomena. In Charles N. Li (ed.), *Subject and topic*, 417–444. New York, NY: Academic Press.

Kuroda, S.-Y. 1972. The categorical and the thetic judgment: evidence from Japanese syntax. *Foundations of Language* 9(2). 153–185.

Ladd, D Robert. 2008. *Intonational phonology*. Cambridge, UK: Cambridge University Press.

Lambrecht, Knud. 1986. *Topic, focus, and the grammar of spoken French*. University of California, Berkeley dissertation.

Lambrecht, Knud. 1996. *Information structure and sentence form: topic, focus, and the mental representations of discourse referents*. Cambridge, UK: Cambridge University Press.

Lambrecht, Knud. 2001. A framework for the analysis of cleft constructions. *Linguistics* 39(3). 463–516.

Law, Ann. 2003. Right dislocation in Cantonese as a focus-marking device. *UCL Working Papers in Linguistics* 15. 243–275.

Lecarme, Jacqueline. 1999. Focus in Somali. In Georges Rebuschi & Laurice Tuller (eds.), *The grammar of focus*, 1–22. Amsterdam: John Benjamins Publishing Company.

Lee, Youngjoo. 2004. *The syntax and semantics of focus particles*. Massachusetts Institute of Technology dissertation.

Bibliography

Li, Charles N. & Sandra Thompson. 1976. Subject and topic: a new typology of language. In Charles N. Li (ed.), *Subject and topic*, 457–490. New York, NY: Academic Press.

Li, Kening. 2009. *The information structure of Mandarin Chinese: syntax and prosody*. University of Washington dissertation.

Lim, Dong-Hoon. 2012. Korean particle 'un/nun' and their syntagmatic, paradigmatic relations [in Korean]. *Korean Linguistics* 64. 217–271.

Maki, Hideki, Lizanne Kaiser & Masao Ochi. 1999. Embedded topicalization in English and Japanese. *Lingua* 109(1). 1–14.

Man, Fung Suet. 2007. *TOPIC and FOCUS in Cantonese: an OT-LFG account*. University of Hong Kong MA thesis.

Marimon, Montserrat. 2012. The Spanish DELPH-IN grammar. *Language Resources and Evaluation* 47(2). 371–397.

Matsui, Tomoko. 1999. Approaches to Japanese zero pronouns: centering and relevance. In *Proceedings of the workshop on the relation of discourse/dialogue structure and reference*, 11–20.

Megerdoomian, Karine. 2011. Focus and the auxiliary in Eastern Armenian. Talk presented at the 37th Annual Meeting of the Berkeley Linguistics Society (BLS), Special session on Languages of the Caucasus.

Mereu, Lunella. 2009. Universals of information structure. In Lunella Mereu (ed.), *Information structure and its interfaces*, 75–104. Berlin/New York: Mouton de Gruyter.

Mitkov, Ruslan. 1999. Multilingual anaphora resolution. *Machine Translation* 14(3). 281–299.

Mitkov, Ruslan, Sung-Kwon Choi & Randall Sharp. 1995. Anaphora resolution in machine translation. In *Proceedings of the 6th international conference on theoretical and methodological issues in machine translation*.

Miyao, Yusuke & Jun'ichi Tsujii. 2008. Feature forest models for probabilistic HPSG parsing. *Computational Linguistics* 34(1). 35–80.

Moeljadi, David, Francis Bond & Sanghoun Song. 2015. Building an HPSG-based indonesian resource grammar (INDRA). In *Grammar engineering across frameworks 2015 (in conjunction with ACL 2015)*, 26–31. Beijing, China.

Molnár, Valéria. 2002. Contrast – from a contrastive perspective. In H. Hasselgrd, S. Johansson, B. Behrens & C. Fabricius-Hansen (eds.), *Information structure in a cross-linguistic perspective*, 147–162. Amsterdam, Netherland: Rodopi.

Montgomery-Anderson, Brad. 2008. *A reference grammar of Oklahoma Cherokee*. Ann Arbor, MI: ProQuest LLC.

Nagaya, Naonori. 2007. Information structure and constituent order in Tagalog. *Language and Linguistics* 8. 343–372.

Nakaiwa, Hiromi & Satoshi Shirai. 1996. Anaphora resolution of Japanese zero pronouns with deictic reference. In *Proceedings of the 16th conference on computational linguistics*, 812–817.

Nakanishi, Kimiko. 2007. Prosody and information structure in Japanese: a case study of topic marker wa. In Chungmin Lee, Matthew Gordon & Daniel Büring (eds.), *Topic and focus: cross-linguistic perspectives on meaning and intonation*, 177–193. Dordrecht: Kluwer Academic Publishers.

Neeleman, Ad & Elena Titov. 2009. Focus, contrast, and stress in Russian. *Linguistic Inquiry* 40(3). 514–524.

Nelson, Gerald, Sean Wallis & Bas Aarts. 2002. *Exploring natural language: working with the British component of the international corpus of English*. Philadelphia: John Benjamins Publishing Company.

Nguyen, Hoai Thu Ba. 2006. *Contrastive topic in Vietnamese: with reference to Korean*. Seoul National University dissertation.

Nichols, Eric, Francis Bond, Darren Scott Appling & Yuji Matsumoto. 2010. Paraphrasing training data for statistical machine translation. *Journal of Natural Language Processing* 17(3). 101–122.

Nichols, Johanna. 2011. *Ingush grammar*. Berkeley, CA: University of California Press.

Ning, Chunyan. 1993. *The overt syntax of relativization and topicalization in Chinese*. University of California, Irvine dissertation.

Oepen, Stephan. 2001. *[incr tsdb()] — Competence and Performance Laboratory. User Manual*. Tech. rep. Computational Linguistics, Saarland University.

Oepen, Stephan, Dan Flickinger, Kristina Toutanova & Christoper D. Manning. 2004. LinGO Redwoods: a rich and dynamic treebank for HPSG. *Research on Language & Computation* 2(4). 575–596.

Oepen, Stephan, Erik Velldal, Jan T. Lønning, Paul Meurer, Victoria Rosén & Dan Flickinger. 2007. Towards hybrid quality-oriented machine translation – on linguistics and probabilities in MT. In *Proceedings of the 11th international conference on theoretical and methodological issues in machine translation*. Skövde, Sweden.

Ohtani, Akira & Yuji Matsumoto. 2004. Japanese subjects and information structure: a constraint-based approach. In *Proceedings of the 18th Pacific Asia Conference on Language, Information and Computation*, 93–104. Tokyo, Japan.

Bibliography

Ortiz de Urbina, Jon. 1999. Focus in Basque. In Georges Rebuschi & Laurice Tuller (eds.), *The grammar of focus*, 311–333. Amsterdam: John Benjamins Publishing Company.

Osenova, Petya. 2011. Localizing a core HPSG-based grammar for Bulgarian. In Hanna Hedeland, Thomas Schmidt & Kai Worner (eds.), *Multilingual resources and multilingual applications, proceedings of german society for computational linguistics and language technology (GSCL)*, 175–180. Hamburg.

Oshima, David Y. 2008. Morphological *vs.* phonological contrastive topic marking. In *Proceedings of chicago linguistic society (CLS) 41*, 371–383.

Oshima, David Y. 2009. On the so-called thematic use of *Wa*: reconsideration and reconciliation. In *Proceedings of the 23rd Pacific Asia Conference on Language, Information and Computation*, 405–414. City University of Hong Kong, Hong Kong.

Ouhalla, Jamal. 1999. Focus and Arabic clefts. In Georges Rebuschi & Laurice Tuller (eds.), *The grammar of focus*, 335–359. Amsterdam: John Benjamins Publishing Company.

Paggio, Patrizia. 1996. *The treatment of information structure in machine translation*. University of Copenhagen dissertation.

Paggio, Patrizia. 2009. The information structure of Danish grammar constructions. *Nordic Journal of Linguistics* 32(01). 137–164.

Partee, Barbara H. 1991. Topic, focus and quantification. *Cornell Working Papers in Linguistics* 10. 159–187.

Partee, Barbara H. 1999. Focus, quantification, and semantics-pragmatics issues. In Peter Bosch & Rob van der Sandt (eds.), *Focus: linguistic, cognitive, and computational perspectives*, 213–231. Cambridge, UK: Cambridge University Press.

Paul, Waltraud & John Whitman. 2008. *Shi . . . de* focus clefts in Mandarin Chinese. *The Linguistic Review* 25(3-4). 413–451.

Pedersen, Ted. 2008. Empiricism is not a matter of faith. *Computational Linguistics* 34(3). 465–470.

Petronio, Karen. 1993. *Clause structure in American Sign Language*. University of Washington dissertation.

Pollard, Carl & Ivan A. Sag. 1994. *Head-Driven Phrase Structure Grammar*. Chicago, IL: The University of Chicago Press.

Portner, Paul & Katsuhiko Yabushita. 1998. The semantics and pragmatics of topic phrases. *Linguistics and Philosophy* 21(2). 117–157.

Poulson, Laurie. 2011. Meta-modeling of tense and aspect in a cross-linguistic grammar engineering platform. *UW Working Papers in Linguistics* 28.

Pozen, Zinaida. 2013. *Using lexical and compositional semantics to improve HPSG parse selection.* University of Washington MA thesis.

Press, Ian J. 1986. *A grammar of Modern Breton.* Berlin/New York/Amsterdam: Mouton de Gruyter.

Prince, Ellen F. 1984. Topicalization and left-dislocation: a functional analysis. *Annals of the New York Academy of Sciences* 433(1). 213–225.

Ramsay, Violetta. 1987. The functional distribution of preposed and postposed 'if' and 'when' clauses in written discourse. In Russell S. Tomlin (ed.), *Coherence and grounding in discourse*, 383–408. Amsterdam: John Benjamins.

Rebuschi, Georges & Laurice Tuller. 1999. The grammar of focus: an introduction. In Georges Rebuschi & Laurice Tuller (eds.), *The grammar of focus*, 1–22. John Benjamins Publishing Company.

Reinhart, Tanya. 1981. Pragmatics and linguistics: an analysis of sentence topics. *Philosophica* 27(1). 53–94.

Rivero, María-Luisa. 1980. On left-dislocation and topicalization in Spanish. *Linguistic Inquiry* 11(2). 363–393.

Rizzi, Luigi. 1997. The fine structure of the left periphery. In Liliane Haegeman (ed.), *Elements of grammar: handbook in generative syntax*, 281–337. Dordrecht: Kluwer Academic Publishers.

Roberts, Craige. 2011. Topics. In Claudia Maienborn, Klaus von Heusinger & Paul Portner (eds.), *Semantics: an international handbook of natural language meaning*, vol. 2, 1908–1934. Berlin, New York: Mouton de Gruyter.

Rochemont, Michael S. 1986. *Focus in generative grammar.* Amsterdam: John Benjamins Publishing Company.

Rodionova, Elena V. 2001. *Word order and information structure in Russian syntax.* University of North Dakota MA thesis.

Roh, Ji-Eun & Jong-Hyeok Lee. 2003. An empirical study for generating zero pronoun in Korean based on cost-based centering model. In *Proceedings of australasian language technology association*, 90–97.

Rooth, Mats. 1985. *Association with focus.* University of Massachusetts, Amherst dissertation.

Rooth, Mats. 1992. A theory of focus interpretation. *Natural Language Semantics* 1(1). 75–116.

Saleem, Safiyyah. 2010. *Argument optionality: a new library for the Grammar Matrix customization system.* University of Washington MA thesis.

Saleem, Safiyyah & Emily M. Bender. 2010. Argument optionality in the LinGO Grammar Matrix. In *Proceedings of the 23rd international conference on compu-*

Bibliography

tational linguistics: posters, 1068–1076. Beijing, China: Coling 2010 Organizing Committee.

Sato, Yo & Wai Lok Tam. 2012. Ellipsis of case-markers and information structure in Japanese. In Stefan Müller (ed.), *Proceedings of the 19th international conference on Head-driven Phrase Structure Grammar*, 442–452. Stanford, CA: CSLI Publications.

Schachter, Paul. 1973. Focus and relativization. *Language* 49(1). 19–46.

Schafer, Amy, Juli Carter, Charles Clifton Jr & Lyn Frazier. 1996. Focus in relative clause construal. *Language and Cognitive Processes* 11(1/2). 135–163.

Schneider, Cynthia. 2009. Information structure in Abma. *Oceanic Linguistics* 48(1). 1–35.

Selkirk, Elisabeth O'Brian. 1984. *Phonology and syntax: the relation between sound and structure*. Cambridge, MA: The MIT Press.

Selkirk, Elisabeth O'Brian. 1995. Sentence prosody: intonation, stress, and phrasing. In John A. Goldsmith (ed.), *The handbook of phonological theory*, 550–569. Cambridge: Blackwell Publishers.

Siegel, Melanie. 1999. The syntactic processing of particles in Japanese spoken language. In Jhing-Fa Wang & Chung-Hsien Wu (eds.), *Proceedings of the 13th Pacific Asia Conference on Language, Information and Computation*, 313–320.

Siegel, Melanie, Emily M. Bender & Francis Bond. 2016. *Jacy: an implemented grammar of Japanese*. Stanford, CA: CSLI Publications.

Skopeteas, Stavros & Gisbert Fanselow. 2010. Focus in Georgian and the expression of contrast. *Lingua* 120(6). 1370–1391.

Slayden, Glenn C. 2012. *Array TFS storage for unification grammars*. University of Washington MA thesis.

Sohn, Ho-Min. 2001. *The Korean language*. Cambridge, UK: Cambridge University Press.

Song, Sanghoun. 2014. Information structure of relative clauses in English: a flexible and computationally tractable model. *Language and Information* 18(2). 1–29.

Song, Sanghoun. 2016. A multilingual grammar model of honorification: using the HPSG and MRS formalism. *Language and Information* 20(1). 25–49.

Song, Sanghoun & Emily M. Bender. 2011. Using information structure to improve transfer-based MT. In Stefan Müller (ed.), *Proceedings of the 18th international conference on Head-driven Phrase Structure Grammar*, 348–368. Stanford, CA: CSLI Publications.

Song, Sanghoun & Emily M. Bender. 2012. Individual constraints for information structure. In Stefan Müller (ed.), *Proceedings of the 19th international conference on Head-driven Phrase Structure Grammar, 329–347. Stanford, CA: CSLI Publications.

Song, Sanghoun, Jong-Bok Kim, Francis Bond & Jaehyung Yang. 2010. Development of the Korean Resource Grammar: towards grammar customization. In *Proceedings of the 8th workshop on asian language resources*. Beijing, China.

Steedman, Mark. 2000. Information structure and the syntax-phonology interface. *Linguistic Inquiry* 31(4). 649–689.

Steedman, Mark. 2001. *The syntactic process*. Cambridge, MA: The MIT press.

Strawson, Peter F. 1964. Identifying reference and truth-values. *Theoria* 30(2). 96–118.

Sturgeon, Anne. 2010. The discourse function of left dislocation in Czech. In *Proceedings of the annual meeting of the berkeley linguistics society*, vol. 31.

Szendrői, Kriszta. 1999. A stress-driven approach to the syntax of focus. *UCL Working Papers in Linguistics* 11. 545–573.

Szendrői, Kriszta. 2001. *Focus and the syntax-phonology interface*. University College London dissertation.

Tamrazian, Armine. 1991. Focus and wh-movement in Armenian. *University College London Working Papers in Linguistics* 3. 101–121.

Tamrazian, Armine. 1994. *The syntax of Armenian: chains and the auxiliary*. University College London dissertation.

Taylor, Heather L. 2007. Movement from IF-clause adjuncts. *University of Maryland Working Papers in Linguistics* 15. 192–206.

Traat, Maarika & Johan Bos. 2004. Unificational combinatory categorial grammar: combining information structure and discourse representations. In *Proceedings of the 20th international conference on computational linguistics*.

Tragut, Jasmine. 2009. *Armenian: Modern Eastern Armenian*. Amsterdam: John Benjamins Publishing Company.

Ueyama, Motoko & Sun-Ah Jun. 1998. Focus realization in Japanese English and Korean English intonation. *Japanese/Korean Linguistics* 7. 629–645.

Valentine, J Randolph. 2001. *Nishnaabemwin reference grammar*. Toronto, Canada: University of Toronto Press.

Vallduví, Enric. 1990. *The informational component*. University of Pennsylvania dissertation.

Vallduví, Enric. 1993. *The Informational Component*. Tech. rep. University of Pennsylvania Institute for Research in Cognitive Science.

Vallduví, Enric. 1992. Focus constructions in Catalan. In Christiane Laeufer & Terrell A. Morgan (eds.), *Theoretical analyses in Romance linguistics*, 457–479. Amsterdam: John Benjamins.

Bibliography

Vallduví, Enric & Maria Vilkuna. 1998. On rheme and kontrast. *Syntax and Semantics* 29. 79–108.

van Valin, Robert D. 2005. *Exploring the syntax-semantics interface.* Cambridge, UK: Cambridge University Press.

Velleman, Dan, David Beaver, Emilie Destruel, Dylan Bumford, Edgar Onea & Liz Coppock. 2012. It-clefts are IT (inquiry terminating) constructions. In *Proceedings of semantics and linguistic theory 22,* 441–460.

Vermeulen, Reiko. 2009. On the syntactic typology of topic marking: a comparative study of Japanese and Korean. *UCL Working Papers in Linguistics* 21. 335–363.

von Fintel, Kai. 2004. Would you believe it? the king of France is back! (presuppositions and truth-value intuitions). In Marga Reimer & Anne Bezuidenhout (eds.), *Descriptions and beyond,* 315–341. Oxford, UK: Oxford University Press.

von Prince, Kilu. 2012. Predication and information structure in Mandarin Chinese. *Journal of East Asian Linguistics* 21(4). 329–366.

Webelhuth, Gert. 2007. Complex topic-comment structures in HPSG. In Stefan Müller (ed.), *Proceedings of the 14th international conference on Head-driven Phrase Structure Grammar,* 306–322. Stanford, CA: CSLI Publications.

Wee, Hae-Kyung. 2001. *Sentential logic, discourse and pragmatics of topic and focus.* Indiana University dissertation.

Wilcock, Graham. 2005. Information structure and Minimal Recursion Semantics. In Antti Arppe, Lauri Carlson, Krister Lindén, Jussi Piitulainen, Mickael Suominen, Martti Vainio, Hanna Westerlund & Anssi Yli-Jyrä (eds.), *Inquiries into words, constraints and contexts,* 268–277. Stanford, CA: CSLI Publications.

Yang, Charles D. 2002. *Knowledge and learning in natural language.* Oxford, UK: Oxford University Press.

Yatabe, Shûichi. 1999. Particle ellipsis and focus projection in Japanese. *Language, Information, Text* 6. 79–104.

Yeh, Ching-Long & Yi-Chun Chen. 2004. Zero anaphora resolution in Chinese with shallow parsing. *Journal of Chinese Language and Computing* 17(1). 41–56.

Yoo, Hyun-kyung, Yeri An & Su-hyang Yang. 2007. The study on the principles of selecting Korean particle 'ka' and 'nun' using Korean-English parallel corpus [in Korean]. *Language and Information* 11(1). 1–23.

Yoshimoto, Kei. 2000. A bistratal approach to the prosody-syntax interface in Japanese. In Ronnie Cann, Claire Grover & Philip Miller (eds.), *Grammatical interfaces in HPSG,* 267–282. Stanford, CA: CSLI Publications.

Yoshimoto, Kei, Masahiro Kobayashi, Hiroaki Nakamura & Yoshiki Mori. 2006. Processing of information structure and floating quantifiers in Japanese. *Lecture Notes in Computer Science* 4012. 103–110.

Yu, Kun, Yusuke Miyao, Xiangli Wang, Takuya Matsuzaki & Junichi Tsujii. 2010. Semi-automatically developing Chinese HPSG grammar from the Penn Chinese Treebank for deep parsing. In *Proceedings of the 23rd international conference on computational linguistics*, 1417–1425.

Zagona, Karen. 2002. *The syntax of Spanish*. Cambridge, UK: Cambridge University Press.

Zeevat, Henk. 1987. Combining categorial grammar and unification. In Uwe Reyle & Christian Rohrer (eds.), *Natural language parsing and linguistic theories*, 202–229. Dordrecht: D. Reidel Publishing Company.

Zhao, Shanheng & Hwee Tou Ng. 2007. Identification and resolution of Chinese zero pronouns: a machine learning approach. In *Proceedings of the 2007 joint conference on empirical methods in natural language processing and computational natural language learning*. Prague, Czech.

Zubizarreta, Maria Luisa. 1998. *Prosody, focus, and word order*. Cambridge, MA: The MIT Press.

Name index

Aarts, Bas, 142, 203, 204
Abeillé, Anne, 155
Alexopoulou, Theodora, 215
Alonso-Ovalle, Luis, 21, 193
Ambar, Manuela, 34, 35, 62, 63, 67, 68
An, Yeri, 13
Arregi, Karlos, 25, 56

Baldwin, Timothy, 3, 177
Beaver, David I., 22, 48, 205
Bender, Emily M., 2–6, 9, 20, 29, 45, 61, 114, 115, 118, 124–126, 128, 133, 139, 155, 156, 162, 194, 196, 197, 212, 233, 236, 237, 250, 252, 253, 261, 265, 266, 271, 274, 276
Bianchi, Valentina, 28, 29, 67, 68, 94, 174, 241
Bildhauer, Felix, 3, 84, 85, 87, 91, 95–99, 104, 124, 152, 158, 159, 215, 216, 220–223
Bjerre, Anne, 87, 176, 177
Bolinger, Dwight Le Merton, 22, 45, 71, 84, 98, 262, 266
Bonami, Olivier, 96
Bond, Francis, 4, 5, 9, 162, 184, 266, 271, 276
Bos, Johan, 96, 100, 101
Bouma, Gerlof, 2
Branco, António, 5
Bresnan, Joan, 4, 93, 102–104, 111, 176, 177, 225, 226
Büring, Daniel, 11, 17, 18, 24, 27, 28, 33, 36, 45–47, 55, 57, 58, 61, 77, 80, 85, 94, 108, 139, 189, 219, 222, 223, 266, 276
Burnard, Lou, 3
Byron, Donna K., 193

Callmeier, Ulrich, 5, 233
Casielles-Suárez, Eugenia, 23, 63, 211
Cecchetto, Carlo, 65, 66
Chafe, Wallace L., 25–27, 65, 154
Chang, Suk-Jin, 39, 84, 85, 87, 89, 94, 123, 191
Chapman, Shirley, 30, 63, 239
Chen, Aoju, 46
Chen, Chen, 194
Chen, Yi-Chun, 194
Choe, Jae-Woong, 124, 159, 222
Choi, Hye-Won, 23, 25, 29, 30, 37, 53, 72, 73, 92, 102, 103, 126, 196, 197, 241
Choi, Incheol, 275
Choi, Sung-Kwon, 193
Chung, Chan, 84, 85, 95, 185, 223–226
Churng, Sarah, 59
Cinque, Guglielmo, 12, 20, 194, 215, 216
Clark, Brady Z., 22, 205
Clech-Darbon, Anne, 203, 208
Comrie, Bernard, 60, 189

Constant, Noah, 47
Cook, Philippa, 87, 95
Copestake, Ann, 3, 5, 14, 83, 105, 105[1], 106, 107, 133, 137, 192, 233, 265, 273
Costa, Francisco, 5
Croft, William, 73, 179
Crowgey, Joshua, 61, 155, 156, 234, 236
Crysmann, Berthold, 5

De Kuthy, Kordula, 84, 85, 87, 94, 223
Delais-Roussarie, Elisabeth, 96
Dipper, Stephanie, 26
Drellishak, Scott, 6, 45, 47, 233, 236, 265
Drubig, Hans Bernhard, 46, 48, 51–53, 57, 59, 76, 189, 222

É. Kiss, Katalin, 16–18, 60, 61, 76, 128, 202, 207, 208
Emonds, Joseph, 29, 181
Engdahl, Elisabet, 11, 12, 21, 47, 48, 60, 76, 83–88, 94, 104, 110, 124, 125, 222, 223
Erteschik-Shir, Nomi, 12–14, 20, 24, 32, 37, 65, 67, 68, 94, 126, 241, 276

Fabb, Nigel, 181
Fan, Zhenzhen, 5, 276
Fanselow, Gisbert, 41, 48, 61, 67, 68
Féry, Caroline, 11, 14, 25, 26, 48, 52, 53, 57, 64–66
Firbas, Jan, 9
Flickinger, Dan, 3, 5, 6, 45, 105[1], 202, 227, 233, 236, 237, 265, 266, 271, 276
Fokkens, Antske, 236
Frascarelli, Mara, 28, 29, 67, 68, 94, 174, 241
Frascarelli, Mare, 215, 216
Frota, Sónia, 46
Fujita, Sanae, 4

Gegg-Harrison, Whitney, 193
Gell-Mann, Murray, 128
Givón, Talmy, 17
Godard, Daniele, 155
Goodman, Michael Wayne, 236
Goss-Grubbs, David, 139
Götze, Michael, 26
Gracheva, Varvara, 23, 153, 208
Grewendorf, Günther, 120
Grishina, Elena, 208
Grohmann, Kleanthes K, 215, 216
Gryllia, Styliani, 17, 37, 39, 40, 68, 72, 79, 93, 110, 190, 208
Gundel, Jeanette K., 11, 12, 14, 16–19, 22, 23, 30, 33–36, 45, 65, 75, 94, 114, 205, 207
Gunji, Takao, 163
Gunlogson, Christine, 192
Gussenhoven, Carlos, 17, 18, 40, 41, 43, 58, 75, 203, 209, 224, 225

Haegeman, Liliane, 28, 171
Haiman, John, 27, 149, 183, 185
Haji-Abdolhosseini, Mohammad, 96
Halliday, Michael Alexander Kirkwood, 12, 22, 48
Han, Chung-Hye, 206
Han, Na-Rae, 193
Hangyo, Masatsugu, 194
Hartmann, Katharina, 57, 58, 79, 80, 222
Hasegawa, Akio, 2, 147, 275

Name index

Hedberg, Nancy, 47, 108, 123, 134, 196, 206, 266
Hellan, Lars, 5
Heycock, Caroline, 28, 65, 115, 123, 149, 171, 173, 174, 181, 185, 196, 275
Hooper, Joan, 29
Horvath, Julia, 61
Huang, C.-T. James, 13, 21, 127, 176, 178, 183, 193

Iatridou, Sabine, 71, 183
Ishihara, Shinichiro, 48, 53, 55, 56, 126, 196
İşsever, Selçuk, 60

Jackendoff, Ray S., 7, 22, 45–47, 84, 98, 108, 232, 262, 266
Jacobs, Joachim, 25
Jacobs, Neil G., 54, 57, 154, 155
Jiang, Zixin, 176
Johansson, Mats, 2
Joshi, Aravind K., 4
Jun, Sun-Ah, 46, 158

Kadmon, Nirit, 47, 108, 266
Kaiser, Elsi, 139
Kaiser, Lizanne, 64, 173, 178, 196, 197
Kamp, Hans, 100
Kawahara, Daisuke, 194
Kiefer, Ferenc, 128
Kihm, Alain, 206
Kim, Jieun, 41
Kim, Jong-Bok, 5, 9, 84, 85, 87, 93–95, 125, 142, 143, 165, 177, 185, 202–210, 223–226, 266, 267, 271, 275, 276
Kim, Taeho, 65–67, 252
King, Tracy Holloway, 3, 102, 103, 206, 275

Klein, Ewan, 96, 97
Ko, Kil Soo, 165
Koenig, Jean-Pierre, 2, 147
Kolliakou, Dimitra, 215
Komagata, Nobo N., 2
Kong, Fang, 194
Krifka, Manfred, 11, 12, 14, 25, 26, 32, 42, 48, 52, 53, 57, 64–66, 94, 193
Kügler, Frank, 46, 48, 60, 76, 222
Kuhn, Jonas, 1, 2, 49, 88, 91, 96, 214
Kuno, Susumu, 25, 28, 36, 111, 171, 176–179
Kuroda, S.-Y., 13, 127, 128
Kurohashi, Sadao, 194

Ladd, D Robert, 46
Lambrecht, Knud, 2, 11–15, 18–28, 34, 57, 65, 66, 85, 87, 110, 112, 124, 126–128, 131, 138, 139, 154, 187, 189, 194, 207, 225, 226, 251
Law, Ann, 65
Lecarme, Jacqueline, 49
Lee, Hyuck-Joon, 158
Lee, Jong-Hyeok, 194
Lee, Sun-Hee, 193
Lee, Youngjoo, 275
Li, Charles N., 21, 53, 127, 154, 193, 198
Li, Kening, 131, 208
Li, Y.-H. Audrey, 13, 176, 178
Li, Yafei, 13, 176, 178
Lim, Dong-Hoon, 28, 174

Maki, Hideki, 64, 173, 178, 196, 197
Man, Fung Suet, 50, 58, 76, 102, 103
Marimon, Montserrat, 5
Matsui, Tomoko, 194

Matsumoto, Yuji, 84, 85, 87, 90, 95
Mchombo, Sam A, 102–104, 111, 176, 177
Megerdoomian, Karine, 60, 190
Mereu, Lunella, 53
Meurers, Detmar, 85, 87
Mitkov, Ruslan, 193
Miyao, Yusuke, 4
Moeljadi, David, 5, 276
Molnár, Valéria, 32
Montgomery-Anderson, Brad, 50, 51

Nagaya, Naonori, 63
Nakaiwa, Hiromi, 194
Nakanishi, Kimiko, 32, 36, 37, 123
Neeleman, Ad, 35, 59, 67, 68, 108, 153, 167
Nelson, Gerald, 142, 203, 204
Ng, Hwee Tou, 194
Ng, Vincent, 194
Nguyen, Hoai Thu Ba, 34, 108, 175, 241
Nichols, Eric, 4
Nichols, Johanna, 57, 67, 68, 74
Ning, Chunyan, 176, 179

Ochi, Masao, 64, 173, 178, 196, 197
Oepen, Stephan, 4, 5, 88, 94, 95, 233, 237, 261
Ohtani, Akira, 84, 85, 87, 90, 95
Ortiz de Urbina, Jon, 60, 156, 190
Osenova, Petya, 5, 237
Oshima, David Y., 31, 47
Ouhalla, Jamal, 34, 203, 206
Øvrelid, Lilja, 2

Paggio, Patrizia, 1, 15, 84–87, 95, 96, 124, 125, 132, 209
Park, Byung-Soo, 177

Partee, Barbara H., 22, 35, 48, 88, 115, 193
Paul, Waltraud, 208
Pedersen, Ted, 4
Petronio, Karen, 59
Pollard, Carl, 3, 83, 105, 165, 206
Portner, Paul, 94, 171, 276
Poulson, Laurie, 51, 236, 239
Pozen, Zinaida, 4, 184
Press, Ian J, 55, 57
Prince, Ellen F., 10, 58, 74–76

Ramsay, Violetta, 27, 149, 183, 185
Rebuschi, Georges, 19, 23, 203, 208
Reinhart, Tanya, 30
Reyle, Uwe, 100
Rialland, Annie, 203, 208
Rivero, María-Luisa, 215
Rizzi, Luigi, 171, 215
Roberts, Craige, 28, 30–32, 65, 173, 174
Rochemont, Michael S., 48
Rodionova, Elena V., 59, 153, 250
Roh, Ji-Eun, 194
Rooth, Mats, 16, 32
Ruhlen, Merritt, 128

Sag, Ivan A., 3, 83, 105, 165, 206
Saleem, Safiyyah, 20, 194, 236, 253
Sato, Yo, 35, 95, 165, 267
Schabes, Yves, 4
Schachter, Paul, 73, 176, 179
Schafer, Amy, 176
Schneider, Cynthia, 52, 131, 222
Selkirk, Elisabeth O'Brian, 219, 224
Sells, Peter, 84, 85, 95, 142, 223–226, 275
Sharp, Randall, 193
Shirai, Satoshi, 194

Name index

Siegel, Melanie, 5, 9, 162, 163, 200, 266, 267, 271, 276
Skopeteas, Stavros, 26, 41, 46, 48, 60, 67, 68, 76, 222
Slayden, Glenn C., 233, 265
Sohn, Ho-Min, 29, 198
Song, Sanghoun, 4, 5, 29, 92, 105, 114, 115, 118, 124–126, 128, 133, 176, 196, 197, 212, 237, 261, 276
Sosa, Juan M., 47
Steedman, Mark, 3, 4, 46, 47, 98–100, 108, 266
Strawson, Peter F., 23
Sturgeon, Anne, 215, 216
Szendrői, Kriszta, 60, 61, 76, 128

Tam, Wai Lok, 85, 95, 165, 267
Tamrazian, Armine, 60, 62, 190
Tanaka, Takaaki, 4
Taylor, Heather L, 183
Thompson, Sandra, 21, 29, 53, 127, 154, 193, 198
Titov, Elena, 35, 59, 67, 68, 108, 153, 167
Traat, Maarika, 96, 100, 101
Tragut, Jasmine, 60
Tsujii, Jun'ichi, 4
Tuller, Laurice, 19, 23

Ueyama, Motoko, 46, 158

Valentine, J Randolph, 74, 76
Vallduví, Enric, 9, 11, 12, 21, 47, 48, 55, 60, 76, 83–88, 94, 104, 110, 124, 125, 132, 222, 223
Vallduví, Enric, 10, 11, 60
van Valin, Robert D., 35, 53, 54, 62
Velleman, Dan, 188, 202, 205

Verhoeven, Elisabeth, 46, 48, 60, 76, 222
Vermeulen, Reiko, 23, 24, 30, 64, 178
Vilkuna, Maria, 10, 11
von Fintel, Kai, 41
von Prince, Kilu, 131, 222

Wallis, Sean, 142, 203, 204
Webelhuth, Gert, 85, 88, 95
Wee, Hae-Kyung, 41
Whitman, John, 208
Wilcock, Graham, 95

Yabushita, Katsuhiko, 94, 171, 276
Yang, Charles D., 21, 193
Yang, Jaehyung, 125, 165, 203, 205, 267
Yang, Su-hyang, 13
Yatabe, Shûichi, 162, 163, 200, 264, 267
Yeh, Ching-Long, 194
Yoo, Hyun-kyung, 13
Yoshimoto, Kei, 84, 85, 87, 95, 97, 275
Yu, Kun, 4

Zaenen, Annie, 102
Zagona, Karen, 53, 132, 215
Zeevat, Henk, 100
Zhao, Shanheng, 194
Zimmermann, Malte, 57, 58, 79, 80, 222
Zubizarreta, Maria Luisa, 53, 55, 92

Language index

Abma, 52, 126, 131, 222
Akan, 46, 53, 57, 76, 152, 179, 222
American Sign Language, 59
Armenian, 60, 62, 189, 190

Basque, 55^8, 56, 60, 61, 152, 155, 190
Bosnian Croatian Serbian, 59, 60, 63, 77, 78, 152
Breton, 55, 57
Bulgarian, 5, 120^{11}, 237
Buli, 52, 53

Cantonese, 50, 51, 66, 66^{17}, 75^2, 76, 102–104
Catalan, 46, 60, 76, 132^{18}, 222
Cherokee, 50, 51, 53
Chicheŵa, 54, 62, 104, 152
Chinese, 5, 20, 20^{10}, 126–128, 131, 146, 179, 208, 222, 231, 276
Czech, 215, 216

Danish, 37, 65, 86, 87, 152, 176
Ditammari, 52

English, 1, 7, 9, 10, 13, 14, 17, 20, 20^{10}, 21, 23, 23^{12}, 26, 29–31, 33, 38, 40, 45–48, 53, 54, 56–58, 61^{14}, 63^{15}, 67, 68, 71, 74, 75^2, 76, 84, 91, 98–100, 103, 108, 110, 112, 120, 123, 124^{12}, 129, 132, 137, 138, 140, 144, 147–149, 158, 159, 162, 166, 167, 171, 173, 174, 177, 179, 180, 185, 216, 219, 220, 222–225, 232, 262, 264–267, 269^4, 270, 275

Finnish, 77
French, 66, 139, 203^{10}, 208
Frisian, 250, 253–255, 257, 258

Georgian, 67, 68
German, 5, 26, 27, 77, 84, 102, 212^{13}, 215, 216
Greek, 39, 68, 79, 109, 215

Hausa, 57, 58, 79, 80, 179, 222
Hungarian, 60, 61, 152

Ilonggo, 73, 179
Indonesian, 5, 276
Ingush, 57, 58, 67, 68, 74, 76, 152
Italian, 12, 20, 39, 174, 215, 216

Japanese, 1, 5, 9, 10, 13, 25, 26, 28, 31, 36, 46, 50, 51, 53, 54, 55^8, 56, 64, 65, 72, 77, 80, 84, 108, 112, 114, 115, 118, 121, 123, 125–128, 137, 147, 153, 158, 159, 161, 162, 163^{17}, 165, 166^{21}, 171, 173, 174, 177, 184, 187, 194^4, 196–198, 201, 212, 217, 246, 249, 254, 262, 265–268, 269^4, 270, 275

Language index

Korean, 5, 9, 10, 13, 20, 20^{10}, 21, 24, 25, 28–30, 33, 37–39, 41–43, 46, 49–51, 53, 54, 55^8, 64–67, 72, 73, 77, 80, 84, 102–104, 108, 114, 115, 121, 123, 125–129, 137, 145, 153, 158, 161, 165, 166^{21}, 174, 177, 184, 187, 194^4, 196–198, 201, 212, 217, 222, 231, 237, 249, 252, 266–268, 269^4, 270, 275, 276

Lakota, 147, 253, 254, 256, 258

Miyako, 253–258
Moroccan Arabic, 206

Navajo, 40
Ngizim, 59
Nishnaabemwin, 74, 76
Norwegian, 5, 205

Paumarí, 30, 239
Portuguese, 5, 34, 62, 63, 67, 68, 77, 152

Rendile, 49, 51–53, 123
Russian, 13, 23^{11}, 35, 59, 67, 68, 77, 78, 102, 108, 109, 119^{10}, 137, 152, 153, 158, 167, 168, 206, 208, 250

Spanish, 5, 20, 20^{10}, 21, 25, 53, 63, 84, 98, 124^{12}, 127^{13}, 132^{18}, 158, 193, 194, 211, 215, 221
Standard Arabic, 34, 206

Tangale, 59
Toba Batak, 54, 62
Turkish, 60, 152

Vietnamese, 34, 108, 109, 123

Wolof, 206

Yiddish, 54, 57, 152, 154, 250, 253–255, 257, 258
Yucatec Maya, 46, 60, 76, 222

Subject index

ACE, 233, 237, 252, 252^5, 265, 265^1
agree, 233, 237, 265^1
[incr tsdb()], 5, 233, 256
LKB, 5, 233, 237, 252^5, 256
LOGON, 95, 96, 96^{10}
PET, 5, 233, 237
info-str, 96, 105^1, 113, 114, 116, 118, 121, 137, 138, 142–145, 147, 149, 168, 172^1, 189, 201, 213, 214, 218, 228, 238, 241–245, 248, 249, 257, 258, 262, 264, 265, 270, 274
mkg, 113, 121, 122, 126, 135, 200, 241, 274
sform, 113, 124–126, 131^{17}, 132, 135, 184, 241, 274
tell-me-about test, 30, 44
wh-fronting, 120^{11}
wh-question, 191
wh-questions, 22, 23, 33, 37, 43, 103, 189, 192, 192^1
wh-test, 38, 77
wh-words, 17, 20, 190, 191, 211

A-accent, 7, 22, 23, 33, 84, 101, 110, 116, 123, 124^{12}, 133, 141, 148, 159, 162, 172, 182, 209, 219, 220, 224–226, 228, 262, 266, 270
aboutness, 44, 46
aboutness topic, 25, 29, 36, 64, 65, 67, 114, 118, 178, 182, 186, 196

adposition, 9, 45, 49–51, 69, 107, 112, 147, 162, 163^{17}, 170, 201, 239, 245, 246, 251, 254, 257, 267, 273
adverbial clause, 149, 171, 183, 185, 186
alternative set, 11, 12^2, 16, 32, 33, 39, 44, 72, 103, 273
alternatives, 2
anti-topic, 65, 66
argument optionality, 20, 187, 193, 194, 217, 244, 253
auxiliary, 62, 144, 145, 155^{14}, 156, 248^4

B-accent, 30, 84, 98, 101, 116, 123, 133, 141, 148, 148^7, 159, 172, 182, 262–264
background, 1, 10–12, 24, 42, 43, 73, 85, 85^1, 89^5, 110, 114, 115, 196, 212, 273
basic word order, 53, 61, 62, 69, 110, 128, 129, 167, 197
binary relation, 95, 96, 110, 113, 115, 121, 133, 142, 171, 273
BURGER, 5, 237

CCG, 4, 99, 102
CLAUSE, 115, 115^8, 116–118, 120, 121, 133, 135, 141, 143–145, 151, 160, 170, 172, 185, 210
clause-final, 35, 57, 59, 63, 67, 69, 77, 78, 108, 152, 153, 167, 170,

Subject index

238, 240, 244, 247, 251, 273
clause-initial, 46, 53, 54, 57, 58, 67, 69, 74, 76, 152–154, 170, 183, 238, 240, 244, 247, 251, 273
CLAUSE-KEY, 115^8, 118, 118^9, 120, 121, 145, 146, 149, 165, 242, 244
clefting, 17, 18, 42, 43, 61^{14}, 73, 75^2, 78, 87^3, 103, 111, 112, 125–127, 129, 142, 143, 154, 176, 179, 180, 187, 202–210, 266^3, 275
complement clause, 171–175, 186
contrast, 1, 2, 10, 11, 23^{11}, 25, 32–37, 39, 43, 44, 49, 64, 67, 68, 72, 92^8, 94, 108, 114, 131, 133, 147, 154^{13}, 174, 181, 184, 191, 198, 208, 251, 273
contrastive focus, 1, 10, 16–19, 19^9, 33, 35, 37, 40, 41, 43, 44, 47, 67–69, 72, 73, 79, 80, 90, 93, 103, 108, 109^3, 110, 134^{19}, 149, 153, 190, 196^5, 208, 223^1, 238, 240, 254, 257, 263
contrastive topic, 12^2, 19, 25, 29, 35, 37, 44, 47, 64, 65, 69, 72, 73, 90, 92, 108, 109, 118, 134^{19}, 147, 174, 175, 196^5, 238, 241, 245, 254
contrastiveness, 11^1, 19, 34, 39, 68, 114, 184, 191, 196^6, 197, 257
control predicate, 107, 141, 144
copula, 42, 112, 119^{10}, 131^{16}, 140, 143, 145, 205–207, 209
correction test, 17, 37, 37^{14}, 41, 44, 72, 208

deletion test, 23, 42, 43
DELPH-IN, 4, 5, 9, 184, 184^8, 222, 233, 237, 265, 265^1, 275, 276

dislocation, 12, 65, 84, 187, 215, 217, 218

ERG, 5, 202, 205, 207, 209, 211, 213, 218, 227^3, 266^2, 271, 276

felicity, 1, 21, 270
felicity-conditions, 2, 18, 21, 31, 61
fixed word order, 244, 247–249
focus, 1, 4^2, 6, 7, 9–11, 11^1, 12, 14–19, 19^7, 20–23, 23^{12}, 24, 28–30, 32–37, 40–42, 42^{16}, 43, 45–48, 48^3, 49–61, 63, 68, 69, 72–75, 75^2, 76–80, 85, 87, 90, 94, 95, 97, 100–103, 108–111, 112^6, 114, 115, 121, 123, 124, 126, 130, 131, 133, 139, 143, 147, 152, 154, 155, 157–159, 162, 167, 175, 176, 179, 180, 182, 186–193, 196, 202, 203^{10}, 205, 211, 213–215, 217, 219–226, 228, 230, 231, 238, 239, 244, 245, 247, 248, 251, 254, 266^3, 270, 273–275
focus projection, 6, 7, 15, 18, 96, 124, 126, 158, 159, 219–228, 231, 274, 275
focus prominence, 17, 97, 139, 220, 221
focus sensitive, 47^2, 48, 190, 193
focus sensitive item, 22, 181, 187, 190, 217, 218, 275
focus sensitive operator, 48, 205
frame-setter, 26, 27, 44, 127, 132, 183
frame-setting, 25, 26, 127, 131, 132, 154, 183, 184, 215
free word order, 59, 167, 251
fronting, 10, 17, 54, 57, 58, 65, 74, 75, 75^2, 76, 80, 103, 114, 115, 152,

154, 155, 171, 173, 174, 180, 187, 214, 215, 217, 218, 266³

generation, 121, 261, 268
GG, 5
grammar engineering, 3, 4, 101, 131, 165, 192, 231, 233, 236, 253, 274
Grammar Matrix, 3, 44, 51⁵, 90, 115⁸, 119, 120, 120¹¹, 131, 139¹, 150¹⁰, 152, 155, 158, 162, 170, 202, 208¹², 233, 237, 252, 256, 258, 265, 274, 275
ground, 9, 85

hanging topic, 215, 216
HPSG, 3, 4, 19⁹, 44, 83–85, 88, 91, 96, 102, 105, 118⁹, 163¹⁷, 172, 198, 216, 219–223, 233, 267, 274

ICONS, 6, 93, 105, 105¹, 108, 110, 115–121, 124, 133, 135, 137, 138, 140, 142, 144, 147–151, 158, 160, 162, 167, 168, 170, 171, 172¹, 183⁷, 186–190, 199⁷, 210, 213, 214, 217, 219, 225, 228–231, 241–245, 249, 252, 258, 261, 263, 265, 265¹, 266, 269, 273, 276
ICONS-KEY, 118, 120, 133, 135, 147, 148, 151, 158, 162, 165, 166, 185, 189, 199⁷, 200, 214, 222, 230, 241, 248
illustrative grammars, 266, 267, 270
Individual CONStraints, 6, 93, 96, 105, 137, 171, 187, 219, 241, 261, 273
INDRA, 5, 276
infrastructure, 94–96, 121

inomissibility, 18, 19, 23

Jacy, 5, 9, 162, 266², 271, 276

KRG, 5, 9, 237, 266², 271, 276

L-PERIPH, 131, 150, 152–154, 168, 184, 247, 274
Language CoLLAGE, 252, 253, 258, 274
left dislocation, 25, 65, 66, 75, 84, 171, 215, 216
lexical markers, 9, 18, 45, 49–53, 69, 72, 80, 92, 93, 123, 124, 165, 201, 217, 238, 239, 251, 252, 263, 267, 273, 275
LFG, 4, 93, 102, 111
lightness, 152, 155, 155¹⁴, 156, 157, 168, 248, 274
LXGram, 5

MKG, 121–123, 124¹², 126, 128, 135, 138, 150, 159, 166, 170, 198–201, 217, 219, 222, 225, 227, 232, 241, 267
MRS, 3, 7, 14, 44, 83–85, 88, 94, 95, 104, 105, 107, 110, 112, 116, 121, 133, 135, 137, 146, 160, 163, 172, 192, 222, 233, 241, 251, 261, 265, 273, 274, 276

narrow focus, 15, 22, 33, 42, 54, 56, 57, 59, 60, 62, 68, 69, 74, 90, 126, 128–131, 155, 168, 169, 205, 223, 248, 256, 257
negation, 27, 36, 38, 40, 103, 188, 193
non-contrastive focus, 10, 14, 16, 18, 33–35, 37, 59¹¹, 62, 68, 79, 110, 113, 134¹⁹, 153, 162, 167, 223¹, 240, 254

Subject index

non-contrastive topic, 25, 35, 64, 67, 123, 134[19], 175, 196[5]
Norsource, 5

passive, 112, 187, 211, 212, 212[13], 213
periphery, 65, 131, 152, 153, 184, 215, 220, 228, 232, 247
postposing, 65, 67
postverbal, 54, 56, 57, 62, 67, 69, 79, 110, 126, 129, 152, 155, 156, 170, 238, 240, 248, 249, 251, 273
preposing, 108
preverbal, 13, 54, 56, 57, 60, 62, 67–69, 74, 76, 79, 110, 126, 152, 155–157, 170, 190, 238, 240, 245, 248, 249, 251, 254, 257, 273
prosody, 23, 45, 47, 48, 48[3], 69, 76, 78, 89, 91, 97, 99, 101, 104, 124, 167, 219, 220, 222, 231, 251, 266, 273
pseudo grammars, 251, 252

quantifier, 47[2], 95, 105, 148[8], 189, 191, 193

R-PERIPH, 150, 152, 153, 168, 247, 274
raising predicate, 107, 141, 144
regression test, 250–253, 274
relative clause, 28, 42, 105[1], 111, 171, 174, 175, 178–182, 186, 202, 207, 209, 266[3]
relative marker, 179
relative pronoun, 111, 112, 138, 176, 177
right dislocation, 39, 65, 66, 84, 215
right dislocation test, 38, 39
root phenomena, 29, 171, 173, 181

scrambling, 37, 53, 56, 103, 118, 121, 123, 125, 126, 154, 187, 196, 197, 199, 201, 267
semantic focus, 14, 16, 17, 17[6], 18, 34, 37, 43, 59[11], 69, 110, 113, 114, 117, 134, 134[19], 141, 148, 153, 172, 191, 198, 228, 254, 257, 262, 263, 265, 267
sentential forms, 124–126, 131[17], 132, 135, 183, 241, 274
SRG, 5
subject-drop, 20, 21, 193, 194
syntactic positioning, 53, 69, 75[1], 127, 152, 163[17], 167, 190, 238, 251, 256, 273

TAG, 4
TARGET, 115, 116, 121, 133, 135, 149, 160, 172, 185
TDL, 158, 205, 237, 241, 242, 244, 246, 247, 258, 266[3], 274, 275
testsuites, 250, 251, 255, 258, 267, 268
topic, 1, 2, 7, 9–12, 12[2], 13–15, 17, 19, 20, 23–37, 41–47, 49–51, 54, 57, 63–66, 69, 72–75, 75[2], 80, 80[3], 85[1], 90, 92, 95, 100, 101, 103, 108, 110–112, 114, 115, 121, 123, 124, 126–128, 132, 133, 139, 147, 149, 150[10], 152–155, 165[19], 171, 173–180, 182–184, 186, 187, 189, 190, 196–199, 201, 211–218, 239, 247, 251, 252, 254, 257, 258, 262, 266[3], 267, 273–276
topic-comment, 13, 15, 65, 122, 125–128, 132, 198, 199, 201
topic-drop, 20, 20[10], 21, 128, 193, 194
topicalization, 65, 74, 75
topicless, 11, 24, 126–128, 131, 177

transfer-based, 88, 94, 121, 261, 268, 270, 274
truth-conditions, 2, 17, 18, 22, 35, 88, 94, 181, 212, 225
TTS, 88, 91, 96, 215[15]

underspecification, 6, 49, 69, 88, 91, 104–107, 109, 114, 123, 124, 135, 159, 167, 172[1], 175, 183, 185, 186, 192, 220, 228, 243, 265, 273

V2 languages, 54, 55, 57, 249, 254, 256–258

wide focus, 15, 22, 90[6], 126, 131, 223

ZHONG, 5, 276

www.ingramcontent.com/pod-product-compliance
Lightning Source LLC
Chambersburg PA
CBHW080633230426
43663CB00016B/2857